Women Migrant Workers

This volume makes the case for the fair treatment of female migrant workers from the global South who are employed in wealthy liberal democracies as care workers, domestic workers, home health workers and farm workers. An international panel of contributors provides analyses of the ethical, political and legal problems faced by those women. Empirical data and case studies inform their original and sophisticated analyses of the systemic, structural factors responsible for the harms experienced by the women workers. The book also proposes realistic and original solutions to the problem of the unjust treatment of women migrant workers, such as social security systems that are transnational and tailored to meet the particular needs of different groups of international migrant workers.

Zahra Meghani is an Associate Professor of Philosophy at the University of Rhode Island.

Routledge International Studies of Women and Place

Series Editors: Janet Henshall Momsen and Janice Monk, University of California, Davis and University of Arizona, USA

1 **Gender, Migration and Domestic Service**
 Edited by Janet Henshall Momsen

2 **Gender Politics in the Asia-Pacific Region**
 Edited by Brenda S.A. Yeoh, Peggy Teo and Shirlena Huang

3 **Geographies of Women's Health**
 Place, Diversity and Difference
 Edited by Isabel Dyck, Nancy Davis Lewis and Sara McLafferty

4 **Gender, Migration and the Dual Career Household**
 Irene Hardill

5 **Female Sex Trafficking in Asia**
 The Resilience of Patriarchy in a Changing World
 Vidyamali Samarasinghe

6 **Gender and Landscape**
 Renegotiating the Moral Landscape
 Edited by Lorraine Dowler, Josephine Carubia and Bonj Szczygiel

7 **Maternities**
 Gender, Bodies and Spaces
 Robyn Longhurst

8 **Gender and Family among Transnational Professionals**
 Edited by Anne Coles and Anne-Meike Fechter

9 **Gender and Agrarian Reforms**
 Susie Jacobs

10 **Gender and Rurality**
 Lia Bryant and Barbara Pini

11 **Feminist Advocacy and Gender Equity in the Anglophone Caribbean**
 Envisioning a Politics of Coalition
 Michelle V. Rowley

12 **Women, Religion, and Space in China**
 Islamic Mosques & Daoist Temples, Catholic Convents & Chinese Virgins
 Maria Jaschok and Shui Jingjun

13 **Gender and Wildfire**
 Landscapes of Uncertainty
 Christine Eriksen

14 **Colonization and Domestic Service**
 Historical and Contemporary Perspectives
 Edited by Victoria K. Haskins and Claire Lowrie

15 **A Political Ecology of Women, Water and Global Environmental Change**
Edited by Stephanie Buechler and Anne-Marie Hanson

16 **Women Migrant Workers**
Ethical, Political and Legal Problems
Edited by Zahra Meghani

Also available in this series:

Full Circles: Geographies of Women over the Life Course
Edited by Cindi Katz and Janice Monk

'Viva': Women and Popular Protest in Latin America
Edited by Sarah A Radcliffe and Sallie Westwood

Different Places, Different Voices: Gender and Development in Africa, Asia and Latin America
Edited by Janet Momsen and Vivian Kinnaird

Servicing the Middle Classes: Class, Gender and Waged Domestic Labour in Contemporary Britain
Nicky Gregson and Michelle Lowe

Women's Voices from the Rainforest
Janet Gabriel Townsend

Gender, Work and Space
Susan Hanson and Geraldine Pratt

Women and the Israeli Occupation
Edited by Tamar Mayer

Feminism / Postmodernism / Development
Edited by Marianne H. Marchand and Jane L. Parpart

Women of the European Union: The Politics of Work and Daily Life
Edited by Maria Dolors Garcia Ramon and Janice Monk

Who Will Mind the Baby? Geographies of Childcare and Working Mothers
Edited by Kim England

Feminist Political Ecology: Global Issues and Local Experience
Edited by Dianne Rocheleau, Barbara Thomas-Slayter, and Esther Wangari

Women Divided: Gender, Religion and Politics in Northern Ireland
Rosemary Sales

Women's Lifeworlds: Women's Narratives on Shaping their Realities
Edited by Edith Sizoo

Gender, Planning and Human Rights
Edited by Tovi Fenster

Gender, Ethnicity and Place: Women and Identity in Guyana
Linda Peake and D. Alissa Trotz

Women Migrant Workers
Ethical, Political and Legal Problems

Edited by Zahra Meghani
Foreword by Maria Jose Alcalá

NEW YORK AND LONDON

First published 2016
by Routledge
711 Third Avenue, New York, NY 10017

and by Routledge
2 Park Square, Milton Park, Abingdon, Oxon OX14 4RN

Routledge is an imprint of the Taylor & Francis Group, an informa business

© 2016 Taylor & Francis

The right of the editor to be identified as the author of the editorial material, and of the authors for their individual chapters, has been asserted in accordance with sections 77 and 78 of the Copyright, Designs and Patents Act 1988.

All rights reserved. No part of this book may be reprinted or reproduced or utilised in any form or by any electronic, mechanical, or other means, now known or hereafter invented, including photocopying and recording, or in any information storage or retrieval system, without permission in writing from the publishers.

Trademark notice: Product or corporate names may be trademarks or registered trademarks, and are used only for identification and explanation without intent to infringe.

*Library of Congress Cataloging-in-Publication Dat*a
Women migrant workers : ethical, political and legal problems /
    edited by Zahra Meghani.
        pages cm. — (Routledge international studies of women and place ; 16)
    Includes bibliographical references and index.
    1. Migrant labor. 2. Women—Employment. 3. Women foreign workers.
I. Meghani, Zahra.
    HD5855.W66 2016
    331.4—dc23   2015014029

ISBN: 978-0-415-53407-9 (hbk)
ISBN: 978-1-315-67726-2 (ebk)

Typeset in Sabon
by Apex CoVantage, LLC

For K
and for my parents and brothers
who have always been a source of love, support and stability
and for my little ones
and for Rani, Fatima and the millions of other women like them

Contents

Foreword: Protecting the Human Rights and Fundamental Freedoms of Migrant Women Workers   xi
MARIA JOSE ALCALÁ
Acknowledgments   xiii

1   Women on the Move   1
ZAHRA MEGHANI

PART I
Circumstances of Injustice

2   "Her Life within the Home": The Construction of Gender and Female International Migrant Workers in the Republic of Ireland   23
GRAHAM FINLAY AND JOANNE M. MANCINI

3   Trapped in a Web of Immigration and Employment Laws: Female Undocumented Home Health Workers in the US   53
ZAHRA MEGHANI

PART II
Uncaring Development Paradigms

4   On a Collision Course: Millennium Development Goals and Mothers' Migration   75
DELALI BADASU AND SONYA MICHEL

5 Global Care Chains: Reshaping the Hidden Foundations of an Unsustainable Development Model 101
AMAIA PÉREZ OROZCO

PART III
Unjust Social Security Systems

6 International Migrant Domestic Workers, National Welfare States and Transnational Social Security Arrangements 131
SARAH VAN WALSUM

7 Gendered Policies, Single Mothers and Transnational Motherhood: Mexican Female Migrant Farmworkers in Canada 154
OFELIA BECERRIL

PART IV
Care for Care Workers

8 "A Place to Call Home": The Catholic Church and Female Foreign Domestic Workers in Singapore 179
THERESA DEVASAHAYAM

PART V
The Way Forward

9 Transnationalization and the Capitalization of Labor: Female Foreign Domestic Workers 199
STUART ROSEWARNE

10 Hopes and Expectations Dashed: Migrant Women, the Informal Welfare State and Women's Labor Force Participation in Greece 224
ANTIGONE LYBERAKI

Contributors 251
Index 255

Foreword: Protecting the Human Rights and Fundamental Freedoms of Migrant Women Workers

Immigration has historically been a foundation on which nations have been built, and today it continues to be—if not more so—an engine for countries' economic growth, prosperity and competitiveness. Globalization, growing inequalities and the rapidly expanded interconnectedness of people and information across disparate points of our planet have led to the worldwide phenomenon of people on the move like never before.

In too many parts of the world, however, immigration has a bad name. It is a 'hot-button' issue, the subject of alarmist and distorted news headlines across the globe, the fuel that politicians wield in electoral campaigns, a stubborn thorn in intergovernmental relations and progress in the United Nations' negotiations. Meanwhile, we witness intensifying discrimination, hate crimes and violence fueled by xenophobia against migrants as daily occurrences in numerous parts of the world. We also know that many such crimes and human rights violations go untold, and are uncounted.

In the fray of these heated discussions on immigration, there is a tendency to overlook the obvious: immigrants, as equal human beings. They are labeled as 'them' and not recognized as an 'us' who share the same concerns and hopes for themselves and their families as we do for ourselves and our loved ones. But people cannot be reduced to labels. The costs in terms of lives lost and injustices perpetrated are all too real, eroding fundamental human rights and human dignity that are the very essence of our shared humanity and of the most basic principles of inclusive, fair and humane democracies.

The dark side of migration shows us how migrants—especially women—face some of the worst neglect and human rights violations resulting from misguided policies and public attitudes, or sheer ignorance about their real-life experiences. In fact, for many years migration had a man's face, with no recognition of the women who migrated with them, much less any gender perspective brought to bear on national immigration policies.

Many women migrate successfully, leaving behind the poverty of limited opportunities and the shackles of oppressive gender regimes in search of expanded freedoms and choices, and improved economic prospects.

Many migrant women will be found in 'hidden' spaces—in private homes as domestic workers, caretakers for children, the ill and the elderly—where they can face heightened risks of exploitation, harassment and sexual abuse; others are enslaved by exploitation and trafficking rings; and many will be in low-income or unregulated jobs without safety or security of their human or labor rights, silenced by the need to send much-needed financial support to their relatives and children back home, or struggling to bring them up as best they can in their adopted countries despite myriad legal and other barriers put in their way.

Nobody can deny that addressing the challenges of migration is very complex and challenging. Surely, with political leadership and resolve, humans in the 21st century are more than capable of arriving at ethical solutions that at a minimum ensure the personal security and protection of the most basic human rights. Care workers and domestic workers are the backbone of more prosperous families and economies around the world. Do public policy makers—and the public at large—ever wonder what goes on behind those closed doors or the personal challenges they face? Are we aware that many of these women working in privileged households may be living in situations of domestic abuse or need help financing the purchase of malaria medication to save their children? That they too have basic needs—for education and health, for their protection from violence, for contraception and other aspects of their sexual and reproductive health and rights, and for access to justice? Does it take macabre cases of murder, sexual violence and forcible entrapment for fear of deportation to bring a more humane lens and policy response to the plight of domestic workers and other migrants?

This volume discusses the ethical, political and legal challenges faced by women migrant workers. It may, hopefully, inspire all readers to work for change, whether in their capacities as voters and employers, in their spaces of influence or, simply, as citizens of the world and fellow human beings.

Maria Jose Alcalá[1]
Director
High-Level Task Force for the
International Conference on Population and
Development Secretariat

NOTE

1. The views expressed herein are my own and do not necessarily reflect the position of the ICPD.

Acknowledgments

Without the support of K, this book would not have been possible. I also need to thank my parents and my brothers for all they have done for me. I am grateful to Samina, Gita and Annie for their help. I am indebted to Janice Monk and Janet Momsen for their help and support.

I would like to acknowledge that the indexing cost of this volume was partially covered by a Project Completion Grant from the University of Rhode Island and a subvention grant from the University of Rhode Island's Center for the Humanities. Finally, I want to acknowledge the contributions of Lisa Eckenwiler who played an integral role in the original conceptualization of this book (including its organizational structure and the identification and recruitment of some of the authors it includes), and who reviewed and contributed to the editing of several chapters.

1 Women on the Move

Zahra Meghani

INTRODUCTION

Over the last three decades, millions of women from poorer countries have crossed borders to find employment in richer nations.[1] Whether they are documented or undocumented, a significant number of them are systematically exploited, dominated, discriminated against, objectified or marginalized in both undemocratic regimes and liberal democracies. Their work and life prospects are constrained by the dominant sexist and racist norms and ethnic and cultural stereotypes. For the same work, migrant women workers employed on the lower tiers of the hierarchy of professions tend to be paid less and receive fewer benefits and protections than their male counterparts or the citizens of the receiving countries. Those injustices are compounded if the immigration policies of the labor-importing nations make it very difficult, if not impossible, for migrant workers in 'low skill'[2] professions to acquire permanent residency or citizenship.[3] Thus those nations use them on terms that benefit their economy and citizens even as they deny them substantive legal status or any political agency.

The women's home countries feel their absence in the short term and the long term in a variety of ways. They experience a significant brain drain as their knowledge and skills are lost to wealthier nations. When the women leave home to work abroad, they have to shift their caregiving responsibilities onto the shoulders of another family member, usually their elderly mother or an adolescent daughter.[4] It is often difficult for migrant workers who are on the lower rungs of the professional hierarchy to visit their families because of the cost of airfare and restrictive immigration and labor policies. Undocumented workers usually do not see their families for years on end because border crossings are a particularly dangerous prospect for them.

The contributors of this volume offer richly nuanced ethical, political and legal analyses and critiques of the treatment of migrant women workers in liberal democracies by drawing on an array of disciplinary perspectives, including those of anthropology, economics, gender studies, geography, history, law, philosophy, political science and sociology. The failure of liberal democracies to treat international migrant workers – especially those who are on the lower tiers of the hierarchy of professions- as the moral equals of their citizens deserves attention because it violates the key ethical principle that justifies the existence of the liberal democratic state. According to that maxim, everyone matters and matters equally (Nielsen, 1985). Commitment to that principle, among other things, means that the state must not deny rights, benefits or protections to members of any group living within its territories on the basis of an arbitrary biological or social characteristic.[5] It should also not give preference to members of one group over another on that basis.

To understand why the exploitation, domination, objectification and marginalization of 'low skilled' international migrant workers is the norm in liberal democracies (such that discrimination against them is even enshrined in the law of those nations), it is useful to analyze the (political) philosophical arguments against open borders because the two issues are deeply entwined.[6] A standard argument against open borders (and in support of the differential treatment that is meted out to noncitizens who live and work within liberal democracies) is that it is necessary to protect the right of the citizenry to engage in self-definition. The case is made, for instance, that if persons who are not a part of the culture that defines a particular nation may enter, live and work in its territories without the acquiescence of those who are a part of it (i.e., citizens), then the ability of citizens to engage in self-determination is undermined (Kymlicka, 2001, p.215; see Wellman (2008) for a more recent variant of this argument).

This argument is erroneous for at least three reasons. First, it is not justified in negatively stereotyping all international migrant workers as the fundamentally different 'other' who are a threat to the ability of citizens to be autonomous. Second, it is not warranted in stereotyping democracies as constituted of a homogeneous culture. Today, most liberal democracies are diverse, comprising of a multitude of cultures (Shaw, 2003). Third, in privileging the right to self-definition of a particular group over the principle of moral equality of all human beings, the argument fails to recognize that it is the status of all persons as moral equals that is the grounds for any group's claim to a right to self-definition. In other words, this argument for protecting the right of groups (within liberal democracies to engage in self-determination) violates the moral principle that is the basis of that group right.[7]

A related argument against open border for liberal democracies (and in support of differential treatment of foreigners who live and work within the territories of those nations) is as follows: States are more likely to be governed democratically and implement social justice policies if its citizens have a sense of common identity that is based on a feature shared by all of them (such as, race, ethnicity, religion, etc.), but which is not their citizenship[8]) (see Miller, 2003, p.270). If noncitizens who do not share that identity become a part of that nation, then that country may no longer remain committed to democratic governance and social justice.

This argument makes the unjustified assumption that functional democracies presuppose a homogeneous citizenry. Most democracies today (as previously argued) are heterogeneous, and yet they are committed to democratic governance and social justice, including the redistribution of wealth. This argument also negatively stereotypes citizens of democracies as persons who tend to need a shared sense of identity (that is not based on their citizenship) in order to practice democratic governance and implement social justice policies. It does not take seriously the possibility that they may be motivated by a commitment to the principle of moral equality of all persons or a sense of common humanity.

A similar argument against open borders that attempts to justify some forms of time de-limited, differential treatment of undocumented and documented persons is as follows: Democracies may be ethically justified in excluding documented workers and irregular noncitizens who have lived within their borders for less than five years from social programs ". . . that are financed by some general tax and that have as their primary goal the transfer of resources from better off members of the community to worse off ones . . . [specifically], income support programs and other programs aimed at poorer members of society such as social housing" (Carens, 2014, p.549; 2013; 2015). During that five-year period, the state has the moral right to deport undocumented persons, but it has an obligation to afford them the same civil, economic and social rights as other workers (except access to the social programs previously mentioned) and a variety of legal rights (Carens, 2014, p.550; 2013). After the five-year period, undocumented persons, provided they have not been convicted of any criminal activity, acquire a right to apply for legal status.[9]

There are problems with this attempt to justify the differential treatment of noncitizens. The proponent of this position, Carens (2010), acknowledges that the five-year condition appears to be arbitrary. Why should undocumented persons not acquire a right to apply for legal status in three or even four years? He contends that it is not the number of years that is of relevance but the passage of time that is of significance because it denotes the unfolding of a human life, including formation of ties of noncitizens to other persons who live in that nation. But the assumption about the forging of connections (over a period of five years that serves as the moral warrant for undocumented persons acquiring a right to apply for legal status) is not justified. The threat of deportation may inhibit undocumented persons from forming relational bonds with others, especially citizens, such that they live fearful, isolated lives in the shadows (Bosniak, 2010). Another problem with this position is that it considers it ethically justifiable for the democratic state to deny food and housing assistance to undocumented persons and documented workers with low or no income (see Carens, 2014, p.551).[10] This stance does not take into account the reality of the existence of documented and undocumented persons who are employed in 'low skill' professions. Most undocumented workers, for instance, tend to be employed in low paying jobs and they may be paid lower than market wages (UN, 2013) *and* given that a number of them remit a portion of their income to support their dependent family members in their nation of origin (IOM, 2013),[11] they may be in difficult financial straits.[12] Thus, denying indigent undocumented persons (and documented workers) access to food and housing assistance cannot be considered morally justified. This stance is also at odds with the UN's Universal Declaration of Human Rights, especially Article 25, according to which "*everyone* has the right to . . . *food, clothing, housing and medical care* . . . (my italics)" (Assembly, 1948). States that are signatories of the declaration have an obligation to respect this right of all persons who live within their borders, not just their citizens. Moreover, by not acknowledging that many migrant workers, including irregular workers, support dependent family members in their nation of origin, this position relies on an abstract conception of them that perniciously overlooks a relevant aspect of their identity. It fails to recognize that they are human beings in relationships that place moral obligations on them.

This volume aims to provide a textured analysis of the problem of the mistreatment of noncitizens in wealthy liberal democracies that is particularly attentive to gender, class, race and ethnicity. It limits itself to analyzing and evaluating the treatment meted out in those nations to female migrant workers from the global South who are employed in the lower (highly gendered) tiers of the professional hierarchy.[13] This population merits special attention because, even though since 1960 women migrants have made up approximately half of the total population of migrants (UNDP 2009, p.25), there is a paucity of aggregated, detailed data on the international migration of women. For instance, the *World Migration Report 2013* of the IOM has only a one-page section on women's migration titled, "Migration and Gender." Although, in contrast, women and international migration is the subject of the *2006 State of World Population* report of the United Nations Population Fund (UNPFA), the United Nations entity does not report on the issue on a regular basis. This collection focuses on women migrant workers who are employed in the informal and unregulated sectors of the economy. They are a particularly vulnerable and marginalized population because they are afforded few, if any, rights, benefits or protections that are extended by the receiving nations to other groups of workers.

This introductory chapter offers a brief discussion of the causes of the South to North labor flow, with particular attention to the role of neoliberal reforms in establishing and maintaining this phenomenon and the economic benefits that host nations receive from the labor of foreign migrant workers. Then, the migration experience of women laborers from the global South are delineated. After that, the contribution of this volume to the literature on the feminization of the global flow of labor is outlined. The chapter concludes with a roadmap to the volume; the five major themes of the collection and the concern of each chapter are identified, and the geographic connections and overlaps between the chapters are sketched.

THE SOUTH TO NORTH LABOR FLOW

International migration has substantially increased as a result of globalization (IOM 2013, p.31). According to the United Nations Development Programme (UNDP), in 2010, the number of people from the global South living outside their birth nation was approximately 174 million, and they constituted an estimated 75 percent of the global population of migrants (IOM 2013, p.58). Whereas the IOM's *World Migration Report 2013* does not distinguish between documented and undocumented international migrants, the UNDP's *Human Development Report 2009* does attempt to calculate the number of migrants who are undocumented. It estimates that there are approximately 50 million undocumented migrants (UNDP, 2009, p.2). In its *2006 State of the World* report (whose theme was international migration and women), the United Nations Population Fund predicted that labor migration would increase given the greater interdependence between nations and the increasing inequality between them (UNPFA, 2006, p.7). It anticipated richer nations needing more workers from the global South to take on low-paying jobs, specifically, work that is "dirty, difficult, demeaning and dangerous" (UNFPA, 2006, p.7). The number of international migrant workers is projected to substantially increase, but sending and receiving nations generally do not have social security systems (i.e., state-based, publically funded social programs to provide for the needs of those with inadequate or no income) that are tailored to meet the needs of those workers and their dependent family members, including young children (see Chapters Four, Five, Six, Seven and Eight, this volume).

In 2009, women migrants numbered about 83 million, constituting 48 percent of the total population of international migrants (UNDP, 2009, p.25). The feminization of the global labor flow began in the 1980s, with a growing number of unmarried and married women migrating without family members (Chammartin, 2005, p.1; UNPFA, 2006, p.22). Both 'push' and 'pull' factors account for the flow of women workers from poorer nations to richer ones. A key pull factor is the increasing number of women in North America, Western Europe and East Asia taking on paid work outside the home, even as the men in those households or families—be they fathers, husbands, boyfriends, brothers, sons, grandfathers, nephews or uncles—fail to do their fair share of care work and domestic work, and there is a dearth of high quality, publicly funded child care and elder care facilities (see Chapters Five, Six and Ten, this volume). Women workers from the global South are being recruited to fill this labor gap in care and domestic work (UNPFA, 2006, p.25). Another 'pull' factor is the widening gap in wages and living standards between nations (IOM, 2013, p.33).

At the other end, there is pressure on poor and middle class women from the global South to find work in richer countries. They are motivated to leave their nation of origin by a complex of factors, such as limited prospects for social advancement, family responsibilities and a "desire to expand their horizons" (UNPFA, 2006, p.22). A dearth of employment opportunities, low wages and poverty in their nation of origin also 'push' them to seek work in richer nations (see Chapter Seven, this volume). The lack of good quality health care and education, corruption and poor governance are other reasons that impel them to leave their nations of origin and seek work elsewhere (IOM 2013, p.33).

Neoliberal reforms in sending and receiving nations have made these pull and push factors stronger (in fact, some of the neoliberal policies function as 'push' or 'pull' forces), but that connection is not acknowledged in key reports about international migration (see, for instance, IOM 2013). Given that the lives of millions of women and men have been and continue to be affected by neoliberal reforms, the relationship between neoliberal policies and international labor migration merits discussion.

Neoliberalism

The development of neoliberalism can be traced to the Mount Perelin Society that was formed at the end of World War II (Harvey, 2005). It consisted of a small group of economists, historians and philosophers who were mentored by economist Friedrich von Hayek (Peet, 2009, p.10). Hayek believed that state regulation of the market would inevitably lead to totalitarian tyranny (von Hayek 1984, 1988), thus he rejected Keynesian economic theory (which espoused state management of the economy) and instead advocated free enterprise and a state that did not intervene in the economy except to protect private property rights (i.e., a 'night watchman' state).

Neoliberalism did not have much credence until the 1970s when it appeared that postwar Keynesian economics lacked the wherewithal to solve the problem of stagflation (Peet, 2009, p.117) and Von Hayek was awarded the Nobel Prize for economics in 1974 (Peet, 2009, pp.11–12). That gave him and other proponents of neoliberalism the opportunity to convince new generations of economists and policymakers of the merits of their theory (Peet, 2009, pp.9–14). As a result of their advocacy efforts, international financial institutions (IFIs) (especially, the World Bank (WB) and the International Monetary Fund (IMF)) have compelled nations of the global South who are their debtors to adopt neoliberal policies (Peet, 2009). Some countries have also voluntarily undertaken neoliberal reforms.

To see how the implementation of neoliberal policies by richer nations has intensified the demand in those countries for migrant women workers from the global South, it is useful to consider the case of Spain. Beginning in the 1980s, Spain shifted from socialism to neoliberalism (Ban, 2011), and one of the consequences of this economic and political shift was that it did not establish an adequate number of high quality, publicly funded elder care and child care facilities that would meet the needs of its citizens (neoliberalism construes care work as the responsibility of individual families, not a societal obligation (see Chapter Five, this volume)). In the past three decades, with increasing numbers of female citizens of Spain entering the paid workforce, and with male citizens refusing to do their fair share of care work,[14] and with a societal norm of undervaluing and underpaying for care work, the demand for foreign female workers who provide child care and elder care services has grown (see Chapter Five, this volume).

With nations of the global South adopting neoliberal policies at the 'urging' of IFIs, middle class and poor women of those countries have been 'pushed' to find work in richer nations. The IFIs have made their loans to poorer countries conditional on the adoption of Structural Adjustment Programs (SAPs)[15] that require the state to more or less function as a 'night watchman' state whose primary responsibility is to protect the property rights of individuals and corporations. Nations that have undertaken neoliberal reforms provide very limited goods and services to their citizens, even if they are mired in poverty (Kirk and Okazawa-Rey, 1998; Harvey, 2005; Gershman, Irwin and Shakow, 2003, pp.168–70; Weisbrot, Baker and Rosnick, 2007, p.179; Peet, 2009; see also Chapters Four, Five, and Six, this volume). Those nations have slashed subsidies for food, fuel and public transportation (Kirk and Okazawa-Rey, 1998, p.188; Peet, 2009, pp.84–5) and government support for education, child care, social welfare and health care has been drastically reduced (Kirk and Okazawa-Rey, 1998; Peet, 2009, pp.84–5). Those countries have also given up control of prices of basic goods and utilities (Kirk and Okazawa-Rey, 1998, p.188), allowing market forces (read: corporations) free rein to establish prices. Whereas the middle class has been affected by the policy changes, the poor (especially mothers and their dependent children) have been disproportionately affected because they are the ones who depend the most on government assistance (Gershman et al., 2003, p.171).

As a result of neoliberal reforms, many women and men have been motivated to seek work in richer countries, leaving behind their families and communities. A number of nations in the South, such as the Philippines, have established institutional frameworks that encourage and facilitate their female citizens' efforts to seek work abroad as domestic workers and care workers because they view them as a potential source of foreign revenue, which could 'correct' trade imbalances (see Chapter Nine, this volume) and be used to service their debt to IFIs. The labor exporting nations also use that flow of foreign revenue as collateral when they attempt to borrow funds (see Chapter Nine, this volume).

This neoliberal end of labor-exporting states is also served by the discriminatory immigration policies of labor-importing nations. They ensure that 'low skill' workers remit their wages to their nations of origin; the policies make it exceptionally difficult or impossible for them to acquire permanent residency (or get visas that would allow their immediate family members to live with them while they work abroad) (see Chapters Six, Eight and Nine, this volume).

The discriminatory immigration and labor policies of labor receiving nations benefit their economies and citizens by making it very difficult for 'low skill' migrant workers to have their families live with them. The policies 'make' the migrant workers into neoliberalism's 'ideal' worker (see Chapter Five, this volume). Specifically, a worker who has no family that could lay claim on her time, attention or energy; she is always fully available to serve her employer's needs and wants (see Chapters Five, Seven, Eight and Nine, this volume). She is not only at the disposal of her employer, she is disposable. She can be forced to return to her nation of origin whenever the receiving nation decides it no longer needs her (see Chapters Two, Seven and Eight this volume). Thus, she, in effect, is reduced to a mere object that exists to be at the service of the labor importing countries.

The WB, the IMF and other IFIs have encouraged international labor migration as a development strategy (see Chapter Four, this volume). But migrant workers and their families have had to shoulder on their own the problems caused within their families by the extended absence of a family member; the IFIs, the labor-exporting states and the labor-importing states have done little or nothing to help them (see Chapters Four, Five, Six and Seven, this volume).

The WB and the IMF are aware that neoliberal reforms entail considerable hardship and suffering for migrant workers and their dependent family members. The WB, for instance, acknowledges that the policies are the cause of "much social pain . . ." (IMF, 1996). Ironically, both IFIs claim that their raison d'être is to help the poor of the global South. The WB lends solely to poorer nations (IMF, 1996) and by 2030 aims to achieve two key goals: to end severe poverty such that no more than 3 percent of the world population will have to survive on less than $1.25 per day, and to encourage the sharing of "prosperity by fostering the income growth of the bottom 40% for every country" (WB, n.d.). The IMF too purports to be motivated by the goal of improving the life prospects of the poor. It claims that it is "committed to the orderly and stable growth of the world economy" because it "will encourage trade, create jobs, expand economic activity, and raise living standards throughout the world" (IMF, 1996).

The advocacy of neoliberal reforms by these two IFIs is traceable to their undemocratic structure. Whereas the owners of the WB are its member nations, who have equity shares in the institution, the Bank is not governed democratically (Suzuki, 2011). The United States (US) is the dominant nation in the organization, and, thus, it has a significant role in defining the terms of the loans made by the WB (Peet, 2009, p.20). Similarly, in the IMF, the US has greater voting power than any other member nation of the organization. The member states of the IMF pay a membership fee or quota subscription, with richer countries paying more than poorer ones. The higher a nation's quota, the greater is its voting power (IMF, 2014). Thus the policies of the financial institution are primarily dictated by the richer member nations, especially the US given its voting clout in the WB and the IMF.

The WB and IMF have been working in conjunction for more than 40 years now. The latter requires that debtor nations in the global South engage in structural reforms of their economies that are espoused by the Bank (IMF, 1996). The reforms, i.e., the SAPs, require that debtor nations allow transnational corporations to engage in trade without being hindered by state intervention that could limit their profits (Peet, 2009, p.21). Additionally, the reforms entail, first, (as mentioned earlier) the reduction of state spending on basic goods and services, second, "the securing of property rights (including those of foreign companies), and [third], the export-orienting of economies to produce hard currency . . ." (Peet, 2009, p.20). These neoliberal reforms ". . . serve to maximize the loan capacity of 'developing countries' . . . [thus ensuring] to the fullest extent possible, [their ability] . . . to repay principal and interest [of the loans made to them by IFIs] . . ." (Peet, 2009, p.20). Moreover, by forcing the debtor nations of the South to devalue their currency so as to generate more export revenues, the IFIs make it harder for them to pay off their loans, because what they owe in terms of their local currency increases (Meghani, 2011). This means that their debt servitude worsens, benefiting their lenders. The WB is a major borrower in the capital markets around the world (IMF, 1996) and the neoliberal policies that it and other IFIs compels poorer nations to adopt as a condition of their loans serve the interests of the global financial markets. So, the real beneficiaries of the neoliberal reforms are the wealthiest of the wealthy, not the poor of the nations of the global South that borrow from the IFIs (2009).

Even as the neoliberal reforms advocated by the WB, the IMF, and other IFIs serve the interest of the capital markets, they have worsened the life prospects of the poor and even the middle class in the nations of the South that are their debtors. Thus these policies have and continue to play a crucial role in establishing and maintaining the flow of undocumented and documented female and male labor from the South to the North.

Contributions of Migrant Workers

In 2010, according to the UNDP, migrants from the South working in the North remitted to their nations of origin approximately US $243 billion (IOM, 2013, p.70),[16] constituting an estimated 56 percent of global remittances (IOM, 2013, p.72). This figure is an underestimate because it does not include monies sent through informal channels (UNPFA, 2006, p.12).

The US Central Intelligence Agency and the European Commission have found that "migration contributes to overall growth, greater productivity and higher employment" for all (UNFPA, 2006, p.17). Female and male migrant workers provide crucial services to the economies of the nations where they work, but that is not always recognized by the citizens of those countries. Those who oppose immigration tend to argue that immigrants deprive them of jobs and depress the wage rate by accepting lower pay than the market rate. Another complaint is that migrant workers are an economic burden on the receiving nations because they take advantage of the social safety net in the nations where they work (IOM, 2011, p.28).

These charges reveal themselves to be baseless when a comprehensive view of the impact of immigrants is taken (UNFPA, 2006, p.17). Empirical studies show that the net effect of the presence of undocumented and documented foreign workers on employment prospects and wages in receiving nations is modest. International migrant workers, especially those with 'low skills,' compete with other similarly skilled migrants for jobs that citizens do not want (UNFPA, 2006, p.17; also see Chapter Ten, this volume). Additionally, while some international migrants compete with citizens for blue-collar work, their effect on the employment prospects of the latter group may be the same as the impact of cheap, labor-intensive imported products (UNFPA, 2006, p.17). Migrant workers may also be compensating for skill gaps within the local population that are attributable to failures in the training or educational system (IOM, 2011, p.28). They might also be responding to the labor market needs of fast growing economies, nations that have declining fertility rates or countries with an aging population (IOM, 2011, p.28).

It is illuminating to consider the impact of undocumented and documented migrant workers in the US. During 2000–7, a third of the growth in America's gross domestic production was attributable to migrants (IOM, 2011, p.29). Data show that the claim that migrants pay little or no taxes or social security is also without merit. For instance, according to the US Social Security Administration (SSA), in 2010, unauthorized immigrants paid $13 billion in payroll taxes but received only approximately $1 billion in benefit payments (Goss et al., 2013, p.3). The SSA also estimated that over the last decade, undocumented workers paid $100 billion into the Social Security Trust Fund but are not likely to benefit from their contributions during their retirement years (Germano, 2014). Immigrants account for approximately 8 percent of the US's total health-care expenditure and government health-care fund, even though they constitute approximately 11 percent of the population (UNFPA, 2006, p.17). In 2008, in the US, the ratio of benefits received from public social services to taxes for citizens was 1.4–1.2 and for immigrants it was 0.8–0.5 (IOM, 2011, p.29).

As the cost of educating and training migrants is borne by their nation of origin, migrant workers cost less to the host nation's economy than the local population of workers (IOM, 2011, p.28). Moreover, if migrants retire to their nation of origin, they pose less of a burden to the country where they were employed than the native population (IOM, 2011, p.28).

In light of the contributions of migrant workers to the economies of receiving nations, the local population's antipathy toward them is not justified. The next section outlines the challenges faced by female foreign migrant workers who are employed in the lower tiers of the hierarchy of professions.

THE MIGRATION EXPERIENCE OF WOMEN WORKERS FROM THE SOUTH

Neoliberal reform has made it easy for products, capital, services, information and ideas to move freely across borders, but humans (especially persons of color with few resources) are subject to numerous restrictions (Davies, 2009). The barriers that persons confront may be profound depending on who they are and the value placed by the labor-importing nations on their skills and the work they perform. The border-crossing experience of women workers is a function of their official status. Documented workers fare better than undocumented ones. The latter group faces considerable dangers, including sexual harassment and assault. Undocumented women may be coerced into performing sex acts as a quid pro quo for 'safe' passage by traffickers or male fellow migrants (UNPFA, 2006, p.31).

The United Nations' International Convention on the Protection of the Rights of All Migrant Workers and Members of their Families aims to ensure that documented and undocumented migrants in any nation are entitled to the same human rights as any other person (UNPFA, 2006, p.17). Its signatories are obligated to make sure that all migrant workers are protected "from enslavement and violence; [have] access to emergency medical care and education for the[ir] children; [afforded] equal treatment as nationals with regard to working conditions; [have] the right to join trade unions and other organizations defending their interests . . ." (UNPFA, 2006, p.17). As of July 2015 (when this chapter was written), the treaty had not been signed, let alone ratified, by Canada, France, Germany, Greece, Ireland, Norway, Spain, the US or the UK (United Nations, 2013). These nations are the wealthy liberal democracies wherein many of the workers from the South seek employment.

As migrants and as women, 'low-skilled' female migrant workers are "doubly disadvantaged" (UNPFA, 2006, p.32). At every stage of the migration experience, they confront more human rights violations than their male counterparts (IOM, 2009, p.9). The circumstances of undocumented women migrant workers can be particularly pernicious depending on their class, race or ethnicity. Not only do they have limited or no access to health care and social services (see Chapters Three and Seven, this volume), their living and work conditions tend to be difficult (IOM, 2009, p.9; see also Chapter Seven, this volume). They are more likely than their male counterparts or documented female peers to be subject to "harassment, intimidation or threats as well as economic and sexual exploitation including trafficking and racial discrimination" (IOM, 2009, p.9).

Gender bias, government policies and employer practices determine the employment prospects of foreign female migrant workers (UNPFA, 2006, p.22; see also Chapters Five and Seven, this volume). For instance, short-term or seasonal labor migration programs are designed with the assumption that the migrant worker will be a single male (UNPFA, 2006, p.32;

Chapter Seven, this volume), and usually the programs aim to meet labor supply shortages in professions that are male dominated, such as farming (see Chapter Seven, this volume). As a rule, women migrant workers—documented and undocumented—can only find work in gender-segregated sectors of the economy that tend to be informal and unregulated (IOM, 2009, p.9; see Chapters Two, Three, Five, Seven, Eight and Ten, this volume). All too often labor laws do not cover professions in which 'low-skilled' women are employed, such as domestic work and care work (see Chapters Two, Three, Five and Ten, this volume), thus the women have few or no rights as workers and little or no bargaining power. Moreover, usually they are not eligible to participate in the state-run social security programs of labor importing nations. Thus, they cannot rely on them for benefits during their old age when they can no longer work (see Chapters Three and Six, this volume). In fact, the labor importing nations thwart the efforts of undocumented workers to set aside monies for their retirement and they make it very difficult for them to be autonomous (see Chapter Six, this volume).

Whereas female and male migrant workers funnel social remittances to their nations of origin (see Chapter Six, this volume), women are more likely to do so than their male counterparts (GFMD, 2010, pp.2–3). They pass on to their families and communities in their nation of origin norms, attitudes, behaviors, ideas, information and knowledge, including the importance of education, good healthcare practices, and health insurance (UNPFA, 2006, p.10, 14; Chapter Six, this volume). They thus play a role in affecting cultural and political change, which encompasses gender justice (UNPFA, 2006, p.14).

Along the global labor chain, a number of state and nonstate actors (such as state regulatory agencies, labor recruitment and placement businesses and money lenders[17]) 'appropriate' a substantial amount of the wages of international workers as they attempt to travel abroad for work or send monies to their families in their nation of origin (see Chapter Nine, this volume). Usually, female migrant workers remit a greater percentage of their wages and salaries than their male counterparts (UNPFA, 2006, p.12; GFMD, 2010, pp.2–3), so this exploitive practice particularly affects them, and especially the subgroup of women who work in the lower tiers of the professional hierarchy and who are underpaid.

Finally, female international workers who are undocumented or employed in 'low skill' jobs have few prospects for a stable, secure, long-term existence in the wealthy liberal democracies where they work. For permanent immigration, a number of rich nations, such as the US and Singapore, have established criteria that are biased against undocumented workers or those employed in 'low-skilled' professions. The standards require that migrant workers be highly educated professionals with considerable proficiency in the official language of that nation (UNPFA, 2006, p 32).[18] In some countries, even the option of family reunification is available only to highly skilled, documented workers. To sum up, in wealthy liberal democracies, female foreign workers who rank low in the professional hierarchy have an existence that is precarious and difficult.

FORGING AHEAD

This collection advances and breaks new ground in the research on international migrant women workers who are employed in the 'low-skill' professions or are undocumented. The discussions of the ethical, political and legal harms experienced by the women (who are employed as farmworkers, home health workers, elder care workers, child-care workers and domestic workers) are informed by data and case studies. This volume thus offers richer analyses than works that are purely theoretical discussions about the feminized global labor flow. It analyzes and critiques the structural, systemic intersecting factors that define the limits of the agency of individual migrant women workers. A number of the chapters examine the role of neoliberal policies and programs in shaping the life and work prospects of the women and their families, thus this volume offers a deeper analysis of the circumstances of migrant women workers than accounts that overlook the impact of that ideology.

By bringing together the original work of researchers from a variety of disciplines, this collection provides a nuanced, multifaceted complex account of the treatment of women workers from the global South in wealthy liberal democratic nations. This volume thus makes the argument that those countries are only nominally committed to gender equality and treating all persons within their borders as moral equals.

In advancing the research on migrant women workers, this collection builds on the important work on the feminization of the global labor flow by Janet Momsen (1999), Barbara Ehrenreich and Arlie Russell Hochschild (2003), Mary K. Zimmerman, Jacqelyn S. Litt and Christine E. Bose (2006) and Seyla Benhabib and Judith Resnick (2009). Taking its impetus from Momsen's volume, it uses case studies that are attentive to the impact of discriminatory and exploitative immigration policies, and structural, systemic, intersecting forms of oppression, specifically, sexism, classism, racism and nationalism.[19] In offering a multidisciplinary perspective on the circumstances of women migrant workers from the global South, this volume mirrors the Ehrenreich and Hochschild anthology (2003). The thematic approach taken in this book is akin to that adopted by Zimmerman, Litt and Bose (2006), but the original works presented here cover female care workers, domestic workers, health-care workers and farmworkers. While this volume has been influenced by Benhabib and Resnick's work (2009) on the national and international laws that shape the lives of female migrant workers, it also addresses a variety of other important issues, including the flaws in the neoliberal development paradigm, the failure of the traditional model of social security to recognize that millions of women from the South are employed as international migrant workers, and the significance of the 2008 global financial crisis for migrant women workers.

A ROADMAP TO THE BOOK

Thematic Connections

This volume is organized into five parts with themes that are interconnected and overlapping. Part one, "Circumstances of Injustice," consists of two chapters that analyze the complex interaction between discriminatory and exploitive immigration laws and employment laws and their oppressive impact on migrant women workers from the global South in Ireland and the US. In Chapter Two, political scientist Graham Finlay and historian JoAnne M. Mancini argue that in Ireland female international migrant workers are vulnerable to exploitation because of immigration policies that are sexist, racist and classist, and a gender-biased social security system. On the basis of their analysis of the treatment of care workers from the Philippines, India and sub-Saharan Africa, they contend that Ireland's immigration policies are designed to reduce those women to objects that the Republic can use and discard as it pleases. Finlay and Mancini hold that Ireland's legal and political institutions should be reformed so that they are respectful of human rights and consistent with the Convention on the Elimination of All Forms of Discrimination against Women. They justify their position by grounding it in Amartya Sen's Capabilities Approach.

In the third chapter, Zahra Meghani, a philosopher, argues that female undocumented home health workers in the US face discriminatory and exploitative laws and regulations at the federal and state level. She makes the case that this constitutes an ethical failure of the liberal democratic state. Meghani also examines the key advocacy efforts of nongovernmental organizations on behalf of care workers to analyze their significance for female undocumented home health workers.

The next set of chapters takes up the theme of uncaring development paradigms. Chapters Four and Five critique the neoliberal model of development adopted by poorer nations that supply care workers to richer countries. In Chapter Four, Delali Badasu, a geography and resource development expert, and historian Sonya Michel criticize Ghana's neoliberal development paradigm because it has led to a failure of the state to address the child care needs of Ghanaian women who have sought work in other nations. Those migrant workers' families have had to cope on their own with the impact of maternal absence on children without any help from the state. As a result, despite the increase in remittances from abroad, Ghana is having considerable difficulty meeting the social development benchmarks of the United Nations' Millennium Goals. Badasu and Michel argue that this failure of care by the state is a serious ethical problem that must be addressed. In Chapter Five, Amaia Pérez Orozco, an economist, argues that the neoliberal development model must be rejected because it engenders and sustains unjust global care chains. Aside from defining the characteristics of unjust care systems, Pérez Orozco uses the case of migration of care workers from Bolivia, Ecuador and Peru to Spain to identify the failings of the dominant development model.

Chapters Six and Seven criticize unjust social protection systems because they do not take into account the needs of migrant women (and men) workers who are employed in 'low-skill' professions. In Chapter Six, Sarah van Walsum, a legal scholar, argues that while wealthier nations have created a transnational social security system for their own citizens by using foreign migrant workers to meet their care needs, they have treated those workers unfairly by not establishing a formal transnational social protection system for them. She makes the case that both receiving and sending nations should eschew the nationalist model of social security. Her theorizing is informed by her research on the strategies used by Ghanaian and Filipina domestic workers in the Netherlands and their family members (who are in Ghana and the Philippines) to provide social security for themselves. Van Waslum criticizes the Dutch state for policies that undermine the efforts of Ghanaian and Filipina low-skilled undocumented migrant workers to meet the needs of their dependent family members (in their nations of origin) and make financial arrangements for their old age. She argues that the social security systems of Ghana, the Netherlands and the Philippines should be expanded and reshaped to meet the needs of international migrant workers who are employed in the lower tiers of the hierarchy of professions.

Chapter Seven by anthropologist Ofelia Becerril is an argument for the need for policies and programs that are specific to the needs of particular groups of international migrant workers and their families. As her case study, she uses female Mexican migrant farmworkers who are mothers with dependent children and who are employed in Canada as part of the Canadian-Mexican Seasonal Agricultural Workers (SAW) program. Besides providing a detailed analysis of the SAW program, she critiques its gendered impact and the failure of Canada and Mexico to ensure that the human rights of female SAW program workers are respected and that they have access to social protection programs that are tailored to meet their needs. Becerril also makes recommendations for policy changes that could improve the working and living conditions of those workers.

The theme of Chapter Eight is care for care workers. Anthropologist Theresa Devasahayam criticizes Singapore's labor rules and policies that deny female foreign domestic workers basic workers' rights. The failure of the state to respect their human rights as workers has exacerbated the women's sense of isolation in Singapore. To alleviate their feeling of detachment and to care for the women, the Roman Catholic Church, a nonstate actor, has attempted to provide a "home" for them. Devasahayam analyzes the institutional values motivating and shaping the organization's attempt to care for female international domestic workers.

16 *Zahra Meghani*

The last two chapters identify new directions for research on the feminization of the global labor flow. In Chapter Nine, Stuart Rosewarne, an economist, argues that the transnational flow of funds entailed by the commodification of reproductive labor is organized through a multilayered institutional architecture. He makes the case that these entities constitute an exploitative global chain along which multiple state and nonstate actors take advantage of female migrant domestic workers by appropriating a significant portion of their wages. Thus there is a need for more research on this global circuit of capitalist exploitation that runs parallel to the global circuit of care. In the tenth and final chapter, economist Antigone Lyberaki discusses the impact of the financial crisis in southern European Union (EU) nations on migrant women workers. Using the case of Albanian care workers and domestic workers employed in Greece, she considers the paradox facing female migrant workers from the global South whose home nations are presently performing better and have brighter economic prospects than the EU nations they migrated to for work. Her work indicates the need for research that tracks the impact of the recent financial crisis on international migrant women workers.

Geographic Connections

The chapters of this volume provide 'snapshots' of the situation of migrant women workers from the global South in a number of wealthy liberal democracies on different continents. Chapters Two, Five, Six and Ten examine the situation of care workers and domestic workers in Ireland, Spain, the Netherlands and Greece, respectively. Chapters Three and Six consider the treatment of female migrant workers in North America, specifically, female undocumented home health workers in the US, and documented migrant farmworkers in Canada who are mothers with young children, respectively. Chapters Eight and Nine shift the focus eastward as they analyze the marginalization of child care and domestic workers in Singapore and Hong Kong.

Poorer countries in South and Central America, South and East Asia, Africa and Eastern Europe are the source nations of the women migrant workers who are the subject of this volume. The population of women discussed in Chapters Two, Four and Six includes citizens of Ghana and other sub-Saharan nations. Migrant women from Mexico and various South American countries (especially Bolivia, Ecuador and Peru) are the concern of Chapters Three, Five and Seven. The injustices faced by women workers from Bangladesh, Cambodia, India, Indonesia, Laos, Malaysia, Mongolia, Mynamar, Nepal, the Philippines and Vietnam are discussed in Chapters Two, Six, Eight and Nine. Albanian migrant women workers who are employed as domestic workers, child-care providers and elder care workers are the focus of Chapter Ten.

CONCLUSION

This volume is not an argument against the migration of 'low skilled' women workers from poorer countries to wealthy liberal democracies. Rather it makes a case for change. In sending and receiving nations, men must take on equal responsibility for care work and domestic work (see especially Chapters Five, Seven and Ten, this volume). There is an immediate need for reform of immigration and employment laws and policies in receiving nations so that migrant workers are not subject to marginalization, exploitation or discrimination (see, for instance, Chapters Two, Three, Six, Seven, Eight and Ten, this volume). The social protection systems of labor-exporting and labor-importing countries need to be reshaped so that they are transnational and tailored to meet the particular needs of different groups of migrant women (and men) workers and their dependent family members (see Chapters Six and Seven, this volume). Both state and nonstate entities (especially transnational financial institutions) must eschew their commitment to the neoliberal paradigm of development and adopt a development model that places the well-being of the poor and marginalized front and center (see especially Chapters Four and Five, this volume). State and nonstate entities should not take advantage of women migrant workers when they travel to other nations for work or when they remit their wages (see Chapter Nine, this volume). Nongovernmental organizations who claim to advocate on behalf of migrant workers should represent their needs and interests even if it means taking a stand that is unpopular or critical of the state (see Chapters Three and Eight, this volume). Additionally, both state and nonstate organizations should conduct research to determine the impact of economic and political policies on migrant women workers and their families (see Chapter Ten, this volume). All in all, liberal democracies should not deny the members of some groups living within their borders freedoms, benefits, opportunities and protections on the grounds that they were born on the 'wrong' latitude and longitude. Otherwise they will continue to cause significant harm to them and give lie to their own claims about their commitment to respecting the human rights of all persons, including the right of women to not be subject to gender-based discrimination.

NOTES

1. "Nation," "country" and "state" are used interchangeably.
2. In many societies, women who lack higher education degrees are channeled into 'womanly' work, i.e., domestic work or care work. It is assumed that this kind of work comes 'naturally' to them (given their biology) and thus requires little or no skill. In reality, care work, for instance, requires a multitude of skills if the dependent charge is to survive and thrive.
3. Canada is one of the exceptions as it permits some care workers to apply for permanent resident status if they meet certain criteria.
4. In some Ghanian families, young children are sent to boarding schools when the mothers migrate for work (see Chapter Four, this volume).

5. It is worth considering that it is solely by convention that in a number of democratic nations, the right to vote has been limited to citizens; it is not a universal norm. For instance, in the US, from 1776 to 1926, noncitizens were permitted to vote in local and federal elections in forty US states and territories (Holding, 2007, p.60). The US Constitution left it up to individual states and cities to determine who should be able to vote; thus, while slaves, women and propertyless white men were denied the right to vote, many constituencies allowed propertied male noncitizens voting rights. The right of noncitizens to vote was rescinded because of the rise in anti-immigration sentiments at the beginning of the twentieth century and the mistrust of foreigners in the wake of World War I (Holding, 2007, p.60).
6. The economic arguments are discussed later.
7. See the detailed account and analysis provided by Benhabib (2004) of an attempt in Europe to resolve this tension.
8. Miller, for instance, contends that when liberals consider the viability of a proposed secession, they should take into account whether the people populating the new state already have a shared sense of identity (2003, p.270).
9. Documented workers' eligibility to apply for permanent residency is not considered problematic by Carens.
10. Carens holds that they should be able to access emergency health care without being at risk of deportation (Carens, 2014, p.551). But he does not engage with the important issue of access to non-emergency medical care for undocumented persons and low income documented workers.
11. According to the IOM (2013), billions of dollars are remitted annually by documented and undocumented migrant workers
12. A similar argument can be made for 'low skill' documented workers.
13. This collection does not, for instance, consider the case of female international migrant workers in undemocratic regimes or the situation of women employed as sex workers because those are cases that deserve extended treatment on their own.
14. Of course, not all women who employ domestic workers have male partners.
15. Since the 1990s, the WB and the IMF have re-named the neoliberal reforms that they advocate "poverty reduction strategies," rejecting the previously used term "structural adjustment policies." But the substance of the policies has remained the same (Schrecker and Labonté, 2007, p. 292).
16. The remittances would be greater but for the exploitative high fees charged by various entities for transferring funds between nations. It can range up to 20 percent of the amount being sent (UNPFA, 2006, p.14).
17. Traveling abroad for work is an expensive proposition for the middle class and the poor of the global South; it entails borrowing from moneylenders at a high interest rate, which they then have to pay using their earnings.
18. Spain and Italy are among the few nations that permit low-skilled workers the option of sponsoring their families (UNPFA, 2006, p.33).
19. This is not to suggest that those are the only forms of oppression or the only ones that matter; but given the limited scope of this project, they are the ones that are covered.

REFERENCES AND FURTHER READINGS

Assembly, U. G. 1948. Universal declaration of human rights. UN General Assembly.
Ban, C., 2011. *Neoliberalism in translation: Economic ideas and reforms in Spain and Romania: Collaboration between the WB and the IMF*. Ph. D. Diss. University of Maryland, Baltimore.
Benhabib, S., 2004. *The rights of others*. Cambridge: Cambridge University Press.

Benhabib, S. and Resnik, J., eds., 2009. *Migrations and mobilities: Citizenship, borders and gender.* New York: New York University Press.
Bosniak, L. 2010. Forum. In: J.H. Carens, ed. 2010. *Immigrants and the Right to Stay.* Cambridge, MA: MIT Press, pp.81–92.
Carens, J. H. 2010. *Immigrants and the Right to Stay.* Cambridge, MA: MIT Press.
Carens, J. H. 2013. *The ethics of immigration.* New York: Oxford University Press.
Carens, J. H. 2014. An overview of the ethics of immigration. *Critical Review of International Social and Political Philosophy*, 17(5), pp. 538–559.
Chammartin, G.M., 2005. Domestic workers: Little protection for the underpaid, [online] Migration Information Source. Available at: <www.migrationinformation.org/Feature/display.cfm?id=300> [Accessed 14 February 2014].
Davies, I., 2009. Latino immigration and social change in the United States: Toward an ethical immigration policy. *Journal of business ethics*, 88 (2), pp.377–91.
Ehrenreich, B. and Hochschild, A.R., 2003. *Global woman: Nannies, maids, and sex workers in the new economy.* New York: Metropolitan Books.
Germano, R., 2014. Unauthorized immigrants paid $100 billion into social security over last decade. *Vice News*, [online] Available at: <https://news.vice.com/article/unauthorized-immigrants-paid-100-billion-into-social-security-over-last-decade> [Accessed 13 April 2014].
Gershman, J. Irwin, A. and Shakow, A., 2003. Getting a grip on the global economy: Health outcomes and the decoding of development discourse. In: R. Hofrichter, ed. 2003. *Health and social justice: Politics, ideology, and inequity in the distribution of disease: A public health Reader.* San Francisco: Jossey-Bass, pp.157–94.
Global Forum on Migration and Development (GFMD), 2010. Uncovering the interfaces between gender, family, migration and development: The global care economy and chains (Annex to Roundtable 2.2 Background Paper), [online] Available at: <https://www.gfmd.org/uncovering-interfaces-between-gender-family-migration-and-development-global-care-economy-and-chains> [Accessed 13 April 2014].
Goss, S. et al., 2013. Effects of unauthorized immigration on the actuarial status of the social security trust funds. *Actuarial Note*, 151, pp.1–5, [pdf] Available at: <http://www.ssa.gov/oact/NOTES/pdf_notes/note151.pdf> [Accessed 26 October 2014].
Harvey, D., 2005. *A brief history of neoliberalism.* New York: Oxford University Press.
Holding, R., 2007. Voting block. *Time Magazine*, 12 April, pp.60–1.
International Monetary Fund (IMF), 1996. *About the IMF: The IMF and the World Bank how do they differ?* [online] Available at: <https://www.imf.org/external/pubs/ft/exrp/differ/differ.htm> [Accessed 15 September 2014].
International Monetary Fund, 2014. *About the IMF: IMF members' quotas and voting power, and IMF board of governors.* [online] Available at: < http://www.imf.org/external/np/sec/memdir/members.aspx > [Accessed 6 December 2014].
International Organization for Migration (IOM), 2009. *Working to prevent and address violence against women migrant workers.* IOM, Geneva, [pdf] Available at: <http://publications.iom.int/bookstore/free/Gender_Report.pdf> [Accessed 14 February 2014].
International Organization for Migration (IOM), 2011. *World migration report: Communicating effectively about migration.* IOM, Geneva, [pdf] Available at: <http://publications.iom.int/bookstore/free/WMR2011_English.pdf> [Accessed 14 February 2014].
International Organization for Migration (IOM), 2013. *World migration report: Migrant well-being and development.* IOM, Geneva. [pdf] Available at: <http://publications.iom.int/bookstore/free/WMR2013_EN.pdf> [Accessed 15 September 2014].

Kirk, G. and Okazawa-Rey, M., 1998. Living in a global economy. In: G. Kirk and M. Okazawa-Rey, eds. 1998. *Women's lives: Multicultural perspectives*. Mountain View: Mayfield Publishing Company.

Kymlicka, W., 2001. *Politics in the vernacular: Nationalism, multiculturalism and citizenship*. New York: Oxford University Press.

Meghani, Z., 2011. A robust, particularist ethical assessment of medical tourism. *Developing World Bioethics*, 11(1), pp.16–29.

Miller, D., 2003. Liberalism and boundaries: A response to Allan Buchanan. In: A. Buchanan and M. Moore, eds. 2003. *States, nations and borders: The ethics of making boundaries*. Cambridge: Cambridge University Press, pp.262–73.

Momsen, J.H., ed., 1999. *Gender, migration and domestic service*. London and New York: Routledge.

Nielsen, K., 1985. *Equality and liberty: A defense of radical egalitarianism*. Totowa, NJ: Rowman & Allanheld.

Peet, R., 2009. *Unholy Trinity: The IMF, World Bank and WTO*. London and New York: Zed Books.

Schrecker, T. & Labonté, R. 2007. What's Politics Got to do With It? Health, the G8, and the Global Economy. In: I. Kawachi & S. Wamala, eds. 2007. *Globalization and Health*. New York, NY: Oxford University Press, pp. 284–310.

Shaw, W. 2003. Relativism in ethics. *Perspectives on ethics*. Boston: McGraw-Hill, pp. 90–5.

Suzuki, E., 2011. Global governance and international financial institutions. *Asia Pac. L. Rev.*, 19 (13), pp.15–36.United Nations, 2005. *Human development report 2005: International cooperation at a crossroads: Aid, trade, and security in an unequal world*, [pdf] Available at: <http://hdr.undp.org/sites/default/files/reports/266/hdr05_complete.pdf> [Accessed 14 February 2014].

United Nations, 2013. *United Nations treaty collection. Chapter IV. Human rights 13. International convention on the protection of the rights of all migrant workers and members of their families*,[online]. Available at: <http://treaties.un.org/Pages/ViewDetails.aspx?mtdsg_no=IV-13&chapter=4&lang=en> [Accessed 14 February 2014].

United Nations Development Programme, 2009. *Overcoming barriers: Human mobility and development* (Human Development Report 2009). UNDP/Palgrave, New York.

United Nations Population Fund (UNFPA), 2006. *State of world population 2006: A passage to hope: Women and international migration*, [pdf] Available at: <http://www.unfpa.org/webdav/site/global/shared/documents/publications/2006/sowp06-en.pdf> [Accessed 14 February 2014].

Von Hayek, F., 1984. *The essence of Hayek*, ed. C. Nishiyama and K. Leube, Stanford, CA: Hoover Institution.

Von Hayek, F., 1988. *The fatal conceit: The errors of socialism*. Chicago, IL: University of Chicago Press.

Weisbrot, D., Baker, D. and Rosnick, D., 2007. The scorecard on development: 25 years of diminished progress. In: V. Navarro, ed. 2007. *Neoliberalism, globalization and inequalities: Consequences for health and quality of life*. Amityville, NY: Baywood Publishing, pp.179–201.

Wellman, C., 2008. Immigration and Freedom of Association. *Ethics*, 11(9), 109–41.

World Bank (WB). 2015. *About: What we do*, [online] Available at: <http://www.worldbank.org/en/about/what-we-do> [Accessed 15 September 2014].

Zimmerman, M.K., Litt, J.S. and Bose, C.E., 2006. *Global dimensions of gender and carework*. Stanford, CA: Stanford University Press.

Part I
Circumstances of Injustice

2 "Her Life within the Home"
The Construction of Gender and Female International Migrant Workers in the Republic of Ireland

Graham Finlay and JoAnne M. Mancini

> *This century will end and the new century emerge with the figure of the migrant at the centre of things. Contained in the essence of the migratory experience are relationships to time and space that have, up to now, been seen as the experience of a minority that, for most policy purposes, could be neglected without cost. . . . At the heart of migration lies the transience of things. It is that transience that explains both the risks and the neglected benefits of having chosen, or of having been condemned to break the inherited links to space, time and cultural certainties. The migratory experience is one of pain . . . One issue immediately suggests itself. It is that of the rights of migrants. If migrants are to possess rights as both human persons and collectivities, their rights attach less to place, nation, race or, indeed property, than they do to persons, individually and collectively.*
>
> Michael D. Higgins, Speech accepting the Sean MacBride Peace Prize, August 30, 1992, (Higgins, 1992). Michael D. Higgins was elected President of Ireland in the election of October 27, 2011.

INTRODUCTION

Ireland's recent history of boom and bust has been characterized by equally volatile flows of people and labor. International migrant workers from a variety of backgrounds were crucial to private industry and to the public sector, particularly health and elder care, and to the increased entry of Irish women into the workforce. Once in Ireland, international migrant workers encountered a number of barriers to equal access to employment rights, to social services, to family reunification, to secure residence and to citizenship. We argue, in this chapter, that these exclusions are evidence of a comprehensive attempt to reduce international migrants to their function as workers, and they have negative effects on their well-being that are easily predictable. These exclusions also present a serious threat of exploitation.[1] Like migration globally, international migration to Ireland has been characterized by the "feminization of migration." Given the increased number of female international migrants and the sectors in which they most often work, these policies and risks take on an explicitly gendered cast that has its origin in the construction of gender in the Republic of Ireland, including its founding and constitutional documents. In these documents, women are explicitly understood primarily as mothers, and female employment is constructed as a risk to this primary role. Although the founding documents can and have been used to argue for greater rights for noncitizen parents of Irish-born children and for a fairer immigration policy generally, they fall short of establishing a fair basis for immigration and work. Accordingly, we recommend an approach based on international human rights instruments, as understood through the capability approach to human rights promoted by Amartya Sen.

In section one we examine the Irish legal and policy context regarding international migration. In section two, we describe the construction of gender in Ireland and the gendered cast of Irish work. Section three analyzes the intersection of Irish policy and the construction of gender and work that causes (easily foreseeable) harms to female international migrant workers. In the following section, section four, we propose a just response to the situation of female international migrant workers, based on international human rights instruments. In section five, we explore a potential ethical basis for this approach, based on Amartya Sen's version of the capability approach. In section six, we explore the benefits of the flexibility of his capability approach. Finally, in section seven we make some concrete policy recommendations for both state and non-state actors and in section eight we consider some potential objections to our approach.

RECENT MIGRATION TO IRELAND AND IRISH MIGRATION POLICY

Although Ireland has always been more diverse than has been acknowledged, the economic boom of the 1990s and early 2000s saw dramatic inflows of people and the crystallization of a complex and differential spectrum of categories for classifying inward international migrants. These include "returned" Irish citizens (a category that includes people whose citizenship derives from the citizenship of a parent or grandparent); citizens of the European Economic Area (EEA)[2] or Switzerland, who are able to work in Ireland without obtaining work permits; migrants from outside the EEA who hold work permits; students (an important source of labor); seekers of asylum; spouses and intended spouses of Irish and EEA citizens; and irregular international migrants, which includes anyone who does not have the legal right to work or live in Ireland.

Statistics are not always available for all categories of migrant, and gender breakdowns are even less accessible. However, the 2006 census recorded 400,000 non-Irish citizens (Pillinger, 2007, p.17). It also included over 100,000 foreign-born Irish citizens living in Ireland. This high figure reflects Ireland's very generous granting of citizenship by descent: regardless of place of birth, any person who has a parent who was born on the island of Ireland (including Northern Ireland, under the jurisdiction of the United Kingdom) is automatically an Irish citizen; and any person with a grandparent born on the island of Ireland can apply for and will normally be granted citizenship. Because this group experiences some of the same barriers that non-Irish international migrants do, in this chapter we consider returning Irish citizens along with the other categories of migrants (NíLaoire, 2008, p.36).

In recent years, migration to Ireland has exhibited some important trends, including the increase of international migrants from within the European Union (EU) and the decrease of both work permit holders and persons seeking and obtaining asylum.[3] These trends reflect external conditions, notably the enlargement of the EU in 2004 to include ten new member states (Cyprus, Czech Republic, Estonia, Hungary, Latvia, Lithuania, Malta, Poland, Slovakia and Slovenia), and they mirror Irish policy. Most obviously, the increase in numbers of migrants from within the EU reflects Ireland's position as one of only three pre-2004 EU states (the others are the United Kingdom and Sweden) that did not erect a work permit requirement for migrants from the ten "accession states." But these trends also reflect another, apparently contradictory aspect of Irish policy: its tendency to erect barriers to permanent settlement and employment for international migrants. Irish policy also does not allow them to access social welfare provisions. Additionally, the Irish state excludes, marginalizes and expels seekers of asylum, who by definition are applicants for permanent residency and whose purpose in migrating is not primarily economic. The state's encouragement of a flexible international migrant labor force, which can be attracted or dispelled as economic needs change, leaves this workforce vulnerable to exploitation. Central to this policy is the discouragement of less 'disposable' noneconomic international migrants, who have or are seeking to have the right to permanent residence.

The Irish policy impetus against permanence of residency and employment is most easily discernible in the case of work permit holders. Until 2006, work permit holders had no clearly defined route to permanent residence and were not ordinarily able to change employers without applying for a new permit. The newly introduced "green cards" permit long-term residency and greater ease of family reunification, but they are only available to small numbers of work permit holders. In order to qualify, international migrants must have salaries over 60,000 euro (when the average industrial wage in the first quarter of 2011 was 35, 237 euro, (Central Statistics Office, 2011)), or work in certain defined sectors, including health care, and earn a salary between 30,000 and 60,000 euro.

Moreover, other recent policies reinforce the bias against permanence for work permit holders. Only jobs that have been subject to a period of advertisement known as the "labor market test" are open to work permit holders. In April 2009, the labor market test was extended to eight weeks. As this condition also applies in the case of work permit holders seeking the renewal of their permits, it has been criticized for driving workers whose permits are expiring into irregular status. Moreover, this change was accompanied by the elimination of the automatic right to work for spouses and dependents of work permit holders (Department of Jobs, Enterprise and Innovation, 2009). This suspension followed another major change in Irish law affecting the status and permanence of work permit holders' families. In 2004, the government initiated a referendum to remove Ireland's automatic provision of citizenship to anyone born in its territory, which passed with a large majority (Mancini and Finlay, 2008). As a result, the Irish-born children of work permit holders and other noncitizens only qualify for citizenship if one or both of their parents meet new residency requirements (which are set by legislation and are open to revision at any time) or through naturalization. As Ireland has one of the lowest rates of acceptance of applications for naturalization in the developed world and very restrictive policies regarding family reunification, the 2004 constitutional change struck a serious blow to permanence for international migrant families.[4]

The tenuous claim to residence for work permit holders has allowed their large-scale replacement by migrants from the EU "accession states" after 2004. As suggested above, Irish policy encouraged this new migration. However, it did so while introducing new barriers to social provision for "accession state" migrants. In order to qualify for nearly any form of social benefit, including pensions, unemployment assistance and the main type of provision for families with children, Child Benefit, migrants from the accession states must meet a Habitual Residency Condition. This Habitual Residency Condition also may apply to returning Irish citizens, who have been refused social protections when they have been found not to meet it (Crosscare, 2010). Recently, however, the cases involving returning Irish citizens have led to deciding officers being given more discretion in terms of whether an individual meets the condition. (Citizens Information Board, 2014). Given that this discretion is largely concerned with citizens perceived to be "Irish," these changes inject a new level of arbitrariness and ethnic preference into the welfare system, to the detriment of migrant workers of other perceived ethnicities. Except for "returning Irish citizens," this Habitual Residency Condition is applied stringently: periods during which international migrant workers are out of work are excluded, as are periods spent on a work permit (in the case of accession state citizens in Ireland before the 2004 enlargement). It is also applied arbitrarily: international migrants can be denied benefits under the Habitual Residency Condition for a variety of reasons,[5] and all decisions are made at the discretion of a Deciding Officer (Department of Social Protection, 2011). As a result, a number of lawsuits have arisen over the denial of social protections and the Free Legal Advice Centre (FLAC) has launched a human rights-based campaign against the discriminatory aspects of the Habitual Residency Condition (Baker, 2011, Free Legal Advice Centre, 2011). Ireland also limits or bars access to social provisions by EU migrants in other ways. The state is seeking to alter EU rules that entitle nonresident children of workers resident in Ireland to Child Benefit at Irish rates. Instead, the state proposes that payment be made according to scales set in the country of residence—scales that are lower due both to the lower cost of living in other states but also because, unlike Ireland, many other EU states divide social supports to children among a variety of programs, of which direct payment is only one component (Smyth, 2011).

As mentioned earlier, the increase in migration to Ireland by citizens of the EU accession states was accompanied not only by a decrease in work permit holders in Ireland, but also by a decline in applications for asylum. There are two reasons why the decline in applications for asylum relates directly to the relationships between labor, migration and permanency. First, international migrants in this category are by definition seeking permanent leave to remain and are unlikely to leave Ireland if the economy declines and the need for international migrant workers diminishes. Second, their economic benefit to the state is less than that of self-identified economic international migrants because the skills they possess are not the basis for their selection. Indeed, if they have been the victims of abuse, they may be unable to work at all.

Here again, the Irish state has been the most important driver of international migrant exclusion, not least because each asylum seeker must individually obtain the state's permission to remain. Statistics reveal that the state generally refuses to grant such permission. In 2010, Ireland's rate of recognition of asylum seekers as refugees in the first instance was 1.38 percent. This was the lowest in the EU. Further, Ireland's overall recognition rate for protection was 6 percent—less than a quarter of the EU average (Smyth, 2010).[6] Irish policy also contributes to the social marginalization of asylum seekers during their time in Ireland and fosters the public perception that asylum seekers are burdensome and alien. During the long period before their cases are heard, asylum seekers are housed in holiday camps, hostels, former military bases and other institutions through a system of "direct provision" that separates them from the general population; they are also prohibited from working or from attending post-secondary educational institutions. Beyond the impression that asylum seekers are a drain on state resources, the government's use of the image of "birth tourists" (non-Irish and, in government rhetoric, nonwhite mothers) in its campaign to pass the 2004 Citizenship Referendum constructed asylum seekers as aliens uncommitted to Ireland and has led to an increase of incidents of racial harassment, most frequently directed at people of African origin (Tormey, 2007).

Finally, recent actions by the state have accelerated the expulsion of international migrants whose applications for asylum fail. In a six-week period in 2011, for example, Acting Minister for Justice Brendan Smith signed 416 deportation orders—including 200 on his last day in office (Lally, 2011).

This reflected not only his administration's eagerness to deport "failed asylum seekers," but also the long term deterioration in legal protections against deportation since the 1990s. This is particularly notable in the case of protections against deportation for the non-EU parents of children who are Irish citizens. Up until the early 2000s, the state generally followed the precedent set in the 1990 case *Fajujonu v. Minister for Justice, Equality and Law Reform* [1990] 2 IR 151. The Supreme Court had declared that the child's right to a family life ordinarily precluded the deportation of non-EU family members unless deportation served the common good. But in the early 2000s the government provoked a test of the *Fajujonu* precedent in the *Lobe and Osayande* case [2003] IESC 3 (sometimes called "*L and O*"). In this case, the Supreme Court ruled that immigration policy could justify the deportation of a non-EU citizen parent (Irish Council for Civil Liberties, 2003); on the basis of this decision, the government ceased the practice of a presumption in favor of letting noncitizen parents of a child who is an Irish citizen remain in Ireland (Corrigan, 2006).[7]

GENDERED CAST OF IRISH WORK

All of these barriers to work and residence for international migrants took on a pronounced gender cast, as will be discussed later in this chapter. But first, it is necessary to note that Irish work has always been profoundly shaped by gender norms. A central theme of Irish political thought, produced alike by men and women, Catholics and Protestants, southerners and northerners, is that both political activity and work compromises women's roles as mothers (Hill, 2003, p.61, 91–2, 95).

However, it may be argued that Catholic social thought has been the most influential source for the construction of gender in Ireland, in that it informed the most significant instrument for the institutionalization of Irish gender roles, the 1937 Constitution. This document has a separate section devoted to "The Family." The principal articles are:

Article 41

1. 1° The State recognises the Family as the natural primary and fundamental unit group of Society, and as a moral institution possessing inalienable and imprescriptible rights, antecedent and superior to all positive law.
   2° The State, therefore, guarantees to protect the Family in its constitution and authority, as the necessary basis of social order and as indispensable to the welfare of the Nation and the State.
2. 1° In particular, the State recognises that by her life within the home, woman gives to the State a support without which the common good cannot be achieved.

2° The State shall, therefore, endeavour to ensure that mothers shall not be obliged by economic necessity to engage in labour to the neglect of their duties in the home.
3. 1° The State pledges itself to guard with special care the institution of Marriage, on which the Family is founded, and to protect it against attack (Bunreacht na hÉireann).

Groups like the Irish Women's Workers Union, the Irish Women's Citizens' Association and Irishwomen's International League criticized the gendered language of the constitution and the policies it implied—like women's exclusion from jury service and the "marriage bar," which required women to resign from civil service posts on marriage (Hill, 2003, p.100)—and urged women to vote against the new constitution. They, however, did not succeed (Hill, 2003, p.101).

The Constitutional equation of "woman" with "mother" has had far-reaching implications for female workers. With Constitutional sanction, some industries denied women work and government agencies emphasized male employment under the doctrine of the "family wage," according to which a man's job is supposed to provide for a family (Mullin, 1991, p.42, cited in Hill, 2003, p.101). These effects have persisted into recent history and to the present day. The civil service marriage bar remained until 1973. Irish women's entry into the workforce in large numbers lagged behind other European countries and working Irish women continue to be segregated in the low-wage and low-status service sectors of the economy (Barry, 2003).

The relegation of care to the private sphere on the basis of the belief that a woman's "life (is) within the home" betrays a tension concerning care work in the state. On the one hand, it sees care work as essential to the "common good." On the other hand, it does not see it as work, but rather as a woman's duty. This finds its clearest expression in the "Carer's Allowance," which is a means-tested social program that provides payments, "free household benefits" (including electricity, heating fuel, telephone rental and television license) and a public transport pass to persons caring for "someone who needs support because of age, physical or learning disability or illness, including mental illness" (Citizens Information Board, 2011). As a result, much of the care work in Ireland is performed by people, mainly women, as a private family obligation rather than as work that accrues labor protections. This allowance is, as a result, particularly vulnerable to cuts in a time of fiscal crisis.

The Carer's Allowance is only one example of a set of social welfare policies that discourage women from working outside the home. Ireland has resisted EU directives concerning extending maternity leave. In contrast to the provision of paid parental leave that prevails on the continent, Ireland has adopted the UK model of unpaid parental leave (Irish Times, 2011, citing Russell, Watson and Banks, 2011). School schedules and child-care provisions are based on the imagined norm of one parent, typically the mother, not working. Child care is expensive and is not tax deductible.[8] Until recently, child care has not received a general subsidy from the state. Moreover, the recent provision of a partial subsidy for part-time child care for attendance at preschool was financed by a reduction in the main state support for dependent children, Child Benefit. In most cases, Child Benefit is paid directly into the mother's bank account. Recent proposals that Child Benefit be taxed or paid in the form of vouchers for local goods and services reinforce the understanding of the Child Benefit as a private payment to low income mothers along the lines of the Carer's Allowance, rather than a universal social entitlement (Keenan, 2011).

Despite these obstacles, the period of the economic boom saw a considerable shift of women into the paid labor force. In keeping with the conception of care in Ireland, much child care is still being provided by family and friends (Department of Justice, Equality and Law Reform, n.d., p.5). Nevertheless, this has led to a considerable growth in for-profit care services, including child and elder care. The new elder care needs have created a rising demand for care workers, often drawn from the Philippines, India and sub-Saharan Africa. The new regulations concerning work permits and the replacement of work permit holders by workers drawn from accession countries has concentrated work permit holders in the health and care sector. In the elder care sector, the workforce consists primarily of women of color drawn from the (above mentioned) sending countries and regions, especially the Philippines and India (Barrett and Rust, 2009, p.8).[9] Access to these jobs is an important opportunity for these international migrant workers, but it has had the effect of creating a new and distinct form of elder care in Irish society, specifically, white Irish patients are cared for by nonwhite carers. In this way, the structure of care, or at least elder care, has increasingly come to resemble the care industry in other developed countries (Barrett and Rust, 2009).

The case of child care is different. There are relatively few international migrant workers holding work permits or people of color employed in this sector, except as nannies or au pairs. The sector as a whole has instead been a site of female Irish entrepreneurship and an important opportunity for Irish women to enter the workforce. The stark difference between elder care and child care is explained by the increasingly restrictive work permit system: In 2003, child-care workers became ineligible for work permits (Ruhs, 2009). Accordingly, child care is divided into two sectors: the formal sector outside the home with full labor protections and the informal sector inside the home with fewer protections and much greater risk of exploitation.[10] This dramatic difference illustrates the powerful effects of the restrictions (that we have highlighted) on international migrant workers' opportunities and the construction of gender in Ireland.

These gender-based disadvantages regarding care work show the paradoxical nature of the construction of gender in Ireland. Officially, the constitution recognizes the importance of care, especially of children, and gives it special standing. This special standing, however, is converted into social programs that perpetuate women's inequality through obstacles to their entry into the workforce. Should women choose to work despite these obstacles, they face high child-care costs, which they may avoid through hiring domestic workers informally—contracting out "their lives within the home." If they have elderly relations, caring for them may depend on the low wages of elder care workers who are disproportionately women of color who are international migrant workers. Many of these care workers have their own responsibilities of care. Far from allowing women greater control over their lives, the Irish regime of care imposes unnecessary costs and burdens, both to Irish women and migrant care workers.

THE GENDERED CAST OF IRISH INTERNATIONAL MIGRATION POLICY

Large numbers of women international migrant workers have found themselves caught up in the complex politics of gender and work in Ireland. Like Irish women, international migrant women tend to work in low-paid sectors, such as cleaning, elder care, hospitality and retail services. Such workers are particularly vulnerable to exploitation, and those on work permits are especially likely to be driven into irregular status by the application of the labor market test. Moreover, many international migrant women on work permits receive salaries that are too low to qualify for a "green card," even if they do work in sectors that are covered by the program.

Family reunification remains a problem for these workers. The feminization of migration has been characterized by women migrating in their own right and alone, leaving any dependent children they have in the care of others in the sending country. This is true of both non-EEA countries such as the Philippines and accession countries such as Latvia. Even if no formal obstacles to family reunification exist for citizens of accession countries, the high cost of living in Ireland and the use of the Habitual Residency Condition discourage many international migrant workers, men and women, from migrating as a family group. Gendered understandings of the family that presuppose a male breadwinner in both the sending country and in Ireland discourage women from claiming their rights as workers and human beings. The new rules removing the automatic right to work of dependent spouses have reinforced such gendered conceptions of the family.

Because Child Benefit is the most important form of state support for dependent children, and women are much more likely to find themselves in the role of caring for dependents, the arbitrary and restrictive use of the Habitual Residency Condition disproportionately affects women and significantly reduces their real income. Proposed changes to reduce Child Benefit payments for international migrants whose children reside outside Ireland to the levels set by the country of residence will worsen the position of female international migrants and their families. Although those international migrants will continue to pay tax at the same rate as Irish workers, they will receive benefits that in many cases will be considerably lower than in Ireland. The proposal, by the Irish Business and Employers Confederation (IBEC), to convert Child Benefit into a voucher for local goods and services was directly targeted at the "repatriation" of Child Benefit to countries outside the state where dependent children of Irish workers reside (Keenan, 2011).

Ireland's hostility to the right to permanent settlement also disproportionately affects women. Not surprisingly, many of the deportation cases of refugee claimants and undocumented workers involve women, often mothers of children who are Irish citizens. The focus on 'sham marriages' was mostly directed at female citizens of EU accession states, particularly from Latvia, who married non-EU men, rather than male EU citizens who married non-EU women. In 2008, the European Court of Justice found that Ireland's plan to deport the non-EU spouses of EU citizens who had not lived together in another member state violated European directives on free movement (*Blaise Beheten Metock and others v. Minister for Justice, Equality and Law Reform* C-127/08, BBC News, 2008). As was widely argued at the time of the citizenship referendum, the removal of birthright citizenship in favor of citizenship by descent "racialized" Irish citizenship. Thus it added the danger of racism to those of gender and economic exploitation, contributing to the multiple vulnerabilities of women of color who are international migrant workers (Lentin, 2007). Finally, the restrictions on travel for people in the asylum process and those attempting to meet the Habitual Residency Condition, combined with Ireland's effective ban on abortion, has led to an increase in unsafe "back alley abortions" involving women who are international migrants who are unable to travel to the United Kingdom for abortion services.[11]

Women who are international migrants are disadvantaged by the gendered construction of work in Ireland, and they are negatively impacted by the courts' tendency to subordinate the rights that derive from the constitutional articles on "The Family" to the interests of the state. This subordination affects citizen women as well as noncitizen women. Although the importance of women's "life within the home" has been cited in defense of policies that treat women and men differently, the Irish courts have found that defending women's fundamental role does not extend to giving them "a share in matrimonial property" or a right to compensation for work performed within the home (*L. v. L.* [1989] ILRM 528, cited in Kelly, Hogan and Whyte, 1994, p.1010–101). In all cases, the state's power to make policy overrides any rights deriving from these constitutional articles.

This privileging of state power especially affects women who are international migrants. Even though the wording of Article 41.1.1 bases the rights of the family in natural law "antecedent and superior to all positive law," and accordingly is applicable to all families regardless of migration status or citizenship, in practice, women's migrant status trumps their maternal or gender status. Thus, although Judge Hamilton in *Northants Co. Council v. A.B.F.* [1982] ILRM 164 said that "The natural law is of universal application and applies to all human persons, be they citizens of this State or not,"[12] the position of the Irish courts has been that the rights of the family are not absolute, but are subject to the state's powers, including the power to imprison citizens and to deport noncitizens (Kelly, Hogan and Whyte, 1994, p.1006). More specifically, Irish courts have ruled that the natural rights of the family and of an individual to family life do not prevent the return of children to foreign jurisdictions (Kelly, Hogan and Whyte, 1994, p.1006), and even *Fajujonu* confirmed that the family rights of citizen children could be subject to the power of the state under aliens' legislation.

The ultimately unsuccessful attempt to use the natural law basis of the Constitution's articles on the family to argue for equal rights for international migrants is paralleled by other attempts to use some of the founding documents of the Irish state to oppose discrimination against international migrants. Activists have used Ireland's republican and nationalist history to argue against the discriminatory treatment of international migrants, especially mothers and children. The declaration, in the Proclamation of the Irish Republic during the Easter Rising in 1916, that the Irish Republic cherishes "all the children of the nation equally" has been invoked by anti-racist groups when they argue against deportation and equality activists have appealed to it to make the case that the Irish state should provide the same support to children who are international migrants (regardless of their legal status) as it does to children who are Irish citizens (Firstworldwar.com, n.d.). Although the Proclamation has no legal standing, it carries considerable moral weight.

ETHICAL TREATMENT OF FEMALE MIGRANT WORKERS IN IRELAND

We have argued that, despite their potential for use as protections against discrimination and exploitation, Irish constitutional rights—and constitutional and republican discourse—provide insufficient protection to female Irish citizen and noncitizen workers. What would constitute a just response to the situation of female international migrant workers in Ireland? Only legal instruments of genuine universal application can be effective. Although a number of such instruments are available, in the form of the main human rights conventions governing migration, only some of them have been ratified or acceded to by Ireland. Of those that have been ratified or acceded to by Ireland, not all have been implemented in Irish law.[13] These include: The International Convention on the Protection of the Rights of All Migrant Workers and Members of their Families (the Migrant Worker's Convention), which entered into force July 2003 (not ratified by Ireland); the International

Labour Organization (ILO) conventions 29 and 182 preventing exploitation (ratified by Ireland) and the nondiscrimination and antiexploitation provisions of the main human rights covenants, all ratified by Ireland: the International Covenant on Civil and Political Rights (ICCPR); the International Covenant on Economic, Social and Cultural Rights (ICESCR); the Convention on the Elimination of All Forms of Racial Discrimination (CERD); the Convention on the Elimination of All Forms of Discrimination Against Women (CEDAW); and the Convention on the Rights of the Child (CRC). Relevant European conventions include the European Convention on Human Rights (ECHR), the European Social Charter and—not signed by Ireland—the European Convention on the Legal Status of Migrant Workers (Irish Human Rights Commission and National Consultative Commission on Racism and Interculturalism, 2004, pp.7–8). Finally, there is ILO Convention 97, the Migration for Employment Convention, ILO Convention 143, Migrant Workers (Supplementary Provision) Convention and the nonbinding ILO Multilateral Framework for a Rights-Based Approach to Labour Migration. We argue that Ireland should ratify all currently unratified instruments and implement them in Irish law, as advocated by both the Irish Human Rights Commission and the National Consultative Commission on Racism and Interculturalism (Pillinger, 2007, p.40).

The ILO Multilateral Framework and CEDAW are the international instruments best suited to addressing the problematic construction of gender and work in Ireland, especially as it affects female international migrant workers. The ILO Multilateral Framework explicitly includes the requirement that states take steps to ensure "that labor migration policies are gender-sensitive" (ILO, 2006, p.12). Its guidelines entail the collection of data and formation of policies that take into account gender issues and the particular vulnerabilities of female international migrant workers (ILO, 2006, p.12, 22). In particular, it argues that states should promote "anti-discrimination policies," conduct "periodic gender-sensitive data collection" and allow "family reunification in accordance with national laws and practice" (ILO, 2006, p.27–8).

Besides ratifying CEDAW, Ireland has also ratified the Optional Protocol to CEDAW that allows individuals to complain to the Committee on the Elimination of All Forms of Discrimination Against Women. In its response to Ireland's most recent submission to the Committee, the Committee outlined a number of "areas of concern" and recommendations. The Committee recommended that Ireland develop a definition of discrimination that is implemented in Irish law. More importantly for the purposes of this chapter, in the latest and in previous responses, the Committee expressed " . . . (concern) at the persistence of traditional stereotypical views of the social roles and responsibilities of women and men in the family and in society at large which are reflected in Article 41.2 of the Constitution and its male-oriented language" (Committee on the Elimination of Discrimination Against Women, 2005, p.4). The Committee recommends that the state replace this language in the constitution with "gender-sensitive language," that the state act to "eliminate traditional stereotypical attitudes" and that it include a constitutional provision that requires the state to pursue "substantive equality between women and men" (Committee on the Elimination of Discrimination Against Women, 2005, p.4). In a recommendation that addressed the ways that state policies disadvantage women, and especially (as we have argued earlier) international migrant women, the Committee called for regular "gender impact analysis" of all policies (Committee on the Elimination of Discrimination Against Women, 2005, p.6). The Committee expressed particular concern about violence against "marginalized and vulnerable groups" including "migrant women, asylum-seeking and refugee women" (Committee on the Elimination of Discrimination Against Women, 2005, p.5). Sharing our understanding of the situation of women in Ireland, the Committee noted that women are concentrated in low-status jobs; the Committee was particularly concerned about how it disadvantaged international migrant women and made them vulnerable to discrimination (Committee on the Elimination of Discrimination Against Women, 2005, p.6–7). It voiced special concern for international migrant domestic workers who are "excluded from the protection against discrimination extended to employees under the Equality Act, 2004" (Committee on the Elimination of Discrimination Against Women, 2005, p.6–7). Finally, it encouraged the state to ratify the Migrant Worker's Convention (Committee on the Elimination of Discrimination Against Women, 2005, p.8).

All of the Committee's recommendations are in accordance with the special character of CEDAW and its implementation. Unlike some of the other international human rights instruments, CEDAW is concerned with the elimination of the effects of discriminatory practices and policies as well as their purposes or the intentions behind them (Steiner and Alston, 2000, p.179). This is to be achieved by modifying "the social and cultural patterns of conduct of men and women, with a view to achieving the elimination of prejudices and customary and all other practices which are based on the idea of the inferiority or the superiority of either of the sexes or on stereotyped roles for men and women" (CEDAW, Article 5). The convention is not only concerned with the actions of the state but also that of non-state individuals and groups (Steiner and Alston, 2000, p.179). Unlike in the ICCPR, for example, it allows, in Article 4, the state to take "special measures" to achieve equality without being guilty of discrimination (Steiner and Alston, 2000, p.179). The inclusion of non-state actors is particularly important for the case of international migrant workers, because it enjoins the state to regulate and monitor employers as well as state bodies. Finally, the areas in which substantive equality is to be sought encompass the many different ways in which women—and especially international migrant women—are vulnerable. In Article 1, these are described as including: "political, economic, social, cultural, civil or any other field" (CEDAW). The inclusion of all potential fields where inequality and discrimination are likely to arise mandates an examination of all potential sources of injustice, from immigration and economic policies to the dangers of racism and sexism, exploitation and violence. Most important is the focus on how these different forms of injustice "intersect." "Intersectionality" is an approach to human rights implementation that considers how discriminations or inequalities in these various fields work together. Thus, instead of seeing a woman of color who is an international migrant worker as "separately disadvantaged" by discrimination based on gender, race or migrant status, the "intersectional" approach examines how these forces work together (Satterthwaite, 2004). This intersectional approach allows other international human rights instruments, which have not always been tied to equality, to be used in ways more analogous to the implementation of CEDAW. The CEDAW and its Committee represent an engaged commitment to gender justice, embodying a substantive conception of equality.

HUMAN RIGHTS, CAPABILITIES AND FEMALE INTERNATIONAL MIGRANT WORKERS

We believe that the discrimination and exploitation experienced by international migrant women in Ireland should be addressed by appealing to Ireland's ratification of the CEDAW and the monitoring body to which individual women in Ireland can appeal and to which Ireland must respond (this approach should also be employed in other countries when appropriate). Ethical approaches to migration issues usually begin with competing moral and political theories that then are applied to a specific case, but we believe that the disadvantages experienced by international migrant women in Ireland and the risks of gender-based exploitation show the appropriateness and relevance of a particular moral and political theory of human rights and equality, specifically, Amartya Sen's capability theory. Capability theory focuses on what people are free to do or to be and uses that lens to examine disadvantages experienced by individuals. With its wide focus on a variety of capabilities and its engagement with inequality, it provides a more sophisticated and penetrating framework for understanding international migrants' rights than the approaches that are often used in debates about migration issues. Such approaches very often restrict their considerations to economic inequality or to conflicts between the right of a state to exclude migrants and the right of migrants to free movement.[14] Capability theory has also paid special attention to women's freedom and equality.

Amartya Sen ties human rights to a powerful theory of equality, freedom and justice, conceptualizing human rights as ethical demands based on the importance of the freedoms to which they are rights (Sen, 2004, p.319). His capability theory emphasizes the freedom (or capability) to achieve valuable states or actions (Sen calls these functionings). Capability theory is advanced by him as a way of understanding equality—through its "informational focus" that allows for comparison of individuals' overall advantage or disadvantage (Sen, 2009, p.232). On the basis of this information, a substantive moral theory of equality can be developed that tracks moral intuitions about what equality means in a world where different people have different abilities to achieve valuable states or actions. Equality consists of people having similar freedom to achieve certain functionings and it becomes possible to compare different individuals' capability sets and consider the distribution of capability within a particular group—up to and including, the whole world—through the theory of social choice. Justice is approached by making the transition to arrangements that are comparatively better, from a capability point of view, than existing arrangements (Sen, 2009, p.16–17). Evaluated from the point of view of capability equality—understood in terms of human rights—it is clear that there is no hard and fast distinction between so-called "negative" rights to not suffer violence and "positive" rights to enjoy access to health care and to avoid poverty.

There is also a political dimension to Sen's theory of human rights. Capabilities have a "process" aspect as well as an "opportunity" facet (what they are opportunities to do). The process aspect of capabilities focuses on the process by which an agent's capabilities are made possible. If someone would, all things being equal, choose to go out on a particular evening, to use Sen's example, it makes a very big difference if she does so of her own volition or if she is commanded to do so by the state or by some private individual or group (Sen, 2004, p.330–31). That other individuals, groups and the state can affect one's capabilities shows how human rights (as capabilities) impose obligations on others. Distinguishing between "perfect" and "imperfect" obligations, Sen argues that we have a perfect obligation to perform or not to perform specific acts, e.g., a perfect obligation not to violate someone's right to bodily integrity. But we also have imperfect obligations to promote people's human rights insofar as it is within our power and depending on the importance of the freedoms in question (Sen, 2004, p.338–40). Although it can be difficult to know what promotes individual human rights in particular cases, it is not the case that individuals or the state have no obligations to promote greater equality as a matter of respect for human rights. Preventable risks of exploitation and predictable threats of disadvantage place an obligation on individuals and, especially, the state to prevent such injustices from occurring. The vulnerabilities of female international migrant workers make ethical demands on all individuals, groups and states, not the least by their interconnection through the global market for labor.

The affinities of Sen's conception of human rights with the implementation of CEDAW are clear. He even says that these imperfect obligations may involve "pressing for, or contributing to, changes in institutions as well as social attitudes" (Sen, 2009, p.383). Rooted as it is in an account of actual, lived equality and inequality, Sen's theory allows "special measures" in the sense referred to in CEDAW to be used to achieve equality, understood as equality of capability. Like the implementation of CEDAW, Sen's focus on the many ways in which individual policies can affect an individual's capability shows the need for regular "gender impact analysis" of all policies. His emphasis on the duties of all individuals, groups and institutions to promote human rights is in accord with CEDAW's broad remit, covering state and non-state actors.

Finally, Sen's theory has a wide informational focus and includes all fields in which women's freedoms are at risk, not merely the political or the economic. We argue that the particular vulnerabilities and multiple forms of disadvantage and discrimination that international migrant women workers face are best recognized by a theory of equality and human rights that looks at the whole of a person's "capability set" and not just individual aspects of their situation. The emphasis on the "process" aspect of capability links the two areas of disadvantage we have explored in this chapter: the non-EEA workers not being afforded the same employment opportunities as EEA workers and the coercive barriers to permanent residency faced by workers on work permits and asylum seekers. Such a theory highlights the connection between state coercion through legal barriers, coercively enforced; economic coercion through widespread gender-based exploitation; and segregation in low-status jobs and cultural coercion through the construction of gender in Ireland.[15]

Sen's comparative approach to justice can allow for incomplete "partial orderings" in which some questions of justice are left unresolved, rather than complete orderings that attempt to work out the exact relationship between promoting the capabilities of citizens, say, and international migrants (Sen, 2009, p.102–5). Although, in many cases, the responsibility to make more just arrangements will fall on states, such obligations are not limited to states and are certainly not limited to the state of which individuals are citizens. Responsibilities, for Sen, involve many potential actors, from states to groups to individuals, within and across national borders. The lack of resolution of Sen's "comparative" approach does not leave female international migrant workers at greater risk of exploitation because, at the very least, the women will receive equal consideration when questions of justice are addressed and, given his emphasis on reducing injustice and the vulnerability of female international migrant workers, their situation may receive special consideration.

BEYOND THE CITIZENSHIP MODEL OF CAPABILITY: A FLEXIBLE DETERMINATION OF THE RELEVANT CAPABILITIES

The loyalties, identities and histories of international migrants may be transnational; the international labor market certainly is. People move for many different reasons, not all of which can be tied to a particular political project or addressed by a specific political community. We have argued that international migrant women workers suffer various vulnerabilities and disadvantages in Ireland, but the solution is not always or necessarily to make them citizens. In a world where people move across borders, there will always be some people outside the political system. Even the relevant international instruments, such as the Migrant Workers Convention and the Declaration on the Human Rights of Individuals Who are not Nationals of the Country in which They Live make a distinction between citizens and other residents of a state (Migrant Workers Convention, Article 42.3). Making such a distinction is compatible with the argument we have made (here and elsewhere) for an open and transparent regime governing access to citizenship for international migrants and their children. Coercive and arbitrary systems are ruled out by their demonstrated risks to individuals' capability sets and permanent residence—which does not necessarily mean citizenship—will very often be a useful means to capability fulfillment. Although we are sympathetic to the claim that all residents of a political community should be able to vote on laws, policies and institutions that affect them, it requires a further argument. In the absence of that argument, we cannot rule out the possibility of a just migration regime, including policies regarding international migrant labor, that does not involve granting full citizenship to all international migrant workers.

A more flexible approach also allows for a more open ended set of capabilities to be considered when attempting to develop just policies regarding female international migrant workers. The important human rights norm of nondiscrimination seems basic to a capability approach, and this will constrain the kinds of means that can be used to promote capability. A concern with the "process" aspect of opportunity will exclude arbitrary coercion as a tool of state policy and make access to justice and due process crucial capabilities. Just such a concern for these capabilities animates the bulk of the articles in the Migrant Workers Convention. Beyond nondiscrimination and noncoercion, though, international migrant workers will benefit from a variety of capabilities, from "basic needs" (such as food and shelter) to cultural expression. International migrants of different types may need different capabilities from the specific to the general, depending on whether they are from the EEA or not, whether they work in the formal or informal sector and whether they have migrated with members of their family or by themselves. Such capabilities could include the ability to access child care, social protections and upskilling (deskilling is a problem for many female international migrants in Ireland), the ability to organize and to access justice at the national or international level. While access to certain crucial goods—that might be made the objects of capabilities—has been the object of our analysis, we do not want to suggest that this list should necessarily be given priority. Rather, we leave the establishment of priorities to female international migrant workers themselves, on the basis of their own politically organized demands. These demands may take the form of political action similar to that of citizens of the receiving country, and they may take a variety of other forms, including engagement with the governments of sending countries, international organizations, national and international human rights institutions, transnational unions and global civil society.

RECOMMENDATIONS

It is, nevertheless, possible to recommend particular policy responses on the basis of the widespread threats experienced by female international migrant workers in Ireland. The following recommendations should not be seen as exhaustive and the possibility of further demands, based on Ireland's ongoing economic, cultural and social changes, should not be ruled out. We have emphasized state action, because the Irish state is the primary agent responsible for making female migrant workers vulnerable, but we also believe that non-state actors can be agents for change.

State Action

Given our analysis, what are the moral obligations of the Irish government with regard to acknowledging the rights of female international migrant workers in Ireland? We believe that it has three responsibilities, which are to not engage in (or allow) discrimination, undertake institutional reforms and change cultural norms and values. We discuss these obligations below.

Antidiscrimination

The Irish state can meet its obligations to avoid discrimination under the various human rights instruments to which it is a state party. Further, it can ratify the Migrant Worker's Convention and the European Convention on the Legal Status of Migrant Workers so that all international migrant workers are treated as the equals of citizens for the purposes of employment and access to cultural, social and educational services (Migrant Workers Convention, Article 43). In domestic legislation, it can include all international migrant workers in the remit of the Equality Act of 2004. When it does so, it could include international migrant status as one of the "grounds" on which direct or indirect discrimination is prohibited under the Equality Act. It should alter its regulations regarding the dependent spouses of work permit holders so that they have independent legal status and should provide greater access to family reunification for all international migrant workers on an equal basis (see Pillinger, 2007, p.4). The government should extend the terms of residence and the fair terms of renewal that are offered to workers with "green cards" to all work permit holders. It should reverse the unfair use of the labor market test. Asylum seekers should be permitted to work, as is the case in Canada and, since 2008, in the United Kingdom.[16] Most important, the Irish state should recognize the "process" aspect of capability and remove the illegitimate coercion that characterizes the treatment of asylum seekers and work permit holders whose permits have expired due to the new rules governing labor market tests. In particular, it should act to reduce the arbitrariness and increase the transparency involved in applications for asylum, social benefits and citizenship.

Institutional Reform
The government should improve the labor inspection regime to provide real access to these protections.[17] There is considerable evidence that low rates of inspection, language barriers and the absence of effective antidiscrimination legislation have led to the serious exploitation of female international migrant workers and have left many more international migrant workers vulnerable to such exploitation (Pillinger, 2006). Improved inspection would directly enhance female international migrant workers' freedom to join and participate in unions, access compensation for injuries sustained on the job and enjoy the employment rights to which they are entitled. It would improve their access to justice generally, including remedy for the worst forms of exploitation. As part of their being brought within the scope of Irish equality legislation, female international migrant workers should be provided access to the institutions that remedy cases of discrimination—including the Equality Tribunal, the Employment Rights Agency (Pillinger, 2007, p.10) and the Labour Court—and supported so that they enjoy real access to justice. Only by setting up institutions concerned with women's equality and not just the violation of their rights, can the government address the social policies and institutions that place female international migrants at risk of gender exploitation.

Cultural Change
As a way of combating the segregation of citizen and noncitizen women in the labor market and to address one of the multiple forms of disadvantage suffered by international migrant women workers, the Irish government should endeavor to change social attitudes and alter the gendered language of the constitution as part of this change. The government should do what the Committee for the Elimination of Discrimination Against Women suggests and promote substantive equality through "special measures" if necessary. These can include affirmative action, particular supports aimed at enhancing women's capabilities through training, access to child care and enhanced maternity leave arrangements. With regard to female international migrant workers, these supports might also include supports for language training, upskilling and cultural expression. The government should merge its efforts to change patriarchal attitudes with its national integration and antiracism strategies (Pillinger, 2007, p.6). It should, as both the ILO Multilateral Framework and the Committee for the Elimination of Discrimination Against Women suggest, conduct regular "gender sensitive" and "migrant sensitive" evaluations of all policies, particularly those that

disproportionately affect international migrants. Only in this way will the government bring to light the material exclusions and negative outcomes that affect female international migrant workers and open up avenues for positive cultural change.

Non-State Actors

Non-state actors also have a role to play in promoting justice for female international migrant workers. Much good work is already being done by nongovernmental organizations (NGOs) engaged with human rights and migrants' rights. These organizations have played a crucial role in informing migrants of their rights, helping them gain access to justice and conducting studies regarding the gender impacts of particular policies and legislation. Such a role is especially important, given that the state has neglected or even abdicated its responsibilities in these areas. Important work has also been done by the Irish Congress of Trade Unions, both by facilitating the self-organization of migrant workers and by exposing the exploitation suffered by migrant workers in Ireland (e.g., Philips, 2011). All such organizations must continue to do this work and to hold the state accountable, given an increasingly difficult funding and organizational environment. But other non-state actors can also contribute. The most obvious group are employers, who should adopt nondiscriminatory practices, including eschewing antimigrant worker policies that the work permit regime allows them to use, especially the labor market test. With regards to providing migrant workers with political voice, Irish political parties should make further efforts to reach out to members of the migrant community, including both EEA and non-EEA citizens. There is evidence that most of the main Irish parties have abandoned their previous efforts in this area, which were, in any case, focused on narrow electoral gains rather than a sustained commitment to inclusion (Fanning, 2011, p.163–4). In this political environment, migrants themselves have an important role to play, through migrant led NGOs like New Communities Partnership.

OBJECTIONS

There are at least two potential objections to our analysis and recommendations. One is a feasibility objection, the claim that, given certain facts about the global economy and the need for cheap labor in developed countries like Ireland, our proposed reforms are not practical. According to that analysis, Ireland is too dependent on cheap labor in certain sectors—especially care, nursing and hospitality—to implement the reforms we have advocated for and retain its competitiveness. In a time of economic crisis, the national budget simply cannot be extended to provide the supports, wages, job security and access to permanent residence that we demand, as a matter of justice, for female international migrant workers. Further, at a time when there is significant emigration by Irish citizens, the government needs to exert even greater control over its noncitizen workforce than during the boom. A similar objection might be lodged against the recommendation that we (and the Committee for the Elimination of Discrimination Against Women) have made that the language of the constitution should be changed as part of an effort to alter the dominant conception of gender in Ireland. In the current crisis, Ireland does not need a divisive constitutional debate.

The second objection is articulated in normative terms. The objection would question our use of the language of rights and human rights to frame the problems facing international migrant workers. Such a critic would argue that because there is no right to enter a country (let alone a human right), international migrant workers justifiably can be treated much worse than Irish citizen workers and sent back to their countries of origin when they are no longer needed by the Irish economy. Attaching restrictive conditions and inferior benefits to the employment of international migrant workers might even be defended in terms of the interests of those workers themselves, with an argument analogous to Nicholas Kristof's defense of sweatshops (2009). Kristof argued that sweatshop jobs should not be criticized because they are superior to those offered in poorer countries. Similarly, a defender of the Irish migrant worker regime might argue that the jobs provided to international migrant workers in Ireland, even if they are not equal in their protections and conditions to those to which Irish citizens are entitled, should not be disparaged, because they are much better than the jobs they could get in their nations of origin and they allow them to make enough money to improve their condition and those of their children and extended families.

We can address both of these (sorts of) objections simultaneously, even though they are based on different premises. Both objections are based on the claim that Irish people's lives—and in the case of the second objection, international migrant workers' lives—will go better if international migrants receive different and inferior treatment, because loss of competitiveness or additional costs will reduce the quality of life of Irish workers (the feasibility objection) or the standard of existence of Irish and migrant workers (the better jobs than in sending countries objection). The latter objection depends on a normative claim that equal consideration in terms of rights or justice does not arise regarding potential migrants, whereas Irish citizens have a special obligations based on rights or justice to compatriots. We take issue with this claim later, but even brief consideration of the contemporary labor situation in Ireland suggests that the prediction of the decline in the Irish or the Irish and non-Irish standard of living is not likely to occur. Ireland will only escape its current fiscal and banking crisis with the aid of the EU; Ireland has been entirely dependent on the EU (represented by the European Commission), the European Central Bank and, until recently, the International Monetary Fund to resolve ongoing fiscal and bank crises (Government of Ireland, 2010). The majority of international migrant workers in the country are citizens of member states of the EU—and are, accordingly, citizens of the EU—and they have the right to freedom of movement. In fact, this freedom is one of the core freedoms of the European project (Central Statistics Office Ireland, 2012). As a country dependent on the EU for its survival, Ireland has no political leverage to try to alter European legislation regarding free movement so that it is more limited or available only to some groups. Indeed, Ireland has been sanctioned by the EU in the past for failing to comply with legislation guaranteeing access to freedom of movement to EU citizens. At a time when many Irish citizens are availing themselves of the right to free movement within the EU and the social protections it guarantees to them in whatever European state they reside, a self-interested commitment to reciprocity militates against Ireland pushing for greater leeway, on the part of member states, to introduce discriminatory measures.

Similar considerations apply to asylum seekers. Ireland is bound by its international commitments to accept genuine refugees and to provide them with all of the protections guaranteed by refugee law and follow the best international practice regarding refugees. The fact of the matter is that Ireland is not bearing the brunt of the refugee burden in the EU, and applications for asylum are much fewer than they were previously. There is no material case for a feasibility objection based on the impact of asylum seekers and Ireland is not, for the reasons stated above, in a position to argue for admitting fewer refugees or weakening refugee protections.

But neither is it in Ireland's interest to discriminate against workers who are on work permits or to look for more "EU" workers among irregular international migrants. Sourcing cheap and potentially exploitable labor may be in a state's interest during a boom, but is counterproductive, politically and economically, during times of high unemployment. In such circumstances, the "dual labor market," with one set of standards for citizens and another for noncitizens—whom Robin Cohen has called the "New Helots"—works against the interests of Irish workers and the Irish state (Cohen, 1987). This is because the threat of displacement of Irish workers is greater when jobs are scarce: New Irish nursing graduates and low-skilled hospitality workers will find their pay and conditions undercut by international migrant workers who are vulnerable to exploitation because they lack access to institutions that will help uphold their rights. In such conditions, a robust labor inspection regime that enforces the minimum wage, health and safety conditions and guarantees workers ability to join unions and exercise their rights creates a well-regulated market that also allows for more positive cultural change in terms of the alteration of sexist and xenophobic attitudes. This makes the task of integration easier and the costs lower.

Attention to the importance of inspection regimes and regulation of the labor market also helps address the objection that questions of human rights and justice are not raised by the presence of international migrant workers. The claim that there is no right to enter and, accordingly, no right to equal conditions rests, we argue, on an overly simplistic understanding of migration. If you ask whether an individual international migrant possesses the right to live in Ireland, with the correlative obligation, on the part of the Irish state, to admit her, then it is the case that some migrants—EEA citizens and asylum seekers—do possess such legal rights, whereas irregular migrants and migrants possessing work permits do not. The question is not whether there is a right to migrate, however, but whether migrants have rights. We have argued, on the basis of existing international human rights instruments, that they do and that these rights, understood as capabilities, should inform their just and ethical treatment. If one abandons this overly simplistic focus on individual cases of migration, then this engagement with migrants needs to be seen for what it is, as engagement with variously regulated political, legal, cultural and, not least, economic processes, requiring a more comprehensive and coordinated response. Such an approach is the only one that makes it possible to scrutinize the details of migration policies and the legitimacy of the barriers faced by and support offered to international migrant workers, with a view to the outcome for all affected persons. Here another aspect of Sen's approach seems especially helpful: his evaluation of institutions and arrangements on the basis of a "goal rights theory," where institutions are evaluated in terms of their effects, not on welfare, but on the non-violation/enjoyment of rights (Sen, 2004). Here, too, we also see the advantages of Sen's "comparative" approach to justice. That there is a better set of arrangements—a well-regulated labor market with equal conditions and freedoms for citizen and noncitizen workers alike—requires that Ireland as a matter of justice change to such arrangements, abandoning the current arrangements (that are defended by those who oppose our position and compare international migrants' conditions in Ireland to those of the sending country).

Those who object to our argument base their position on the claim that migrants will be comparatively better off in Ireland than they would be at "home," even if they experience conditions of life and work that are inferior to those enjoyed by Irish citizens. But if international migrant workers would be still better off under the system we propose, then, assuming our reply to the feasibility objection holds, our opponent should by his or her own lights endorse a move to our proposed arrangement.

CONCLUSION

Despite the severe recession and fiscal crisis that began in 2008, Ireland remains a wealthy country, albeit one that is experiencing outflows of citizen and noncitizen workers rather than the dramatic inflows that characterized the boom. As the second "most globalized economy" in the world after Hong Kong, Ireland is deeply immersed in complex global processes involving the movement of capital, ideas, goods and labor (Irish Independent, 2011). Ireland is relying on its openness to these processes to extricate itself from its current situation. A just response to the movement of people in and out of Ireland, sensitive to the way that gender informs these movements, is crucial for the success and legitimacy of Ireland's policies.

NOTES

1. By understanding migrant workers' situation in Ireland in terms of their vulnerability to exploitation or the threat of exploitation, we hope to appeal to the literature, in the theory of equality, about the role of vulnerability (Goodin, 1985) and to the notion of "standard threats" to individuals' enjoyment of the substances of their human rights, developed by Henry Shue (1996) and widely accepted in theorizing about human rights. We also adopt this terminology because, although there are a number of accounts of individual and group exploitation in Ireland, countrywide data is difficult to acquire. More important, the threat of exploitation affects a wider group than actual exploitation.
2. The European Economic Area includes the 27 states of the EU, Iceland, Liechtenstein and Norway.
3. Mac Éinrí and White (2008) provide a good overview of the history of migration to Ireland until 2008, although it was published before the 2008 crisis and the resulting outflow of people from Ireland.
4. In 2009, "47 per cent of applications were refused," compared to "9 per cent in the United Kingdom and less than three per cent in Canada," (Fanning, 2011, p.167).
5. Fanning, 2011, pp.134–8, 152. The changes lead to an increase in homelessness among migrant workers.
6. Irish acceptance rates have increased recently and are approaching the European average. It is not clear if this is a long-term trend and, if so, what the causes are. The reasons for the change may be new steps to deal with the backlog of asylum applications, a greater number of applications from Syrian nationals (which will largely succeed given the crisis in that country) or the decline in applications itself. For the latest statistics, see Bitoulas, 2014. We are grateful to Dr. Karen Murphy for identifying these latest statistics.
7. More recently, the European Court of Justice's decision in *Zambrano v. Office national de l'emploi* [2011] C34/09 declared that an EU state cannot refuse residence or a work permit to the non-EEA parents of a minor EU citizen. The government is now reviewing such cases on this basis (*Immigration Council of Ireland*, 2011, see also *Irish Government News Service*, 2011). By January 24, 2012, over 850 non-EU parents have been granted residence in Ireland out of 1000 cases that have been reviewed on the basis of the decision. An additional six parents who had left Ireland following a deportation order have been given visas to reenter Ireland (Duncan, 2012).
8. For the expensive cost of child care see Barry (2003, p.9).
9. In 2001, "about two-thirds of the new nurses registering in Ireland were from other countries, mainly Australia, India, the Philippines, South Africa and the United Kingdom" (Barrett and Rust, 2009, p.12, citing Stewart, Clark and Clark, 2007). Barrett and Rust also note that Ireland is one of the countries "employing the greatest number of Filipino nurses" (Barrett and Rust, p.12, note 5). It should be noted that Barrett and Rust do not disaggregate nurses engaged in social care and nurses in other lines of health work. Much of elder care in Ireland is provided in facilities run by the state health service.

10. For a description of particular cases of exploitation as a domestic worker, see Pillinger, 2007, p.67 and Migrant Rights Council of Ireland, 2010, p.3. As noted below, domestic workers are particularly vulnerable, because they are not covered by Ireland's equality legislation, the Equality Act of 2004.
11. Holland, 2004. We are grateful to Thomas Murray for reminding us of this phenomenon. This has not been changed by the passage of the "Protection of Life During Pregnancy Act" of 2013, itself required by the *A, B and C v. Ireland* decision of the European Court of Human Rights, one of the plaintiffs being a non-Irish EU citizen.
12. Hamilton accordingly ruled that an English father who had brought his child to Ireland to avoid loss of custody was protected by these constitutional principles (Kelly, Hogan and Whyte, 1994, pp.999–1000).
13. This latter case is particularly true of the Convention on the Rights of the Child (CRC), ratified by Ireland without reservation in 1992. Attempts to implement the CRC in Ireland have been drawn out since 2006, when the need for a referendum on its implications for Irish law was first mooted by the government. That referendum was passed on November 12, 2012, but legislation has been held up by lawsuits challenging the conduct of the referendum. In any case, the legislation will, in all likelihood, not fully implement the CRC in Irish law.
14. Many debates in the ethics of migration have been carried out from what Pogge calls an "interactional" perspective, one that emphasizes ethical interactions between individuals and sometimes individuals and states (1992, p.50). Such approaches find it hard to address the peculiar problems of justice posed by the experience of international migrant workers and female international migrant workers in particular, where the politics and economics of global population flows, the international market for labor and socially constructed attitudes to gender and the family form the basis of complex institutions and processes that lead to female international migrant workers' vulnerability to gender-based exploitation. Such theories also cannot articulate the engaged commitment to substantive equality embodied in the implementation of CEDAW. For examples of the interactional approach both for and against more open borders, see Carens, 1987and Wellman, 2008.
15. Sen, however, is not the only capability theorist interested in gender justice. Martha Nussbaum (2000) has also highlighted the specific capability deficits that women face in various situations and how their gender is a crucial factor in their disadvantage. We prefer Sen's theory because Nussbaum's theory is insufficiently committed to a "cosmopolitanism from below," which would take into account the multiple historical engagements that different groups and, in particular, marginalized groups use to navigate their condition (see e.g., Gasper, 2006, Pieterse, 2006). Sen's theory is less likely to fall prey to that mistake, because he does not provide a canonical list of capabilities, let alone a priority rule for weighing trade-offs between the central capabilities and others. The other reason we have reservations about Nussbaum's theory is that it does not appear to be able to address the question of who has the responsibility to foster the capabilities of persons who move from one state to another. For instance, her "Ten Principles for the Global Structure" (Nussbaum, 2006, pp.315–24) does not seem to recognize the existence of international migrants. This is one consequence of the statist cast of Nussbaum's capability approach to justice.
16. Following a ruling by the High Court in the UK based on the European Convention of Human Rights (Doward and Hinsliff, 2008). Ireland and Denmark are the only EU member states who have failed to ratify the 2003 EU Directive

on the Minimum Standards for the Reception of Asylum Seekers. Gráinne Mellon argues that, "The Reception Directive, as it is known, lays down the minimum conditions for asylum seekers and provides that they must be allowed to work after a year of waiting for a decision, or before" (2011).
17. Currently there are 71 labor inspectors for a workforce of 2.25 million. There has been a loss of 20 percent of inspectors over two years, down from the 90 inspectors agreed between trade unions and government in 2007. Even the agreed inspectorate is unsuited to the task of eliminating the exploitation of migrant labor (Millar, 2010).

REFERENCES AND FURTHER READINGS

Baker, N., 2011. Growing number of child benefit residency cases. *Irish Examiner*, 6 April, [online] Available at: <http://www.examiner.ie/ireland/growing-number-of-child-benefit-residency-cases-150534.html> [Accessed June 24, 2011].

Barrett, A. and Rust, A., 2009. Projecting the future numbers of migrant workers in the health and social care sectors in Ireland. *ESRI Working Paper No. 275*, [pdf] Available at: <http://www.esri.ie/UserFiles/publications/20090114112135/WP275.pdf> [Accessed November 4, 2011].

Barry, U., 2003. *Review and reform of EU Equality Law: Ireland, women's education*. [pdf] Research and Resource Centre, University College Dublin. Available at: <http://research.mbs.ac.uk/european-employment/Portals/0/docs/gendersocial/CNE_IE.pdf> [Accessed June 29, 2011].

BBC News, 2008. Court backs EU citizens' spouses, 25 July. [online] Available at: <http://news.bbc.co.uk/2/hi/7525472.stm> [Accessed Nov. 10, 2011].

Bitoulas, A., 2014. Population and social conditions. *Eurostat*, [pdf] 14 March. Available at: <http://epp.eurostat.ec.europa.eu/cache/ITY_OFFPUB/KS-QA-14-003/EN/KS-QA-14-003-EN.PDF> [Accessed July 29, 2014].

Bunreacht na hÉireann. [online] Available at: <http://www.taoiseach.gov.ie/upload/static/256.htm> [Accessed June 25, 2011].

Carens, J., 1987. Aliens and citizens: The case for open borders. *The Review of Politics*, 49 (2), 251–273.

Central Statistics Office, 2011. *Earnings and labour costs*. [online] Available at: <http://www.cso.ie/quicktables/GetQuickTables.aspx?FileName=EHQ03.asp&TableName=Earnings+and+Labour+Costs&StatisticalProduct=DB_EH> [Accessed November 4, 2011]

Central Statistics Office Ireland, 2012. *Census 2011: Visitors*. [pdf] Available at: <http://www.cso.ie/en/media/csoie/census/documents/census2011pdr/Pdfpercent203percent20Commentary.pdf> [Accessed April 15, 2012].

Citizens Information Board, 2011. *Carer's allowance*. [online] Available at: <http://www.citizensinformation.ie/en/social_welfare/social_welfare_payments/carers/carers_allowance.html> [Accessed November 4, 2011].

Citizens Information Board, 2014. *Residence requirements for social assistance in Ireland*. [online] Available at: <http://www.citizensinformation.ie/en/social_welfare/irish_social_welfare_system/social_assistance_payments/residency_requirements_for_social_assistance_in_ireland.html> [Accessed July 29, 2014].

Cohen, R., 1987. *The new helots*. Aldershot: Avebury.

Committee on the Elimination of Discrimination Against Women, 2005. [pdf] *Concluding comments: Ireland*. 33rd Session, July 5–22, 2005. Available at: <http://www.un.org/:womenwatch/daw/cedaw/cedaw33/conclude/ireland/0545060E.pdf> [Accessed June 30, 2011].

Convention on the elimination of all forms of discrimination against women. [online] Available at: <http://www.un.org/womenwatch/daw/cedaw/text/econvention.htm#intro> [Accessed June 30, 2011].

Corrigan, C., 2006. All our children: Child impact assessment for Irish children of migrant parents. [pdf] *Children's Rights Alliance Report.* Available at: <http://www.childrensrights.ie/files/AllOurChildrenCADICRpt0406.pdf> [Accessed June 24, 2011].

Crosscare (Social Protection Agency of the Catholic Archdiocese of Dublin), 2010. *Submission to the Joint Oireachtas Committee on social protection on the habitual residence condition and returned emigrants.* [pdf] Available at: <http://migrant-project.ie/documents/CrosscareSubmissiontotheJointOireachtasCommitteeonSocialProtectionontheHabitualResidenceCond.pdf> [Accessed June 15, 2011].

Department of Jobs, Enterprise and Innovation, 2009. Changes to work permits arrangements, April 2009, [online] Available at: <http://www.djei.ie/labour/workpermits/revisedworkpermitarrangementspercent20-percent20junepercent202009.htm> [Accessed June 15, 2011].

Department of Justice, Equality and Law Reform, n.d. *Developing childcare in Ireland.* [pdf] Available at: <http://www.justice.ie/en/JELR/Childcare.pdf/Files/Childcare.pdf> [Accessed November 4, 2011].

Department of Social Protection, 2011. *Habitual residence condition—guidelines for deciding officers on the determination of habitual residence.* [online] Available at: <http://www.welfare.ie/EN/OperationalGuidelines/Pages/habres.aspx#7.1> [Accessed June 22, 2011].

Doward, J. and Hinsliff, G., 2008. Ruling frees asylum seekers to work. *The Observer*, [online]14 December. Available at: <http://www.guardian.co.uk/politics/2008/dec/14/ruling-frees-asylum-seeker-work> [Accessed July 1, 2011].

Duncan, P., 2012. Over 850 non-EU parents get residency. *The Irish Times*, [online] 24 January. Available at: <http://www.irishtimes.com/newspaper/frontpage/2012/0124/1224310673916.html> [Accessed February 16, 2012].

Fanning, B., 2011. *Immigration and social cohesion in the Republic of Ireland.* Manchester: Manchester University Press.

Firstworldwar.com, n.d. *Primary documents—proclamation of the Irish Republic. 24 April 1916.* [online] Available at: <http://www.firstworldwar.com/source/irishproclamation1916.htm> [Accessed June 29, 2011].

Free Legal Advice Centre, 2011. *Not every child in Ireland gets the children's allowance.* [pdf] Available at: <http://www.integratingireland.ie/userfiles/File/Database/Childpercent20Allowancepercent20Campaign.pdf> [Accessed June 24, 2011].

Gasper, D., 2006. Cosmopolitan presumptions? On Martha Nussbaum and her commentators. *Development and Change*, 37 (6), pp.1227–46.

Goodin, R., 1985. *Protecting the vulnerable.* Chicago: University of Chicago Press.

Government of Ireland, 2010. *EU/IMF programme of financial support for Ireland: programme documents.* [pdf] Available at: <http://www.merrionstreet.ie/wp-content/uploads/2010/12/EUIMFmemo.pdf> [Accessed April 16, 2012].

Higgins, M., 1992.The challenge of building the mind of peace . . . asserting the humanistic vision. *The Irish Review*, 13, pp.131–42.

Hill, M., 2003. *Women in Ireland: A century of change.* Belfast: The Blackstaff Press.

Holland, K., 2004. Crisis pregnancies among non-nationals increasing. *Irish Times*, [online] Available at: <http://www.irishtimes.com/newspaper/ireland/2004/0709/1086274535009.html> [Accessed June 29, 2011].

Immigration Council of Ireland, 2011. Immigration information update—the 'Zambrano' case. [online] Available at: <http://www.immigrantcouncil.ie/newsbulletin/2011/475-ici-news-bulletin-issue-84> [Accessed June 24, 2011].

International convention on the protection of the rights of all migrant workers and members of their families. [online] Available at: <http://www2.ohchr.org/english/law/cmw.htm> [Accessed June 30, 2011].

International Labour Organization, 2006. *ILO multilateral framework for a rights-based approach to migration.* [pdf] Available at: <http://www.ilo.org/public/english/protection/migrant/download/multilat_fwk_en.pdf> [Accessed June 30, 2011].

Irish Council for Civil Liberties, 2003. *Submission to Joint Oireachtas Committee on justice, equality, defense and women's rights supreme court decision in the case of D.L., A.O. & Ors v Minister for justice, equality and law reform*, 23 January. [online] Available at: <www.iccl.ie> [Accessed June 24, 2011].

Irish Government News Service, 2011. *Statement by minister for justice, equality and defense, Mr Alan Shatter, TD, on the implications of the recent ruling of the Court of Justice of the European Union in the case of Ruiz Zambrano*, 21 March, [online] Available at: <http://www.merrionstreet.ie/index.php/2011/03/statement-by-minister-for-justice-equality-and-defense-mr-alan-shatter-td-on-the-implications-of-the-recent-ruling-of-the-court-of-justice-of-the-european-union-in-the-case-of-ruiz-zambrano/> [Accessed June 24, 2011].

Irish Human Rights Commission and National Consultative Commission on Racism and Interculturalism, 2004. *Safeguarding the rights of migrant workers and their families.* [pdf] Available at: <http://www.ihrc.ie/download/pdf/safeguarding_rights_migrants.pdf> [Accessed June 29, 2011].

Irish Independent, 2011. Ireland ranked as 2nd most globalised economy in the world. *Irish Independent Online*, [online] 16 January. Available at: <http://www.independent.ie/business/irish/ireland-ranked-as-2nd-most-globalised-economy-in-the-world-2511772.html> [Accessed April 15, 2011].

Irish Times, 2011.Work and pregnancy. *Irish Times*, [online] 28 June. Available at: <http://www.irishtimes.com/newspaper/opinion/2011/0628/1224299679233.html> [Accessed June 29, 2011].

Keenan, B., 2011. IBEC: Use "smart" card to pay child benefit. *Irish Independent*, [online] 30 September. Available at: <http://www.independent.ie/national-news/ibec-use-smart-card-to-pay-child-benefit-2892430.html> [Accessed November 4, 2011].

Kelly, J.M., Hogan, G. and Whyte, G., 1994. *The Irish constitution.* Dublin: Butterworths.

Kristof, N., 2009. Where sweatshops are a dream. *New York Times*, 14 January, [online] Available at: <http://www.nytimes.com/2009/01/15/opinion/15kristof.html> [Accessed November 9, 2011].

Lally, C., 2011. Minister ordered 200 deportations on final day. *Irish Times*, 6 June, [pdf] Available at: <http://search.proquest.com/docview/1008576492/fulltextPDF/B47C27573ECD4F1CPQ/1?accountid=14507> [Accessed November 6, 2014].

Lentin, R., 2007. Illegal in Ireland, Irish illegals: Diaspora nation as racial state. *Irish Political Studies*, 22(4), pp.433–53.

Mac Éinrí, P. and White, A., 2008. Immigration into the Republic of Ireland: A bibliography of recent research. *Irish Geography*, 41(2), pp.151–79.

Mancini, J.M. and Finlay, G., 2008. Citizenship matters: Lessons from the Irish citizenship referendum. *American Quarterly*, 60(3), pp.575–99.

Mellon, G., 2011. Deprivation of permission to work: Asylum seekers and Article 8 ECHR. [online] Available at: <http://www.humanrights.ie/index.php/2011/03/24/deprivation-of-permission-to-work-asylum-seekers-and-article-8-echr/> [Accessed July 1, 2011].

Migrant Rights Council of Ireland, 2010.Ending the race to the bottom: Changing the balance for migrant workers in Ireland. *Policy Paper* [pdf] Available at: <http://www.mrci.ie/media/File/MRCIpercent20PPpercent20Endingpercent20thepercent20Racepercent20topercent20thepercent20Bottom.pdf> [Accessed November 10, 2011.]

Millar, S., 2010. Inspectors must prosecute firms that exploit migrant labour. *Irish Examiner*, [online] 12 January, Available at: <http://www.examiner.ie/ireland/inspectors-must-prosecute-firms-that-exploit-migrant-labour-109463.html#ixzz1Qu12Vfqd> [Accessed July 1, 2011].

Mullin, M., 1991.Representations of history, Irish feminism and the politics of difference. *Feminist Studies*, 17, pp.29–50.

NíLaoire, C., 2008. Complicating host-newcomer dualisms: Irish return migrants as home-comers or newcomers? *Translocations: Migration and Social Change* [online], 4(1), pp.35–50. Available at: <http://www.translocations.ie/volume4_issue1.html> [Accessed June 15, 2011]

Nussbaum, M., 2000. *Women and human development*. Cambridge: Cambridge University Press.

Nussbaum, M., 2006. *Frontiers of justice*. Cambridge, MA: Harvard University Press.

Philips, S., 2011.Towards a strategy for the inclusion of migrant workers in trade unions. *Irish Congress of Trade Unions*, [pdf] Available at: <http://www.ictu.ie/download/pdf/ictu_migrant_workers_a5.pdf> [Accessed April 12, 2012].

Pieterse, J., 2006. Emancipatory cosmopolitanism: Towards an agenda. *Development and Change*, 37(6), pp.1247–57.

Pillinger, J., 2006. An introduction to the situation and experience of women migrant workers in Ireland. *The Equality Authority* [online] Available at: <http://www.equality.ie/getFile.asp?FC_ID=279&docID=577> [Accessed June 30, 2011].

Pillinger, J., 2007. *The feminisation of migration: Experiences and opportunities in Ireland*. [online] Immigrant Council of Ireland, Dublin. Available at: <http://www.immigrantcouncil.ie/research-publications/archive/359-the-feminisation-of-migration-experiences-and-opportunities-in-ireland> [Accessed June 24, 2011].

Pogge, T., 1992.Cosmopolitanism and sovereignty. *Ethics*, 103(1), pp.48–75.

Ruhs, M., 2009. *Ireland: From rapid immigration to recession*. [online] Available at: <http://www.migrationinformation.org/Feature/display.cfm?ID=740> [Accessed November 4, 2011].

Russell, H., Watson, D. and Banks, J., 2011. Equality authority and crisis pregnancy. *Programme report, pregnancy at work: A national survey*. [online] Available at: <http://www.equality.ie/index.asp?locID=105&docID=970> [Accessed June 30, 2011].

Satterthwaite, M., 2004. Women migrants' rights under international human rights law. *Feminist Review*, 77, pp.167–71.

Sen, A., 2004. Elements of a theory of human rights. *Philosophy and Public Affairs*, 32(4), pp.315–56.

Sen, A., 2009. *The idea of justice*. Cambridge, MA: Harvard University Press.

Shue, H., 1996. *Basic rights*. Princeton: Princeton University Press.

Smyth, J., 2010. State has EU's lowest rate of granting refugee status. *Irish Times*, [online] 10 July. Available at: <http://www.irishtimes.com/newspaper/ireland/2010/0710/1224274420878.html> [Accessed June 24, 2011].

Smyth, J., 2011. State seeks to change EU child benefit rule. *Irish Times*, [online] 21 March. Available at: <http://www.irishtimes.com/newspaper/ireland/2011/0321/1224292709236.html> [Accessed June 24, 2011].

Steiner, H.J and Alston, P., 2000. Comment on CEDAW's substantive provisions. *International human rights in context*. Oxford: Oxford University Press.

Stewart, J., Clark, D. and Clark, P., 2007. Migration and recruitment of healthcare professionals: Causes, consequences and policy responses. *Focus Policy*

Brief, 7, pp. 1–8. [online] Available at: <http://focus-migration.hwwi.de/typo3_upload/groups/3/focus_Migration_Publikationen/Kurzdossiers/PB07_Health.pdf> [Accessed July 14, 2015].

Tormey, A., 2007. 'Everyone with eyes can see the problem': Moral citizens and the space of Irish nationhood. *International Migration*, 45(3), pp.69–100.

Wellman, C. H. 2008. Immigration and Freedom of Association. *Ethics*, 119(1), pp. 109–141.

3 Trapped in a Web of Immigration and Employment Laws
Female Undocumented Home Health Workers in the US[1]

Zahra Meghani

INTRODUCTION

In the United States, over 90 percent of home health workers are women. Undocumented and documented home health workers travel to the residence of their elderly, disabled or chronically ill clients to provide them with clinical and caregiving services.[2] The value of their work is undeniable, but they are underpaid. Most home health workers live below or near the poverty line, undocumented home health workers face additional challenges. Caught in a complex web of immigration and employment laws and policies, they are exploited and denied workers' rights. This chapter analyzes and criticizes this ethical failure of the democratic state. It also evaluates the advocacy efforts of nongovernmental organizations (NGOs) on behalf of care workers, with particular attention to their significance for undocumented home health workers.

The first section provides a brief account of the nature of the work performed by home health workers. The characteristics of undocumented home health workers and the challenges they face are delineated. In the next part, the history of the profession is described and the immigration and employment laws applicable to undocumented workers are outlined. Then, the hierarchy of workers created by neoliberalism—a technology of governance—is discussed and the 'place' of undocumented workers in that structure is analyzed. Following that, the efforts of two NGOs to remedy the ethical failure of the democratic state to treat undocumented home health workers and care workers as the moral equals of other workers are examined.

HOME HEALTH WORKERS

Home health workers perform multiple low-level clinical tasks for their elderly, disabled or chronically ill clients. They administer their medication, monitor their blood pressure and assist in the performance of range-of-motion exercises (Boris and Klein, 2006, p.82; Hess and Henrici, 2013, p.5). In addition, they help their clients with daily life activities, such as bathing, dressing and eating (Hess and Henrici, 2013, p.5). The duties of home health workers include clinical and personal care for their adult clients, but the profession is often mistakenly equated with domestic work that is relegated to wives or the care work performed by mothers for their young children (Boris and Klein, 2006, p.81).

In the US, home health workers are grouped under the larger category of direct care workers (DCWs), which includes certified nurse aides and personal care attendants (PHI, n.d., *About PHI*).[3] They are employed in institutional facilities, community based settings and households (Hess and Henrici, 2013, p.1, footnote 1). Documented and undocumented home health workers are disproportionately women of color (Boris and Klein, 2007, p.5). There are not much data available about undocumented home health workers, but it may be assumed that its members are reluctant to identify themselves, fearing arrest, imprisonment and deportation. Some inferences can be made about the group and its circumstances using the available data about the foreign-born DCWs population. An estimated 20 percent of DCWs were born outside the US and an approximate fourth of those are undocumented workers. Persons from Mexico and Central America make up 33 percent of that group and people from the Caribbean and Africa constitute 18 percent and 20 percent, respectively (Martin et al., 2009, p.27).

Undocumented home health workers tend to be employed in home settings where they are less likely to be required to provide documentation verifying that they have the state's permission to work (Hess and Henrici, 2013, p.13). Many DCWs (including, presumably, female undocumented home health workers) live in urban areas and work in suburban home settings (Salter and Vilner, 2006, p.5). The New York-Northeastern New Jersey urban areas have the greatest concentration of foreign-born home health workers; they constitute 74 percent of the larger population of home health workers (Hess and Henrici, 2013, p.5). In Florida's Miami and Hialeah, foreign-born home health workers make up 83 percent of the total number of home health workers and in Fort Lauderdale, Hollywood and Pompano Beach 79 percent. In Texas's McAllen, Edinburg, Pharr and Mission, they constitute almost 70 percent of the total number of home health workers. In California, in Los Angeles and Long Beach, they number 61 percent of the total population of home health workers and 56 percent of San Francisco's, Oakland's and Vallejo's. Foreign-born home health workers comprise 53 percent of the total number of home health workers in Washington, DC, Virginia, Maryland and San Diego in California (Hess and Henrici, 2013, p.5).

Undocumented women home health workers generally earn less than their documented counterparts as they often work as "live-ins" (Hess and Henrici, 2013, p.13; Hondagneu-Sotelo, 2001). Female undocumented domestic and home health workers are more likely to be victims of thefts and other crimes than their documented peers (Hondagneu-Sotelo, 2001).

It is because they work in households performing the work that is expected of females, their employers tend to place excessive demands on them—such as expecting them to work additional hours for no pay or do work that they are not required to do—on the grounds that they are "part of the family" (Clare, 2005). This vulnerability to exploitation and their failure to report crimes is partly attributable to their fears of deportation (Hess et al., 2011).

Given the low pay of undocumented DCWs, it is very likely that they do not have retirement benefits or health insurance coverage. Only 30 percent of DCWs that are employed in home settings have health insurance coverage (Regan, 2008). Most home health workers do not earn enough to purchase health insurance on their own. If their employers do offer health insurance coverage with the condition that they pay for a portion of the cost, it is unlikely that they can afford the premium cost because they are not even assured of a minimum wage (more on this later). Home health workers who are American citizens may be able to access Medicaid (a health insurance program funded jointly by federal and state governments that covers certain groups of poor or disabled persons) if they meet the eligibility criteria of their state of residence. But undocumented home health workers, regardless of their impoverished circumstances, do not qualify for Medicaid coverage because of their undocumented status. The lack of health insurance coverage is a serious problem. Uncontrolled chronic health conditions such as diabetes and hypertension are more prevalent among persons without health insurance than those who have consistent access to health care (Wilper et al., 2009). In general, DCWs have one of the higher rates of work related injury among various professions (PHI, 2011, *FACTS 4*, p.5). Home health workers have a 20.5 per 10,000 workers chance of suffering injuries while on the job (OHS, 2010).

Undocumented persons living near or in poverty without health insurance tend to rely on hospital emergency rooms or free clinics for medical care. The 1986 Emergency Medical Treatment and Labor Act mandated that no hospital emergency room turn away patients experiencing a medical crisis, even if they cannot pay for it (Warner, 2012). However, once patients stabilize, hospitals do not have the responsibility to continue providing care to them. Patients are also billed for emergency care. So undocumented persons can get care at a hospital emergency room if they have a medical crisis, but then they face very high medical bills, because even simple diagnostic or surgical procedures can easily run into tens of thousands of dollars.

For nonemergency medical care, undocumented persons (including, presumably, undocumented home health workers) generally rely on free health-care clinics, assuming such clinics are available where they live. In the US, there are more than 1,100 such facilities, which provide care to approximately 1.8 million patients. Forty percent of those who utilize these facilities are immigrants (Darnell, 2010). Free clinics are nonprofit community health-care providers,[4] which offer medical care to low-income, uninsured, or underinsured patients at little or no cost (Liebert and Ameringer, 2013, p.3). They are staffed by volunteer medical professionals, including doctors, dentists, nurse practitioners, nurses, dental hygienists and mental health professionals, and they are dependent on private individual donors, foundations and corporations for funding (they cannot bill any government-funded insurance program or health insurance company for the services they provide) (Liebert and Ameringer, 2013, p.3). Thus the ability of the clinics to serve their patients depends on the availability of volunteer medical professionals and the largesse of private donors. In other words, the primary source of health care for undocumented persons is unreliable.

It is undeniable that home health workers, both undocumented and documented, face considerable difficulties. Their circumstances are not a matter of bad luck; rather, they are the product of laws and government policies.

A HISTORY OF THE HOME HEALTH WORK PROFESSION

The New Deal and Home Health Workers

The origins of the profession of home health work can be traced to the New Deal. Between 1933 and 1936, the US introduced a number of domestic economic initiatives to pull the nation out of the Great Depression. The New Deal included a program that aimed to assist families whose primary (female) caregiver was incapacitated or ill, while providing jobs for poor women who were unemployed (Boris and Klein, 2006, p.84). The program paid the women to go into those homes and fill in for the mothers and wives by performing a variety of domestic tasks as well as care work for the elderly and the disabled.

The federal program appeared to have been motivated by the idea that poor, unemployed women needed to be rehabilitated. The assumption was that they would become productive members of society and learn to care for themselves and their families by helping the elderly and the disabled avoid institutional care (Boris and Klein, 2006, pp.84–5). This conception of poor women on welfare is consistent with the general cultural assumption in the US that welfare recipients are morally or psychologically deficient (Fraser and Gordon, 1994, p.111).

The New Deal labor regulations considered home health workers and nurse companions to be domestic servants because the work they performed was in the home. The construal of home health workers as domestic workers (even though the former provided certain health-care services unlike the latter) had substantial ramifications. In 1935, when the Social Security Act was passed, all workers categorized as domestic workers were excluded from coverage. This failure of inclusion was significant in terms of gender, race and class as the vast majority of domestic workers were women on welfare and African Americans and immigrant women of color (Boris and Klein, 2006, p.84). It was in 1950 that domestic workers were permitted to contribute to the program and draw benefits from it, provided they met certain criteria (Kollmann, 2000). In 1954, the eligibility criteria were revised, allowing more domestic workers to enroll in the program (Kollmann, 2000). Today, home health workers are covered under the Social Security Act, but undocumented home health workers by virtue of their undocumented status cannot access this crucial benefit.

Labor Laws and Home Health Workers

Aside from state policies and programs, the US employment regime had a critical role in shaping the home health worker profession. Employment laws fall under the National Labor Relations Act (NLRA). Passed in 1935, the Act governs labor entities and protects the right of employees as individuals to organize with other workers and engage in some forms of collective action (Griffith, 2009, pp.128–9, 142). The NLRA does not apply to domestic workers, individual contractors and certain other categories of workers (NLRB, n.d.). Undocumented and documented home health workers are not covered by the Act because they are classified as domestic workers.

In 1938, the federal government passed the Fair Labor Standards Act (FLSA) to ensure a minimum living standard for all workers by establishing a minimum wage, overtime pay and other protections. However, domestic workers were not covered under the FLSA, and it was only because of the activism of second wave feminists, alliance of professional women, civil rights activists and trade unionists that in 1974 the FLSA was extended to include household workers, including housekeepers, full-time nannies, chauffeurs and cleaners (Boris and Klein, 2006, p.84; May, 2011, p.176). They became entitled to a minimum wage and overtime pay. However, the 1974 amendment excluded home health workers; it construed them as "companions to the elderly or the infirm" who were analogous to babysitters. The exception it permitted was the subgroup of home health workers who were employed by a "large enough organization" (i.e., home care agencies) (Boris and Klein, 2007, p.6). But in 1975, the Department of Labor ruled that that group was also not covered under the FLSA (Boris and Klein, 2006, p.84).

Following the 1975 ruling, home health workers sought to change the FLSA so that they could be covered under it. A relatively recent effort that received considerable media attention was made in 2002 by Evelyn Coke, a home health worker in New York. She filed a suit against her employer, Long Island Care at Home, because for a number of years the small home care agency had been paying her less than minimum wage and no overtime pay (Perry, 2008, p.1185). The Jamaican immigrant had been a home health worker for twenty years, working at times three consecutive 24 hour shifts, assisting her elderly charges by monitoring their medication, helping them bathe, dress and cooking for them (Martin, 2009). Some weeks she worked more than 70 hours, yet for her efforts she received $7 an hour rather than the (higher) minimum wage and no overtime pay.

In 2007, *Long Island Care at Home v. Evelyn Coke* was decided by the US Supreme Court. The justices ruled that the Department of Labor had the authority to not include home health workers in the category of workers covered by the FLSA. Transcripts of the court's arguments revealed that the decision was motivated by the concern that families would not be able to afford elder care in their homes if they had to pay home health workers at least the minimum wage and overtime pay (Boris and Klein, 2007, p.5). In other words, the court considered the well-being of the women employed as home health workers—who are predominantly poor women of color and (documented and undocumented) immigrants—to be secondary to that of the families that employed them. So counties and states who employed home health workers continued to treat them as independent contractors rather than employees who were entitled to the same rights and benefits as other state and county employees (Boris and Klein, 2006, p.84). Moreover, home care agencies that employed home health workers had the endorsement of the federal government to pay them less than the minimum wage and deny them overtime pay.

In 2001, the Clinton administration attempted to amend the FLSA to include home health workers (Whittaker, 2008, pp.10–11) but the effort failed. In 2011, President Obama promised to extend the FLSA to home health workers and, in September 2013, the Act was changed to include direct care workers, including home health workers, giving them the right to minimum wages and overtime pay. Undoubtedly, this was an important step by the federal government toward the fair treatment of home health workers. But it is unlikely that undocumented home health workers will benefit from this change in employment law given the complex interplay between US employment laws and immigration laws. In the following section, their complicated interaction with respect to undocumented workers is outlined.

IMMIGRATION LAWS, EMPLOYMENT LAWS AND UNDOCUMENTED WORKERS

Historically, the US labor and employment regime has considered US citizens, permanent residents and (documented and undocumented) foreign workers on American soil to be equals (Griffith, 2009, p.128). Its stance is predicated on the belief that unless the rights of each and every worker are protected, the rights of all workers are at stake (Griffith, 2009, p.128). All workers in the US must be afforded the same individual and collective rights to avoid the prospects of an underclass of employees (Griffith, 2009, p.159). So, the NLRA applies to documented and undocumented workers, but, as mentioned earlier, it does not cover home health workers.

Undocumented Workers and the Immigration Reform and Control Act

Unlike labor and employment laws, immigration laws consider the documented or undocumented status of foreign nationals in the US to be of significance and, thus, grounds for treating them differently than American citizens. In 1952, the US Congress enacted the federal statute, the Immigration and Nationality Act (INA). The INA determined the conditions under which foreigners could immigrate or naturalize, including work in the US (Griffith, 2009, p.128). In 1986, Congress passed the Immigration Reform and Control Act (IRCA), which marked a substantial change in US immigration policy. Combating the employment of undocumented persons became the key concern of immigration law (Griffith, 2009, p.139).[5] With the implementation of IRCA, the hiring of undocumented workers was criminalized (Garcia, 2012, p.665). Employers who knowingly hired undocumented workers were subject to civil and criminal action, but IRCA did not effectively "prohibit undocumented aliens from seeking or maintaining employment" (Griffith, 2009, p.140). US employers could continue to employ undocumented persons who were completely "off the books" (Griffith, 2009, p.140).

The IRCA placed on the shoulders of US employers the responsibility of monitoring and discouraging undocumented workers. They were required to verify that the workers that they hired were eligible to work in the US. This abdication of responsibility by the federal government has had profound consequences for undocumented workers. That Act created a power relationship between US employers and their undocumented workers that privileged the former group, while undermining the latter group. Employers could hire them at rates lower than the prevailing market wages and require them to work under conditions that were exploitative and dangerous (Griffith, 2009, p.140).

Undocumented workers attempting to organize have been fired by their US employers (Garcia, 2003, p.741). The federal government imposes a nominal penalty on employers for violating undocumented workers' right to organize. They have to "post a notice to employees stating that the employer violated the NLRA" (Garcia, 2003, p.748). So, while the NLRA considers undocumented workers to be employees who have claim to the same rights and protections as US citizens who are employees, IRCA is able to effectively undermine those entitlements and protections (Garcia, 2003, p.748).

Moreover, with the passage of IRCA, undocumented workers have experienced a significant wage penalty. The wages of undocumented workers who were able to become permanent residents rose by 40 percent, "even when controlling for factors like education, language ability, and length of residency in the United States" (Weber, 2010, p.619, footnote 27; Rivera-Batiz, 1999, pp.100–6). The wages of those who remained undocumented did not increase.

In some respects, IRCA's stance on the status of undocumented workers was foreshadowed in the Supreme Court's 1984 decision in *Sure-Tan, Inc. v. NLRB*. The case involved an employer who called the Immigration and Naturalization Services on his undocumented employees who were attempting to organize. The Court ruled that undocumented workers qualified as employees under the NLRA, and, thus, they had the same rights as other US employees, regardless of their immigration status in the country (Garcia, 2012, p.665). But it also held that the former undocumented employees could not lay claim to back wages or be reinstated *because* they had already been deported (Garcia, 2003, p.745).

The IRCA's influence on the highest court in the US can be seen in the 2002 decision in the *Hoffman Plastic Compounds Inc. v. NLRB* ruling. The case involved the termination of an undocumented worker without due cause. The majority on the Supreme Court ruled against undocumented workers. The decision was motivated by the fear that if undocumented workers were recognized as entitled to back pay following illegal termination, it would encourage the violation of immigration laws (Garcia, 2010, p.659). The court clearly privileged immigration law over the NLRA. The ruling seems to have created a climate wherein employers feel emboldened to exploit and threaten undocumented workers and discourage them from organizing (Garcia, 2012, p.667). It relegated undocumented workers to a second class status by denying them the right to reinstatement following illegal termination and any claim to back pay (Garcia, 2012, p.659; also see Griffith, 2009, p.141, 143).

In general, the devaluation of the worth of the work performed by undocumented workers is rooted in the biased conception of that group as "born lawbreakers" (Garcia, 2003, p.748). No other group that violates the law is conceptualized in terms that make illegality a fundamental part of their identity. Executives who break the law or individuals who evade taxes are not called "illegal executives" or "illegal taxpayers" (Garcia, 2003, p.748). Yet undocumented workers are termed "illegal aliens" as though the violation of immigration laws is their defining feature (Garcia, 2003, p.750–1).

Presumably, emboldened by IRCA and the federal government's failure to protect the fundamental rights of undocumented workers, a number of US states have passed a variety of punitive laws that target that population. Some of those laws are identified in the section that follows.

Undocumented Workers and State Laws

In 2008, undocumented persons were 4 percent of the population of the US and they constituted 5.4 percent (8.3 million) of the nation's workforce (Passel and Cohn. 2009, p.i, iii); yet in 2007, an exceptionally high number of state-level legislations targeting undocumented persons were passed. That phenomenon can be attributed to the year 2008 being a presidential election year. It is not uncommon in the year preceding a presidential election for political parties to use the presence of undocumented persons in the US as an issue to define their stance and garner public support and, thus, votes. In 2007, Colorado, Maine, Minnesota, Mississippi and Utah passed laws that disqualified undocumented workers from receiving unemployment insurance benefits, even though the workers had paid and would have to continue paying unemployment insurance premiums and state and federal taxes (Colorado HB 1286; Maine LD 1015; Minnesota SB 0167; Mississippi SB 2448; Utah SB 103). Colorado, Idaho, Indiana and Texas enacted legislation that made it a requirement that applications for benefits be accompanied by proof of legal residency (Colorado HB 1314; Idaho SB 1157; Indiana SB 504; Texas SB 589). So undocumented workers are unable to apply for public assistance. Minnesota passed legislation that barred undocumented persons from receiving general medical care that was funded by the federal or the state government (Minnesota HB 1078). (The only exception was emergency care.) Nevada and Oregon also enacted legislation that rendered undocumented workers ineligible for workers' compensation regardless of the harm they might have experienced while on the job (Nevada AB 496; Oregon HB 2244 and SB 202).

Florida, Indiana, Kansas, Louisiana and North Dakota have effected legislation that require noncitizens to provide documentation of their legal status in the US in order to obtain a driver's license (Florida SB 2114; Indiana SB 463; Kansas SB 9; Louisiana HB 766; North Dakota SB 2112). Consequently, undocumented workers cannot acquire a driver's license in those states. They cannot drive themselves to a medical clinic (Liebert and Ameringer, 2013, p.6), a grocery store or a post office without taking the risk of being arrested for driving without a license. They are also unable to use banks because they need formal identification documents such as a driver's license or a valid passport to open a bank account. So they have to rely on check cashing facilities that charge exorbitant fees and interest rates. As a result, some undocumented workers carry their cash earnings on them, which makes them prime targets for criminals.

UNDOCUMENTED WORKERS IN THE NEOLIBERAL HIERARCHY OF WORKERS

Not all state laws applicable to undocumented persons are punitive, but the general tendency at the state and the federal level has been to create laws and policies that make the US an increasingly hostile environment for undocumented workers. Racism appears to be at work because most of these workers are from the global South. In 2010, of the total of number of undocumented persons, those from Mexico constituted 58 percent (6.5 million), Central America 11 percent (1.3 million), South America 7 percent (775,000), Caribbean 4 percent (500,000), South and East Asia accounted for 11 percent (1.3 million) and nationals of various African countries approximately 3 percent (400,000) (Passel and Cohn, 2011, p.11, 21). These laws and policies are also class biased because approximately 47 percent of undocumented adults (ages 25–64) do not have a high school education (Passel and Cohn, 2009, p.iv). Moreover, undocumented persons tend to be employed in low-skilled jobs in the agriculture, construction, leisure/hospitality and services sectors of the economy (Passel and Cohn, 2009, p.14). They make up 25 percent of the farmworkers population in the US, 19 percent of building, grounds keeping and maintenance workforce and 17 percent of those employed as construction workers. Undocumented workers constitute 12 percent of the US population of food preparation workers and servers, 10 percent of production workers and 7 percent of transportation and material moving workers (Passel and Cohn, 2009, p.15).

To understand the biases shaping US policies and laws that apply to undocumented workers, Aihwa Ong's notion of neoliberalism is a useful tool. Her conception of neoliberalism is different from "neoliberalism" as a political philosophy.[6] In contrast to that notion of neoliberalism, Ong has proposed that "neoliberalism" (with a lower case "n") should be understood as a technology of governance that the state uses to create hierarchies of workers to optimize productivity (Ong, 2006, p.6). This means of governance is used by democratic states and authoritarian ones. The state establishes a hierarchy of workers by affording privileges to certain kinds of workers, while denying those benefits and basic entitlements and protections to other types of workers (Ong, 2006, pp.6–7). The former class of workers is treated as a positive exception to the norm such that they are deemed worthy of more than the standard workers' protections and benefits. The group of workers categorized as the negative exception to the norm is regarded as deserving of few, if any, of the basic workers' rights that the state guarantees to the general population of workers.

In the US, both at the federal and state level, the government treats undocumented workers as exceptions in the negative sense to the norm for workers. In fact, as mentioned earlier, criminality is inscribed as an intrinsic part of their identity (Garcia, 2003, p.751). They are considered unworthy of the basic rights of workers and denied access to key benefits and protections. The state's refusal to afford basic workers' rights to undocumented workers is an instance of neoliberal exception that allows it and US employers to exploit them. When domestic workers or home health workers are not paid (at least) a minimum wage or overtime pay, it profits their employers and their clients. The advantage to the state is that it earns the loyalty of the populations who are the beneficiaries of the practice of treating undocumented and documented home health workers as exceptions in the negative sense to the norm of workers.

Any democratic state that creates a hierarchy of workers such that some groups are denied their basic rights as workers fails ethically in a significant way. The raison d'être of any democracy is a commitment to the principle of the moral equality of all persons (Nielsen, 1985). Liberal democracies are beholden to respect all persons within their borders (over whom they have authority) as moral equals. Among other things, it means that they are ethically obligated to not deny the members of any group their human rights on the basis of an arbitrary biological or social difference between them and some other population. Thus no liberal democracy is justified in discriminating or exploiting the undocumented workers employed within its borders.

NGOS AS MORAL AGENTS

Given the ethical failure of the state to treat DCWs fairly, a number of NGOs have attempted to advocate on their behalf. In this section, the advocacy efforts of the Paraprofessional Health Institute (PHI) are delineated, with particular attention to their significance for undocumented home health workers. The PHI is an NGO that describes itself as the "nation's leading authority on the direct-care workforce (including home health workers)" (PHI, n.d., *About PHI*). The activism of the Caring Across Generations campaign on behalf of undocumented caregivers is also examined. The campaign is a collaborative initiative undertaken by the National Domestic Workers Alliance, the Service Employees International Union, Hand in Hand: The Domestic Employers Association, Direct Care Alliance, 9 to 5 Winning Justice for Working Women, National Council on Aging, AFSCME (a public services employees union), Ohio Organizing Collective, Virginia New Majority Education Fund, Bend the Arc: A Jewish Partnership for Justice, Jobs With Justice and PHI (CAG, 2013).

PHI

The PHI describes itself as an organization that aims to nurture the dignity, respect and autonomy of those in need of care and the DCWs that provide care to them. As approximately 90 percent of DCWs are women, a primary aim of the organization is to help "unemployed women and their families... achieve economic independence" by providing them with "entry-level, in-service, and incumbent worker training curricula to strengthen training for direct-care" (PHI, n.d., *About PHI*). To that end, it collaborates with care providers, those who need care, worker organizations and policy makers.

In recent years, PHI has undertaken two key advocacy initiatives on behalf of DCWs, including home health workers. Its efforts to secure minimum wage protection and health insurance coverage for DCWs are briefly outlined below.

Minimum Wage Protection for DCWs
As discussed earlier, historically, the FLSA did not cover DCWs. Thus, they were not assured a minimum wage or overtime protection. Consequently, according to PHI, approximately 45 percent of the direct care

workforce has had to rely on public assistance for meeting the daily needs of their families (PHI, 2011, *FACTS 3*). Policy makers justified denying minimum wage and overtime pay to direct care workers on the grounds that, while "they would love to pay workers more, . . . it would mean having less money to provide care for people with disabilities and elders" (Surpin and Sturgeon, 2013). No doubt as a result of the advocacy efforts of PHI and other such entities, as of September 2013, DCWs, including home health workers, are guaranteed a minimum wage and overtime pay. The population of DCWs that will benefit from this change consists of those persons who are employed by health-care agencies and who are US citizens, because labor laws are in their favor if they are denied minimum wage or overtime pay. But given IRCA and the Supreme Court's *Hoffman Plastic Compounds Inc. v. NLRB* ruling, it is unlikely that undocumented home health workers can rely on the government or the courts to ensure that they receive at least minimum wage and overtime pay. In other words, the fact that home health workers are now covered under the FLSA may not have any significance for undocumented home health workers.

Health Insurance Coverage for DCWs
The PHI has been a strong and vocal proponent for health insurance coverage for DCWs. It has been especially concerned about DCWs employed in home settings because 70 percent of them lack health-care insurance (Regan, 2008). For a variety of reasons many DCWs do not have health insurance. Employers either do not offer coverage or only provide it to employees who work full time or who have worked for them for a long period of time. Some DCWs also go without coverage because they cannot afford the premiums given their low wages or because the premiums are exorbitant because, as a profession, they tend to be at high risk for work-related injuries (PHI, 2013, *Health Coverage*).

With the passage of the 2010 Patient Protection and Affordable Care Act (ACA) as well as the Health Care and Education Act, PHI has been "monitoring federal and state implementation of the Affordable Care Act, and the impact on direct-care workers" (PHI, 2013, *Health Coverage*). The NGO has also been providing information to long-term care employers and DCWs about ACA coverage criteria and helping employers choose health insurance coverage for their employees that will meet their needs. Additionally, it has been working with its allies in the health-care and long-term-care sectors with the aim of ensuring the implementation of the ACA. Moreover, it has been encouraging states to use federal monies to increase Medicaid coverage so that more low low-income populations get access to health care (PHI, 2013, *Health Coverage*). If individual states expand Medicaid coverage to include persons who earn less than 138 percent of the poverty level, then more than 350,000 DCWs could get health insurance (PHI, 2013, *Health Coverage*).[7] Moreover, DCWs with a higher level of income but who are still poor would be eligible to purchase health insurance through the state or federal exchanges that are being created as part of the ACA.

Medicaid coverage may now be available to a greater number of DCWS than previously, but undocumented DCWs, including undocumented home health workers, remain ineligible for Medicaid coverage by virtue of their undocumented status (Lee, 2013). The lack of affordable health insurance coverage for this group of DCWs is not mentioned in key PHI reports on the problem of health insurance coverage for DCWs.[8] Those reports also do not discuss the possibility that the ACA might result in the closure of some free clinics, which are the major source of medical care for undocumented persons. It is likely that the ACA will mean an increase in the demand for primary care physicians because millions of uninsured Americans will get access to health care, contributing to the worsening of the shortage of physicians who are available to volunteer at free clinics, possibly resulting in their closure (Liebert and Ameringer, 2013, p.8). The silence of PHI on the issue of access to health care for undocumented DCWs is revealing. The population of DCWs that seems to be the organization's advocacy efforts' focus is US citizens or persons who have been (legal) permanent residents for at least five years.[9]

The Caring Across Generations (CAG) Campaign

The CAG campaign describes itself as representing the interests of elderly Americans, persons with disabilities, their families and their caregivers. It aims "to protect all Americans' right to choose the care and support they need to live with dignity" (CAG, 2013). One of the dimensions of CAG's multifaceted campaign is an initiative to advocate for legal status and a path to citizenship for undocumented caregivers of elderly and disabled US citizens (CAG, 2013).

The CAG's advocacy on behalf of undocumented home health workers and other low-wage DCWs is informed by the reality of their circumstances. Recognizing that many undocumented home health workers may be paid in cash by their clients, the organization takes the stance that eligibility for legal status and citizenship should not be contingent on those workers' ability to provide pay stubs as evidence of their employment (CAG, 2013). The CAG also holds that undocumented home health workers should be eligible to apply for legal status and immigration without being subject to "onerous fines, application fees, or English language requirements" (CAG, 2013, *About Us*). The organization is aware that the substantial English language proficiency requirement and high application fees or fines are biased criteria that favor a certain class of undocumented workers who have access to considerable resources and who are fluent in English. In contrast to that group of undocumented workers, undocumented home health workers have very limited resources. Their low wages makes it unlikely that they will be able to pay significant fines or high application fees, and they may not be in the financial position to work fewer hours in order to take English language classes.

There are two parts to the legislative proposal developed by CAG outlining the path to legal status for undocumented home health workers and other DCWs (Hess and Henrici, 2013, p.15). First, workers would be eligible for temporary legal status and work authorization upon providing evidence of employment in a private home. In the second step, workers with temporary legal status would become legal permanent residents provided they completed job-training requirements and remained employed as home health workers for a specified minimum period of time. Recognizing that employers of home health workers could be abusive and given the power imbalance between the undocumented workers and their employers, CAG intends to "create a method for workers to obtain certification for the specified criteria without having to rely on validation from their employer" (Hess and Henrici, 2013, p.15). The campaign also means to guide the workers to legal status even if she is unemployed or "employed in jobs with unacceptable working conditions. Finally, the (CAG) plan proposes that undocumented caregivers be entitled to the same protections provided under current federal and state employment laws as documented workers in the US" (Hess and Henrici, 2013, p.15).

An Analysis of Advocacy Strategies

It has been argued that PHI's advocacy does not focus on the particulars needs of the undocumented home health workers; its concern appears to be the population of DCWs who are US permanent residents or citizens. In contrast, the CAG campaign has an initiative that is aware of and responsive to the specific challenges faced by undocumented caregivers. But both advocacy efforts, as evident from their websites, share in common two key features. First, they make a powerful moral appeal to the public's and policy makers' feeling of compassion for and sense of duty toward family members and fellow citizens who are elderly, disabled or chronically ill and who need the assistance of DCWs. For instance, PHI's website, *About PolicyWorks* (n. d.), states: "By 2016, we will need 4 million direct-care workers to provide long-term services and supports . . . Unless we take action now to invest in the direct-care workforce and improve the quality of these essential jobs, *we will face a caregiving crisis that could jeopardize the quality of life for millions of Americans who need support with daily activities. In addition, failure to act will put further strains on already overburdened American families* (my italics)." Similarly, the CAG's "About Us" website asserts that the "Caring Across Generations (campaign) brings together aging Americans, people with disabilities, workers, and their families to *protect all Americans' right to choose the care and support they need to live with dignity* (my italics)."

There is another feature that is common to the two advocacy efforts. The PHI's strategy is to make the case that the welfare of the elderly, the disabled or the chronically ill who need care services depends on DCWs, *therefore* health-care workers should be assured of a minimum wage, overtime pay and health-care coverage. Similarly, the CAG campaign approach is to argue that there should be a pathway to documented status for undocumented caregivers *because* they provide crucial services to US citizens who are elderly, disabled or chronically ill. In other words, both advocacy efforts employ the same strategy – they make the argument that home health workers should be provided with workers' rights (and undocumented home health workers should have the opportunity to become documented) *because* the well-being of elderly American citizens depends on them. This strategy might be an effective one for persuading politicians because elderly American citizens are a politically significant population; they are more likely to vote than many other demographics.[10] In contrast, historically, DCWs and, especially, undocumented home health workers, have been treated by elected officials as if they are morally and politically virtually inconsequential; they consigned them to the lower, if not the lowest, rung of the hierarchy of workers by denying them coverage under the FLSA.

It is significant that neither PHI nor the CAG campaign makes the argument that care workers should be afforded the same rights as other workers by virtue of the fact that they are human beings. In other words, they do not make any appeals to the universal rights of workers. This may be a strategic decision because public support for workers' rights has waned with the ascendancy of neoliberalism in the US that began in the Reagan years (Harvey, 2005, p.25).[11] It is also worth considering that PHI and the CAG campaign do not argue that affording DCWs with worker's rights is an issue of gender, race and class equity because most of those workers are women of color who are poor—a historically marginalized population. In the US, gender and racial inequities remain contentious issues, and their existence is routinely decried and denied (see, for instance, Wyly and Ponder, 2011). Moreover, while there is a sharp and increasingly widening class disparity, a significant majority of Americans (65 percent) choose to subscribe to the American Dream (i.e., the idea that prosperity and success are within the reach of any hardworking individual) (Center for the Study of the American Dream, 2011). In light of a pervasive national tendency to deny the reality of racial, gender and class inequalities, PHI and the CAG campaign could be read as making pragmatic choices by avoiding advocacy arguments that would be considered provocative by the majority of the populace. However, in making advocacy appeals that align with and do not antagonize the dominant ideology about gender, class and race, those NGOs might also be reinforcing and putting their imprimatur on them.

CONCLUSION

This chapter makes the case that undocumented home health workers in the US are caught in a complex web of immigration and the labor laws, which enable and encourage discrimination against them and the exploitation of their labor. This constitutes a serious ethical violation of the principle of moral equality that is the raison d'être of the liberal democratic state. It is also argued that the moral agency of NGOs who attempt to advocate on behalf of documented and undocumented home health workers may be constrained by pragmatic considerations.

NOTES

1. This chapter builds on Meghani and Eckenwiler (2009) and Meghani (2014).
2. The term "home health workers" is used in this chapter although "home health aides" is also employed to refer to this group of workers. "Home care workers" is not used because it is open to the misreading that these workers perform domestic work.
3. The term DCWs does not refer to health-care workers who have advanced education, such as physicians, dentists, nurses and therapists (Hess and Henrici, 2013, p.1, footnote 1; Martin et al., 2009).
4. Free clinics are not the same as community health centers. The community health center boards have to consist of a majority from the patients that are from the community they serve. They offer "comprehensive primary health care services as well as supportive services (education, translation and transportation, etc.) that promote access to health care" (US Department of Health and Human Services. Health Resources and Services Administration. n.d. *Primary Care: The Health Center Program: What is a Health Center?*). Fees are based on patients' ability to pay. They are eligible to receive federal dollars (ibid.).
5. In a more recent coauthored paper (2012, p.4), Griffith has argued that IRCA provides some degree of protection to documented and undocumented workers.
6. Neoliberalism as a political philosophy has two key elements (Ong, 2006, p.12). First, it assumes that the free play of market forces results in a more equitable division of public resources than government regulations. Second, it advocates for a form of individualism that valorizes competitiveness and acquisitiveness, while construing persons primarily as consumers, who are responsible for the choices they make under conditions of a free market (Ong, 2006, p.12).
7. However, a number of states with high levels of poverty that are controlled by the Republican party have refused to accept additional funds from the federal government to expand their Medicaid coverage to cover more indigent persons and their families (Tavernise and Gebeloff, 2013).
8. Such as "Health Coverage" (2013), "FACTS 3: America's Direct-Care Workforce" (2011), "FACTS 4: Health Care Coverage for Direct-Care Workers" (2011), "The Invisible Care Gap: Caregivers without Coverage" (Regan, 2008), "Fact Sheet: Health Insurance Vital to Job Retention" (2007), "Medicaid Matters . . . to the American People" (2011), "Medicaid Matters . . . for Managed Long-Term Services and Supports" (2012), "When Michigan's Caregivers Lack Coverage: Findings from a Survey of Michigan's Home Help Workforce" (2007), "Is New York Prepared to Care? A Comprehensive Coverage Solution for Home Care Workers" (2009), and "Beyond Reach? Michigan Long-Term Care Employers Are Struggling to Provide Health Coverage for Employees" (2008).

9. Legal permanent residents who have been in the US for less than five years and whose income is at or below 400 percent of the federal poverty level are eligible for subsidized health-care coverage but not Medicaid (Lee, 2013).
10. It is unclear whether the government takes seriously the concerns of the disabled who need assistance from DCWs.
11. For instance, in the 1950s, about one third of the US workforce was unionized, but in 2010, union membership had shrunk to 8 per cent in the private sector (Garcia, 2012, p.671).

REFERENCES AND FURTHER READING

Boris, E. and Klein, J., 2006. Organizing home care: Low-waged workers in the welfare state. *Politics and Society*, 34(1), pp.81–108.
Boris, E. and Klein, J., 2007. Laws of care: The Supreme Court and aides to elderly people. *Dissent*, 54.4, pp.5–7.
Caring Across Generations (CAG), 2013. *About us.* [online] Available at: <http://www.caringacross.org/about-us/> [Accessed 17 February 2014].
Center for the Study of the American Dream. 2011. *The second annual state of the American dream survey.* Xavier University. [pdf] Available at: <http://www.xavier.edu/americandream/programs/documents/Final-American-Dream-Survey-PowerPoint.pdf> [Accessed 17 February 2014].
Clare, S., 2005. Finding dignity in dirty work: The constraints and rewards of low-wage home care labour. *Sociology of Health and Illness*, 27(6), pp.831–54.
Colorado, House Bill 1286. 2007.
Colorado, House Bill 1314. 2007.
Darnell, J.S., 2010. Free clinics in the United States: A nationwide survey. *Archives of Internal Medicine*, 170(11), pp.946–53.
Florida, Senate Bill 2114, chapter 147. 2007.
Fraser, N. and Gordon, L., 1994. A genealogy of 'dependency': Tracing a keyword of the U.S. welfare state. *Signs*, 79(2), pp.309–36.
Garcia, R.J., 2003. Ghost workers in an interconnected world: Going beyond the dichotomies of domestic immigration and labor laws. *University of Michigan Journal of Law Reform*, 36, pp.737–65.
Garcia, R.J., 2012. Ten years after Hoffman Plastic Compounds, Inc. v. NLRB: The power of a labor law symbol. *Cornell Journal of Law and Public Policy*, 21, pp.659–75.
Griffith, K., 2009. US migrant worker law: The interstices of immigration law and labor and employment law. *Comparative Labor Law & Policy Journal*, 31, pp.125–62.
Griffith, K. L. and Lee, T. L., 2012. Immigration advocacy as labor advocacy. *Berkeley Journal of Employment and Labor Law*, 33(1).
Harvey, D., 2005. *A brief history of neoliberalism.* Oxford: Oxford University Press.
Hess, C. and Henrici, J., 2013. *Increasing pathways to legal status for immigrant in-home care workers.* Washington, DC: Institute for Women's Policy Research.
Hess, C., Henrici, J. and Williams, C., 2011. *Organizations working with Latina immigrants: Resources and strategies for change. Report# I922.* Washington, DC: Institute for Women's Policy Research.
Hondagneu-Sotelo, P., 2001. *Doméstica: Immigrant workers cleaning and caring in the shadows of affluence.* Berkeley, CA: University of California Press.
Idaho, Senate Bill 1157. 2007.
Indiana, Senate Bill 463, Act 184. 2007.
Indiana, Senate Bill 504. 2007.

Kansas, Senate Bill 9. 2007.
Kollmann, G., 2000. *Social Security: Summary of major changes in the cash benefits program.* Washington, DC, USA. [online] UNT Digital Library. Available at: <http://digital.library.unt.edu/ark:/67531/metacrs6366/> [Accessed 25 August 2013].
Lee, E.Y., 2013. A simple guide to the Affordable Care Act for immigrants. [online] Think Progress. Available at: <http://thinkprogress.org/immigration/2013/10/01/2708441/affordable-care-act-immigrant-types-coverage/> [Accessed: 15 December 2013].
Liebert, S. and Ameringer, C.F., 2013. The health care safety net and the Affordable Care Act:
Implications for Hispanic immigrants. *Public Administration Review.* doi: 10.1111/puar.12147.
Louisiana, House Bill 766. 2007.
Maine, LD 1015. 2007.
Martin, D., 2009. Evelyn Coke, home care aide who fought pay rule, is dead at 74. *New York Times,* 9 August, p. A18.
Martin, S. et al., 2009. *The role of migrant care workers in aging societies: Report on research findings in the United States.* [pdf] Institute for the Study of International Migration, Georgetown University. Available at: <http://www12.georgetown.edu/sfs/docs/20101201_Elder_Care_Report.pdf> [Accessed 17 February 2014].
May, V.H., 2011. *Unprotected labor: Household workers, politics, and middle-class reform in New York, 1870–1940.* Chapel Hill: University of North Carolina Press.
Meghani, Z., 2014. Justice for the 'other' caregivers: Addressing the epistemic dimension of injustice. In: M. Rawlinson, W. Vandekerckhove, R. Commers and T. Johnston, eds. 2014. *Labor and global justice: Essays on the ethics of labor practices in the age of globalization.* Lanham: Lexington Books, pp.123–39.
Meghani, Z. and Eckenwiler, L., 2009. Care for the caregivers?: Transnational justice and undocumented non-citizen care workers. *International Journal of Feminist Approaches to Bioethics,* 2(1), pp.77–101.
Minnesota, House Bill 1078. 2007.
Minnesota, Senate Bill 0167. 2007.
Mississippi, Senate Bill 2448. 2007.
National Labor Relations Board (NLRB), (n.d.). Home: Rights we protect: Employee rights. [online] Available at: <http://www.nlrb.gov/rights-we-protect/employee-rights> [Accessed: 15 December 2013].
Nevada, Assembly Bill 496. 2007.
Nielsen, K. 1985. *Equality and liberty: A defense of radical egalitarianism.* Totowa: Rowman & Allanheld.
North Dakota, Senate Bill 2112. 2007.
Occupational Health and Safety (OHS), 2010. *Guide addresses top hazards for home health aides.* [online] Available at: <http://ohsonline.com/articles/2010/02/04/guide-addresses-top-hazards-for-home-health-aides.aspx?admgarea=ht.Ergonomics> [Accessed 17 February 2014].
Ong, A., 2006. *Neoliberalism as exception: Mutations in citizenship and sovereignty.* Durham, NC: Duke University Press.
Oregon, Bill 2244/ Senate Bill 202. 2007.
Paraprofessional Healthcare Institute (PHI). n.d. *About PHI.* [online] Available at:<http://www.phinational.org/about> [Accessed 17 February 2014].
Paraprofessional Healthcare Institute (PHI). n.d. *About PolicyWorks.* [online] Available at:<http://phinational.org/policy/about/about-policyworks> [Accessed 13 July 2014].

Paraprofessional Healthcare Institute (PHI). 2007. *Fact Sheet: Health Insurance Vital to Job Retention*[online] Available at: <http://phinational.org/sites/phinational.org/files/clearinghouse/RetentionFactSheet.pdf> >[Accessed 8 July 2015].
Paraprofessional Healthcare Institute (PHI). 2007. *When Michigan's caregivers lack coverage: Findings from a survey of Michigan's home help workforce.* [pdf] Available at: <http://phinational.org/sites/phinational.org/files/research-report/hchcw_misurvey.pdf> [Accessed 18 February 2014].
Paraprofessional Healthcare Institute (PHI). 2008. *Beyond reach? Michigan long-term care employers are struggling to provide health coverage for employees.* [pdf] Available at: <http://phinational.org/sites/phinational.org/files/hchcw-mi-survey-factsheet.pdf> [Accessed 18 February 2014].
Paraprofessional Healthcare Institute (PHI). 2009. *Is New York Prepared to Care? A Comprehensive Coverage Solution for Home Care Workers.* [pdf] Available at: <http://phinational.org/sites/phinational.org/files/clearinghouse/NY-HCAcoverage 2009.pdf> [Accessed 18 February 2014].
Paraprofessional Healthcare Institute (PHI). 2011. *FACTS 3: Who are direct care workers?* (February 2011 update.) [pdf] Available at: <http://www.phinational.org/sites/phinational.org/files/clearinghouse/NCDCW%20Fact%20Sheet-1.pdf> [Accessed December 16, 2013].
Paraprofessional Healthcare Institute (PHI). 2011. *FACTS 4: Health care coverage for direct-care workers: 2009 data update.* [online] Available at: <http://phinational.org/sites/phinational.org/files/clearinghouse/facts4-20110328.pdf> [Accessed 18 February 2014].
Paraprofessional Healthcare Institute (PHI). 2011. *Medicaid matters . . . to the American people.*[pdf] Available at: <http://phinational.org/sites/phinational.org/files/clearinghouse/medicaidmatters2-20110526.pdf> [Accessed 18 February 2014].
Paraprofessional Healthcare Institute (PHI). 2012. *Medicaid matters . . . for long-term services and supports.* [pdf] Available at: <http://phinational.org/sites/phinational.org/files/medicaidmatters-20110408.pdf> [Accessed 18 February 2014].
Passel, J.S. and Cohn, D., 2009. *A portrait of unauthorized immigrants in the United States.* [pdf] Pew Hispanic Center. Washington, DC. Available at: <http://www.pewhispanic.org/files/reports/107.pdf> [Accessed 17 February 2014].
Passel, J.S. and Cohn, D., 2011. *Unauthorized immigrant population: National and state trends, 2010.* [pdf] Pew Hispanic Center. Washington, DC. Available at: <http://www.pewhispanic.org/files/reports/133.pdf> [Accessed 17 February 2014].
Perry, M.F., 2008. Avoiding mead: The problem with unanimity in Long Island Care at Home, Ltd. v. Coke. Harvard Journal of Law & Public Policy, 31(3), pp.1183–94.
Regan, C., 2008. *The invisible care gap: caregivers without health coverage: Caregivers without health care.* [pdf] Available at: <http://phinational.org/sites/phinational.org/files/clearinghouse/PHI%20CPS%20Report%20May%2008.pdf> [Accessed 18 February 2014].
Rivera-Batiz, F.L., 1999. Undocumented workers in the labor market: An analysis of the earnings of legal and illegal Mexican immigrants in the United States. *Journal of Population Economics*, 12, pp.91–116.
Salter, V. and Vilner, M.A., 2006. *Conversations about the future of direct-care workforce research.* PHI. [pdf] Available at: <http://phinational.org/sites/phinational.org/files/clearinghouse/Research%20Conversations.pdf> [Accessed: 12 January 2012].
Surpin, R. and Sturgeon, J., 2013. *Reflections on the companionship exemption.* [online] Available at: <http://phinational.org/blogs/reflections-companionship-exemption> [Accessed: 12 January 2012].

Tavernise, S. and Gebeloff, R., 2013. Millions of poor are left uncovered by health law. *New York Times*, 2 October, p. A1.

Texas, Senate Bill 589. 2007.

US Department of Health and Human Services. Health Resources and Services Administration. n.d. *Primary care: The health center program: What is a health center?* [online] Available at: <http://bphc.hrsa.gov/about/> [Accessed 18 February 2014].

Utah, Senate Bill 103. 2007.

Warner, D.C., 2012. Access to health services for immigrants in the USA: From the Great Society to the 2010 Health Reform Act and after. *Ethnic and Racial Studies*, 35(1), pp.40–55.

Weber, D.P., 2010. (Unfair) advantage: Damocles' sword and the coercive use of immigration status in a civil society. *Marquette Law Review*, 94, pp.613–78.

Whittaker, W.G., 2008. *The Fair Labor Standards Act: Continuing issues in the debate* (RL34510). Washington, DC: Congressional Research Service. [online] Available at: <http://digitalcommons.ilr.cornell.edu/key_workplace/519/> [Accessed 18 February 2014].

Wilper, A.P., et al.,2009. Hypertension, diabetes, and elevated cholesterol among insured and uninsured U.S. adults. *Health Affairs*, 28(6):w1151.

Wyly, E. and Ponder, C.S., 2011. Gender, age, and race in subprime America. *Housing Policy Debate*, 21(4), pp.529–64.

Part II
Uncaring Development Paradigms

4 On a Collision Course
Millennium Development Goals and Mothers' Migration

Delali Badasu and Sonya Michel

> Remittances by themselves cannot guarantee the realization of the right to quality education and health care, nor surmount gender discrimination . . .
> —Rossi et al., 2006

INTRODUCTION

When it comes to ending poverty around the globe, the "development community" and the world's wealthy nations are on a collision course. Since the 1990s, development policy makers have largely concurred that women must play a key role in any plan to end world poverty, through both paid employment and their work as mothers. Yet while those seeking to encourage the world's "emerging economies" to rally around the Millennium Development Goals (MDG), the so-called "rich countries" are systematically drawing women—many of them mothers—to migrate as paid care providers, leaving their own families behind. Drained of critical care resources, poor countries are finding it difficult, if not impossible, to reach those lofty goals. This chapter examines the contradiction between these two trends, using Ghana as a case study.

The MDG, proclaimed by the United Nations in 2000, include, inter alia, ending poverty and hunger, providing universal primary education and significantly improving child health and reducing child mortality—all by 2015. To this end, international and nongovernmental organizations (IOs and NGOs, such as the United Nations' Children's Fund (UNICEF), World Vision and Save the Children) have been pouring money and expertise into the nations of the global South, working with local governments to establish schools and clinics and improve food supplies. But such resources remain inert unless "targeted" families can tap into them: children must regularly attend school, visit clinics and eat nutritious meals. For this to occur, vigilant adults must provide a link between children and valuable resources.

While child-rearing patterns vary widely from one society to another, in most societies it is mothers who are expected to perform this vital function. Yet, in many families in developing societies, scores of mothers are physically absent. For the past several decades, hundreds of thousands of women, many of them mothers, have been migrating from poorer countries to wealthier ones in search of employment. Contrary to accusations that they are abandoning their children (Parreñas, 2005) or turning them into "Euro-orphans" (Lutz, 2012), these "transnational mothers" believe that they are fulfilling their maternal responsibilities by earning much-needed cash for better food, clothing, shelter and, especially, improved chances for an education (Segura, 1994). But because they are not on hand to oversee their children and ensure that they are taking advantage of the resources on offer, these benefits often fail to materialize.

To be sure, fathers, siblings, grandmothers, aunts and other female extended family members, along with "other-mothers" and hired care workers do their best to replace the care mothers previously provided (Badasu, 2011), but the results are uneven. Fathers may refuse to fill in or do so only intermittently (Parreñas, 2001; Badasu et al., 2009; Oppong, 2004a); relatives and other-mothers—often friends and neighbors—have other responsibilities; hired workers still need supervision. Local communities and institutions are more likely than national governments to try to compensate for lost care resources, but they too are stretched thin.[1] Even with the aid of NGOs and IOs, they cannot provide the level of social services necessary to attend to the daily needs of thousands of children who have one or more parent abroad. As a result, in societies where maternal migration is high, so too are rates of school absenteeism and dropouts (especially for girls; see Mapp, 2010, chaps. 7–8; Rossi et al., 2006), failure to receive regular vaccinations (Hildebrandt and McKenzie, 2005) and children wandering the streets without regular supervision (Schmalzbauer, 2004).

The social dilemma of the sending countries of the global South is closely but asymmetrically related to the uneven development of welfare states in the global North. Here, too, women have been entering paid employment in greater numbers than ever, disrupting the traditional gender division of labor that assigned the bulk of care work to wives, mothers, daughters, sisters, grandmothers and daughters-in-law. But some of the national governments of the global North have been more proactive in addressing the "care deficit." From the 1970s on, countries in northern Europe have worked to design welfare states that would help women achieve "work-family balance," and for a while it appeared that the "adult-worker model," with both parents "activated" in the labor market, would become the norm (Lewis and Giullari, 2005). By the late 1990s, however, under the sway of neoliberalism and economic strain, these same welfare states were forced to retrench (Mahon, 2002; Daly, 2011), returning many care responsibilities to the other women in the family. Other "rich" countries, such as the United States and those of Southern Europe, such as Greece, Italy and Spain, never developed robust welfare states in the first place, leaving care work as a private responsibility to be handled through the family or the market (Bettio et al., 2006; Michel, 2010; Michel and Peng,

2012). But in these countries, population aging and economic crisis have pushed resources to the limit.

Shifting demographics have, in fact, exacerbated the care deficit in all of these countries. As populations age and birth rates fall, dependency ratios have become dramatically skewed. Not only are there fewer young people—and women—available to care for the elderly, but native-born workers increasingly eschew this type of work. (This has been less true in the well-developed welfare states, where both elder- and child-care work are professionalized, but even they have begun to experience care worker shortages as governments retrench.) All over the global North, families have been turning to migrant care workers, not only because they were willing to accept low wages, live in their employers' households and work long hours, but also because they are thought to be "naturally" kind and sympathetic (Pratt, 1997; Bettio et al., 2006; Michel and Peng, 2012). And from many parts of the global South, cash-starved mothers have migrated to meet the demand, leaving their own unpaid care responsibilities behind. Unpaid care includes maternal care (mainly for offspring and fostered children), sick care and care for aged parents and other aged extended family members, all for which no remuneration is received.

Together, the social conditions of North and South form what scholars call "the migration-development nexus"—a dynamic relationship that has been deeply inflected by neoliberal thinking.[2] To understand the place of women, children and families within the nexus, we must bring two literatures into dialogue: gender and development, and gender and welfare states. In what follows, we first discuss a "social investment" paradigm that has shaped welfare states in the North. Next we examine how that paradigm has shaped development policies over the past several decades, assessing the effects of what has been called the "migration-development nexus" on the realities of transnational mothering of the children who remain in countries of origin. We pay special attention to their educational achievement because it is an area that has been deemed essential to reversing poverty by both development experts and transnational mothers. We then look at Ghana as a case study of families' powers of resilience and adaptation of both families and individuals, focusing on its social setting, demographic dynamics and the behaviors associated with the movement of labor to the global North as well as human well-being. The choice of Ghana is appropriate because it belongs to the West African subregion where both internal and international migration are common and have long been a way of life (Manuh et al., 2005; Manuh, 2006). Moreover, fostering has also been a characteristic feature of the traditional societies, as well as the contemporary population of Ghana. Furthermore, Ghana is in the process of adopting a policy to manage the migration process and its outcomes for the benefit of the country as a whole and the individual migrants and their families, with an overall objective of reducing poverty and promoting human development in the country. We conclude by offering some policy recommendations.

DEMOGRAPHIC ASYMMETRIES AND THE SOCIAL INVESTMENT PARADIGM

As noted above, the demographic profiles of the global South and the global North differ markedly. Their distinctive population structures contribute to the movement of labor from the one to the other (Badasu 2011). The global South generally has a youthful and rapidly increasing population with high fertility levels due mainly to relatively low levels of female education. The global North, on the other hand, has low fertility and an aging population that necessitate admission of migrant labor to fill the gaps in the labor market. While the national birth rates of the global South continue to be robust, those of the North have been shrinking, in many cases below replacement rate. At the same time, life expectancy is rising much more quickly in the North than in the South. As a result, the proportion of children (under age 15) in the populations of poorer countries is far higher than in richer ones, while for elders (65 and over), the reverse is true.[3] In sub-Saharan Africa, for example, 43 percent of the population is under 15, while in the countries of Europe, the proportion hovers between 13 and 15 percent; worldwide the average is 27percent (Population Reference Bureau, 2011). With large numbers of the elderly to support, many destination countries have stepped up their immigration quotas, not only to bring in care providers but also to replenish their labor forces and keep revenues flowing into pay-as-you-go pension funds.

Late-twentieth-century fertility declines across most of the global North have prompted great concern among IOs.[4] At the Organisation for Economic Co-operation and Development (OECD), for example, this was one of the trends leading to a much-cited 2007 study, *Babies and Bosses*. Attributing falling birth rates to parents' inability to reconcile work and family, the report warned of critical consequences, not just personal but also social and economic:

> If parents cannot achieve their desired work/family life balance, not only is their welfare lower but economic development is also curtailed through reduced labour supply by parents. A reduction of birth rates has obvious implications for future labour supply as well as for the financial sustainability of social protection systems. As parenting is also crucial to child development, and thus the shape of future societies, policy makers have many reasons to want to help parents find a better work/family balance.[5]

In the view of the OECD, it seemed that nothing less than the entire way of life enjoyed by the citizens of the global North was at stake.

The OECD did not, however, counsel greater spending outright on social services for children and families, but rather promoted policies that would both encourage female employment and increase "human capital"

(OECD, 2006; 2009). Under the terms of what scholars came to label the "social investment" paradigm (Giddens, 1998; Jenson and St. Martin, 2006; Mahon, 2009), the OECD and other IOs, principally the World Bank (2007), envisioned societies in which families and states would work together to ensure children's futures through a combination of public services, such as child care and elder care, designed to free all adults for paid work and tax incentives to encourage parents to save privately for children's education and their own old age. The paradigm persisted even as birth rates failed to rebound, the proportion of the elderly continued to increase and, then in late 2007, the Great Recession hit.

DEVELOPMENT DISCOURSES, THE SOCIAL INVESTMENT PARADIGM AND THE DAILY REALITIES OF TRANSNATIONAL MOTHERING

Applications of the social investment paradigm were not limited to the global North but also extended to the global South, shaping the MDG project as it was rolled out. The United Nations' final report, *Investing in Development* (2005), framed the project's goals in neoliberal terms, again entwining the individual's good with that of the larger economy and society (p.4):

> The Goals are ends in themselves, but for [extremely poor] households they are also capital inputs, the means to a productive life, to economic growth, and to further development. A healthy worker is a productive worker. A better educated worker is a productive worker. Improved water and sanitation infrastructure raises economic output per capita through various channels, such as reduced illness. So, many of the Goals are part of capital accumulation, defined broadly, as well as desirable objectives in their own right.

The MDG dovetailed snugly with what the World Bank (1999) dubbed a "New Poverty Agenda," culminating a decade of thinking about development that sought to shift the emphasis away from older models of charity, relief, direct aid and subsidies, toward self-sufficiency and "empowerment." At the level of social policy, this meant "co-responsibility"—active partnerships between parents, families and helping agencies—that would avoid the stigma of charity and the passivity attached to being a recipient or even a client of social services (Molyneux, 2006; Jenson, 2012).

Bringing in parents and families was itself a new wrinkle. While conversations about fighting poverty among IOs began in the 1970s, it was not until the 1990s that the United Nations and its development agency, the United Nations Development Programme, began calling upon governments, policy planners and practitioners to recognize social issues in development (United Nations, 1995; see also Zinsser, 2002). The idea that human development was perhaps a better indicator of progress than economic growth brought into focus the need to invest in human resources for child and adult survival and general human well-being. Since then, development experts have considered factors such as nutrition and health to be essential for human well-being, and they have also begun to recognize the key role played by parents—especially mothers—in making progress in this area.

To implement policies based on these insights, UNICEF and other IOs turned to academic specialists in international nutrition and public health. In 1994, for example, UNICEF held a joint colloquium on "Care and Nutrition of the Young Child" with the Division of Nutritional Sciences at Cornell University. Planners of the event made certain to emphasize the idea that the delivery of adequate food and health to children is ultimately determined by the care provided them (Garza, 1995; Ramakrishnan, 1995). International nutrition expert Michael C. Latham (1995, p.282), one of the organizers, pointing out that "the three underlying causes of malnutrition in children are inadequate food, inadequate health, and inadequate care," noted that care was the least investigated of all three factors. Many countries had adequate knowledge about their food situation and health facilities and services, he said, but they knew very little about how children were cared for. This was especially important for very young children who could not feed themselves but had to depend on others for nourishment—not just for breastfeeding (which the experts strongly encouraged be done until the child is two years old) but also for "complementary" and "replacement" or "weaning" foods (Ramakrishnan, 1995, p.289). But care was also important for promoting "good psychosocial development" in older children, which was related to continuing good nutrition (Latham, 1995, p.284).

The colloquium's participants took a rather broad view of nutrition problems, attributing them not so much to ignorance as to larger social, cultural and economic trends. According to Latham (1995),

> in Africa, as well as most of Asia and Latin America, an erosion of traditional caring practices in the 1990s has contributed more to malnutrition than wrong—or inappropriate—caring practices. Traditional caring practices have been altered or eroded, often for the worse, as a result of modernization or westernization, as well as increasing urbanization. (p.283)

But when it came to gender, their view was considerably narrower. While acknowledging that in developing societies it was common for members of extended families, including husbands, grandmothers and older siblings, as well as nonrelatives, to become involved in care, Latham and his colleagues largely assumed that mothers would serve as the primary caregivers, particularly for infants. Latham (1995) expressed concern about the effects of paid employment, which often separated mothers and infants for long periods every day, and proposed maternity leave and workplace child care as remedies (p.283). Notably, however, none of the experts at this colloquium mentioned migration as a cause of extended mother-child separation; although by this time, nearly half of the world's migrants were female (Zlotnick, 2003) and many of them were mothers. Indeed, earning money for children's needs was usually what motivated them to migrate in the first place (Piper, 2005). For transnational mothers, none of the remedies Latham proposed would be of any use.

He also called for "empowering mothers" by ensuring their rights, such as control over their own money, and also through practical measures such as reducing their workloads and providing nearby clean water supplies (Latham, 1995, pp.284–5). Maternal and child health expert Usha Ramakrishnan, one of the few women present at the meeting, urged policy makers to recognize "the role of alternative caregivers, especially fathers" (1995, p.291) and take special pains to develop policies that would include them and help them contribute effectively to children's well-being, but like her male colleagues, the bulk of her analysis focused on working with mothers.

Sociologist Maxine Molyneux and political scientist Jane Jenson have criticized this approach to social policy as a form of "neomaternalism." According to Jenson (2012),

> [it] ... foregrounds "the child" and places women, often in the guise of "parents," in the background, [placing] great responsibility on mothers, for good parenting and childrearing practices. In all of this, women as anything other than mothers [e.g. workers, political actors, community leaders, etc.] disappear from policy discourse. (p.2; for a more detailed discussion, see Jenson, 2009)[6]

For Molyneux, the problem is that such policies

> depend upon women fulfilling their "traditional" social roles and responsibilities ... [They] unambiguously rest on normative assumptions concerning "women's roles," so that the work women undertake in ensuring that children's needs are met, is taken for granted as something that mothers "do." The social relations of reproduction remain unproblematized, with the work performed simply naturalized. (2006, p.438)

But perhaps this approach is not as limiting as Jenson and Molyneux argue. Consider the point that sociologist Laura Balbo made long ago, namely, that women fill a critical gap—act as a kind of "social glue"—when they act as liaisons between their families and public services. According to Balbo, women provide "organizational work ... the keeping in touch with the many outside agencies which deliver services, the sorting out, the piecing and patching, and the creation of orderly patterns" (Balbo, 1987, p.51).

Indeed, for Balbo, such activities constitute a form of service to the state (in Balbo's case, to the "capitalist state").

Balbo also recognized that these activities performed an important emotional function:

> Unless something is added to material goods in order to link them to what a specific individual expects or wants, personal needs are not satisfied . . . Being there to wait, to listen, to respond, to attend to the needs and desires of others; to worry when difficulties are anticipated; to deal with one's own sense of guilt when problems are not successfully resolved; this is servicing. (Balbo, 1987, p.53; quoted in Lewis and Giullari 2005, p.84)

For social policy analysts Jane Lewis and Susanna Giullari, Balbo's insights underscore the idea that care cannot become fully "commodified"—that some element of it will always exceed the limitations of commodified care (cf. also Hochschild, 2003 and 2012). Invoking another important concept of Balbo's, "*doppia presenza*" (double presence, not to be confused with "double day"), they point to "uneasy accounts of mothers who report that they are thinking simultaneously about their jobs and about whether their children are being looked after properly" (Lewis and Giullari, 2005, p.84).

Here, Lewis and Giullari as well as Balbo are thinking about wage-earning mothers who live and work in the same home as their children. But what if we extrapolate their responses to transnational mothers? "Uneasy" only begins to describe the feelings of women whose doppia presenza spans borders, oceans and continents (Hondagneu-Sotelo and Avila, 1997; Schmalzbauer, 2004; Pratt, 2012), and whose double day begins with many hours of caring for someone else's children or elderly relatives and ends with trying to provide support to their own loved ones via phoning or text messaging or an Internet service like Skype, which permits users to communicate by using a webcam. Whether this takes the form of helping with homework, mediating between a child and a father or "other-mother" or discussing the child's situation with a teacher or social worker, the results are likely to leave mothers feeling dissatisfied at best, anxious at worst. And often they must dissemble, hiding their emotions lest employers feel they are not focusing fully on the children or the elderly they are being paid to care for (Pratt, 2012, Ch.1).

Emotional Tangles

Closely paralleling mothers' anxieties are the emotions of children left behind. Depending on their age, they may have more or less understanding of why their mothers are gone; but even if they can grasp (literally as well as figuratively) the material benefits their mothers are providing, they may not feel comforted. As one young Filipina told sociologist Rhacel Parreñas (2005),

My mother's love was not enough. I would have wanted her next to me, so I could feel her love . . . I know she loves me because she is working hard over there. She is working hard so that we could have everything we want and everything we need . . . But still, I want her to be with me here every day. (p.124)

Sociologist Leah Schmalzbauer (2004) and geographer Geraldine Pratt (2012) have reported similar findings in their research.

One of the saddest ironies of the migration-development nexus is that children may feel so distressed by their mothers' absence that they cannot function well in school—the very thing for which their mothers are striving. Transmigrant mothers (those maintaining ties with their countries of origin, families and children while working in their destination countries (Glick Schiller et al., 1995)) not only provide cash for school fees but also use their own sacrifices to motivate children to study harder. They may, for example, let their children know that they have taken a second job or gone to a food bank in order to save more money to send them. For some children, these messages work as intended; in others, they engender feelings of resentment and guilt—hardly conducive to focusing on schoolwork. Teachers sometimes take the initiative to comfort children who are visibly distressed by their mothers' absence, but few schools provide guidance counseling on a regular basis. When counselors are on hand, they tend to focus on the "troublemakers" and often end up blaming their disruptive behavior on parental absence (Parreñas, 2005, pp.49–50). Drawing only on anecdotal evidence, Filipina counselors told Parreñas that children with absent fathers tended to do better than those with absent mothers (2005, pp.50–1).

Mothers' absence particularly affects school-age girls, who may be kept home to care for younger siblings (Mapp, 2010, p.149)[7]—duties that take time away from homework. Girls' inability to complete school not only brings disappointment to their hardworking mothers, but also undermines two MDGs: universal primary education and gender equality. Transnational migrant women's social capital in, and ties to, their nation of origin ensures that their children are provided care by others. In the lives of many women migrant workers' children, the key caregiving figure is the grandmother, usually on the maternal side. By encouraging (if not actually supervising) their studies, preparing food and sending them off to school each day, these women serve as the kind of social glue that keeps children connected to resources (Schmalzbauer, 2004, p.1324). Notably, however, these women also take responsibility for other children who may be less well supervised. In the Honduran community studied by sociologist Leah Schmalzbauer, for example, the grandmother of one child with a migrant mother also looks out for several other children left behind in the care of an older sibling who herself has to work, supplying them with snacks when there is no food at home (2004, p.1324). Women like this clearly subscribe to a sense of mutual responsibility—"what goes around comes around," as anthropologist Carol Stack put it succinctly many years ago (Stack, 1974).

But there can be emotional complications. Children may end up becoming more attached to their other-mothers than their biological ones; and if the opportunity arises for families to reunite, children may feel conflicted about separating from the women who have cared for them perhaps longer than their natural parents, thereby experiencing a second trauma. Both children and adults may become confused about who is actually in charge: the other-mother on the spot, or the mother who is toiling abroad to support them financially. Often, children end up playing adults off against one another, but insofar as authority is closely related to a child's sense of security, long-term anxiety may offset any temporary gains (Schmalzbauer, 2004, p.1325).

Surprisingly, few scholars have attempted to analyze the emotions of children left behind. The literature on migration—even on care migration—often ignores the fact that many (how many is not clear) female migrant workers are mothers (Hondagneu-Sotelo and Avila, 1997; Parreñas, 2001; Schmalzbauer, 2004; Castles and Miller, 2009, pp.235–8; and Pratt, 2012 are notable exceptions). Only a few scholars have systematically studied the impact of women's absence on the children left behind (Levitt, 2001; Artico, 2003; Parreñas, 2005), and even fewer have sought to match up migrants abroad with their own children at home (Schmalzbauer, 2004 is a notable exception). In one intriguing study, geographer Brenda Yeoh and her colleagues found that as part of their emotional coping strategies, both children and parents create "imaginary ties" to one another that transcend extended periods of absence and geographical distance (Yeoh et al., 2005).

We are more likely to find close examinations of relationships between transnational mothers and their children in popular culture—the fiction film *Mammoth* (2009), directed by Lukas Moodysson; Mona Simpson's novel *My Hollywood* (2010); and documentaries such as Nilita Vachani's *When Mother Came Home for Christmas* (1996) and Alan Grossman and Áine O'Brien's *Promise and Unrest* (2010). The films use the device of alternating scenes between the migrant worker and her family back home, while the novel's narrative voice alternates between the Filipina nanny and her employer. All depict the mixed blessings of migration—the alienation that seems inevitably to develop between the absent parent and her children after many years' separation, despite the material benefits her work has made possible. This outcome comports with the findings of Parreñas (2005) and Pratt (2012). It should be noted that Parreñas attributes much of the difficulty to rigid gender ideologies that produce exaggerated expectations on children's part—expectations that are bound to be disappointed by actual mothering practices (2005, Introduction).

Perhaps scholars of gender and migration, the majority of whom are feminist, shy away from examining the emotional dimensions of transnational motherhood because they do not want to contribute, however inadvertently, to the kind of "mother blaming" that has become common in some countries of origin. Sociologist Helma Lutz (2012), for example, has shown how a handful of unfortunate incidents among migrants' children has led to an outburst of accusations against migrant mothers in the Ukraine. There is, however, a fine line between mother blaming, on the one hand, and understanding the conditions that motivate women to migrate, as well as their intentions and goals in doing so, on the other. Only by squarely acknowledging the consequences of maternal absence on families can communities and policy makers begin to address them. We suggest that for many countries, including Ghana, the expected benefits of mothers' employment, such as support for their families and for the economies of their countries of origin, obscure any challenges that their absence may create. Moreover, in Ghana, the cushioning effect of the social context (the social capital in particular) of female migration means that only the positive impacts are perceived.

THE MIGRATION-DEVELOPMENT NEXUS AND CARE: THE CASE OF GHANA

In present-day Ghana, we can see how the tensions between the need for wage-earning abroad and for care at home play out. As indicated in an earlier section, we have chosen Ghana as a case study for two reasons. First, it is a country where, as in the rest of the West African subregion, both internal and external migration for employment, as well as child fostering, are common (Goody, 1982, 1975). Second, a number of studies have noted the impact of internal migration on kin support for child care (e.g., Badasu, 2004, 2012; Baataar, 2012; Oppong, 2004b; Oppong et al., 2012; and Nukunya, 1969). These studies identify dwindling kin support for child care as a consequence of migration. Third, transmigrant mothers or parents frequently leave children behind (at the time of departure) or send them home later to be raised by extended family members or hired domestic workers (Tetteh, 2008; Yeboah, 2008). These children—referred to as "posted babies" (Tetteh, 2008)—receive care within a context of reciprocal social relations between migrants and their societies of origin. Providing what have come to be recognized as a form of "reverse remittances," members of home communities render a range of services to migrants, including care for children, elders and the ill (Mazzuccato, 2011; Henry, 2009).[8] They do so out of a strong sense of family solidarity and bonds of reciprocity (Baataar, 2012; Nabigne, 2012; Sackey, 2009).

Although prevalent throughout West Africa (and also in the African Caribbean; see Chamberlain, 2006), the traditional practice of fostering and the principle of reciprocity that sustains child care by nonbiological parents, runs counter to the prevalent assumption in the global North that mothers should serve as the primary care givers. In Ghana and elsewhere in the subregion, the social capital of mothers or parents that ensures care for children includes kin and nonrelatives. Consequently, a mother may or may not be the primary care giver of her children. These patterns are overlooked by feminist development analysts, who assume that the biological mother is always the primary care giver to the child (Folbre,1996 and 2004; Moore, 1994). The practices of care suggest that theorists, researchers and policy makers need to rethink development policies that are directed at child well-being in circumstances where mothers are migrants.

Ghanaian Migration in Context

Migration has long been a way of life in Ghana as in sub-Saharan Africa generally and West Africa in particular since time immemorial, as recounted in the oral history of various ethnic groups. In most instances, it has been perceived as a survival or preventive strategy. The case of the Akan ethnic group who make up the bulk of Ghanaian emigrants illustrates this pattern. An Akan popular proverb states, *"anomaento a, obua da"* (if a bird does not fly, it goes hungry). Since the late 1970s, however, the downturn in the economies of sub-Saharan African countries (as in many other developing countries) and its consequences for human well-being have resulted in migration on an even larger scale. In Ghana, the volume of emigration between the 1970s and the first decade of the twenty-first century was particularly high, so high that the movement of the late 1980s was referred to as an exodus. Most unfortunate for Ghana, the predominant occupation of the female emigrants was health work, particularly nursing, which led to a nursing shortage within the country (Anarfi et al., 2005; Nyonator, 2005). Such migration by women (largely without their children) was possible because of the social acceptance of fostering of children and delegation of maternal roles.

Ironically, for many years, Ghana was itself a major destination for immigrants; in 1960, foreign nationals made up 12 percent of the total population. In 1969, however, the government implemented an anti-immigration measure, the "Aliens Compliance Law," requiring all foreign nationals to leave the country. Since that time, foreigners have composed less than 3 percent of the population. Meanwhile, scores of Ghanaians have been leaving the country in search of employment (Ghana Statistical Service, 2005). Several estimates of Ghanaian emigrants living abroad have been given. It is popularly believed that about three million Ghanaians live abroad, but most official sources indicate lower figures. The difference is probably accounted for by irregular migrants, who are seldom captured in official figures. In 2011, the World Bank estimated that close to one million Ghanaians (824,900, representing 3.4 percent of the total population) live in the diaspora. Their top ten destinations were Nigeria, Cote d'Ivoire, the United States, the United Kingdom, Burkina Faso, Italy, Togo, Germany, Canada and Liberia (World Bank, 2011). According to the 2010 Ghanaian Population and Housing Census, 250,623 Ghanaian emigrants were living abroad for six months or more—64 percent of them male, 36 percent female. Their major destinations were Europe (37.7 percent) other African countries (35.8 percent) and the Americas (23.6 percent) (Ghana Statistical Service, 2012, p.5). Data from the Ministry of Foreign Affairs indicates that in 2009, 107,487 Ghanaians had registered with Ghana Missions in 33 countries, with the total number of emigrants estimated at more than half a million (Quartey, 2009).

Emigration first began to pick up in the late 1970s, when Ghana, like many other developing countries, experienced an economic downturn, and employment opportunities, especially in the formal sector and in urban areas, became scarce. Would-be internal migrants who might have previously found jobs in Ghanaian cities began to seek greener pastures abroad. They traveled to other African countries, such as Nigeria, South Africa, Botswana and Zimbabwe, to Asia, Saudi Arabia in particular (Twum-Baah, 2005) and to North America and Europe, especially the United Kingdom, Germany, Holland, Italy, Greece and Spain (Arthur, 2008; Smith, 2008; Asiedu, 2005). Ghana's health sector experienced the greatest loss, as a mass exodus of skilled workers departed, leaving it with inadequate personnel to provide services (for a similar situation in South Africa, see Pillinger, 2011). Nurses figured prominently among female labor migrants who moved, with or without their families.

The wave of emigration coincided with a period of dwindling investment in social programs. In response to the economic crisis, the Ghanaian government, following the neoliberal economic prescriptions of the Washington Consensus (Williamson, 1989), implemented a series of economic policies known as Structural Adjustment Programs (SAPs). Intended to ameliorate the effects of worsening economic conditions, the SAPs instead created more hardship. While focusing on market-driven economic policies, liberalization of trade and privatization of public enterprises, they removed public subsidies for social services and shrank funding for education (Mapp, 2010, pp.146–7). Other impacts of the SAPs included reduced opportunities for employment as large corporations were privatized and the size of their labor force was pruned in order to increase their profits. For some unemployed workers, migration became an option. It would take two more decades, until the late 1990s, for Ghanaians to see signs of economic improvement, but the social programs never recovered from the loss of financial support (Twum-Baah, 2005; Manuh, 2006).

Even today, the removal of some subsidies from the educational and health sectors has made access to services financially inaccessible to some Ghanaians. It is no wonder that large proportions of remittances sent by Ghanaian emigrants to families are spent on school fees and health expenditures. As a result, it has been argued that remittances contribute to human development in Ghana.

Meanwhile, in global policy circles in the late 1990s, the strict dictates of the Washington Consensus were beginning to give way to the social investment paradigm and with it a dawning insight that migration, specifically its positive impacts, could contribute to development in poor sending economies (Castles, 2008). Here the focus was on remittances and how they could not only reduce poverty but also contribute to human well-being. Thus the migration-development nexus was born.

In order to make it an integral part of the country's development agenda, Ghana began drafting a policy to manage migration as a tool for development. The Ministry of Interior and its partners, including the Ghana Immigration Service (GIS), the Ministry of Foreign Affairs, the Centre for Migration Studies (CMS) at the University of Ghana and the International Organization for Migration (IOM), among others, have held stakeholders meetings to seek public views before the policy is finalized. Policy makers anticipate that the large Ghanaian migrant community will become engaged in helping to realize the policy's goals. In addition to sending remittances, members of the Ghanaian diaspora have already been investing in the country, and policy makers believe that their commitment to citizenship, national identity and social protection will spur them on to do even more. Within this agenda, however, migration-related care does not feature as an important area of concern. Instead, the emphasis is on macroeconomic issues centered on economic development, leaving the social context of migration, deliberately or otherwise, to the attention of migrants themselves.

Compensating for Policy Neglect

In the absence of governmental policy, Ghanaian society has adapted to the care needs of migrants' children in several different ways. Transnational migrants not only maintain ties with kin and friends, but they also engage in economic and social spaces in their home country by donating to community development projects (particularly schools, clinics and hospitals) and engaging in chieftaincy affairs or local government as well as national political debates and other issues. Through such ties, they have been able to delegate care for children who are left behind to the children's grandparents, extended family, hired domestic workers or friends (see, for example, Awumbila et al., 2011; Mazzucato, 2011; Wong, 2006; and Tetteh, 2008). More often than not, entire families do not migrate at the same time; immigration restrictions may prevent adult workers from bringing family members with them or the cost may be too great for everyone to travel at once. Thus families plan to move in different stages (Yeboah, 2008). When fathers leave children behind with their mothers, care provision tends to be much easier (Tetteh, 2008). But in many transnational families, both parents eventually migrate, leaving one or more children left behind under the care of an extended family member or paid domestic worker. In the Netherlands, for example, globalization and development scholar Valentina Mazzucato (2011) found that half of the 22 Ghanaian migrants she interviewed had children who were being raised at home by someone other than the parents (see also Tetteh, 2008).

In addition to leaving children in the care of other families, anecdotal information indicates an increase in the number of boarding institutions (mostly international schools) in Accra, the capital city, and other large towns. These schools cater to Ghanaian migrants who do not want to raise their children abroad where they might become assimilated into the host society, but prefer to have them to grow up in Ghana, preferably in an urban setting where they can get a good education and also be immersed in Ghanaian culture (Tetteh, 2008). (There is also evidence that such schools have emerged in Sri Lanka and Turkey, for similar reasons. See Vachani, 1996 and Billstein, 1988).[9]

The practice of sending children to be raised by nonbiological parents is not, in fact, unprecedented in the West Africa. Unlike the rest of Africa, many of the region's societies, including Ghana, have a long-standing tradition of child fostering, particularly in times of crisis, such as divorce, death or unstable or tragic family conditions and also for apprenticeship purposes (Ardayfio-Schandorf and Amissah, 1996; Goody, 1975, 1982; Fiawoo, 1978).[10] West Africans regard care and socialization not as an individual responsibility but as a communal one. It is a kinship obligation to foster children of one's kin; and children in need, according to kinship practices, have a right to be fostered (for similar patterns in the African Caribbean, see Chamberlain, 2006). Fostering is also done with the motive of strengthening kinship ties (Nukunya, 1969) and avoiding the wrath of ancestors and deceased parents when orphans are neglected. Some children, research suggests, fare even better when fostered than they would being raised in conditions of deprivation by their biological parents (Isiugo-Abanihe, 1985). These fostered children may have deprivations in their natal homes because of poverty or insufficiency of resources to meet their material needs. Fostered children, according to studies such as Appiah (2001), receive the same care as the biological children of their foster parents, because cultural values discourage unequal treatment of children. Fostering in traditional settings is a source of social protection for many children. In recent years, as economic and social insecurities have deepened and governments have failed to implement social protection policies to address care deficits, West Africans have come to depend even more on social capital and informal sources of social protection, such as fostering. Remittances serve to reinforce informal social protection (Wong, 2006, p.359); as migrants maintain personal ties with gifts, they are reciprocated with child care. Ghanaian migrants depend on social networks and social capital as protection against the vulnerabilities and risks associated with the migration process, starting with the initial decision to migrate, moving on to problems encountered in destination countries and even continuing with the return to their country of origin or relocating to other destinations. Indeed, the knowledge that such resources exist may be what motivates them to take the risk of migrating in the first place.

A Realistic Appraisal of the Future of Fostering

In Ghana today, the social context of migration, particularly the practice of fostering, suggests that female migration and the associated delegation of their care roles at their origin may not be questioned so long as the benefits are economically sound. Women's contribution to the remittance flow is financially rewarding to them, their children, family and others, including the government as it receives tax on remittances sent through financial institutions. Female migrants are also empowered by the earnings capability attained at destination areas. So some in Toronto can say "this is not Ghana" to their husbands/partners who desire to exercise their power in the conjugal relations as in Ghana (Manuh, 1999).

But even if fostering, as part of the migration process, helps move women toward gender equality, we must still analyze the practice from the perspective of children and the goal of development. Indeed, in recent years, the practice has changed. For one thing, Ghanaian society has undergone considerable sociocultural transformation, as the twin processes of modernization-migration and urbanization have undermined solidarity and family ties; this was noted by Nukunya (1969) over four decades ago and more recently by Oppong et al. (2012). These changes have in turn led to an increase in nonkin fosterage in the country (see Afriyie, 2010; UNICEF (2011). The rise of boarding facilities at both the primary and secondary school level that are patronized by transnational migrant families also gives evidence of this new pattern of care.

Within traditional kin-based, foster-care settings, too, things are changing. Child fostering is becoming more burdensome for the female kin of migrants as women are generally sharing a greater burden of productive work in addition to the reproductive work (this is especially true for women in urban areas), and they are also receiving dwindling support from kin abroad (Baataar, 2012; Oppong, 2004b). Moreover, siblings, who used to be a great source of care, are less available as mandatory attendance at school becomes the norm. With the transformation of the practice, the values once associated with fostering also appear to be changing. For example, foster parents traditionally felt an obligation to devote equal attention to their own children and to those in their care. Nonkin and institutional caregivers are not imbued with such values. Moreover the pupil-teacher ratio in institutions does not compare favorably with that in traditional foster parent settings. Under these conditions, fostering may no longer be offering adequate support for female migration.

The irony of the situation, of course, is that many of the migrant mothers of children left behind or sent to Ghana as "posted babies" are providing care for children or the aged at the destination areas for low wages, often below the minimum, while not being able to provide their own children with maternal care. In her study of Ghanaian transnational migrants residing in the Netherlands, Valentina Mazzucato (2011) labels fostering of children and other services rendered by persons at the origin of transnational migrants as "reverse remittances." She also shows how transnational caring arrangements may go wrong and the implications at both ends. She notes that

> if a child caring arrangement fails, this affects the migrant's ability to participate in a host country's society. In [one case], the breakdown prevented her from doing the job well. [In another], childcare constituted] a crisis event for a migrant, and resolving it required mobilizing a migrant's Ghanaian network. . . . [In the first case, an] aunt lost track of] a migrant's] child and [in the second], the caregiver in Ghana died, leaving the minor without care. The missing child ha[d] to be found in one case and a new caregiver in the other. Network members in Ghana were relied upon to help resolve these crises, and they had to devote substantial amounts of their time to do so. They helped the migrant trace her daughter in one case and in the other were asked to take over the childcare. (Mazzucato, 2011, p.458)

As Mazzucato points out, these cases and others like them demonstrate "how aspects of migrants' lives taking place in their home country should be taken into account in studies on migrant integration" (Mazzucato, 2011, p.458). Many other studies also note the social risks of migration for children and even spouses left behind by migrants (see, for example, Cortés, 2007).

CONCLUSION

Scholars of development celebrate the gender-egalitarian dimension of the MDG, not just in its explicit call for gender equality (Goal #3), but also in its emphasis on "gender mainstreaming"—integrating women into the very heart of the project. Development expert Craig Murphy (2006), for example, claims that

> [b]y adopting [the MDGs], many powerful institutions—both governmental and intergovernmental—have come to embrace an egalitarian, human-centred view of development that was not common-place in the 1970s. Moreover, these institutions have accepted the central role of women, and of their empowerment, in any attempt to achieve the society-wide development goals . . . (pp.210–11; quoted in Jenson, 2012, p.6)

Such a view elides women's roles in the migration-development nexus and the fact that migration has the potential to undermine development goals such as the MDGs by extracting a crucial element of the process: mothers' care. This is not to sentimentalize that resource. The fact that we raise the issue of care deficit should not be read as suggesting that women should not migrate (a position that pseudofeminist critics allege limits women's right to mobility).[11] Rather, we seek to point out that the goals of the "development community" and the realities of welfare state underdevelopment, both North and South, are mutually contradictory and to urge the rich economies of the global North to address that contradiction, both directly and through assistance to sending countries.

We propose a number of policy initiatives. On the destination side, several measures seem to make sense: more readily available multiple-entry, long-term visas for care workers (which would enable them to go back and forth legally) along with requirements that employers provide annual, or better, semiannual paid vacations and plane fare; changes in immigration laws to allow for timely family reunification for migrants who seek to settle in destination countries (van Walsum, 2009; Boyd, 2011; Parreñas, forthcoming); visas for family members of those who plan to work in those countries only on a temporary basis; and improvements in wages and working conditions for care providers, both to ensure the fair treatment of migrant workers and to attract more native-born workers.

On the sending side, remedies are not so apparent. We would not seek to limit women's migration, if for no other reason than the fact that remittances are crucially needed, and women, while earning less than men, tend to remit more of their income (Piper, 2005, pp.12–13). But at the same time, we realize that neither money nor formal social services may fully compensate for a parent's absence for some children, depending on their experience of fostering. Visits may help to mitigate some of the emotional pain of separation, but they can also reproduce the trauma of departure over and over again. Circular migration (Lutz, 2011a and 2011b) can ease tensions and anguish by lessening the time between visits, but this is feasible only when sending and receiving countries are close by, when immigration laws permit frequent reentry and when migrants can afford the travel expenses (for one very successful, but probably unusual, example of a family's circular migration between the US and Mexico, see Lima, 2001). We recognize that when it comes to policy, "one size does not fit all" (Daly, 2012). The case of Ghana demonstrates that a nation of strong communities and close-knit extended families, imbued with a powerful sense of reciprocity and culturally accustomed to nonparental care, can develop robust compensatory practices either by adapting old ones, such as fostering, or initiating new ones, such as boarding schools. But how long can this last? The case of Ghana, as described above, along with others, such as the Philippines (Parreñas, 2005), remind us that the cultures of sending countries (like those everywhere) do not remain static. Northern patterns, such as the trend toward nuclear families, may seep into the South, eroding the commitment to extended-family values, and migrants may reduce remittances as they begin to put down roots in destination countries, disrupting the balance between cash flowing in one direction and services in the other (Echazarra, 2011).

In the end, the "grand bargain" of the migration-development nexus rests on an equation between labor outflows and cash remittances: Sending countries may lose critical labor power and even suffer from brain drain, but these losses will be balanced by remittances—social as well as financial—that will increase human as well as financial capital. The assumption is that this situation will be temporary and that eventually, as a result of both remittances and shifts in the global economy, some form of worldwide economic equilibrium will be achieved, thereby reducing the need for labor migration and restoring the integrity of the nation's population.[12] But this rosy scenario leaves out an essential dimension of the process: the care drain and its consequences in the present. Without the social glue provided—yes, alas, in the absence of a miraculous gender revolution—by women, by *mothers*, development in the sending countries will be curtailed, and the outflow of caring power will continue.[13] This will, of course, work to the advantage of the rich countries of the global North, whose welfare states will continue to thrive, subsidized by low-paid care labor from the global South. But it will push off into the ever-receding future the prospect of achieving the Millennium Development Goals.

NOTES

1. In many countries of the global South, this is partly the result of the "New Federalism," a policy promoted in the 1990s by powerful IOs such as the World Bank and the International Monetary Fund; see Kunz (2011, pp.72–3).
2. Kunz (2011, pp.1–7) cautions against reifying what she calls the "migration-remittances-development nexus," and advocates deconstructing, problematizing and historicizing the concept, particularly from the perspective of gender. We agree and argue that it is also important to include children in the process.
3. The demographics of the more rapidly developing "BRIC" countries (Brazil, Russia, India and China) do not exactly fit this pattern; life expectancy in Brazil, for example, is rising, although its birth rate is, for the moment, keeping pace, so the proportion of the population that is elderly is not as great as it is in, say, Europe (see http://data.worldbank.org/indicator/SP.DYN.LE00.IN). By 2050, however, the UN Population Division predicts that 80 percent of the elderly will live in the global South; see http://www.un.org/esa/population/publications/popfacts/popfacts_2012-4.pdf; also W. Lutz et al., 2008.
4. The United States has long been the exception to this pattern, largely due to high rates of immigration and high fertility among immigrants, especially Hispanics. Recently, however, Hispanic birth rates have fallen dramatically, suggesting that the overall US birth rate may soon converge with those of Europe (Saulny, 2013).
5. This quotation comes from a synthesis report: http://www.oecd.org/document/45/0,3343,en_2649_34819_39651501_1_1_1_1,00.html
6. Jenson (2012) and Molyneux (2006) both focus on a specific type of policy that has become common in Latin America known as "conditional cash

transfers," which are designed to incentivize mothers to fulfill certain obligations, such as taking their children to school.
7. For a historical example of such "little mothers," see Michel, 1999 (pp.74–5).
8. These scholars criticize the conceptualization of remittances as a one-way flow, indicating that the social space of transnational migrants is embedded within a network of reciprocal social relations. For this reason, remittances have to be examined as a two-way flow of gifts.
9. There is also historical evidence of parents using orphanages for similar purposes, particularly in cases of death or divorce, so they could work (cf. Michel 1999, Ch.1.)
10. It should be noted that fostering, although somewhat unique in Africa, is not unknown in other parts of the world. Schmalzbauer (2004) emphasizes the prevalence of "other-mothers" in Honduras, and "child-shifting" in the Caribbean. (Cf. also rural-urban patterns among extended African American families in Billingsley (1994, Chs. 1–2).
11. See, for example, the comments of Michael Clemens, senior fellow at the Center for Global Development and Manuel Orozco, director for the Remittances and Development Program at Inter-American Dialog, in the program on "Careworkers around the world" (Kojo Nnamdi Show, 2012). Interestingly, the WHO has called for limiting the migration of health care workers to prevent further brain drain in that sector without receiving such criticism.
12. To be sure, historically, this has often been the case. Italy, a major sending country in the late nineteenth and early twentieth century, has become a major destination for labor migrants, particularly care workers. Mexicans, the dominant group of immigrants to the US, both legal and undocumented, are now returning home in droves as the economy there improves.
13. Development experts point to another essential link: "Government intervention and civil society initiatives are crucial to maximizing the social benefits and minimizing the social costs of migration and remittances" (Rossi et al., 2006).

REFERENCES AND FURTHER READINGS

Afrifa, 2010. *Childcare in foster homes: Public policy on institutionalized fosterage in Ghana*. In: University of Ghana, *Faculty of Social Studies, University of Ghana colloquium*. Legon, Ghana December 7, 2010.
Ardayfio-Schandorf, E. and Amissah, M., 1996. Incidence of child fostering among schoolchildren in Ghana. In: E. Ardayfio-Schandorf, ed. 1996. *The changing family in Ghana*. Accra: Ghana Universities Press.
Anarfi, J., Kwankye, S.O. and Ahiadeke, C., 2005. Migration, return and impact on Ghana: A comparative study of skilled and unskilled transnational migrants. In: T. Manuh, ed. 2005. *At home in the world?: International migration and development in contemporary Ghana and West Africa*. Accra: Sub-Saharan Publishers.
Appiah, E.N., 2001. *Health and nutritional status of children left behind by female migrants: A case study of Amansie-East District of Ghana*. MPhil. University of Ghana.
Arthur, J.A., 2008. *The African diaspora in the United States and Europe: The Ghanaian experience*. Hampshire: Ashgate.
Artico, C., 2003. *Latino families broken by immigration: The adolescents' perspective*. New York: Lfb Scholarly.
Asiedu, A., 2005.Some benefits of migrants' return visits to Ghana. *Population, Space and Place*, 11, pp.1–11.

Awumbila, M. O. et al., 2011. *Sociocultural dimensions of migration in Ghana.* Technical papers, No. 3, Centre for Migration Studies, University of Ghana.

Baataar, C., 2012. Dwindling kin support for child care among the Dagara. In: C. Oppong, D. Badasu and K. Waerness, eds. 2012. *Child care of a globalizing world: Perspectives from Ghana.* Bergen: BRIC.

Badasu, D.M., 2004. "Child Care Among Ewe Migrants in Accra: Cases of Crisis." *Institute of African Studies Research Review*, 16, pp.17–37.

Badasu, D.M., 2011. Understanding the neglect of migration-related care consequences in Ghana. In: *World women's congress*, Ottawa, Canada 4–8 July 2011.

Badasu, D.M., 2012. Maternal education, child care and well-being among Accra migrants. In: C. Oppong, D. Badasu and K. Waerness, eds. *Child Care in a Globalizing World: Perspectives from Ghana.* Bergen: BRIC.

Badasu, D.M., Codjoe, S.N.A. and Frimpong Ainguah, F., 2009. Child care strategies among young migrants at destination areas. In: J.K. Anarfi and S.O. Kwankye, eds. 2009. *Independent child migration in Ghana.* Accra: Sundel Services.

Balbo, L., 1987. "Crazy quilts": Rethinking the welfare state debate from a woman's point of view. In: A. Showstack Sassoon, ed. 1987. *Women and the state.* London: Unwin Hyman, pp. 45–71.

Bettio, F., Villa, P. and Simonazzi, A., 2006. Changing care regimes and female migration. Journal of European Social Policy, 16 (3), pp.271–85.

Billingsley, A., 1994. *Climbing Jacob's ladder: The enduring legacy of African American Families.* New York: Touchstone Books.

Billstein, H., 1988. An Islamic boot camp: The Khomeini from Cologne. *Die Zeit*, February 12. Trans. Tes Howell. In: D. Göktürk, D. Gramling and A. Kaes, eds. 1988. *Germany in transit: Nation and migration, 1955–2005*, Berkeley: University of California Press, pp.200–2.

Boyd, M., 2011. Bringing care workers to Canada: Canada's migration policies. In: S. Michel, ed. 2011. *Women, migration, and the work of care.* Washington, DC: Woodrow Wilson Center. [pdf] Available at: <http://www.wilsoncenter.org/sites/default/files/Women%2C%20Migration%20and%20the%2Work%20of%20Care.pdf > [Accessed 7 July 2014].

Castles, S., 2008. Comparing the experience of five major countries. In: S. Castles and R. D. Wise, eds. 2008. *Migration and development: Perspectives from the South.* Geneva: International Organization for Migration (IOM).

Castles, S. and Miller, M.J., 2009. *The age of migration: International population movements in the modern world.* 4th ed. New York: Palgrave Macmillan.

Chamberlain, M., 2006. *Family love in the Diaspora: Migration and the Anglo-Caribbean experience.* New Brunswick, NJ and London: Transaction Publishers.

Cortés, R., 2007. Women and children left behind in labor sending countries: An appraisal of social risks. *Global report on migration and children.* [pdf] Available at: <http://www.childmigration.net/files/Rosalia_Cortes_07.pdf> [Accessed 7 July 2014].

Daly, M., 2011. What adult worker model? A critical look at recent social policy reform in Europe from a gender and family perspective. *Social Politics*, 18 (1), pp.1–23.

Daly, M., 2012. Making policy for care: Experience in Europe and its implications in Asia. *International Journal of Sociology and Social Policy*, 32 (11/12), pp.623–35.

Echazarra, A., 2011. Accounting for the time pattern of remittances in the Spanish context. Remesas.org working paper no. 5 (January). [online] Available at: <http://www.remesas.org/WP5-2011.html.> [Accessed 7 July 2014].

Fiawoo, D.K., 1978. Some patterns of foster care in Ghana. In: C. Oppong, ed. 1978. *Marriage, fertility and parenthood in West Africa.* Canberra: Australian National University Press.

Folbre, N., 1996. Engendering economics: New perspectives on women, work, and demographic change. In: M. Bruno and B. Pleskovic, eds. 1996. *Annual world bank conference on development economics, 1995*. Washington, DC: World Bank, pp.127–53.

Folbre, N., 2004. *Who pays for the Kids? Gender and the structures of constraint.* New York: Routledge.

Garza, C., 1995. UNICEF-Cornell colloquium on care and nutrition of the young child—introduction. *Food and Nutrition Bulletin*, 16 (4), p.281.

Ghana Statistical Service, 2005. *2000 population and housing census: Demographic, economic and housing characteristics, total country.* Accra: Ghana Statistical Service.

Ghana Statistical Service, 2012. *2010 Ghana population and housing census: Summary report of final results*. Accra: Ghana Statistical Service.

Giddens, A., 1998. *The third way: The renewal of social democracy*. Cambridge, UK: Polity Press.

Glick Schiller, N., Basch, L. and Blanc, C.S., 1995. From immigrant to transmigrant: Theorizing migration. *Anthropological Quarterly*, 68 (1), pp.48–65.

Goody, E.N., 1975. Delegation of parental roles in West Africa and the West Indies. In: T.R. Williams, ed. 1975. *Socialization and communication in primary groups*. Mouton: The Hague.

Goody, E.N., 1982. *Parenthood and social reproduction: Fostering and occupational roles in West Africa*. Cambridge: Cambridge University Press.

Henry, S., 2009. Strapped immigrants seek "reverse remittances." *Associated Press*. [online] Available at: <http:www.sfgate.com/business/article/Strapped-immigrants-seek-reverse-remittances-3227022.php>. [Accessed 7 July 2015].

Hildebrandt, N. and McKenzie, D.J., 2005. Effects of migration on child health in Mexico. *Policy Research Paper #3573*. World Bank. [online] Available at: < http://elibrary.worldbank.org/doi/abs/10.1596/1813-9450-3573>. [Accessed 7 July 2015].

Hochschild, A., 2003. *The managed heart: Commercialization of human feeling.* 20th anniversary. Berkeley: University of California Press.

Hochschild, A., 2012. *The outsourced self: Intimate life in market times*. New York: Metropolitan Books.

Hondagneu-Sotelo, P. and Avila, E., 1997. "I'm here but I'm there": The meanings of Latina transnational motherhood. *Gender and Society*, 11 (5), pp.548–71.

Isiugo-Abanihe, U.C., 1985. Child fosterage in West Africa. *Population and Development Review*, 11 (1), pp.53–73.

Jenson, J., 2009. Lost in translation: The social investment paradigm and gender equality. *Social Politics*, 16 (4), pp.446–83.

Jenson, J., 2012. The new maternalism: What has happened to women in social policy design? In: Institute for the Study of Human Rights, *Workshop on deconstructing and reconstructing "mother."* Columbia University, New York 30 November 2015. [online] Available at: hrcolumbia.org/gender/bibliography. Accessed January 4, 2013].

Jenson, J. and St. Martin, D., 2006. Building blocks for a new social architecture: The LEGO^T paradigm of an active society. *Policy and Politics*, 34(3), pp.429–51.

Kojo Nnamdi Show, Careworkers around the world, 2012. [online] WAMU Radio. 15 August 2015. Available at: <http://thekojonnamdishow.org/shows/2012-08-15/care-workers-around-world/transcript.> [Accessed 7 July 2014].

Kunz, R., 2011. *The political economy of global remittances: Gender, governmentality, and neoliberalism*. New York: Routledge.

Latham, M.C., 1995. UNICEF-Cornell colloquium on care and nutrition of the young child Overview. *Food and Nutrition Bulletin*, 16(4), pp.82–5.

Levitt, P., 2001. *The transnational villagers*. Berkeley: University of California Press.

Lewis, J. and Giullari, S., 2005. The adult worker model family, gender equality and care: The search for new policy principles and the possibilities and problems of a capabilities approach. *Economy and Society*, 34(1), pp. 76–104.

Lima, F.H., 2001. Transnational families: Institutions of transnational space. In: L. Pries, ed. 2001. *New transnational social spaces: International migration and transnational companies in the early twenty-first century*. New York: Routledge.

Lutz, H., 2011a. Circular migrant domestic and care workers in Germany and Austria. In: Woodrow Wilson International Center for Scholars. *United States studies, women, migration, and the work of care*. Washington, DC. [pdf] Available at <:http://www.wilsoncenter.org/sites/default/files/Women%2C%20Migration%20and%20the%20ork%20of%20Care.pdf.> [Accessed January 3, 2013].

Lutz, H., 2011b. *The new maids: Transnational women and the care economy*. London: ZedBooks.

Lutz, H., 2012. The Euro-orphan debate and the reaction to transnational motherhood. In: Institute for the Study of Human Rights, Workshop on deconstructing and reconstructing "mother." Columbia University 30 November 2012.

Lutz, W., Sanderson, W.C. and Scherbov, S., 2008. A world of simultaneous population growth and shrinking unified by accelerating aging. *Population Network Newsletter, POPNET* 39(Winter 2007/08). International Institute for Applied Systems Analysis.

Mahon, R., 2002. Toward what kind of "social Europe"? *Social Politics*, 9 (3), pp.343–79.

Mahon, R., 2009. Babies and Bosses: Gendering the OECD's social policy. In: R. Mahon and S. McBride, eds. 2009. *The OECD and transnational governance*. Vancouver: University of British Columbia Press.

Mammoth. 2009. [film] Directed by Lukas Moodysson. Sweden: Svenska Filminstitutet.

Manuh, T. 1999. "This place is not Ghana: Gender and rights discourse among Ghanaian men and women in Toronto." *Ghana Studies*, 2, pp.77–96.

Manuh, T., 2006. *An 11th Region of Ghana? Ghanaians Abroad*. Inaugural Lecture. Ghana Academy of Arts and Sciences.

Manuh, T., Asante, R. and Djangmah, J., 2005. The brain drain in the higher education sector of Ghana. In: T. Manuh, ed. 2005. *At home in the world?: International migration and development in contemporary Ghana and West Africa*. Accra: Sub Saharan Publishers.

Mapp, S., 2010. *Global child welfare and well-being*. New York: Oxford University Press.

Mazzucato, V., 2011. Reverse remittances in the migration-development nexus: Two-way flows between Ghana and the Netherlands. *Population, Space and Place*, 17, pp.454–68.

Michel, S., 1999. *Children's interests/mothers' rights: The shaping of America's child care policy*. New Haven: Yale University Press.

Michel, S., 2010. Domestic workers' unhappy thanking: States are slow to grant basic rights to those who care for other people's families. *Baltimore Sun*, 23 November. [online] Available at: http://articles.baltimoresun.com/2010-11-23/news/bs-ed-domestic-workers-20101123_1_minimum-wage-thanksgiving-table-county-official. [Accessed 7 July 2015].

Michel, S. and I. Peng. 2012. All in the family? Migrants, nationhood, and care regimes in Asia and North America. *Journal of European Social Policy*, 22 (4), pp.406–18.

Molyneux, M., 2006. Mothers at the service of the new poverty agenda: Progresa/oportunidades, Mexico's conditional transfer programme. *Social Policy & Administration*, 40 (4), pp.425–49.

Moore, H.L., 1994. *Is there a crisis in the family?* Geneva: UN Research Institute for Social Development.

Murphy, C., 2006. *The United Nations development programme: A better way?* Cambridge: Cambridge University Press.
Nabigne, E., 2012. 2012. Helping them grow their teeth: Care and conflict among the Dagaaba of Northern Ghana. *Research Review* (supplement), 16, pp.77–83.
Nukunya. G.K., 1969. *Kinship and marriage among the Anlo Ewe.* London School of Economics Monographs on Social Anthropology. No.37. London: Athlone Press.
Nyonator, F. and Dovlo, D., 2005. The health of the nation and the brain drain in the health sector. In: T. Manuh, ed. 2005. *At home in the world? International migration and development in contemporary Ghana and West Africa.* Accra: Sub-Saharan Publishers, pp.227–49.
OECD, 2006. *Starting strong II: Early childhood education and care.* Paris: OECD.
OECD, 2007. *Babies and bosses*, vols. 1–5. Paris: OECD.
OECD, 2009. *Doing better for children.* Paris: OECD.
Oppong, C., 2004a. Globalization and disruption of mother care. *Institute of African Studies Research Review*, New Series, 17 (1), pp.25–47.
Oppong, C., 2004b. Social capital and systems of care: Some contrasting evidence. *Institute of African Studies Research Review, New Series* (supplement), 16, pp.1–15.
Oppong, C., Badasu, D. and Waerness, K. eds., 2012. *Child care of a globalizing world: Perspectives from Ghana.* Bergen: BRIC.
Parreñas, R.S., 2001. *Servants of globalization: Women, migration, and domestic work.* Stanford: Stanford University Press.
Parreñas, R.S., 2005. *Children of global migration: Transnational families and gendered woes.* Stanford: Stanford University Press.
Parreñas, R.S., Forthcoming. Permanent and transitional guest workers: Variations of partial citizenship among migrant Filipina domestic workers in the Diaspora. In P. Kettunen, S. Michel and K. Petersen, eds. (forthcoming). *An American dilemma? Race, ethnicity and the welfare state in the US and Europe.* Cheltenham Glos, UK: Edward Elgar.
Pillinger, J., 2011. Quality health care and workers on the move. Ferney Voltaire, France: Public Services International, International Migration and Women Health and Social Care Workers Programme. September.
Piper, N., 2005. *Gender and migration.* Global Commission on International Migration. [pdf] Available at: <https://www.iom.int/jahia/webdav/site/myjahiasite/shared/shared/mainsite/policy_and_research/cim/tp/TP10.pdf.> [Accessed 7 July 2014].
Population Reference Bureau, 2011. *2011 world population data sheet.* [online]. Available at: <http://www.prb.org/Publications/Datasheets/2011/2011-world-population-data-sheet.aspx.> [Accessed 7 July 2014].
Pratt, G., 1997. Stereotypes and ambivalence: The construction of domestic workers in Vancouver, British Columbia. *Gender, Place & Culture: A Journal of Feminist Geography*, 4(2), pp.159–78.
Pratt, G., 2012. *Families apart: Migrant mothers and the conflicts of labor and love.* Minneapolis: University of Minnesota Press.
Promise and Unrest. 2010. [film] Directed by Alan Grossman and Aine O'Brien. Ireland: FOMACS.
Quartey, P. 2009. *Migration in Ghana: A Country Profile 2009.* Geneva: International Organization for Migration.
Ramakrishnan, U., 1995. UNICEF-Cornell colloquium on care and nutrition of the young child—planning. *Food and Nutrition Bulletin*, 16 (4), pp.186–92.
Rossi, A., Jesperson, E. and Saab, R., 2006. Children, youth, and migration. In: United Nations, *UN conference on international migration and development.*

Turin, Italy 30 June 2006. [pdf] Available at: <http://www.un.org/esa/population/migration/turin/Turin_Statements/UNICEF.pdf.> [Accessed 7 July 2014].
Sackey, B., 2009. Family networking and relationships in the care of the seriously ill. In: C. Oppong et al., eds. 2009. *Care of the seriously sick and dying: Perspectives from Ghana*. Bergen: BRIC.
Saulny, S. 2013. Hispanic pregnancies fall in U.S. as women choose smaller families. *New York Times*, [online] 31 December. [online] Available at: <http://nytimes.com/2013/01/01/health/us-birthrate-disespecially-forhispanics.html?_r-0>. [Accessed 31 December 2013].
Schmalzbauer, L., 2004. Searching for wages and mothering from afar: The case of Honduran transnational families. *Journal of Marriage and the Family*, 66 (December), pp.1317–31.
Segura, D.A., 1994. Working at motherhood: Chicana and Mexican immigrant mothers and employment. In: E.N. Glenn, G. Chang and L.R. Forcey, eds. 1994. *Mothering: Ideology, experience, and agency*. New York: Routledge.
Simpson, M. 2010. *My Hollywood*. New York: Alfred A. Knopf.
Smith, L., 2008. *Tied to migrants: Transnational influences on the economy of Accra, Ghana*. African Studies Collection, vol. 5. Leiden: African Studies Centre.
Stack, C., 1974. *All our kin: Strategies for survival in a Black community*. New York: Harper and Row.
Tetteh, E.K., 2008. Voices of left-behind children: A study of international families in Accra, Ghana. M.A. University of Ghana.
Twum-Baah, K., 2005. Volume and characteristics of international Ghanaian migration. In: T. Manuh, ed., 2005. *At home in the world? International migration and development in contemporary Ghana and West Africa*. Accra: Sub-Saharan Publishers.
UNICEF, 2011. *The state of the world's children*. [pdf] New York: UNICEF. Available at: <http://www.unicef.org/sowc2011/pdfs/SOWC-2011-Main-Report_EN_02092011.pdf.> [Accessed 27 June 2013].
United Nations, 1995. *The Copenhagen declaration and programme of action: World summit for social development*. [online] New York: UN. Available at: <http://www.un.org/documents/ga/conf166/aconf166-9.htm.> [Accessed 7 July 2014].
United Nations, 2005. *Investing in development: A practical plan to achieve the Millennial Development Goals—Overview Report*. [online] New York: United Nations. Available at: <http://www.unmillenniumproject.org/reports/index_overview.htm.> [Accessed 7 July 2014].
Van Walsum, S., 2009. Transnational mothering: National immigration policy and European law: The experience of the Netherlands. In: S. Benhabib and J. Resnik, eds. 2009. *Migrations and mobilities: Citizenship, borders, and gender*. New York: NYU Press.
When mother comes home for Christmas. 1996. [film]. Directed by N. Vachani. Greece and Germany: Filmsixteen, Greek Film Center and Zweites Deutsches Fernsehen (ZDF).
Williamson, J., 1989. What Washington means by policy reform. In: J. Williamson, ed. 1989. *Latin American readjustment: How much has happened?* Washington, DC: Institute for International Economics.
Wong, M., 2006. The gendered politics of remittances in Ghanaian transnational families. *Economic Geography*, 82, pp.355–81.
World Bank, 1999. World development report 2000/1: Attacking poverty. [pdf] Washington, DC: World Bank. Available at: <http://siteresources.worldbank.org/INTPOVERTY/Resources/WDR/approutl.pdf.> [Accessed 7 July 2014].
World Bank, 2007. *Early childhood development from measurement to action: A priority for growth and equity*. [online] Washington, DC: World Bank. Available

at: <http:/siteresources.worldbank.org/INTECD/Resources/ECDBook2007.pd> [Accessed 7 July2014].

World Bank, 2011. *Migration and Remittances Fact Book*, second edition. [e-book] Available at: <http://siteresources.worldbank.org/INTLAC/Resources/Factbook2011-Ebook.pdf> [Accessed 27 June 2013].

Yeboah, I., 2008. *Black African neo-diaspora: Ghanaian immigrant experiences in the Greater Cincinnati, Ohio Area*. Lanham, MD: Lexington Books.

Yeoh, B., Huang, S. and Lam, T., 2005. Transnationalizing the "Asian" family: Imaginaries, intimacies, and strategic intents. *Global Networks*, 5 (4), pp.307–15.

Zinsser, J.P., 2002. From Mexico to Copenhagen to Nairobi: The United Nations decade for women, 1975–1985. *Journal of World History*, 13 (1), pp.130–68.

Zlotnick, H., 2003. *The global dimensions of female migration*. [online] Washington, DC: Migration Policy Institute. Available at: <http://www.migrationinformation.org/Feature/display.cfm?ID=109.> [Accessed 7 July 2014].

5 Global Care Chains
Reshaping the Hidden Foundations of an Unsustainable Development Model[1]

Amaia Pérez Orozco

INTRODUCTION

The operation of global care chains render visible the unfairness of the care systems that serve as the foundation of the current hegemonic, unsustainable development model. Identifying how these systems work and how they are being reshaped is the goal of this chapter, which aims to move beyond the somewhat polarized and contradictory visions embodied in the current discourses on global care chains. My larger objective is to argue that there should be public dialogue in countries that are part of the global care chain about the kind of life that is worth living and which is deserving of care.

The discourse on women migrant workers has multiple strands, one of which focuses on family disintegration and the related series of social harms in origin countries. It blames those ills on the women who migrate for work. This kind of blame argument is made by conservative (religious) factions and activists opposed to neoliberalism. It also circulates among the very people involved in global care chains (Herrera, 2012). Some macrolevel feminist analyses, conducted primarily by Western researchers, stress the fact that the care crisis in richer countries is producing a care drain in the origin countries of the women migrant workers. As Salazar, Jiménez and Wanderley put it, the "elderly's care needs in Spain are covered by Bolivian women who leave their children behind to be cared for by elderly women" (2010, p.17). In contrast, other feminist research emphasizes family reintegration and the ability of women to reconstruct caring relationships across borders. This discourse analyzes individuals' agency and microlevel social relationships. It focuses on emotional work, its key role in caring and the provision of care under conditions of geographic separation.

Which of these discourses holds the *truth*? Indeed, are the meanings and impacts of global care chains that straightforward? Based on the research results of the project, "Building Networks: Latin-American Women in Global Care Chains,"[2] this chapter addresses those questions. It examines migration from Bolivia, Ecuador and Peru to Spain. An initial motivating hypothesis of the project was that blaming women for various serious social ills is a means (whether conscious or not) of hiding structural problems that surface when women shift their social position. Thus the aim of the project was twofold: elucidating what, if any, systemic failures the existence of global care chains rendered visible in the origin countries (i.e., Bolivia, Ecuador and Peru) and the destination nations (i.e., Spain), while avoiding theoretical assumptions that refused to recognize women's agency (and so were at risk of being appropriated in conservative discourses on women's migration). For the sake of the latter goal, the answers to research questions on systemic issues (e.g., whether women's migration and their work in the care sector was reinforcing, transforming or weakening preexisting, unfair care systems) were based on the concrete and embodied experiences of the women who are part of the global care chains.

In the first part of this chapter, the concept of global care chains is introduced to clarify its link to the notion of sustainability of life. In the second section, it is argued that the analysis of the processes of sustaining life reveals a latent conflict between them and capital accumulation. The third section elaborates on that conflict and its connection to the denial of the vulnerability of life. I argue that this conflict and denial are at the heart of the prevailing development paradigm. I use the case of care chains between Bolivia, Ecuador, Peru and Spain to illuminate how unfair care systems serve as the invisible foundation of this unsustainable development model. The fourth section provides background information on global care chains between those countries. I argue that a double crisis is at the heart of their formation: a care crisis in Spain and a crisis of social reproduction in Bolivia, Ecuador and Peru. The situation of migrant domestic workers in Spain is described briefly. The fifth section analyzes the impact and meaning of these care chains in terms of three dimensions: (i) the lack of societal responsibility for care and social reproduction, (ii) the operation of a gender mandate and (iii) the existence of a systemic link between care and inequality. These conditions are presented as the defining elements of unjust care systems. I close the chapter by arguing that global care chains provide a strategic 'location' for engaging with questions about the life that is worth living and which is worthy of care.

GLOBAL CARE CHAINS: THE CONCEPT

Global care chains were first defined by Hochschild as "a series of personal links between people across the globe based on the paid or unpaid work of caring" (2000, p.131). In this chapter, I use the concept of global care chains in a slightly different way to refer to the transnational networks that are formed for the purpose of maintaining daily life.[3] These networks consist of households that transfer their care giving tasks to other households on the basis of power axes, such as gender, race, ethnicity, social class and place of origin. In order to link this concept to processes of sustaining daily life, I employ a broad notion of care that includes all activities that regenerate physical and emotional health for everyone—not just for people in dependent situations—and that are performed both in the domestic and public spheres. Caring involves "practices aimed at taking responsibility for sexed bodies, recognizing that (dis)affections cut across these practices and that they constitute relationships in and of themselves" (Precarias a la deriva, 2006, p.108). Conceiving global care chains in this way allows us to raise the question whether the socioeconomic system is achieving what feminist economists would say is its ultimate goal—daily (re)production of embodied well-being (Picchio, 1992; 2003; Carrasco, 2011). It also enables us to ask whether or not a public responsibility toward it is articulated.

Are (global) care chains a new phenomenon? In a sense, they are not. First, it is generally argued that the difficulties in reconciling *work* and *family/personal* life experienced by women in the global North is a recent phenomenon caused by their increased participation in the paid labor force, but the reality is that working class and rural women in virtually every country have a long history of facing that challenge. Second, the (domestic and international) migration of women is not a new phenomenon and women migrants have usually found work in the domestic employment sector. Third, domestic work is neither a new labor sector nor one that is unique to the global North. The International Labour Organization (ILO) estimates that only 7 percent of domestic workers are employed in *developed countries* (2011). Low wages and poor working conditions have invariably characterized the sector (ILO, 2010; Razavi and Staab, 2010), and poor women are overrepresented among domestic workers.

In most countries, care arrangements have always been linked to inequality. Exploitation of domestic workers is a long-standing and widespread phenomenon. Indeed the ILO (2010, p.5) recognizes that:

> Domestic work is one of the oldest and most important occupations for many women in many countries. It is linked to the global history of slavery, colonialism and other forms of servitude. In its contemporary manifestations, domestic work is a global phenomenon that perpetuates hierarchies based on race, ethnicity, indigenous status, caste and nationality.

Care has always been transferred, usually on exploitive terms, at the very least along lines of inequality. Any examination of the impact of care chains must also consider how current care arrangements are the result of past asymmetrical transfers of care. Inquiries into the operations of care chains between the global South and North should be accompanied by an examination of similar processes in the South-South migration corridors and rural-to-urban internal migration patterns.

What is new is the process of *globalization of care*. This is a multifaceted phenomenon consisting of at least three processes (Orozco, 2010): the internationalization of care work and the formation of global care chains (this is the most visible facet of the globalization of care and the focus of this chapter); the increased involvement of supranational actors (such as, multinational corporations, international cooperation agencies and multilateral agencies) in the provision of care or in defining the conditions under which care can be provided; and the outsourcing of part of the care industry to less expensive locations. Understanding how care is being globalized makes it possible to analyze the ways in which care systems are interconnected on a global scale. This interconnection implies that fairer care systems cannot be achieved by acting at the national level alone and it raises questions about the **appropriateness** of understanding care rights based on national citizenship. Examining and understanding the globalization of care also allows for the identification of the coexistence of different social conceptions of care (i.e., the notion of care depends on a certain "culture of care," and cultures of care vary from country to country, over time and among social groups (Vega Solís, 2009)), which opens up the possibility of interrogating the social discourses that legitimatize exploitative care arrangements.

A LATENT CONFLICT ABOUT THE SUSTAINABILITY OF LIFE

Recognizing care implies acknowledging the vulnerability of life. Life is precarious; it is possible, but not certain. Life must be cared for in order to exist. As Butler argues, "Life requires various social and economic conditions to be met in order to be sustained as life" (2009, p.14). It could be said that taking care of life is a basic element of what Butler calls "enabling conditions" (2009, p.21). Along the life cycle our care needs vary, as does our ability to take care of ourselves as we become involved in mutually caring relationships and take on responsibility for attending to those whose capacity to take care of themselves is reduced or nonexistent (i.e., children, the elderly, persons who are ill or disabled). But we always need care, and as healthy, nondisabled, nonelderly adults we can almost always simultaneously give and receive care. Care shows that life is interdependent (Carrasco, 2011; Gil, 2011): The only way to deal with vulnerability is together with others, as our vulnerabilities mean that we can be affected by what happens to others. The precariousness of our existence leaves us exposed to "... those we know and to those we do not know; a dependency on people we know, or barely know, or know not at all" (Butler, 2009, p.13). As Gil explains, "Interdependence, as a bond that ties us to one another, lies at the heart of every life [. . .] Even if we live dispersed lives, swimming in differences, losing ourselves among fragmented stories, life is not possible without this common dimension of experience" (2011, pp.39–40).

Although vulnerability and interdependence are basic conditions of human existence, the social contract that Escobar (2010) terms the "modernizing project" imposes a hegemonic normative ideal of self-sufficiency onto individuals. The violence of this harmful ideal and the violence that must be perpetrated to sustain it are at stake in the deployment of global care chains. The illusion of self-sufficiency underlies what feminist economists call the *mushroom* (male) *worker*,[4] and even the *mushroom* (male) *citizen* who is supposed to be party to that social contract. *He* acts independently in the realm of public life. In economic terms, *he* sustains *him*self thanks to what *he* buys in the market. *He* is the one who works (in the market) and, thus, sustains the economy. This is the embodiment of a wider unidirectional relationship: Markets sustain society, and individuals depend on the good performance of business enterprises. *He* is a he because this notion of separateness and self-sufficiency is a component of masculinity (regardless of whether *he* is recognized as a man or a woman).

This figure of a rational, independent *he* acting in the realm of the market is an illusion. The figure of the mushroom worker who has no care needs (i.e., a healthy, nondisabled, nonelderly, entirely self-sufficient adult) and no care responsibilities (*he* does not have to provide care to another person such that there are conditions or limits on *his* ability to meet the needs of the labor market) is a myth. This conception of the citizen-worker renders invisible *his* care needs, and it relies on the existence of a hidden sphere where *his* care and all the rest of the needed care that *he* does not take responsibility for is provided by others (who are almost always women). In other words, it is based on the naturalization of the process by which *he* receives care but which is not recognized. Care as work, a dimension of life and a socially meaningful task is denied. This series of illusions not only ignores the vulnerability of each individual, it also fails to recognize that this person's interdependence places an ethical obligation on him to provide care to others. Instead, his care needs are met through unequal transfers of care responsibilities in terms that exploit those who provide the care. In addition, no collective structures (either public institutions or otherwise) to deal with vulnerability are created. As Gil puts it, "Interdependency is not something good in and of itself because it does not hold any specific content; rather, it is an internal lever for us to question the assumptions upon which contemporary life is built" (2011, p.306).

Such a violent discourse, which denies the basic conditions of existence, is the basis of a socioeconomic system in which life is put at the service of the process of capital accumulation. Markets (i.e., capitalist markets) follow their own logic: The force driving the economic process is the valuation of capital. In this process, producing the resources needed for sustaining life is, at best, a means for a different end. The commodification of life (including intimate life) is a key means for expanding the areas where capital valuation can occur. The commodification of certain dimensions of care and for certain segments of the population is yet another way of doing it.

Nonetheless, there will always be dimensions of life that cannot be made profitable, particularly those that have to do with vulnerability. There will be lives that cannot be used for profit making, and there will be situations in which destroying life will be more lucrative than sustaining it. In all of those cases there is a fundamental contradiction between guaranteeing the process of capital accumulation and guaranteeing the process of sustaining life, with life being understood in its most holistic sense, embracing all of its dimensions and all lives. By definition, capitalist economies prioritize capital accumulation. This prioritizing might be described as locating markets at the epicenter of the socioeconomic system. This means that what is collectively guaranteed is the process of capital accumulation, which discourages the public assumption of responsibility for sustaining life. The diverse dimensions of the welfare state (health and education systems, pension schemes, care provision) represent public assumption of responsibility for the maintenance of certain aspects of life. But the commitments of the welfare state are always in conflict with the driving force of markets. In other words, welfare states are an inadequate, doomed attempt at resolving the irreconcilable contradiction between the vulnerability of life and the process of capital accumulation.

However, life goes on and it must be sustained, but the question is how and where. The argument put forth by feminist economists is that this responsibility has been privatized. It is being shifted out of the public realm and pushed into and relegated to the private-domestic sphere where it is being fulfilled by families using their personal resources (e.g., social and family networks, the purchase of services in the marketplace). Responsibility for sustaining life is also feminized. It is tied to femininity under the gender mandate or, more precisely, the *reactionary ethos of care*. This discourse understands care as a female responsibility, and even as a crucial dimension of female identity. This ethos helps to organize the division of labor and to build gendered identities.[5] Taking responsibility for life in a system where life is not a priority—and where doing so makes you less and less like the mythical self-sufficient citizen—is not a free choice, but an obligation. This responsibility is also made invisible; it is assigned to those who are in subaltern positions and relegated to spheres that are not publicly and politically negotiated. From such marginal spaces, the larger social structure cannot be questioned, nor can it be politically challenged. Those who provide care are deprived of any power to question socioeconomic priorities. These three moves (privatizing, feminization and the rendering invisible of the responsibility for sustaining life) make up the three defining dimensions of unfair care systems.

These elements define the (hetero)patriarchal, capitalist way of organizing the economy that is part of the modernizing project and, by extension, the hegemonic model of development. Care is used as a tool at the service of the *higher objective* of development, which is understood as the expansion of markets and the monetized spheres of the economy.

The domestic work sector, as long as it entails caregiving in exchange for money, destabilizes this structure, as it locates the task of responding to the vulnerability of life in a reality where vulnerability is not supposed to exist. The conflict between capital accumulation and the vulnerability of human life that makes care crucial is either hidden or ignored by the discourse that blames social ills on migrant women workers. Paraphrasing Sassen (2000), it could be said that global care chains instantiate the conflict between capital and the sustainability of life. Additionally, they reveal that the hegemonic model of development (in terms of social reproduction) is unsustainable because it requires the expansion of unjust care systems for its continued existence.

A CONFLUENCE OF CRISES: THE CONTEXT IN WHICH GLOBAL CARE CHAINS OPERATE

Social Reproduction Crisis and Care Crisis

The context in which global care chains between Bolivia, Ecuador, Peru and Spain have been formed and function can be described as the confluence of two crises: a crisis of social reproduction in Bolivia, Ecuador and Peru and a care crisis in Spain.[6] The term "crisis" is meant to denote a state of affair wherein living processes are put at risk. Thus, in this chapter (and the research project it is based on), the use of the term "crisis" is deliberate as the aim is to position the issue of sustaining daily life at the heart of public debate on the economic crisis. Currently, the possibility of meeting expectations of material and emotional reproduction are in a state of crisis in the three origin countries.[7] In other words, access to the diversity of resources necessary to fulfill individuals' needs and desires is uncertain, if not impossible. In Spain, which, at least ostensibly, was supposed to be in a period of *economic growth* when the project was implemented and until the financial breakdown in 2007–8, a certain dimension of social reproduction, specifically, care provision, was undoubtedly at risk, as it was often deficient and unsatisfactory.[8]

In Latin America, Structural Adjustment Programs (SAPs) were implemented during the 1980s. SAPs were a package of policies aimed at opening the countries up to global competition. They entailed the privatization of welfare mechanisms and public enterprises, and the withdrawal of the state from its role as guarantor of basic living conditions. The SAPs resulted in the so-called *lost decade* of the 1990s in Latin America, a decade when social development vanished and indicators regarding absolute and relative poverty, illiteracy and infant and maternal mortality rates worsened. In order to meet daily needs and fulfill their responsibilities, households deployed a variety of survival strategies, with women playing the lead role as the primary or ultimate guarantor of their households' well-being. The survival strategies were also globalized, as migration became a widespread solution to the crisis. During the 1990s and 2000s, Bolivia, Ecuador and Peru underwent what Sassen calls the feminization of global survival circuits (2000). Migration became *feminized*. The term *feminization of migration* refers not only to the number of women migrating, but also to their reason for migrating, i.e., "the sustained increase in the proportion of women migrating independently in search of employment" (Pérez Orozco et al., 2008, p.36). In particular, Latin American women led the migration outflows to European nations because of job opportunities in those countries' care sectors. However, they were not just motivated by economic and work-related reasons. The other key factors were a desire for greater autonomy, a wish to escape violent or unsatisfactory relationships or a search for professional opportunities commensurate with their higher level of education. In other words, migration was a decision that was an expression of personal agency and motivated by structural constraints upon their ability to achieve their life plans in their home nations (Pérez Orozco et al., 2008).

On the whole, a significant number of Bolivian, Ecuadorian and Peruvian women migrated to Spain. Initially, all of these migration flows were significantly feminized (in 1998, 60.2 percent, 67.4 percent and 62.6 percent of immigrants from each country, respectively, were women). Women were the pioneers in their families, and they helped the men to migrate. By the end of 2008, the proportion of women had decreased to 55.3 percent, 50.8 percent and 50.0 percent, respectively.[9]

Over the last two decades, the hegemonic model of the organization of care collapsed in Spain. Today, in Spanish society, the traditional division of labor and normative family model (with male breadwinner and female caregiver) no longer exists (Pérez Orozco, 2006; Vega Solís, 2009; Carrasco and Domínguez, 2011). This is due to a variety of factors: changes in women's roles in the economy and life choices, patterns of urban expansion, population aging, a labor market that has become flexible and the increasing organization of socioeconomic activities and structures as for-profit markets. Some improvements in public services and benefits have been made (more on this later); however, they are insufficient to meet current care needs. The inadequate response of public institutions, coupled with insufficient changes in men's gender roles, has meant that households have to resolve care arrangements on their own. Households have done so through the transfer of care tasks between women. Women have attempted to meet their families' care needs at the expense of their quality of life or careers, grandmothers have had to take on care work or households have employed domestic workers. The care services market is underdeveloped; thus the commodification of care provision is limited to domestic work. Hiring a domestic worker is an increasingly common *reconciliation strategy*, which families use to cover a variety of situations. Domestic workers are hired to care for children on a regular, full-time basis, or they are employed as live-in care providers for the elderly or they are hired on a part-time basis to perform domestic chores for adults who work, etc. Domestic work is not only a consequence of the care crisis, but also a result of the aspirations related to performance of social class. The care crisis has produced changes in the societal conceptions of decent care that prioritize individualized and commodified solutions.

Domestic Work in Spain

The number of domestic workers in Spain had been declining since the mid-1980s, but then started to increase dramatically in the mid-1990s.[10] According to the Economically Active Population Survey, there were 414,000 domestic workers in 1987, 344,000 in 1997 and 764,500 in 2007. This increase was attributable to the arrival of migrant women (the feminization of the sector has remained constant: Women accounted for 90.2 percent of domestic workers in 1987, 88.4 percent in 1997 and 90.7 percent in 2007). Overall, by 2008 approximately 60 percent of domestic workers in Spain were migrants. Domestic work is an important labor sector for foreign migrant women in Spain: 51.8 percent of Bolivian women, 21.7 percent of Ecuadorian women and 22.1 percent of Peruvian women in Spain labored as domestic workers in 2007. They were primarily adults (two-thirds of them were 21–40 years old) with a relatively high level of education (more than half had completed secondary school). Most of them (83 percent) were participating in the labor market prior to migrating, but only a few had been employed as domestic workers.

Until early 2012, domestic work in Spain was governed by a special labor regulation, which was different from the regular labor norms that are applicable to most sectors. This was called the Special Domestic Work Regime (*Régimen Especial de Empleados de Hogar*, or REEH in Spanish), and it was worse than general labor regulations and also worse than the regulations that applied to *special* sectors, such as self-employment, agriculture and mining. The REEH rendered domestic workers ineligible for contributing to any social security scheme if they worked less than 19 hours per week;[11] it denied them access to unemployment benefits; it also did not allow them sick leave until the 29th day of their illness; it exempted employers from the responsibility to abide by regulations that would have required them to ensure that domestic workers had a safe work environment, and it did not recognize that domestic workers may face occupational hazards. Moreover, it permitted employers to fire workers at will and it set much lower wages and severance pay for domestic workers than other workers, even though they worked longer hours. Thus REEH could be considered a form of indirect sex-based discrimination.

Migrant domestic workers' lives are shaped by labor laws and their status as foreign migrants in Spain. The domestic work sector is governed by discriminatory labor regulations, and the little protection the regulations may afford domestic workers is not available because the rules are not implemented. There are no mechanisms for the enforcement of domestic workers' labor rights. The lives of the workers are also determined by migration rules, which tie migration status to labor status. These migration rules have been tightened since Spain entered the EU (Zaguirre, 2010). An irregular migration status affects migrants' daily lives in multiple ways, including the job opportunities available to them, the conditions they labor under and the possibility of family reunification or trips home. On the whole, according to Zaguirre, "these [migrant domestic] workers face a labyrinth of legal obstacles that prevent them from accessing a basic standard of labor rights and social protection. This is due to the combination of two sets of regulation that mutually reinforce one another, provoking worrisome situations of vulnerability: the Foreign National Law and the one that regulates domestic work" (2010, p.23).

THE REARTICULATION OF UNJUST CARE REGIMES

Do global care chains create new problems for care provision and social reproduction in Bolivia, Ecuador and Peru? Do they resolve the deficit in care provisioning in Spain? No, the care chains between Spain and Bolivia, Ecuador and Peru do neither of those things. Rather, they signify the rearticulation of unjust care systems that predated the feminization of global migration. Any care system can be said to be unfair when it has three characteristics: (i) a lack of social responsibility for care and social reproduction, (ii) the operation of a *gender mandate* that materially and symbolically links care with women and the feminine and (iii) the existence of a systemic link between care and inequality. These features of unjust care chains are discussed below.

Lack of Social Responsibility for Care and Social Reproduction

Neither in Bolivia, Ecuador and Peru nor in Spain is there a collective or public system dedicated to creating the conditions for decent care arrangements and for socializing the risks of life vulnerabilities (e.g., old age, disability, sickness, childhood). Households assume caregiving tasks by using their personal financial resources; they purchase care services and they rely on unpaid care work. So global care chains do not lead to societal responsibility for care. Instead, care is reprivatized: It is private because it remains the responsibility of households, and it continues to be private because it is increasingly commodified.

Doubly Private: Families and Commodified Care Work
Global care chains are primarily and ultimately guaranteed by kinship bonds. Families, understood as "the result of permanent adjustment in response to changing circumstances and not as fixed structures of social organization" (Herrera, 2012, p.75), are in charge of care. How they cover this responsibility varies, from performing it directly (undertaking unpaid care work) to managing its transfer when a domestic worker is hired. This occurs in the origin and destination countries.

When women emigrate from Bolivia, Ecuador and Peru, the care work they used to perform is delegated to a dispersed women-led network, mostly within the extended family. Care is spread out as a result of migration. This happens longitudinally, with both extremes of the generational chain (grandmothers and granddaughters or grandsons) becoming very active in care provisioning, as well as transversally, with the involvement of aunts, godmothers, cousins, sisters-in-law and nieces. These family care arrangements have to be dynamic and flexible, as they are constantly adapting to fit new circumstances.

Is care being commodified in origin countries as a consequence of these processes? Apparently, this is not happening directly. Hiring a domestic worker is not a priority expenditure, although there are some cases where it is. It is much more common for relationships to become psuedocommodified (e.g., a distant relative receives some money in exchange for helping perform specific chores or covering certain situations). A recurring element in these care arrangements is that they have a monetary dimension: Someone takes charge of children or the elderly, but the migrant pays for the upkeep of both dependents and the caregiver. In general, origin countries are undergoing a broader commodification of social reproduction. Remittances play a critical role by allowing families to purchase basic needs, such as education, health, social protection and housing, which would otherwise be inaccessible to them. In this way, remittances have become the primary means by which families make up for the lack of public services.

In Spain, the nuclear or small-size family is in charge of providing care for family members. The loss of the extended family (and other social) bonds, and the shift toward a more individualistic way of life have motivated families to employ domestic workers. The hiring of domestic workers is characterized by a change in discourses about care; family members now have less resistance or ethical qualms about the transfer of care responsibilities to domestic workers. But does this mean that familist discourses are losing their currency in Spain? Such discourses understand care in terms of intimate relationships, not work. They hold that the best care is provided within personal relationships that are special, individualized and motivated by love. In that sense, the domestic worker is like one of the family; the proof of good care is the love that develops between the domestic worker and the family. Familism now extends beyond the boundaries of the domestic sphere. For example, the expectation is that the elderly who move into an assisted living facility or nursing home will continue to receive the daily, individualized care that a domestic worker used to provide to them in their homes. Thus familist discourses are being reconfigured in Spain; arrangements have shifted from the direct provision of care by family members to its supervision by them.

While the Spanish family continues to be the locus of care provision, care is becoming commodified. The hiring of a domestic worker is an indicator of this process. A variety of employer households can be identified, ranging from the upper class (who tend to hire more than one live-in worker for the performance of a variety of tasks, such as cooking, caring for the children and cleaning) to the middle class (e.g., young professionals who hire someone to do the household chores, or couples who need child care) and the lower middle class (e.g., blue-collar workers who hire someone to take care of older family members while they are at work). Thus the domestic worker plays a different role for and fulfills different needs or expectations of her employers. She serves as the marker of social status, her hiring buys her employers free time or time to devote to their personal lives or careers and she meets urgent needs or fills specific gaps in care or domestic work needs.

The Absence or Twisted Presence of the State

The absence of social protection and public services is a reason why people migrate. Migrants from Bolivia, Ecuador and Peru regularly cite providing for the education and medical costs of their families and saving for retirement (to compensate for nonexistent pension schemes) as key reasons for or benefits from their migration. Migrant households' testimonies clearly reveal the failure of the state to provide those essential social welfare goods and services. The state also does not meet care needs. It is remarkable that no public institutions are mentioned by the migrants or their transnational household members when they explain how they organize their daily lives and make care arrangements. For example, in semirural Bolivia, the lack of public transportation to schools is a matter of importance for migrant workers and their families. Migrant families compensate for this failure of the state on a semicommodified basis, e.g., they pay a teenage neighbor to take their children to school. The state is also conspicuously absent when families need help in urgent situations, such as in some cases of mental illness. Another way in which the state is absent is when it fails to respect sexual and reproductive rights of individuals and provide them with access to birth control. Unplanned, early pregnancies often destabilize the existing care arrangements of transnational families; the families have to readjust care arrangements, which often results in the migration of other members of the household, even the new mothers themselves.

Welfare policies in Ecuador, Bolivia and Peru tend to be targeted at specific populations; none of those nations have a single welfare regime. As a result, the state becomes a kind of paternalistic sponsor of its citizenry, dividing society into different strata depending on the rights, needs and abilities of different groups that it recognizes. This segmentation is captured by the notion of "worlds of welfare" that coexist within each Latin American country (Martinez Franzoni, 2007). In this web of worlds of welfare, migrant households usually fall through the cracks: They are neither the poorest for whom the policies are meant, nor are they the better off who can access privatized healthcare and social security systems. Child care, when available, tends to be provided through targeted policies and frequently relies on volunteer work. Care services for the elderly and people with disabilities are still in an embryonic phase. Migrant households' experiences reveal the absence of the state vis-à-vis the wider provisioning of welfare services and the concrete provisioning for care needs. As Herrera (2012) notes, this absence is not new; what is new is the disconnection between the rhetoric of postneoliberal governments (especially in Ecuador and Bolivia) and the reality of their policies.

In Spain, the lack of public responsibility for care is also a key factor leading to the formation of care chains that extend to other nations. However, it would not be entirely accurate to say that the state has either withdrawn from or been absent in care provisioning. Recent years have seen an expansion of public care services and benefits (at least up until cuts in social spending were implemented in 2010). Benefits easing the combination of paid work and unpaid care work have been expanded (maternity and paternity leaves, family care unpaid leaves of absence, flexible working arrangements, voluntary reduced working time). In addition, a right to receive care in situations of dependency has been established by Act 39/2006 for the Promotion of Personal Autonomy and Attention to Persons in a Situation of Dependency (known as the "Dependency Law"). Nevertheless, the implementation of these promising policies has been hindered by various serious deficiencies; namely, the policies are insufficient (Campillo Poza, 2010) and segmented, leading to the exclusion of broad swathes of the population, and they rely on women's unpaid or poorly paid labor. Indirectly, the policies have made hiring domestic workers a desirable option, because either they leave some needs unaddressed (e.g., the needs of those who are dependent but who are not officially recognized as "dependent," lack of public preschools) or they are deficient (e.g., services require co-pay). They have also directly promoted the private hiring of domestic workers, primarily through a variety of financial benefits and tax exemptions. Finally, the Dependency Law recognized that monetary compensation should be given to the family member who performed care work for her or his family, albeit not as a professional care worker. According to this benefit, a family member would be paid less than the minimum wage in return for her or his taking responsibility for attending to all of the care needs of a dependent person. This figure was supposed to be an "exception to the rule," but it ended up accounting for more than half of all the benefits and services provided under the new law. Typically, female caregivers were the ones providing this kind of 24/7 care services. This benefit was also frequently (and unofficially) used by families to hire a domestic worker, without a formal employment contract.

Migration policies have been instrumental in creating a pool of *mushroom workers* by linking residency permits to migrants' labor situations and making it increasingly difficult for the workers' family members to join them (Zaguirre and Orozco, 2011). Migrant domestic workers are thus *fully available* to provide for the needs of Spanish citizens. Although the Spanish state is "absent" in that it has not assumed any direct responsibility for addressing the care needs of its citizens, it has actively created conditions such that households must seek private ways to resolve their care and social reproduction needs. Thus the state has been a "twisted presence."

To sum up, in origin and destination countries, there is a vicious cycle wherein the state's absence or twisted presence contributes to migration and the hiring of domestic workers by households. As care provisioning for certain segments of the population (that could not otherwise cover their needs) is not recognized as public responsibility, it creates gaps that migrant workers help fill. These segments of the population are (members of) Latin America's deprived middle class who migrate to Europe and Spanish middle-class families that hire domestic workers as a response to the care crisis.

The Operation of a Gender Mandate

All along the global care chains, women make care arrangements and serve as the primary caregivers. Men are present throughout the chains as beneficiaries of care, but are consistently absent as primary caregivers, appearing only on the periphery of the circle of care provisioning.

In Spain, although a transfer of care work takes place, care still remains a woman's responsibility. Apart from the fact that the domestic worker is usually a woman, women play a critical role in shaping and sustaining the entire care arrangement. In the case of the elderly, care work generally falls on the shoulders of the domestic worker and a main caregiver who is usually the (female) spouse, a daughter or a daughter-in-law. Both women form a split nucleus around which care is organized. In the case of children, mothers rarely feel that their decision to transfer care responsibilities is legitimate when care work does not conflict with their job duties. But when it does come into conflict with their job, a diverse range of nonmutually exclusive resources is deployed: family networks (consisting primarily of grandmothers), public resources (extracurricular activities, school cafeterias, etc.) and the private hiring of a domestic worker. The mother is the person responsible for making all of the pieces fit together. In addition, adult women tend to resist externalizing all the tasks that were previously considered to be female duties (e.g., single women hire domestic workers less frequently than do single men; heterosexual couples transfer fewer tasks to domestic workers than single person households, and it is usually the woman who performs the 'left over' work). To sum up, a woman is in charge of hiring, supervising and establishing the conditions of paid care; a woman is also responsible for doing all the tasks that the domestic worker does not do (even when the bulk of care work is transferred, there is still a significant amount of unpaid work that remains). Women are always the backbone of care arrangements as well as the ones who provide care directly. Men and women feel differently legitimated to transfer their care responsibilities.

When women migrate, they look for someone to do their care work for them. They do so following a "classificatory sequence" (Salazar, Jiménez and Wanderly, 2010, p.115) marked by gender, family bonds and time availability (which is a function of employment status).[12] Following Parreñas (2005), it could be said that global care chains are built on a tradition of the expansion of maternity and the immobility of paternity. The latter term refers to the fact that fathers who remain in charge tend to do so either as a formality while another woman is actually in charge, or for a short period (when migrating to meet their wives, moving into a new household, etc.). Other male relatives, such as uncles and grandfathers, are also absent as primary caregivers. The only case in which the primary caregiver is a man is the situation in which the oldest son remains in charge of younger brothers and sisters. In such situations, their masculinity is often questioned by their peers.

In terms of the expansion of maternity, all along the global care chains new maternities are emerging (Herrera, 2012, p.210). These include "transnational maternities" (mothering from a distance), "replacement maternities" (referring to the women who take over care in the nations of origin of the migrant worker and the domestic workers caring for their employers' children), "teenage maternities" (when an older daughter takes care of her younger siblings or when migrant workers' daughters become young mothers, creating new needs that must be provided for), "extended maternities" (when migrants' mothers help their daughters by taking charge of their children), etc.

Thus, in all countries, paraphrasing Vega Solís (2009), care arrangements are a triangulation between mother, daughter and the (female migrant) domestic worker. Global care chains entail an expanded version of motherhood that is not strictly biological. It is also motherhood under surveillance, as women involved in transfers of care are subject to scrutiny: Are they properly caring for *their loved ones*? Or are they shirking their obligations or natural destiny as good mothers/caregivers? Community, family, the Catholic Church (and other religious institutions), schools, employers—everyone keeps an eye on them. This goes beyond biological maternity. For example, blaming daughters for abandoning their elderly parents is common. Ratzinger, the former head of the Catholic Church, articulates the nonbiological notion of motherhood that underlies this reactionary ethos of care:

> This intuition is linked to women's physical capacity to give life. Whether lived out or remaining potential, this capacity is a reality that structures the female personality in a profound way. [. . .] Although motherhood is a key element of women's identity, this does not mean that women should be considered from the sole perspective of physical procreation. [. . .] This means that motherhood can find forms of full realization also where there is no physical procreation. (2004)

This gender/motherhood mandate permeates public policies. In origin countries, motherhood has been a matter for public intervention since the 1920s; and the "mother-child dyad," which recognizes mothers as the main or even sole caregivers, "has left profound marks in public policy" (Herrera, 2012, p.30). During the implementation of neoliberal policies in the 1990s, there was a burst of women-led volunteer work aimed at collectively guaranteeing minimum living conditions. When social policy returned (after the horrific effects of its 10-year absence), it used those women's *volunteer* work to reach broad swathes of the population at a relatively cheap cost. This is a defining feature of the so-called New Social Policy, as Molyneux (2007) makes clear in the title of her article, "Mothers at the Service of the State?." This abuse and exploitation of half-volunteer, half-paid labor is characteristic of many of the targeted care services available nowadays in Bolivia, Ecuador and Peru; similarly, women's roles as caregivers is the backbone of the main antipoverty policy: conditional cash transfers.[13] In Spain, the Dependency Law was based almost entirely on women's unpaid care work. Finally, it should also be noted that home-work life reconciliation rights are mostly aimed at women (availability of maternity and paternity leaves is very unbalanced), and it is women who exercise them.

Thus global care chains rely on a closely monitored, reformulated and enforced gender mandate. This mandate obligates women (as do the duties of motherhood) to assume the role of the ultimate guarantor of the reproduction of the family by performing any work that remains undone, whether in the nuclear family or in the wider family or societal network. The women do so often at the expense of their own needs or desires. So the ultimate limitation on women's search for independence through paid employment is the tendency of society and the state to assign responsibility for the well-being of others to them. According to reactionary ethos of care, "the true woman is the one who is emotionally prepared to provide care, the one who is trained to do so efficiently and who asks for little or nothing in return" (Anderson, 2012, p.23). Global care chains tell the story of women who are subjected to this reactionary ethos of care but who are contesting it.

The Systemic Link between Care and Inequality

There is a systemic link between care and inequality. This vicious cycle produces unfair transfers of care from certain population groups to others, with access to care being a key differentiating element between them. Moreover, privileged social groups have access to decent care[14] at the expense of other groups, who are only able to access precarious care services. So the question must be asked whether this is a feature of global care chains.

For transnational households, migration is a double-edged sword. On the one hand, they may experience improvements in access to health and education services and to decent material living conditions (including the means to meet the preconditions of care). But the question is whether the remittance inflows are leading to inflation in the communities of origin and, thus, putting nonremittance recipient households at risk. This is a common phenomenon in regions with high migration rates (Pérez Orozco et al., 2008). On the other hand, direct care is put at risk because of the conditions under which care must be undertaken by those remaining in charge. Usually, care responsibilities are transferred to women who are already overloaded with obligations (e.g., they have jobs and families). Alternatively, the responsibility is transferred to women who have finished their reproductive cycle (i.e., elderly women who worked as caregivers for a long time and who should now be cared for themselves) or persons who are not yet ready to perform caregiving work (usually young girls and occasionally young boys). This state of affairs, in conjunction with the emotional stress of separation, creates vulnerability such that any unexpected change (for instance, an illness, a cessation of remittance flows or an unforeseen pregnancy) might lead to the "collapse of family cooperation" (Anderson, 2012).

The extent to which migration is a vulnerability factor is closely linked to the existence of a "culture of migration." In places with established migration flows, migrants' families may be familiar with other migrant families' experiences with rearranging care, thus normalizing such challenges. However, when a cultural discourse construes the nuclear family and cohabitational motherhood (mother and child living under the same roof) as the norm, it stigmatizes those who do not fit that mold or hinders their ability to exercise their rights. It also depends on whether there are public resources available to address care needs. So migration may increase the vulnerability of either the migrant households or the nonmigrant ones. To sum up, migration is another factor that widens inequalities that affect the wider community.

In destination countries, the situation of migrant domestic workers is emblematic of the care-inequality nexus. Their work is a key resource that is utilized to compensate for the shortcomings of the state, but that places the migrant workers at high risk regarding care arrangements for their own families. First, domestic work is a site of frequent human rights violations, both of labor rights and broader socioeconomic and care rights. Labor rights are violated due to the aforementioned discriminatory regulation and to its systematic infringement. The health of domestic workers and their ability to care for themselves are put at serious risk by the regulations and the physical and emotional difficulty of the work. The very character of domestic work (which is used as a preferred resource to cover the gaps and times during which it is most difficult for employer households to reconcile paid work and care) makes it difficult to combine this job with domestic workers' own care responsibilities. Moreover, domestic workers' motherhood is penalized. Maternity leave and related protections (pregnancy risk leave, breastfeeding breaks, rule prohibiting the firing of women workers because of their pregnancies) are not available to domestic workers. It is also usually not possible for domestic workers to have their children join them in Spain because the criteria for family reunification are very difficult for them to meet. Secondly, this multidimensional violation of rights is compounded for migrant workers in general. Migration tends to translate into poor labor conditions because of the segmentation of the labor market along racial and ethnic lines, with fewer job alternatives available for migrants, despite their greater financial needs. The intersection of domestic work regulations and migration policies creates a series of specific vulnerabilities. All of this results in migrant women workers having a narrower range of care resources at their disposal.

Global care chains reveal the conflicts involved in the transfer of care needs or responsibilities. Some are able to access better living conditions or improve their market position (becoming closer to the ideal of the mushroom worker), while the vulnerability of those who have assumed the care responsibilities (and must simultaneously meet their own care needs) is increased. These unequal positions are defined by social class (according to one's market position), gender (according to one's position in the heterosexual matrix), race and ethnicity (according to the position one occupies on the racial and ethnic stratifications) and migration status (according to one's position within a system of global hegemony). In this sense, analyzing the home-work life *reconciliation* difficulties faced by domestic workers and their employers and the strategies used by the two groups reveals the common nature of the problems and the difference in their ability to access care. The conflict is the same for both women as are the strategies they deploy. However, the range of resources available to them to do so (i.e., money, family help, information and entitlement to public services and benefits) and the final outcome are very different, with the arrangements being much more precarious in the case of migrant domestic workers.

A final point that must be stressed is that once global care chains start operating, they rarely stop. Migration as a project of upward mobility is fragile in and of itself. An intergenerational reproduction of the role of caregiver (both paid and unpaid) is more common than intergenerational class mobility. Many domestic workers bring other female relatives (frequently their daughters) along with them to work in the same sector. At the same time, although migrants may see domestic work as a first job that they will quit as soon as possible, many end up being unable to leave that labor sector. Improvements in labor conditions and even intrasector mobility (toward more professionalized care work) are feasible. However, escaping the care sector proves to be a difficult task. Global care chains continue to absorb those who are vulnerable into new care chains, while doing the same with those in more privileged positions.

Although the shape and functioning of global care chains is quite dynamic in response to varying circumstances on the employers' side (mainly changing care needs, standard of living expectations and purchasing power), employers often believe that they cannot do without care workers. While a sudden situation (such as an illness or a new child) can result in the transfer of care, there is not a similar process of return to the earlier arrangement (e.g., when the child grows up). In other words, the experience of having a domestic worker tends to create a need for such help. This can be understood as an instance of "the social construction of needs" (Pérez Orozco and Gil, 2011, p.178).

This commodification of what constitutes (good) care is linked to a change in social discourses about domestic work that tend to put a new twist on the historical (standard) discourses that legitimize and naturalize inequality. Today, two discourses are vying with one another to establish their hegemony over Spanish society: servile familism versus neoservile professionalism. Familism and professionalism vary in their recognition of care as an intimate relationship (familism) or as work, which might clash with professional career (professionalism). They set different labor conditions for domestic work: differentiating (or not) between tasks and clarifying which ones are required, recognizing (or not acknowledging) required qualifications, negotiating labor conditions based on contractual terms or emotional ones, etc. However, both tend to justify inequitable transfers of care.[15] Servility implies the naturalization of the division of society into two social strata: those who are *naturally* worthy of receiving care, and those who must care for them and be grateful for doing so (i.e., they must be grateful for being welcomed into the home where they perform care work and for being treated with *affection* by their employers). Neoservility justifies this division in capitalist terms. According to the rhetoric of free exchange and equal opportunity, some people want to buy care (for various reasons, the legitimacy of which should not be questioned), while others want to sell it. It should not be a matter of concern that the exchange takes place within a labor market segmented by class, race, ethnicity and sex and under social or even legal norms that systematically undervalue care work.

Whether or not polite rhetoric is used, the words of a Spanish male employer make the point clear: "Who am I kidding? I mean, without judging me or anything. I believe that as long as I can, I would prefer not to get down on my knees to clean toilets [laughs]. If there weren't bourgeoisie like me, who refuse to clean toilets, the poor would die of hunger. I mean, in a way we make the world go round. I'm trying to justify my ways [laughs]."

In broad terms, the chains reveal the shared need—but unequal resources—to cover care needs; and global care chains show that in the absence of collective mechanisms to break the vicious cycle between care, inequality and vulnerability, this nexus will continue to exist and be reproduced on a global scale. The sexual division of labor is being internationalized, and individuals' locations in an unequal global order is a factor that increasingly determines who can get decent care, how they can access it and at whose expense. Ultimately, unjust care systems are being refashioned and are increasingly interdependent on a global scale.

UNJUST CARE SYSTEMS: THE BASIS FOR SOCIALLY UNSUSTAINABLE DEVELOPMENT MODELS

Rather than merely transferring a deficit in care provisioning, new care arrangements and strategies are creating a "new geography of inequality"

(Herrera, 2012, p.27). These arrangements are distinguishable by their private character, which are attributable either to the state's absence (or twisted presence) or to the public promotion of pseudocommodified, cheap solutions for care needs. Another characteristic of these care arrangements is that they are women led, which allow men to benefit from them even as they neglect their care responsibilities. Participants along global care chains are positioned differently in terms of their ability to establish decent care arrangements and to introduce into public debates privately experienced care problems: In Spain, the care need problems of employers are a matter of concern for trade unions, the government and the public, but migrant domestic workers' problems caused by labor regulations, migration policies or the situation of their transnational families remain largely unacknowledged by the Spanish state and society.

I have argued in this chapter that a growing global pool of *mushroom (care) workers* is available because there is inequality. Migration is an increasingly important axis in enabling the creation of such a pool and in determining the conditions under which people can make care arrangements. Undoubtedly, such conditions include vulnerability in destination countries and a complicated impact in origin countries. Transnational migration from the global South to the North creates new forms of and channels for exclusion and inequality.

Global Care Chains: Now You See Them, Now You Don't

Domestic work is a very sensitive indicator of two critical questions: to what extent is a society committed to publically providing for the care needs of its population and what is the level of social inequality in accessing decent care (within that society)? (And relatedly, what degree of inequality in accessing care is considered to be acceptable, or legitimate, by that society?[16]). Taken a step further, we can say that privatized domestic work indicates the non-existence of social responsibility for sustaining life and inequality among individuals in being able to live a life worth living.[17] As the volume of domestic work increases, the degree of public responsibility for care and living conditions decreases, resulting in increasing inequality. The existence of global care chains render visible structural problems related to both of those questions. Those problems affect society as a whole, but their gravity for individuals varies immensely.

Global care chains expose shared structural problems, but they also help to obscure them by allowing individuals to address care needs with their personal resources within a framework of inequality. Those chains draw certain *vanishing lines* (i.e., they involve processes that destabilize to some extent the status quo and, thus, open up possibilities for questioning it). Among them, at least two should be stressed. First, the origins of care chains are rooted in earlier destabilization of gender roles. In other words, in a certain sense they are an expression or a consequence of women's rebellion against the traditional gender roles. In Spain, the rhetoric of equality is nowadays commonplace; women do not want to be solely responsible for care, but men and society as a whole have yet to assume their share of the work. Often, a domestic worker is hired in the interest of either avoiding this conflict or not acknowledging its existence. In Bolivia, Ecuador and Peru, prior changes in women's lives and expectations are factors enabling their migration as well as a reason to migrate. Second, global care chains explicitly show that care transfers are taking place instead of hiding them, thus they open up spaces for negotiating their content and conditions. Remittance flows have raised the question of whether commodification of caregiving relationships is occurring in Bolivia, Ecuador and Peru. Is care being offered in exchange for money? The answer to this question is complicated. Migrant households' experiences show that every relationship and the functioning of all households involve a monetary dimension, but they cannot be reduced to it. Furthermore, the provision of care has to be analyzed in more sophisticated terms than the limiting dichotomy of altruism (caring for free, caring for love) versus selfishness (caring for money). Examining care arrangements in light of migration might allow for a more nuanced discussion that elucidates the (un)fairness of these exchanges.

The approach to care must fulfill two conditions so as to take advantage of these *vanishing lines*. First, care must be recognized as a dimension of well-being, as work and as the critical *cohesive factor* sustaining daily life. Second, it must be recognized that care is performed within a network of unequal social relations that organize its very provision. Anderson affirms that while care is an "emic" concept "in the sense of being used in natural [daily] language" (2012, p.201), global care chains or the social organization of care are not. Those terms, in contrast, are "ethical and analytical" concepts that "stem from our approach as observers and researchers" (Anderson, 2012, p.201). People involved in global care chains recognize care needs, but rarely recognize care transfers. Instead, they speak about the rearticulation of intimate relationships. This tendency is illustrative of the wider phenomenon of keeping the organization of care invisible and private, even when it is explicitly transferred and, thus, changes one's living conditions. Therefore, in this chapter, the use of the concept of global care chains is deliberate, with the analytical, ethical and political aim of rendering visible not just care, but also its unfair organization and the complications in conceptualizing it.

However, recognizing care as work, like any other job that can be professionalized and sold in the marketplace, is also problematic. Casting care as work within a framework characterized by segmented labor markets and by the hegemonic discourse of equal opportunity, and where the externalization of care takes place as a commodity and not a public good, is a way of reinventing the legitimacy of unfair care transfers. Buying domestic work (a personal service to provide for your own needs or care responsibilities) is increasingly seen as a critical dimension of a life that is worth living. The fiction of symmetrical exchange allows those who benefit from it at the cost of others to evade any ethical or political discomfort about its (un)fairness.

Thus it is not just a matter of rendering care visible. It is a question of what is understood as care and under what set of socioeconomic relations its existence is recognized. Care is a notion that crosses multiple boundaries: work/life, labor/consumption, selfishness/altruism, giving/receiving, market/nonmarket. In that sense, it is a concept that has what Haraway (1992) would call the "promises of the monsters." These "monsters" are terms that are 'located' at the boundaries of hierarchical dichotomies that one wants to deconstruct. 'Care' is a "monster" that might help one interrogate the discursive structure by means of which current unfair care systems are made intelligible. Salazar, Jiménez and Wanderly affirm that "care is at the heart of citizenship and of development processes. . . . Care questions the ethical approach to development that is imposed in a given society" (2010, pp.28–9).

In this chapter, I have argued that global care chains are a strategic location from which questions can be asked about the priority that the maintenance of life deserves and receives. The problems that women involved in care chains face derive from their simultaneous involvement in the process of capital accumulation and the processes of caring for and sustaining life. Their experiences bring to light three issues. First, the conflict between capital accumulation and life sustainability is becoming more pronounced, among other reasons, because of the commodification of intimate life. Second, collective structures are at the service of the market processes; in other words, there is not social responsibility for sustaining life, but there is a public responsibility for ensuring the process of capital accumulation. Third, the responsibility for caring and sustaining life is privatized (pushed into the domestic realm), feminized (under the gender mandate and the reactionary ethos of care) and hidden (i.e., relegated to subjects who are denied the power to position their experiences as common social problems; this dimension has a direct link with the care-inequality nexus). Unfair care systems serve as the root of such unsustainable development models.

What Kind of Life Do We Want to Take Care of?

This is the precise moment to raise such questions in the nations involved in the global care chain. On the one hand, Ecuador and Bolivia have made explicit political moves toward changing their development priorities. The common public goal is no longer development (a notion tied to market expansion), but *sumak kawsay/suma q'amaña*,[18] which could be translated as collective well-being/living well (Escobar, 2010). Moreover, public discussions about that notion are now underway.[19] Questions about the priority that care should receive and what constitutes good care should be part of these discussions on collective well-being/living well.

Spain, on the other hand, is facing a deep multidimensional crisis that is worsening the care crisis and is beginning to develop into a social reproduction crisis (Agenjo Calderón, 2011; Ezquerra, 2011; Pérez Orozco, 2011). The crisis makes blatantly obvious the conflict between the process of capital accumulation and life sustainability. Current political *anticrisis* policies in Spain are flagrantly biased; they aim at generating revenue by means of a direct attack on the living conditions of the middle class, the working class and the poor. Policies are being introduced that entail sharp cuts in public expenditure on care services. For example, the Dependency Law has more or less been suspended. Despite its weaknesses, it was a move toward the articulation of a certain public responsibility for care. The quick and targeted attack on that law reveals the serious conflict that underlies the economic system. The crisis provides a critical opportunity for raising two questions for Spanish society. First, what does a life that is worth living look like (how is living well to be collectively defined)? Second, how should a collective and democratic responsibility for establishing the conditions of such a life be organized?

The political and socioeconomic events that are occurring at both extremes of global care chains—the sending and the receiving nations—are a momentous window of opportunity to begin debates that engage with the following questions: What is a life worth living? What are the ethical and political values that should form its foundation? Should this foundation be a consumerist model according to which it is impossible to fulfill all needs? Or should it be based on an individualist approach to life that seeks to resolve everything within a nondemocratic and increasingly isolated household (i.e., an approach that is not open to imagining other social networks that could work)? Should an individual's aspiration be to insert her or himself into a labor market, which is characterized by a refusal to recognize that workers are interdependent living bodies?

All of these are the foundational issues that under the current hegemonic development model define the notion of a life worth living and shape the global care chain. But this paradigm of development is not only unsustainable, it is unfair. Therefore, the ultimate question is not just about how fairer globalized care systems can be fostered, but also about the kind of life that we—members of Spanish society—want to take care of. The answer to such a question cannot come from any exhaustive research or brilliant theory, but from a radically democratic debate.

NOTES

1. This chapter was edited by Allison Petrozziello.
2. The project, "Building Networks: Latin-American Women in Global Care Chains," was developed by the International Research and Training Institute of the United Nations for the Advancement of Women (UN-INSTRAW); four

additional research teams were contracted (Postgrado en Ciencias del Desarrollo, Universidad Mayor de San Andrés in Bolivia; Facultad Latinoamericana de Ciencias Sociales-Ecuador in Ecuador; Centro de Investigaciones Sociológicas, Económicas, Políticas y Antropológicas de la Pontificia Universidad Católica in Peru; and Centro de Estudios de la Mujer in Chile). The project focused on interregional migration from Bolivia, Ecuador and Peru to Spain as well as intraregional migration from Peru to Chile. It had two components: research (assessing the impacts of the creation of global care chains on development in destination and origin countries) and policy dialogue (promoting policies to defend the rights that are violated in the formation and functioning of global care chains). A comparative analysis of the five case studies as well as four other intraregional studies (migration from Nicaragua to Costa Rica and from Paraguay to Argentina) can be found in Molano Mijangos, Robert and García Domínguez (2012). This chapter focuses solely on the findings about interregional migration flows. The related research reports can be found in Salazar, Jiménez and Wanderley (2010), Pérez Orozco and Gil (2011), Anderson (2012) and Herrera (coord.) (2012).
3. This chapter also draws from the work on global care by Yeates (2005), Benería (2008), Benería, Deere and Kabeer (2012) and Razavi and Staab (eds.) (2012).
4. Carrasco et al. (2004) use the metaphor of the mushroom worker when referring to the denial of care work. It is rooted in feminist critiques of Hobbes' conception of the adult citizen who comes into being fully formed: "[C]onsider men as if but even now sprung out of the earth, and suddenly, like mushrooms, come to full maturity, without all kind of engagement to each other" (Hobbes, 1651 cited in Pateman, 1989, p.446). The economic version of the mushroom citizen is embodied in the idea of the *homo economicus*, which has being sharply criticized by feminist economists (England, 1993; 2003; Hewitson, 1999).
5. There could hardly be a better definition of this discourse than the one provided by Ratzinger, the former head of the Catholic Church: "Among the fundamental values linked to women's actual lives is what has been called a 'capacity for the other.' Although a certain type of feminist rhetoric makes demands 'for ourselves,' women preserve the deep intuition of the goodness in their lives of those actions which elicit life, and contribute to the growth and protection of the other" (Ratzinger, 2004).
6. The concepts of care crisis and crisis in social reproduction are slightly different from the notion of multiple crises of care which, according to Zimmerman, Litt and Bose (2006), have been wrought by globalization: care deficits in families when women perform paid work, commodification of care, influence of multilateral organizations in adjudicating care arrangements and intensifying global stratification systems. Regardless of the exact term that is used, there is a common understanding that the focus should not be on markets, but on living processes.
7. The concept of social reproduction refers to the daily and embodied experience of well-being, and not to macroeconomic performance data. Emigration is linked more closely to a crisis in social reproduction than it is to any economic (market) crisis. This explains phenomena such as the increase in emigration from Peru during the 2000s while economic growth rates were high (Anderson, 2012). People react to the factors that affect their lives most directly, and these are not linked as closely to macroeconomic data as those writing from an economistic perspective would have us think.
8. This discussion about the current care crisis should not be taken to imply that previously care provision was appropriately and fairly organized. The term "crisis" is used to highlight the failure of past mechanisms that tended to obscure deep-seated social conflicts about care provisioning.

9. Data prepared by Valentín García from the following original sources: Observatorio Permanente de la Inmigración (OPI), Anuario Estadístico de Inmigración from multiple years and Instituto Nacional de Estadística (INE), Padrón Municipal multiple years.
10. All the data on domestic work in Spain was compiled by the author and Valentín García using data from INE, Encuesta Nacional de Inmigración 2007 and Encuesta de Población Activa, multiple years; and data from the Social Security database.
11. It is estimated that 60 percent of all domestic workers did not work on a regular contract basis in 2007. However, not all situations in which domestic workers were not affiliated to any social security scheme had an irregular labor status. It was possible to be *formally* working in the informal economy. This is a clear example of the symbiotic relationship between the formal and informal economies (Sassen, 1998; Gavanas, 2010).
12. For the Ecuadorian case study, time use data was available. The last Time Use Survey (Armas, Contreras and Vásconez, 2009) provided data disaggregated by migration status, which was used to uncover the following pattern. Differences were found regarding who the main caregivers were in households with and without members who had migrated, with a higher proportion of caregivers over the age of 46 or under 18 (mainly, those who have not yet entered the paid labor force or women—primarily grandmothers—who had never entered it). It should be noted that a higher proportion of men was found among those under the age of 18 years, revealing that the only case in which men's role tended to change was among the younger males in the family.
13. For a thorough discussion of the debate on whether they constitute financial recognition of women's unpaid role as caregivers or serve as a mechanisms to solidify gender roles, see Rodríguez Enríquez (2012)
14. The notion of decent care refers to situations in which individuals access care that is sufficient (it satisfies their needs), freely chosen (individuals have decision-making power) and satisfactory (care arrangements fulfill what the individual considers as important).
15. The opposite discourse would be (class) egalitarianism, which is aware that the transfer of care tends to happen on the basis of unequal class positions. It should also be noted that all of these discourses share a key aspect: the naturalization of the gender mandate (Pérez Orozco and Gil, 2011).
16. According to Jiménez Tostón, "Domestic work can be used as a thermometer to measure what inequality is like and the dynamics inside unequal relationships" (2001, p.73).
17. The feminist economists' notion of life sustainability on which this chapter draws is fruitfully linked to the capabilities approach initially proposed by Amartya Sen and later expanded upon by feminist economists (e.g., Agarwal, Humphries and Robeyns, eds., 2005).
18. There is not a single term to define this alternative notion to development, which proves the vivacity of the ongoing discussion: *sumak kawsay* in Quichua, *suma q'amaña* in Aymara, *buen vivir* in Spanish in Ecuador, *vivir bien* in Spanish in Bolivia.
19. Civil society is reclaiming that this debate on what constitutes living well should occur more in political and social terms and not be led by governments themselves.

REFERENCES AND FURTHER READINGS

Agarwal, B., Humphries, J. and Robeyns, I. eds., 2005. *Amartya Sen's work and ideas: A gender perspective*. London: Routledge.

Agenjo Calderón, A., 2011. Lecturas de la crisis en clave feminista: Una comparación de la literatura en torno a los efectos específicos sobre las mujeres. *Papeles de Europa*, 23, pp.70–100.

Anderson, J., 2012. *La migración femenina peruana en las cadenas globales de cuidados en Chile y España: Transferencia de cuidados y desigualdades de género.* Santo Domingo: UN-Women.

Armas, A., Contreras, J. and Vásconez, A. 2009. *La economía del cuidado, el trabajo no remunerado y remunerado en Ecuador.* Quito: Comisión de Transición, INEC, AECID and UNIFEM.

Benería, L., 2008. The crisis of care, international migration, and public policy. *Feminist Economics*, 14(3), pp.1–21.

Benería, L., Deere, C.D. and Kabeer, N., 2012. Gender and international migration: Globalization, development, and governance. *Feminist Economics*, 18(2), pp.1–33.

Butler, J., 2009. *Frames of war: When is life grievable?* London: Verso.

Campillo Poza, I., 2010. Políticas de conciliación de la vida laboral y familiar en los regímenes de bienestar mediterráneos: Los casos de Italia y España. *Política y Sociedad*, 47 (1), pp.189–213.

Carrasco, C., 2011. La economía del cuidado: Planteamiento actual y desafíos pendientes. *Revista de Economía Crítica*, 11, pp.205–25.

Carrasco, C. and Domínguez, M., 2011. Family strategies for meeting care and domestic work needs: Evidence from Spain. *Feminist Economics*, 17 (4), pp.159–88.

Carrasco, C., Mayordomo, M., Domínguez, M. and Alabart, A. 2004. *Trabajo con mirada de mujer. Propuesta de una encuesta de población activa no androcéntrica.* Madrid: Consejo Económico y Social.

England, P., 1993. The separative self: Androcentric bias in neoclassical assumptions. In: M.A. Ferber and J.A. Nelson, eds. 1993. *Beyond economic man: Feminist theory and economics.* Chicago: University of Chicago Press, pp.37–53.

England, P., 2003. Separate and soluble selves: Dichotomous thinking in economics. In: M.A. Ferber and J.A. Nelson, eds. 2003. *Feminist economics today: Beyond economic man.* Chicago: University of Chicago Press, pp.33–60.

Escobar, A., 2010. Latin America at a crossroads: Alternative modernizations, post-liberalism, or post-development? *Cultural Studies*, 24 (1), pp.1–65. [pdf] Available at: <http://www.sidint.net/docs/EscobarPaper.pdf> [Accessed 8 October 2011].

Ezquerra, S., 2011. Crisis de los cuidados y crisis sistémica: La reproducción como pilar de la llamada economía real. *Investigaciones Feministas*, 2, pp.175–87.

Gavanas, A., 2010. *Who cleans the welfare state? Migration, informalization, social exclusion and domestic services in Stockholm.* [pdf] Stockholm: Institute for Future Studies. Available at: <http://www.iffs.se/wp-content/uploads/2011/06/who-cleans-the-welfare-state.pdf> [Accessed 3 February 2012].

Gil, S.L., 2011. *Nuevos Feminismos: Sentidos comunes en la dispersión: Una historia de trayectorias y rupturas en el estado español.* [pdf] Madrid: Traficantes de Sueños. Available at: <http://traficantes.net/index.php/content/download/28063/260518/file/mov_11_FINAL.pdf> [Accessed 20 November 2011].

Haraway, D., 1992. The promises of monsters: A regenerative politics for inappropriate/d others. In: L. Grossberg, C. Nelson and P.A. Treichler, eds. 1992. *Cultural studies.* New York: Routledge, pp.295–337.

Herrera, G. coord., 2012. *Familias transnacionales, cuidados y desigualdad social en Ecuador.* Santo Domingo: UN-Women.

Hewitson, G.J., 1999. *Feminist economics: Interrogating the masculinity of rational economic man*, Northampton, MA: Edward Elgar Pub.

Hobbes, T., 1651. Philosophical rudiments concerning government and society. In Sir W. Molesworth, ed. 1841. *The English works of Thomas Hobbes of Malmesbury.* London: John Bohn.

Hochschild, A.R., 2000. Global care chains and emotional surplus value. In: W. Hutton and A. Giddens, eds. 2000. *On the edge: Living with global capitalism.* London: Jonathan Cape, pp.130–46.
International Labour Organization, 2010. *Decent work for domestic workers. Report IV(I)*. Geneva: ILO.
International Labour Organization, 2011. *Global and regional estimates on domestic workers.* Policy Brief 4. [pdf] Available at: <http://www.ilo.org/wcmsp5/groups/public/—-ed_protect/—-protrav/—-travail/documents/publication/wcms_155951.pdf> [Accessed 11 May 2012].
Jiménez Tostón, G., 2001. Servicio doméstico y desigualdad. *Géneros*, 8 (24), pp.72–80.
Martínez Franzoni, J., 2007. *Regímenes de bienestar en América Latina.* Madrid: Fundación Carolina-CeALCI.
Molano Mijangos, A., Robert, E. and García Domínguez, M., 2012. *Cadenas globales de cuidados: Síntesis de resultados de nueve estudios en América Latina y España.* Santo Domingo: UN-Women.
Molyneux, M., 2007. Change and continuity in social protection in Latin America: Mothers at the service of the state? *Gender and Development Program Paper*, 1. UNRISD.
Orozco, A. 2010. *Global care chains: Towards a rights-based global care regime.* Santo Domingo: UN-Women.
Parreñas, R., 2005. *Children of globalization: Transnational families and gendered woes.* Stanford: Stanford University Press.
Pateman, C., 1989. 'God hath ordained to man a helper': Hobbes, patriarchy and conjugal right. *British Journal of Political Science*, 19 (4), pp.445–63.
Pérez Orozco, A., 2006. *Perspectivas feministas en torno a la economía: El caso de los cuidados.* Madrid: Consejo Económico y Social.
Pérez Orozco, A., 2011. Crisis multidimensional y sostenibilidad de la vida. *Investigaciones Feministas*, 2, pp.29–53.
Pérez Orozco, A. and Gil, S.L., 2011. *Desigualdades a flor de piel: Cadenas globales de cuidados. Concreciones en el empleo de hogar y articulaciones políticas.* Madrid: UN-Women.
Pérez Orozco, A., Paiewonsky, D. and García Domínguez, M., 2008. *Crossing borders II: Migration and development from a gender perspective.* Madrid, Santo Domingo: Ministerio de Igualdad, UN-Women.
Picchio, A., 1992. *Social reproduction: The political economy of the labour market.* Cambridge: Cambridge University Press.
Picchio, A., 2003. A macroeconomic approach to an extended standard of living. In: A. Picchio, ed. 2003. *Unpaid work and the economy: A gender analysis of the standards of living.* London: Routledge, pp.11–28.
Precarias a la Deriva, 2006. Precarización de la existencia y huelga de cuidados. In: Mª. J. Vara, ed. 2006. *Estudios sobre género y economía.* Madrid: Akal, pp.104–34.
Ratzinger, J., 2004. *Letter to the bishops of the Catholic Church on the collaboration of men and women in the church and in the world.* Vatican. [online] Available at: <http://www.vatican.va/roman_curia/congregations/cfaith/documents/rc_con_cfaith_doc_20040731_collaboration_en.html> [Accessed 7 April 2012].
Razavi, S. and Staab, S. 2010. Underpaid and overworked: A cross-national perspective on care workers. *International Labour Review*, 149 (4), pp.407–22.
Razavi, S. and Staab, S. eds., 2012. *Global variations in the political and social economy of care: Worlds apart.* London: Routledge.
Rodríguez Enríquez, C., 2012. Políticas de atención a la pobreza y las desigualdades en América Latina: una revisión crítica desde la economía feminista. In: V. Esquivel ed., 2012. *La economía feminista desde América Latina. Una hoja de ruta sobre los debates actuales en la región.* Santo Domingo: UN-Women.

Salazar, C., Jiménez, E. and Wanderley F., 2010. *Migración, cuidado y sostenibilidad de la vida*. La Paz: CIDES-UMSA, UN-INSTRAW.
Sassen, S., 1998. *Globalization and its discontents: Essays on the new mobility of people and money*. New York: New Press.
Sassen, S., 2000. Women's burden: Counter-geographies of globalization and the feminization of survival. *Journal of International Affairs*, 53 (29), pp.503–24.
Vega Solís, C., 2009. *Culturas del cuidado en transición. Espacios, sujetos e imaginarios en una sociedad de migración*. Barcelona: Editorial UOC.
Yeates, N., 2005. Global care chains: A critical introduction. *Global Migration Perspectives*, 44. [online] Global Commission on International Migration. Available at: <http://www.unhcr.org/refworld/docid/435f85a84.html> [Accessed 7 September 2012].
Zaguirre, A., 2010. La política migratoria y la normativa de extranjería desde una perspectiva de género y de cuidados. El caso de España. *Gender, Migration and Development*. Working Paper 7. Santo Domingo: UN-Women.
Zaguirre, A. and Orozco, A., 2011. Lavoro di cura. In: I. Peretti, ed., 2011. *Schengenland. immigrazione: Politiche e culture in Europa*. Roma: Casa editrice EDIESSE.
Zimmerman, M.K., Litt, J.S. and Bose, C.E., 2006. Globalization and multiples crises of care. In M.K. Zimmerman, J.S. Litt and C.E. Bose, eds., 2006. *Global dimensions of gender and carework*. Palo Alto, CA: Stanford University Press, pp.9–29.

Part III
Unjust Social Security Systems

6 International Migrant Domestic Workers, National Welfare States and Transnational Social Security Arrangements

Sarah van Walsum

There is considerable scholarship on the neoliberal dynamics of globalization, labor relationships and migration, but very few scholars have broadened their analysis to include related shifts in the so-called reproductive spheres of care, sexuality, gender and intergenerational relationships. At the same time, while scholarship on gender and migration frequently addresses the latter issues, it generally lacks a broader vision that includes the global dynamics in the sphere of so-called productive labor (i.e., paid labor performed outside of the home). One of the few researchers who have developed an integrated approach is Anne Stewart in *Gender, Law and Justice in a Global Market* (2011). In this chapter, I expand on her analysis by discussing the practices that migrants have developed to meet their commitments to their kin and to secure their own futures given global neoliberal dynamics. It is my conviction that, in trying to conceive of new approaches to social security, care and migration, it is essential that nations take into account the initiatives that the migrant workers have developed on their own, because to be successful, any form of regulation must take into account existing norms and practices. It is likely that regulatory efforts that counteract or frustrate existing and viable strategies will be counterproductive. Moreover, in trying to conceive of new approaches to social security that are not nationalist, states may learn much from the transnational arrangements that migrant workers have already in place.

As Fiona Williams put it in her 2009 report for the United Nations (UN), the case of migrant domestic workers poses a particular challenge to the nationalist paradigm that still informs debates on migration and social security in the so-called "Western welfare states" (p.26). These migrants, like many other migrants, are compelled to develop cross-border social security arrangements for their own benefit and that of their kin. Moreover, as domestic workers and providers of home-based care, they are becoming integral to the social security systems of their country of employment and those systems, as a result of the presence of these workers, are becoming transnational in character. They thus stand at the forefront of more general developments that have been transforming the paradigmatic institutions upon which national welfare states have been constructed. (These paradigmatic institutions include the notions of national solidarity, the full-time, permanent employment contract, the "gender contract" between male breadwinner and female caregiver and the nuclear family as administrative and consumer unit).

In this chapter, I briefly discuss the challenges to the nationalist paradigm of the welfare state—in the sending and receiving nations—posed by the existence of international migrant workers. I argue that a reduction in formally regulated employment and in state-financed services in the global South has driven people to migrate. The migrant workers who have ended up in the global North find themselves in a worker-employer relationship that is increasingly precarious because of factors such as temporary labor contracts (or (quasi) self-employment) and state retraction from formally regulated social security and services (cf. Resnik, 2013). The latter development has particularly affected international migrants, because in a number of receiving nations, claims to social security and public services are increasingly dependent on legal status. I argue that the shifts in gender and family relationships have also played an integral part in these dynamics, and they have implications for the financial security and care needs of a growing number of households in both the North and the South.

My findings are primarily based on interviews conducted in 2008 and 2009 with migrant domestic workers residing in Amsterdam whose nation of origin were Ghana and the Philippines, respectively. The information from these interviews was supplemented with visits with family members in Ghana and the Philippines.[1] The study revealed the tensions that can arise in the current neoliberal context between the aspirations of migrant workers, their transnational family commitments and nationalist state policies (both in the country of origin and in the country of residence of the migrant workers). In addition, it showed how migrants strove to negotiate those tensions and the effect of increasingly restrictive immigration policies on their options.

I argue that by including foreign migrants in national social insurance systems and services, receiving states not only give them access to specific forms of financial security and provisions of care, they also give them access to knowledge and experiences that they can share with and elaborate on with their families in their nation of origin. Depending on the political context of those nations, those shared experiences may even influence the social policies of those countries. By excluding foreign migrants from their national social insurance systems and services, receiving states deny them access to particular forms of financial security and provisions of care and render them more dependent on employers, increasing the possibility and scope of their exploitation. Extended family or other social networks may offer alternative sources of security (both in the country of employment and in the country of origin), but such commitments should not be taken for granted. When a migrant's appeals for support are deemed excessive, inappropriate or undeserved by their extended family or other support systems, they may well be ignored, leaving the migrant socially isolated and possibly destitute.

The challenge will be to conceive of an alternative model of social security that does not rely on the institutions in which the postwar welfare state was grounded (i.e., the nuclear family, the full-time, permanent employment contract and the nation), but is rooted in and seeks to amplify the transnational links between persons sharing common concerns and interests. Can such networks be mobilized in an equitable way to achieve a global regime of redistribution of care and economic resources? If so, how might we imagine the role of national state institutions within such a regime? Saskia Sassen has argued that even if national state institutions are changing under the force of current processes of globalization, it does not mean they are losing their relevance (2006). While examining the coping strategies migrant workers are trying out to see if they are suited to a transnational, neoliberal context and the ways in which they might support each other in such endeavors, it is important to not lose sight of the ability of state regulations to aggravate or neutralize relationships of power, or facilitate or undermine relationships of affect.

CURRENT CHALLENGES TO THE WELFARE STATE

Development as Welfare under Pressure

James Ferguson (2006) has argued that the paradigm for international development advocated by the UN from its inception until the 1970s was one of nation-building. Although most of the newly independent nations did not have resources for more than rudimentary welfare provisions, public services such as education and health, arguably, were considered to be key to the nation-building processes (cf. Anderson, 1991; Pandey and Geschiere, 2003; Fraser, 2009). This connection is well expressed, for example, by Prince Nico Mbargain in his 1977 song "Free Education in Nigeria." Since the 1980s, the nationalist welfare state paradigm of the UN has been largely replaced by the neoliberal state-and-society paradigm of the International Monetary Fund (IMF) and World Bank (WB). This paradigm sees development not as the project of a developmentalist state, but as a societal process that is held back by a state that claims too much control over too many services and resources. Thus Structural Adjustment Programs (SAPs) were imposed to "liberate" market forces so that they could do their development magic (Ferguson, 2006, p.97). Under these programs, nation-building investments, such as free education and public health care, were drastically cut. In countries like Ghana and the Philippines, school fees were introduced and rose steadily, and hospital care too became increasingly expensive and provided only on the basis of the so-called "cash and carry" system—meaning patients had to pay before they could be treated. As the need for cash increased, so did migration—to urban centers or beyond.

In the global North, the so-called industrial nations are also in a period of fundamental change (Sassen, 2006) as they have adopted neoliberal policies.

According to Saskia Sassen, the nationally oriented model of the democratic welfare state (i.e., that of democratically elected bodies passing legislation aimed at protecting citizens against the vicissitudes of life) had more or less prevailed within those countries during the decades following the Second World War; but since the 1980s, it has been giving way to a more globally oriented model of governance. As powerful economic actors (specifically, transnational companies and financial institutions) have come to transcend national boundaries, they have divided the process of production over various locations, all the while shifting the locus of various elements in their productive processes. As a result, the role that state actors can play in organizing, controlling and regulating economic activities and transactions has changed. In trying to attract and hold down increasingly mobile capital, national governments now tend to give more priority to the demands of transnational businesses than to national social issues. Sassen posits that this has largely been achieved by privatizing what was previously public and denationalizing what were once state responsibilities and national policy agendas (Sassen, 2006, p.412; see also Resnik, 2013).

Shifts in Employment and Gender Relationships

Anne Stewart (2011, p.75) has argued that the shift in government priorities (discussed above) has affected the nature of the welfare state in the global North. Its former role in underpinning and supporting the "traditional" labor contract of the male breadwinner citizen, who has social benefits and public services, has changed. Within the neoliberal paradigm, poverty is redefined as social-economic exclusion and, thus, addressing poverty means ensuring that individuals can access the market, rather than legislating systems of collectively financed support. Individuals (both men and women) are expected to avail themselves of the opportunities provided by the market. If they do not, the welfare state (through the social security and welfare systems) limits its responsibilities to subsistence support.

The welfare state's responsibilities have shrunk as a result of the increasingly flexible worker-employer relationship. Although social security provisions are still tailored to meet the needs of the full-time, permanently employed male breadwinner, a growing number of workers do not conform to this model, either because they are employed on a temporary or part-time basis, or because they are self-employed.[2] As a result, they fall outside the scope of the employers' wider social responsibilities and the related state commitments. Consequently, the level of labor protection and social security once provided to the male breadwinner in the global North has become illusory for a growing number of households.

Both men and women must now engage in paid labor as individual workers to support their households, but the redistribution of domestic work and care work responsibilities remains unresolved. Although some couples have been able to redistribute child-care and domestic work among themselves, in most cases this has proved problematic either because of the micropolitics of gender relationships, or because of time constraints or, in the case of single-parent families, because there is no partner to share them with (Fudge and Owens, 2006, p.3 cf. Hochschild, 1989; Stacey, 1991). As more and more women have started to switch from unpaid work in the home to paid work on the national labor market, the demand for paid domestic workers and providers of home-based care (whether for children, the elderly or the infirm) has increased (Lutz, 2008).

In the global South, SAPs have led to drastic cuts in public employment, resulting in a significant loss of formal employment. This has particularly affected women, for whom formally regulated jobs were often scarce to begin with (Stewart, 2011, Chapter 4; Ferguson, 1999, Chapter 5). International competition moreover seems to favor the maintenance, in the global South, of informal relationships of production—including outsourcing of work to households—rather than formally regulated employment relationships with state-based benefits (Stewart, 2011, p.12, 29).

In a context where the role of the state is highly limited, family-based provisioning remains paramount (Stewart, 2011, p.21). Such family commitments, however, can be subject to various, sometimes conflicting, pressures. James Ferguson has, for example, documented the tensions that can arise between pressure on individual migrant workers from extended family members to conform to a rural ethos and family commitments and the migrant workers' own urban aspirations to achieve a more individualist and cosmopolitan lifestyle (Ferguson, 1999, Chapter 4). Stewart too observes that normative systems of mutual support (as referred to by Ferguson) may be at odds with wider socioeconomic changes associated with the development of market cultures, including the gendered, nuclear family as a consumer unit (Stewart, 2011, p.105, 113 cf. Maher, 1974).

Contested Regulation of an International Market in Domestic Work

Given the commodification of basic services (like health and education) and the precarious worker-employer relationship in the global South, it is interesting to note that SAPs and the fiscal measures promulgated by international financial institutions (over the last two decades) have been geared toward promoting a market in domestic work and care work in transitional and the global South countries, where state provisions for child and elderly care are frequently absent (Stewart, 2011, p.195, 301). Moreover, through the General Agreement on Trade in Services, the World Trade Organization is trying to facilitate the restructuring of care activities as commodified services so that they can be traded more easily on the global market (Stewart, 2011, p.31). Some states, such as the Philippines, moreover, have been active in promoting their female populations on the global labor market as providers of care and household services (Guevarra,

2010). Together with the social and economic pressures (described above), such regulatory initiatives have contributed to the female citizens of those countries seeking work abroad as paid caregivers and domestic workers. The migration of these women has in turn led to shifts in the division of labor and gender relationships in the households they leave behind.

The shift toward a free global market in services also causes tensions between international trade interests and nationalist social and labor policy in migrant receiving countries. Businesses that employ international migrant workers risk losing their competitive advantage when they are confronted with national legislation that requires wage parity and the inclusion of those workers in the national social security regime (Stewart, 2011, p.195). In an attempt to negotiate the tensions between free trade aspirations and nationalist regimes of social security and labor protection, proposals have been put forward to separate long-term migration for permanent settlement purposes from temporary or circular trade-related migration by persons who provide services. In the European Union (EU), the long-term residence regime is primarily available to "highly skilled" migrants—mostly men—or migrants from privileged nations, such as the EU member states, the US, Canada, Australia and New Zealand. To the extent that the temporary or circular migration regime has been implemented, it generally applies to "low-skilled" migrants—many of them women—from the global South (De Lange and Van Walsum, 2014).[3]

Although it is a public secret that irregular migrants—usually women—play a growing role in the provision of domestic work and care work in the private homes of EU citizens, there is strong public resistance—particularly in the more northern states like the Netherlands—to proposals for legalizing temporary or circular migration for care workers and domestic workers. The fear is that it will lead to the creation of pools of flexible and relatively inexpensive migrant labor, to the disadvantage of local workers with permanent contracts and full benefits.[4] Consequently, in those nations where the debate on admission policies remain in a deadlock, many if not most of the migrants employed in the care work and domestic work sectors are still forced to lead a clandestine existence, entailing (for those without forged documents) radical exclusion from formally regulated employment and no access to social security or other social benefits (Vonk, 2013).

Although legal temporary or circular migration could release "low-skilled" migrant workers from the ignominy and stress of having to live in the shadow of the law, it is unlikely that it would bring much improvement in terms of social security for them, given that they would not be eligible for permanent settlement (De Lange and Van Walsum, 2014). Whether they remain undocumented or are granted a temporary resident status, migrant domestic workers and care workers will therefore be largely excluded from the national social security regimes of the countries where they have found employment. But even international migrant workers with permanent resident status or citizenship may be working under precarious conditions, because domestic work has been excluded from the protections granted to breadwinner-employees because it is seen either as "women's work," or as service provided by an independent contractor.

Migrant domestic workers thus may be subject to three modes of exclusion: as (irregular) migrants; as providers of services that are strongly associated with women's "natural" work in the home and, therefore, undervalued; and as workers who are considered by the state to be nonemployees and hence excluded from the financial guarantees that the welfare state has traditionally granted to breadwinners and their dependent family members. Additionally, although their social security in their country of employment is at least a focal point of struggle, their ties of affect and their related commitments to dependents in their nation of origin receive little or no attention (see, for example, ILO, 2011).

TRANSNATIONAL SOCIAL SECURITY ARRANGEMENTS: THREE EXAMPLES[5]

The fact that migrant domestic workers are excluded on multiple grounds from the forms of social security traditionally associated with the welfare state does not necessarily mean they are not protected at all. My research revealed that in a transnational context, new dynamics of social security have been created. These social security systems rely on social structures other than those that underpinned the postwar welfare state: the standard (full-time, permanent) employment contract, the associated "gender contract" and nuclear family and the "imagined community" of the nation. In this section, I discuss three cases of transnational social security arrangements; the first case is about coverage of health risks and other calamities affecting migrants' kin in their nation of origin, the second one is about migrant workers' efforts to make transnational arrangements for housing and (paid) care for dependent family members and the third case is about migrant workers making financial provisions for their return to their country of origin. The first case explores the (possible) cumulative gains that can accrue from including migrants (who maintain transnational contacts and commitments) in the official social security schemes of receiving nations. The second case examines how exclusion from or lack of state provisions can worsen the tensions between autonomy and dependency for migrant workers who are domestic workers or who provide home-care services. The third explores how the convergence of restrictive migration policies with other regimes of exclusion can undermine migrant workers' transnational strategies to secure financial independence.

Although my main focus is on irregular resident migrant workers (i.e., migrant workers who have not been given a resident permit), I have also included legal resident migrants in my empirical descriptions and analysis. I can thus examine how the difference in legal status impacts social security arrangements of international migrant workers within specific social structures. I argue the issue is not only whether a particular state participates in the social security arrangements of a specific group of persons living and working within its territory, but also how it does this and, more specifically, how its involvement intersects with other (transnational) social structures that are also part of those arrangements. I show that the transnational social security arrangements that are taking shape, involve interwoven networks and institutions in which state actors and concerns of national welfare do play a role, but in various ways and to differing degrees.

Transnational Migrants and National Health Care Benefits

Until recently, the hospitals in Ghana worked on a "cash and carry" system. Patients who were unable to pay did not receive any care. In the event of an emergency, there might be considerable pressure on migrants living abroad to provide their family members in Ghana with the necessary funds to access health care (Smith, 2007, p.181). Starting in the early 1990s, mutual health insurance schemes organized on a local basis started to develop in various districts in Ghana. In 2007, these local initiatives were taken over by the Ghanaian government and successfully applied nationwide.[6]

Prima facie, these developments appear to be relevant only to the social protection of persons in Ghana, and not in the Netherlands, but a closer look reveals that they have had important implications for the material security of Ghanaian migrants residing in the Netherlands. They are now better able to manage their savings for their own present and future needs. They no longer have to cover all the medical costs of chronically ill relatives or plunder their savings or borrow funds on short notice to cover the costs of a medical emergency in Ghana.

Some anthropologists have suggested that paying premiums for insurance is not something people in rural African societies are readily inclined to do (Kabki, 2007, p.22). Lothar Smith, however, has reported on extended families that have set up calamity funds, primarily meant to cover funeral costs in Ghana. What is interesting to me is the initiating role that migrant family members living in more affluent nations have played in setting up these schemes. Quoting one of his informants, Smith explains:

> In origin the calamity fund was organized in recognition of the fact that those abroad were too often called upon for any problem, with those in Ghana demanding their financial support when those who are abroad might actually be out of a job or in other financial difficulties. Therefore, to add to their financial support of such events like funerals, the calamity fund was created. We have agreed within the family that those in the village pay 2,000 Cedi in the case of women, or 5,000 Cedi for men, per month [i.e., 20 and 50 Eurocent]. Family members in Kumasi have to pay higher contributions, and those in Accra pay even more. Finally those who are abroad will pay the highest monthly contribution . . . (Smith, 2007, p.194)

My data indicates that Ghanaians are not averse to paying for health insurance once they have settled in the Netherlands. On the contrary, informants who were documented and statutorily obliged to pay never complained about that fact; and one woman who was undocumented, and therefore excluded from regular insurance, had taken out tourist insurance so that she would at least be covered in the event of an accident. Smith even reports of a man who, after having returned to Ghana, continued to pay premiums in the Netherlands to cover the insurance of his wife and child who had stayed behind in the Netherlands and for himself as well.[7]

Ineke Bosman (a Dutch doctor who had been practicing in the Brong Ahafo region since the 1970s) was one of the people who was instrumental in establishing, in the 1990s, the collective health insurance programs. During an interview, she reported that she had initially experienced difficulty convincing people in her district to spend their precious *cedis* on insurance premiums,[8] even though they were well aware of the disadvantages of the "cash and carry" system and eager for a better alternative. In the end, the more affluent members of extended families, who would normally be appealed to in emergency situations, played a crucial role in convincing the villagers to give the system a chance. Although Dr. Bosman could not confirm that family members living abroad had been among those exerting such pressure, the parallels between her account and that of Smith concerning the funeral funds is striking.

It seems likely to me that migrants living abroad would indeed have been included in family discussions on health insurance such as those described by Dr. Bosman. It also seems probable that they would have brought into these family discussions their own experiences with the health insurance schemes in their country of residence. Legal resident migrant family members in particular would have been in a position to encourage their families to participate in a Ghana-based insurance system, because they would have been insured themselves and, hence, familiar with the workings of such a system.

This example shows how the social protection offered to migrants who have been included in the institutional arrangements offered by the Dutch state can reach beyond the borders of the Dutch nation. The indirect positive effects on the social protection of dependent kin in the migrants' countries of origin can, in turn, help strengthen the economic position of the migrants in the Netherlands, because they will be under less pressure to provide financial relief in emergency situations.

Transnational Arrangements for Housing and (Paid) Care

Having delineated how the social protection regimes in migrants' countries of origin and their countries of residence can intersect, I now examine the implications for migrants who have been excluded from institutional forms of social protection in their countries of employment. The focus here is on migrant domestic workers and their efforts to build a home for themselves in their nation of origin, their role in the maintenance of homes in their country of employment and the part they play in care arrangements in both localities.

Ironically, measures designed to exclude irregular migrants from various facets of Dutch society have in fact driven many of them into the heartland of that society, its citizens' private homes. As restrictions on the employment of irregular migrants in other sectors came to be more vigorously enforced, more and more irregular migrants—both men and women—have responded to the increasing demand for paid help in the home where such state controls are rare due to privacy considerations. In this context of intimacy, some may succeed in deriving a degree of social protection from their relationship with their employers. My data show that some Filipino domestic workers, who counted a relatively large number of professionals among their employers, were able to access medical care via their employers or their employers' social networks. Moreover, all domestic workers reported using their employers' networks to find new opportunities for employment.

Dutch authorities have not only sharpened measures against the illegal employment of migrant labor, in an effort to gain more control over the low-cost housing sector, Dutch housing corporations have become more active in tracking down people who sublet illegally.[9] Immigration authorities may be involved in these controls so that, in the event the person who is subletting illegally proves to be without legal resident status, he or she can be arrested and placed in an alien detention center. As a result, domestic workers with irregular status may prefer working on a live-in basis. One of my informants reported that she knew of several Filipinas who worked as live-in domestics in an affluent suburb outside of Amsterdam where the houses are roomier than in the Dutch city centers and, thus, are more conducive to such arrangements. Formerly, according to her, these women would have been eager to leave a live-in arrangement because of the limited privacy and personal freedom. They would have moved into the city, found a place to stay and looked for work on a live-out basis. The women she spoke to more recently, however, seemed reluctant to leave their employers' homes because of the increased risks involved in illegally subletting an apartment in the city—one of the few housing arrangements available to irregular migrants. Rumors circulated of Filipinos being caught during housing control investigations, handed over to the immigration authorities and deported. In this context of increased controls, providing domestic services on a live-in basis has become more attractive despite the limits on privacy and the greater dependency on the employer.

In migrants' country of origin, too, issues of shelter and care are often intertwined. Lothar Smith reports that Ghanaian migrants in the Netherlands have constructed dwellings in their hometowns to express their success as migrants and their commitment to their extended family and to secure a home for themselves for their own old age, in a place where they expect to be looked after and kept company by their kin (Smith, 2006; see also Mazzaliet et al., 2006, pp.42–3).

My own data confirms Smith's findings concerning the Ghanaian case (Van Walsum, 2010). The link that he describes between migrant workers' investment in real estate and in their future care also emerged in my research about Filipino migrants. One woman told how she had been able to purchase a lot in a suburb of Manila and build a house there within six years of coming to the Netherlands as an au pair. Once the house was completed, she had her mother move into it, thus ensuring the house would be looked after in her absence, while saving herself the cost of paying for her mother's rent in Manila. This retirement investment was, however, put under pressure by family commitments. Concerned that her mother, who had developed diabetes, would need care and help in the home, the migrant worker invited her unemployed younger brother, his wife and their two children to join her mother in the house. By having her brother move into her house, my informant could release him and his family from the overcrowded and run-down home that they had been sharing with his wife's widowed mother, siblings and in-laws, while ensuring her own mother of the help and care that she increasingly needed. So, while she had initially invested in a home of her own, this woman ended up accommodating her family members' needs.

Arguably, in doing so, she was also investing in her own future, because her brother's children might feel indebted to her and inclined to support her and care for her in her old age. Not everyone who goes abroad can count on such support upon returning, however. My data also yielded cases of migrants who have spent their entire adult lives abroad working in private homes and who subsequently returned to care for their aging parents but had no relatives that they could count on to look after them in their old age. One Filipino woman who was in her early fifties had spent most of her adult life working in Malaysia, Singapore and Hong Kong as a domestic worker. Although she had work authorization in those countries, she had never been entitled to settle permanently in any of them. She had never married and had no children of her own, and she returned to the Philippines to look after her aging mother. She had three sisters, but they were married and settled abroad with families of their own, so she worried about her own future after her mother passed away.

These cases show that issues of housing, care, autonomy and dependency are intertwined. For persons in need of care, it is important that care providers share their home or at least have ready access to it. For persons aspiring to be autonomous, a home of one's own is an important way to ensure their privacy and freedom. Migrant domestic workers who cannot secure independent housing may feel compelled to move in with their employers and, as a result, find themselves in a position of increased dependency vis-à-vis those employers. A lack of welfare benefits and care provisions in their country of origin can force them to share the houses they have had built there with family members, even if they have invested in those houses to ensure their own autonomy when they return to their nation of origin (see also Van Walsum 2011).

Transnational Financial Arrangements for Return to the Country of Origin

As the populations of the more affluent nations age, those societies are becoming increasingly dependent on the care labor and household services being provided for them by young adult migrant workers—mostly women—from Eastern Europe, sub-Saharan Africa, South America and South East Asia (Lutz, 2008). To the extent that these migrants are unable, because of live-in work arrangements or restrictive migration policies, to engage in close physical contact with their kin, establishing or maintaining a family remains problematic for them. Making suitable arrangements for support, care and company for these and other migrant workers in their old age is arguably one of the most urgent social security and migration issues.

For migrants who are excluded from the formal social security schemes in their nation of employment, and who are unable or unwilling to rely solely on the future support of family in their nation of origin, commercial insurance or other financial products can be a solution. Under the auspices of the Filipino Ministry of Labor and organizations such as UNICEF and Oxfam-Novib, some Filipino nongovernmental organizations (NGOs) have set up projects that link (undocumented) migrants in Europe to rural financial institutions in the Philippines (ERCOF, 2005–14). These institutions finance development projects that are screened for their business potential by microfinance experts and are covered, to a degree at least, by insurance funded by COS, a Dutch NGO that is active in the field of development in the global South (see also Anonuevo et al., 2008).

Although they were not formally involved in the development project, interviews with Filipino state actors (including the Filipino consulate in the Netherlands) revealed that they follow it with interest and sympathy through informal networks. The financial position of returning migrants is a topic of concern for the Filipino Ministry of Labor. The worry is that some may return worse off than they left. While documented migrant workers can be approached through consular officials abroad and encouraged to continue contributing to national social insurance schemes, irregular migrants are harder to track down and include in such schemes. Transnationally coordinated investment projects like the one described here are an alternative strategy for ensuring some financial security for these migrants when they return to the Philippines.

Irregular migrants taking part in this project are, however, hampered in their participation by the fact that, as irregular migrants, they are excluded by Dutch law from regular banking transactions. In order to send their money abroad, they either have to access the bank account of a legally resident compatriot, take part in a collective bank account run by a legally resident member of some association (cf. Moerbeek, Tinnemans and Kara-agach, 2012 pp.52–7) or rely on family members in the Philippines to transfer remittances to their accounts there. Their ability to secure funds for their personal future needs thus remains dependent on the loyalty and honesty of their kin or members of other social networks. State control of transnational banking, which is closely linked with state control of migration, hence worsens the exclusion of irregular migrants from state regulated forms of social protection by complicating the realization of alternative arrangements through transnational financial transactions. Migrants are forced to depend on people in their networks who enjoy a more secure position. This example also shows that state-based exclusion can block migrant workers' aspirations and efforts to be more autonomous (c.f. Van Walsum, 2013).

DISCUSSION: DYNAMICS OF EXCLUSION, DEPENDENCY AND POWER

As the examples discussed in this chapter make clear, irregular migrants, although excluded from national social security regimes, are a part of an array of social relationships that are transnational in scope. Some of these are closely connected to their position on the transnational labor market and include employers, associations of particular categories of migrant workers (such as migrant domestic workers) and trade unions (more on this later). Others involve more long-term reciprocal relationships, such as those between kin, among persons sharing a common place of origin or between members of a particular faith association. The possibilities offered through social or employment networks might be supplemented, on the one hand, by commercial alternatives provided by brokers, often via the Internet and, on the other hand, by Dutch religious institutions and NGOs—some of which might be (partially) financed or at least condoned by local authorities (Engbersen et al., 2002; Van der Leun, 2003).[10]

Even as these various networks provided access to financial support or care in the absence of state provisions, they also structured power relationships between migrant workers and other persons. For instance, exclusion from state provision for social security limited the autonomy of the persons in my study, and it broadened the possibility and scope of their exploitation and abuse.

Dependency in Employment

Employers' generosity is a double-edged sword. A worker whose employer has provided for her health care, shelter or other basic needs will feel indebted and dependent as a result. As Marchetti has argued, the dependency vis à vis the employer that results from the worker's undocumented status forces her into a dialectic consisting of favors and gifts on the part of the employer, and expressions of gratitude from the worker. With few alternatives to the favors provided by their employers, undocumented migrant workers find it difficult to assert their rights and avoid servility (Marchetti, 2005, p.77–84).

In the Netherlands, irregular migrants are not excluded from the protections provided by labor law, even if their employment is unauthorized. These protections include claims relevant to their social protection, such as the right to minimum wage and the right to paid sick leave. Since 2006, migrant domestic workers, including those with irregular status, have been able to join the Dutch trade union movement. Through the trade union, they are educated in their rights vis à vis their employers and so they may feel strengthened in their negotiations with their employers. One of my informants, for example, was successful in negotiating paid vacations with at least some of her employers. Another became more assertive in her salary negotiations after joining the union. More important perhaps, through their involvement in the trade union movement, migrant domestic workers have acquired some voice in a slowly emerging Dutch political debate on the status of household services and home-based care (FNV, 2012).

However, as various forms of exclusion from formal social protection accumulate, migrant domestic workers with irregular status can be forced to depend more on their employers, not just for income but also for access to medical care and shelter, and so they are at risk of becoming more vulnerable and their ability to negotiate with their employers weakens. One of the Filipino women I interviewed was an active member of an organization of domestic workers and of a Dutch trade union. She worried about Filipino domestic workers who had elected to continue working on a live-in basis with a single employer out of the fear that working for multiple employers on a live-out basis might render them at greater risk for apprehension and deportation.[11] Whenever she approached such workers to encourage them to organize, they generally refused, saying their employers would not approve. Other research also indicates that multiple forms of dependency vis à vis employers make workers vulnerable to exploitation, even when they are documented workers. Irregular labor migrants who only depend on their employers for their salary and can rely on other social relationships for needs such as housing or health care, can in fact be in a better position to negotiate their terms of employment than regular migrants who are multiply dependent on their employers (Van den Berg-Eldering, 2007; Pool, 2011).

Dependency in Social Networks

Although there are obvious and undeniable differences between my Ghanaian and Filipino informants, both groups depended on and facilitated systems of mutual support provided through (combinations of) extended family, friends, hometown associations, church congregations and even political ties. The extent to which they could gain access to social networks in both their countries of origin and their countries of residence, and the degree to which they could rely on receiving support from those social networks was not self-evident, however, and depended on, among other things, many variables such as shared histories and the extent to which support was deemed by others to be justified and deserved (cf. Böcker, 1994; Ferguson, 1999; Van Walsum, 2000). Thus, like employment relationships, relationships based on reciprocity can involve a high degree of dependency, with the accompanying risk of abuse (Staring, 2001; Bashi, 2007; Moerbeek, Tinnemans and Karaagacli, 2012, pp.35–51).

Under extreme pressure, informal structures of mutual support can collapse (Finch, 1989; Von Benda-Beckmann, 1994; Ferguson, 1999). When an individual who is in the position to help an undocumented migrant worker feels that her need for support exceeds what is appropriate, a painful silence can develop between them, filled with unexpressed resentment, misunderstanding and feelings of powerlessness on the part of the latter (Van Walsum, 2000). Legally settled migrants may avoid newcomers so as to not have to face their neediness, and irregular newcomers may feel forced to dissemble so as to not embarrass the legally settled members of their extended family, faith group or other social networks.

The collapse of an irregular migrant's social support structure not only affects that particular individual, but also the settled migrants or citizens with whom he or she is closely linked. When an irregular migrant with Dutch children is unable to provide them with sufficient shelter, food and clothing, it can result in loss of custody and placement of those children in institutional care or foster homes, thus profoundly affecting the family life of these Dutch children, as well as that of their destitute migrant parent and his or her family members in the country of origin.

When social networks (such as those based on kinship, faith or place of origin) are unwilling or unable to support migrant workers in their needs, irregular migrants may turn to local authorities, forcing them to confront the following normative question (Van der Leun, 2003): To what degree can they deny migrant workers their basic needs solely on the grounds that they lack the formal right to reside in the Netherlands? Current Dutch case law that has resulted from this confrontation suggests that there is a limit—however minimal—to the extent to which the state can exclude irregular migrants from formal modes of social protection. The Dutch Supreme Court (Hoge Raad) has, for example, called on the Dutch state to provide some form of shelter to undocumented migrants with young children, as long as the families are not under a deportation order[12] (see also Vonk and Van Walsum, 2012, pp.30–1).

Increasingly, modern communications technology is facilitating long distance communication and thereby impacting transnational social relationships. As many irregular migrants are unable to travel due to visa restrictions or the high costs of international travel, they rely on long distance communication to maintain their social networks, supervise the care of their dependents, convey their emotional involvement, control the distribution and spending of their remittances and manage any property or business interests they might have in their nations of origin. Digital payment systems that work via mobile phones could, moreover, make it easier for irregular migrants to circumvent restrictions on their use of formal banking institutions (Van Walsum, 2010).

But if modern communication technology has done much to facilitate international communication, enforced separation can nonetheless weaken claims to future support and care. It makes it impossible, for example, for migrants to attend important ritual celebrations, such as funerals, where mutual ties of commitment and solidarity are enacted and confirmed. Similarly, marital bonds must be maintained without physical contact, resulting in forced infertility or—if a child is born from an adulterous relationship—possibly divorce. Certainly, in societies where people rely on their children for care and support in their old age, such complications have implications for the social security of migrant workers and their family members as they age.

CONCLUSION: BEYOND THE NATIONAL WELFARE STATE?

As less affluent nations have been retracting state support for the education and health of their expanding populations, often under the pressure of international organizations like the WB and the IMF, their young adult citizens have been leaving in growing numbers to work in more affluent countries. They thus have been able to supply the necessary funds to their families to compensate for the reduced state subsidies for housing, education and health care. In that process, they not only challenge the nuclear family model as an administrative unit of the modern state, but also the notion of the nation as a bounded entity in sole control of its citizens' welfare.

At the same time, the female members of more affluent populations have reduced the amount of unpaid care that they devote to housework and the dependent family members in their households, and they have joined their male family members in the labor market. Depending on their means and available networks, they engage other family members or underpaid workers—increasingly female foreign migrants—to take over their tasks in the home. Although in different ways and to a lesser degree than in poorer countries, in the more affluent nations, too, the modernist ideal of the nuclear family as the cornerstone of both the welfare state and the consumer society is in competition with more complex and diffuse household arrangements (cf. Stacey, 1991). Care labor that was formerly provided in the context of (nuclear) family has increasingly become commodified in a transnational market of services.

The Intersection of Community and Market

As labor relationships become more flexible and chains of production and services become increasingly complex, the distinctions between employers, employees, self-employed and consumers become more diffuse. Each of these players is caught up in, and trying to cope with, the insecurities of the fragmented, mobile and volatile markets of today. This suggests that the increase in precarious work may not just be a simple maneuver on the part of employers to avoid having to conform to the relatively costly norm of full-time and permanent employment, it may also be an expression of fundamental and structural changes in the way production and services are currently being organized (cf. Knegt, 2008; Zimmerman et al., 2006; Fudge and Owens, 2006; Conaghan et al., 2002). As market and community relationships merge and mingle at the global level because, for example, of the commodification of care, shifts are liable to occur within the power relationships involved.

Some of the more creative initiatives undertaken by trade unions that organize domestic workers have included employers or consumers of care services as actors morally engaged with those workers, albeit in the context of complex and asymmetrical power relationships. Cranford has, for example, described how, in Los Angeles, unionized domestic workers and patients' organizations have dismantled the traditional employer-employee relationship between households and providers of household services or home-based care. Care-receivers maintained authority over the work performed in their homes and on their bodies, but state-run health centers took on the administrative responsibilities of employers. The latter paid the workers' salaries, reported their salaries to the tax department and managed their claims for sick leave benefits. When the state threatened to introduce cuts in health care, the union and the patients' organizations joined forces to successfully campaign against the cuts. Where interests diverged, however, providers of household services or home-based care and the receivers of these services looked after their own, for example by organizing their own training sessions on dealing with discrimination on the grounds of gender or race (Cranford, 2011). Similarly, in a report on an unorthodox union initiative to organize migrant domestic workers in Israel, Mundlak and Shamir indicate that some form of cooperation with employers is crucial and that traditional trade union approaches (which are based on the conflict of interest between employees and employer) are unproductive (2011).

Nisha Varia (2011, pp.284–5), who has done research for Human Rights Watch on the protection of migrant domestic workers in Asia and the Middle East, observes that migrants' groups, both within these host countries and in the migrants' countries of origin, are growing in size, diversity and sophistication, and they are entering into alliances with each other, with local human rights organizations, women's rights groups, trade unions and the media, and with UN agencies like the ILO. She describes a number of imaginative and innovative campaigns that have been developed by migrants' rights organizations to raise public awareness about the situation of (migrant) domestic workers and to develop their rights.

Identifying *with* Rather Than *As*

One of the most exciting and innovative aspects of Anne Stewart's work is her attempt to formulate an alternative approach to organizing solidarity based on concepts of responsibility, accountability, engagement and solidarity (Stewart, 2011, p.65). Following Iris Marion Young (2004), she proposes the formation of new coalitions of actors who are intent on developing more than just transnational relationships of care brought together through the social and economic processes associated with global supply chains (Stewart, 2011, p.310). José Medina, similarly inspired by Young, has put forward the idea of transnational solidarity based on social connections. Citing Scheman (1997), Medina describes the social connection model of solidarity as relying on identification *with* others, rather than *as* others (Medina 2012, p.17). An example can be found in a long-term and broadly conceived art project carried out in the Netherlands called the "Grand Domestic Revolution." The artists involved in this project expressed their identification with, among others, international migrant domestic workers. The artists, many of whom were of foreign origin, identified with foreign migrant domestic workers' status as aliens; with their precarious and uninsured position as workers; with their involvement—through their work—with matters of emotion, affect and aesthetic; and with the political and economic marginalization that such involvement implies in this neoliberal age (CASCO, 2010).

Medina, moreover, emphasizes that in the chains of concern that emerge, there must be awareness that the oppressed should not carry the biggest burdens. Rethinking solidarity hence not only requires tracing chains of connection across national borders and between the spheres of market and community, but also examining the power structures within and between the various interacting networks of market and community, between global North and global South. We need to not only identify opportunities for institutionalizing engagement and solidarity, but also look for ways to enforce responsibility and accountability. This is a formidable project. It means tapping into the bonds of affect between providers and receivers of care without losing sight of the complex power relationships between them. It means linking the talents and resources of independently operating workers without losing the organizational clout of union solidarity. It means mobilizing cross-border bonds and commitments in ways that counterbalance, rather than reinforce, global inequality.

Rethinking the Role of the State

This alternative approach with its focus on transnational connections through interlinking market transactions and community ties does not exclude state institutions. As our three case studies have shown, even where social security arrangements are not state driven, the context of state regulation remains relevant. It affects the degree to which migrants, who have been excluded from state regulated national forms of social protection, can initiate, develop and profit from alternative transnational forms of social protection, such as those described in this chapter. The microfinance scheme in the Philippines is being supported informally by highly placed state actors there, but is also being frustrated to a degree through Dutch state policies that exclude irregular migrants from bank transactions. The collective health insurance schemes in Ghana have now been taken over by the Ghanaian state—their initial success may well have been supported by the fact that Ghanaian migrants who were legal residents in the welfare states of the EU with well-developed social security systems had become familiar with their mandatory health insurance schemes. States that rely—officially or unofficially—on the labor of foreign migrant domestic workers from the global South to resolve care issues in their own societies can compromise those persons' future care needs by restricting their ability to have a family life. The retraction of formal state regulated alternatives can worsen irregular migrants' dependency on their employers, family or other support networks, increasing their risk of abuse by them. It can also place their transnational networks under pressure by forcing aspiring migrants to bank on a level of support from legally settled migrants that the latter may not consider fair or proper.

As Adam McKeown (2008) has documented in his historical study of the American exclusionary clauses regarding Asian migrants, exclusionary immigration regimes actively aim to discredit and disrupt transnational networks of social relationships. My research shows that as migration control becomes increasingly linked to exclusion from contractual relationships—those involved in opening a bank account, taking out insurance or renting an apartment, for example—immigrants are forced into an increasingly dependent position vis à vis their employers, extended family or other social networks, making it difficult if not impossible for them to realize their aspirations for a more autonomous existence.

The lesson that can be learned from the initiatives developed by the migrant workers in my study is that arrangements for social security are being created by migrant workers that transcend national borders and do not rely on permanent, full-time employment or the nuclear family unit. Policy makers, trade unions and market actors struggling to come to terms with the uncertainties and inequities of the current global economy might derive inspiration from these workers' initiatives to create social security arrangements for themselves and their kin, combining and recombining stronger and weaker ties worldwide to family, employers, community leaders, NGOs, state actors and market agents. They would do well to build on such alternative strategies rather than undermine them. To reach that point, however, receiving and sending states and the other powerful actors involved will have to fundamentally question and disaggregate the linchpins of the postwar welfare state family, employment and nation, and then reassemble the pieces to counter the new asymmetries of power that are emerging in the current neoliberal global context.

NOTES

1. For this research, I collected data through semistructured interviews with 15 Ghanaian and 17 Filipino domestic workers in Amsterdam. Subsequently, I spent three weeks, respectively, in Ghana and the Philippines. During each of these periods, I stayed with or interviewed family members of five informants from, respectively, the Ghanaian and the Filipino segments of the Amsterdam sample. This research was funded by the Dutch Research Council (NWO) as part of the collaborative ESF/EUROCORES project: Migration and Networks of Care in Europe.
2. In the Netherlands, labor market authorities estimate that at least 30 percent of the workforce is currently "flexibly employed" (Hilbers, Houwing and Kösters, 2011). About 40 percent of the working women in the Netherlands have a temporary contract (Cörvers, Euwals and De Grip, 2011).
3. Arguably, employees of transnational companies who are transferred to the EU form an intermediate category.
4. Such fears are not unfounded. See the decision of the Haute Autorité de lutte contre les discriminations et pour l'égalité (HALDE) No. 2008–283, 15 December 2008: CODETRAS (Collectif de défense des travailleurs étrangers dans l'agriculture) v. l'administration des Bouches-du-Rhône. Available at: <www.halde.fr> [Accessed: 5 July 2012].The case concerned the structural employment, by French agricultural enterprises, of Moroccan migrant workers who had been repeatedly admitted on temporary visas over the course of numerous years. The HALDE ruled that these workers were in effect being excluded from permanent employment on the grounds of their migrant status.
5. These findings have been discussed in Vonk and Van Walsum 2012, Vonk and Van Walsum 2013 and De Lange and Van Walsum 2014.
6. Research on the history of this national health insurance scheme was conducted by Professor Irene Agyepong of Legon University, Accra Ghana.
7. Smith, 2007, p.181. Because registration in the Dutch municipal registrars is a prerequisite for regular health insurance in the Netherlands, I assume this man was still legally resident in the Netherlands.
8. The *cedi* is the Ghanaian currency.
9. See, for example, "Corporatie boekt zege op onderverhuurder," *NRC Handelsblad* (Dutch daily newspaper) 19 July 2008 [page unknown].
10. Staring (2001) has described the emergence of financial services and labor and housing brokerages within the Turkish community in the Netherlands. Some of my Ghanaian and Filipino informants reported finding jobs or homes via Turkish brokers.
11. Besides the risks involved in having to sublet lodgings illegally, there is also the risk of being apprehended while traveling to and from work. In February 2010, 30 undocumented domestic workers were apprehended and placed in alien detention following a joint control action carried out by the bus company transporting them from their place of residence to the suburb where their employers lived and local police charged with migration control (Marjon Bolwijn: Illegale werksters land uitgezet. *De Volkskrant* (Dutch daily newspaper) 16 December 2011 p.1, 4 and 5).
12. Hoge Raad 21 September 2012, LJN BW5328.

REFERENCES AND FURTHER READINGS

Anderson, B., 1991. *Imagined communities*. London: Verso.
Anonuevo, A.T., Dizon-Anonuevo, E.M. and Gonzales, E., 2008. *Coming home: Migration and reintegration reference materials*. San Pablo City, Laguna: Atikha Overseas Workers and Communities Initiative.
Bashi, F., 2007. *Survival of the knitted: Immigrant social networks in a stratified world*. Stanford: Stanford University Press.
Böcker, A., 1994. *Turkse migranten en sociale zekerheid: Van onderlinge zorg naar overheidszorg?* Amsterdam: Amsterdam University Press.
CASCO, 2010. *The grand domestic revolution goes on*. Utrecht: CASCO. Office for Art, Design and Theory.
Conaghan, J., Fischl, M.R. and Klare, K., 2002. *Labour law in an era of globalization: Transformative practices and possibilities*. Oxford: Oxford University Press.
Cörvers, F., Euwals, R. and De Grip, A., 2011. *Labour market flexibility in the Netherlands*. The Hague: CPB Netherlands Bureau for Economic Policy Analysis.
Cranford, C.J., 2011. Towards flexibility with security (im)migrant care workers: A comparative analysis of personal assistance services in Toronto and Los Angeles. In: Oxford University, *Making Connections: Migration, Gender and Care Labour in Transnational Context*. Oxford, United Kingdom, 14–15 April 2011.
De Lange, T. and Van Walsum, S., 2014. Institutionalizing Temporary Labour Migration in Europe: Creating an 'In-between' Migration Status. In: L.F. Vosko, V. Preston and R. Latham, eds. 2014. *Liberating temporariness? Migration, work, and citizenship in an age of insecurity*. Montreal & Kingston: McGill-Queen's University Press, pp.126–51.
Engbersen, G. et al., 2002. *Illegale vreemdelingen in Nederland: Omvang, overkomst, verblijf en uitzetting*. Rotterdam: RISBO/Erasmus University.
ERCOF, 2005–14. *Economic resource center for overseas Filipinos*. [online] Available at: <http://www.ercof.com/>.
Ferguson, J., 1999. *Expectations of modernity: myths and meanings of urban life on the Zambian Copperbelt*. Berkeley: University of California Press.
Ferguson, J., 2006. *Global shadows: Africa in the neoliberal world order*. Durham: Duke University Press.
Finch, J., 1989. *Family obligations and social change*. Cambridge, UK: Polity Press.
FNV, 2012. (Federatie van Nederlandse Vakbeweging). FNV Vakbond van Huishoudelijk Werkers. *Schimmenspel. Hoe Nederland hopeloos achterloopt als het gaat om de rechten van huishoudelijk werkers*. Amsterdam: FNV Bondgenoten.
Fraser, N., 2009. Feminism, capitalism and the cunning of history. *New Left Review*, 56, pp.97–117.
Fudge, J. and Owens, R., 2006. Precarious work, women and the new economy: the challenge to legal norms. In: J. Fudge and R. Owens, eds. 2006. *Precarious work, women and the new economy: The challenge to legal norms*. Oxford: Hart Publishing, pp.3–27.
Guevarra, A.R., 2010. *Marketing dreams, manufacturing heroes: The transnational labor brokering of Filipino workers*. New Brunswick, NJ: Rutgers University Press.
Hochschild, A., 1989. *The second shift*. New York: Viking Penguin Books.
Hilbers, P., Houwing, H. and Kösters, L., 2011. De flexibele schil—Overeenkomsten en verschillen tussen CBS- en UWV-cijfers. *Sociaaleconomische trends*, 2nd quarter, pp.26–33.
International Labor Organisation (ILO), 2011. *International Labor Conference Convention no. 189 and Recommendation no. 201 concerning decent work for domestic workers, 2011*. Geneva: International Labor Organisation (ILO).
Kabki, M., 2007. *Transnationalism, local development and social security: The functioning of support networks in rural Ghana*. Leiden: African Studies Centre.

Knegt, R., 2008. *The employment contract as an exclusionary device: An analysis on the basis of twenty-five years of developments in the Netherland*. Antwerp: Intersentia.

Lutz, H., ed., 2008. *Migration and domestic work: A European perspective on a global theme*. Aldershot: Ashgate.

Maher, V., 1974. *Women and property in Morocco: Their changing relation to the process of social stratification in the Middle Atlas*. Cambridge: Cambridge University Press.

Marchetti, S., 2005. *We had different fortunes: Relationships between Filipina domestic workers and their employers in Rome and Amsterdam*. Master's Thesis. University of Utrecht.

Mazzali, A., Muliro, A., Zarro, A. and Zupi, M., 2006. *It's our problem too: Views on African migration and development. Major outcomes of an International Workshop, a Multidisciplinary Delphi Consultation and Interviews* [research paper]. Rome: Centro Studi di Politica Internazionale (CeSPI).

Mbargain, P.N. and Jazz, R., 1977. *Free education in Nigeria*. [album online] Available at: <http://www.youtube.com/watch?v=WgmTuTMs1-c>.

McKeown, A., 2008. *Melancholy order: Asian migration and the globalization of borders*. New York: Columbia University Press.

Medina, J., 2012. Communicative democracy and solidarity across racial and sexual differences. In: University of Amsterdam and VU University Amsterdam, *Inclusion and democracy revisited: normalisation and difference in 21st century Europe*. Amsterdam, The Netherlands, 5 July 2012.

Moerbeek,. S, Tinnemans, W. and Karaagach, D., 2012. *Over de grens*: Een onderzoek naar migranten zonder papieren en transnationale vormen van sociale zekerheid. Amsterdam: BMP (Stichting Bevordering Maatschappelijke Participatie).

Mundlak, G. and Shamir, H., 2011. Organizing migrant care workers: The trade union option. In: Oxford University, *Making Connections: Migration, Gender and Care Labour in Transnational Context*. Oxford, United Kingdom, 14–15 April 2011.

Pandey, G. and Geschiere, P., 2003. The forging of nationhood: The contest over citizenship, ethnicity, and history. In: G. Pandy and P. Geschiere, eds. 2003. *The forging of nationhood*. Delhi: Manohar, pp.7–27.

Pool, C., 2011. *Migratie van Polen naar Nederland in een tijd van versoepeling van migratieregels*. Den Haag: Boom Juridische uitgevers, Centrum voor Migratierecht Radboud Universiteit Nijmegen.

Resnik, J., 2013. 'Globalization (s), privatization(s), constitutionalization, and statization: Icons and experiences of sovereignty in the 21st century. *International Journal of Constitutional Law*, 11 (1), pp.162–99.

Sassen, S., 2006. *Territory, authority and rights*. Princeton: Princeton University Press.

Scheman, N., 1997. Queering the center by centering the queer: reflections on transsexuals and secular Jews. In: D.T. Meyers, ed. 1997. *Feminists rethink the self*. New York: Westview, pp.124–62.

Smith, L., 2006. A home in the city: transnational investments in urban housing. In: Research Committee on Sociology of Migration, *ISA XVI World conference of Sociology*. Durban, South Africa, 23–30 July 2006.

Smith, L., 2007. *Tied to migrants: transnational influences on the economy of Accra, Ghana*. Leiden: Africa Studies Centre.

Stacey, J., 1991. *Brave new families: Stories of domestic upheaval in late twentieth century America*. New York: Basic Books.

Staring, R., 2001. *Reizen onder regie: Het migratieproces van illegale Turken in Nederland*. Amsterdam: Het Spinhuis.

Stewart, A., 2011. *Gender, law and justice in a global market*. Cambridge: Cambridge University Press.
Van den Berg-Eldering, M., 2007. *Huishoudelijk personeel rechteloos? Buitenlands huishoudelijk personeel in dienst van diplomaten: Een overzicht van de rechtsbeschermingperikelen onder het Nederlands recht*. Master's Thesis Law. VU University Amsterdam
Van der Leun, J., 2003. *Looking for loopholes: Processes of incorporation of illegal immigrants in the Netherlands*. Amsterdam: Amsterdam University Press.
Van Walsum, S., 2000. *De schaduw van de grens: Het Nederlandse vreemdelingenrecht en de sociale zekerheid van Javaanse Surinamers*. Deventer: Sanders Instituut/Gouda Quint.
Van Walsum, S., 2010. Migrants, banks and security issues in a context of globalisation. In: University of Maastricht, *Critical Perspectives on Security*. Maastricht, The Netherlands, 27–8 May 2010.
Van Walsum, S., 2011. Migration and the regulation of care. Notes from a transnational field of enquiry. In: Oxford University, *Making Connections: Migration, Gender and Care Labour in Transnational Context*. Oxford, United Kingdom, 14–15 April 2011.
Van Walsum, S., 2013. Ken uw klant. Migranten, banken en beveiliging in tijden van globalisering. *Cultuur en Criminaliteit*, 3 (a), pp.32–46.
Varia, N., 2011. Sweeping changes? A review of recent reforms on protections for migrant domestic workers in Asia and the Middle East. *Canadian Journal of Women and the Law*, 23 (1), pp.265–87.
Von Benda Beckmann, F. and Von Benda-Beckmann, K., 1994. Coping with insecurity. *Focaal: Journal of Global and Historical Anthropology*, 22/23, pp.7–31.
Vonk, G., ed., 2012. *Cross-border welfare state: immigration, social security and integration*. Antwerpen: Intersentia.
Vonk, G. and Van Walsum, S., 2012. Access Denied: Towards a new approach to social protection for formally excluded migrants. In: G. Vonk, ed. 2012. *Cross-Border Welfare State: Immigration, Social Security and Integration*. Antwerpen: Intersentia, pp.3–59.
Vonk, G. and Van Walsum, S., 2013. Access denied. Towards a new approach to social protection for formally excluded migrants. *European Journal of Social security*, 15 (2), pp.124–50.
Williams, F., 2009. *Claiming and framing in the making of care policies: The recognition and distribution of care*. New York: United Nations Research Institute for Social Development.
Young, I.M., 2004. Responsibility and global labor justice. *Journal of Political Philosophy*, 12(4), pp.365–88.
Zimmerman, M.K., Litt, J.S. and Bose, C.E., eds., 2006. *Global dimensions of gender and carework*. Palo Alto, CA: Stanford University Press.

7 Gendered Policies, Single Mothers and Transnational Motherhood
Mexican Female Migrant Farmworkers in Canada

Ofelia Becerril[1]

INTRODUCTION

This chapter examines the impact of the policies governing Canada's Seasonal Agricultural Workers (SAW) Program for Mexican migrant farmworkers who are mothers. A key question that is explored is: What changes occur in the families of those women? It is argued that they experience multiple transformations, including the formation of transnational families and the expansion of the frontiers of motherhood into the realm of transnational mothering. The case is made that Canada and Mexico must create policies and programs that are tailored to meet the needs of this group of short-term migrant women workers and their dependent children.

Part one contains a description of the methodology that was used in the research project that was the basis of this chapter, and part two provides a profile of the Mexican women in the SAW Program. The third section examines the transnational Mexican families that are the result of Canada's policies that apply to migrant farmworkers. In part four, the transnational mothering practices of Mexican women who are part of the Program are described and analyzed. Section five discusses the gendered impact of Canada's policies. The final section of the chapter offers some recommendations for policy changes that could improve the work and life conditions of Mexican women migrant workers and their dependent children.

METHODOLOGY

Theoretical Framework

This chapter adopts a theoretical approach that uses gender and transnational migration to analyze the migratory experience of female Mexican farmworkers in the SAW Program in Canada. That framework examines the interaction between the destination society and the society of origin by stressing human agency, subjectivity and the strategies that the migrants use to provide care for their families. From that theoretical lens, transnational practices are social processes by which migrants function in the domains of social, political and economic action, and these arenas transcend geographical, political and cultural borders (Glick-Schiller, Basch and Blanc-Szanton, 1992). This analysis also conceptualizes transnational migratory circuits as the dynamic formation and the constant movement of people, money, goods, information, organizations, ideologies, signs and real or symbolic values across territorial borders (Rouse, 1988; Goldring, 1992). These circuits are historical and geographical anchors that react to the multivalent logics of the local, regional, national and global dynamics (Rivera, 2008). The analysis of the impact of gender-differentiated labor policies governing Mexican female seasonal farmworkers is based on the conceptual framework proposed by Aihwa Ong (1987). According to it, through their changing positions in family, at work and in the wider society, women can design and implement tactics to counter the images imposed on them and, thus, reconstruct their own images. The experiences and practices of the SAW Program workers who are mothers and heads of households are examined using that conceptual paradigm.

Nowadays most scholars understand gender as a principal organizer of migration (Georges, 1992; Hondagneu-Sotelo, 1994). As a social system, gender molds the migratory patterns of men and women and their experiences in the destination countries (Hondagneu-Sotelo, 1994). It is also acknowledged by most researchers that the variables of gender, class, race and ethnicity should be analyzed simultaneously in the context of migrants' experiences (Pessar, 1999). This chapter uses that approach to understand the migratory patterns of employment of Mexican female workers in the SAW Program in Canada. That strategy reveals the impact that temporary employment has on those workers and their family dynamics.

Data Collection

By drawing on quantitative and qualitative data, I examine Canada's temporary work visa program and labor policies' gendered impact on female Mexican migrant workers who are mothers. I conducted fieldwork in 2002–4 and 2009 in Leamington and Niagara-on-the-Lake, Ontario, Canada, and in 2010–11 in Guanajuato, Michoacán and Estado de Mexico, Mexico. I use a microsocial approach and ethnographic mixed methods, including participant observation, interviews, life stories and statistical reports of the SAW Program (STPS from Mexico, HRSDC and CIC from Canada) to analyze the practices, social relationships, working conditions, experiences and meanings that the women migrants construct about their work and life. The study is based on 28 anonymous semistructured interviews with women workers from different Mexican geographical communities while they were working in Leamington and Niagara. In-depth interviews of 20 other Mexican migrant women were conducted in Mexico. Moreover, there were open-ended interviews with representatives of farmers and the institutions that administer the SAW Program in both countries. Representatives of social organizations that provide services to migrant farmworkers in Canada were also interviewed. The interviews took place in the farms and the women's housing in Canada, at the workshops for workers who were migrant mothers, in the women's homes in Mexico and in the places where they engaged in social interaction in both countries. Participant observation was also treated as data.

PROFILE OF FEMALE MEXICAN MIGRANT WORKERS IN THE SAW PROGRAM

Compared to four decades ago, today Mexican migrant agricultural workers are employed in a variety of food production processes rather than just harvesting. Moreover, they have longer work trajectories than they did previously and long-term employment contracts. They also constitute a stable (nominal)[2] group of workers, and they are distributed throughout a larger area in rural Canada than previously. When the SAW Program began, only male migrant farmworkers were part of it. In 1989, female workers from Mexico were permitted to join the Program, but progress has been slow. The number of women workers increased from 37 to 67 in the 1989–97 time span, and 145 to 280 in the 1998–2001 period, and from 398 to 662 in the 2006–12 time span. In 2009, out of a total of 23,375 SAW Program employees, only 740 (2.5 percent) were female workers and 620 of those were Mexican women (CIC, 2010; STPS, n.d.). In summary, in 2012 women workers represented 3.8 percent of 17,626 Mexican workers; in 1989 they were only 0.8 percent of the total of 4,414 workers.

This section identifies the geographical origins in Mexico of the women in the SAW Program. The Canadian provinces and the agricultural sectors where they work are also tracked. Their age, education level, marital status and dependency obligations are delineated because they are determinants of the impact on them and their families of Canada's policies governing international migrant farmworkers.

Origins

In 2012, the migratory flows of female workers originated mainly from Estado de Mexico (14.3 percent), Tlaxcala (12.2 percent), Puebla (10.7 percent), Guanajuato (8.3 percent), Oaxaca (4.9 percent), Veracruz (4.8 percent), Morelos (4.5 percent), Michoacán (4.5 percent) and other rural areas (35.8 percent). Today, women workers come from every state in the Mexican Republic, in contrast to 2001, when they came from just thirteen central states, following the general pattern of the temporary migrants in the Program.

Destinations in Canada

The SAW Program employers have chosen to limit employment opportunities for female migrant workers to five provinces, mainly in the Niagara region and the Leamington area in Ontario. In contrast, male Mexican farm laborers can find employment in nine provinces that have agricultural facilities. In 2000, almost all migrant women farmworkers (91 percent) were concentrated in Ontario. A decade later, female migrants can be found in five provinces: Ontario (39.9 percent), British Columbia (25.8 percent), Alberta (19.3 percent), Quebec (8.8 percent) and Saskatchewan (6.1 percent). Particularly important is the fact that British Columbia increased its employment of Mexican women from 2.5 percent in 2005 to 25.8 percent in 2010 and Alberta from 10.1 percent to 19.3 percent in the same period. In 2010, of the total of 621 female Mexican workers in the Program, 67.5 percent were nominal women workers, while of the total of 15,809 male Mexican workers, 69.5 percent were nominal male workers.

Employment Sector

Mexican women workers are employed in fruit farms (65.2 percent), greenhouses (19.8 percent), nurseries (14.4 percent) and vegetables farms (0.6 percent); men work in vegetable and legume fields, greenhouses, fruits farms, nurseries, tobacco farms and ginseng farms. They are also employed in tree production facilities and at meat and paste canning factories, and some of them work as beekeepers. Female workers are employed on 71 farms, mainly in Fraisebec, Tangaro Ventures, Belmor Farms, Meadwbrook Greenhouses, Abe Epp & Family, Lakeshore, J W Bouw Greenhouses, Brar Brothers Farms, Central Botanical Gardens, Oyen Greenhouses, Great Northern Hydroponics, Ricciardelli Orchards, Sun Ray Orchards, Seaway Farms, Rosa Flora, Konkle Farm & Greenhouses, Andrewes Farms, AVB Greenhouses and Meyers Fruit Farms (HRSDC, 2010). An analysis of the dynamics of worker mobility by gender shows that, while the first flow of female Mexican workers arrives in Canadian fields in January (12 percent) for planting and crop maintenance, male workers begin work in February (16 percent). Most of the female workers have worked for four to fourteen seasons in Canada. I estimate that 67.2 percent of women have contracts for 101 to 360 days per year. The majority of them start their contracts between January and July, while men begin their contract between March and August. The women's contracts end between September and November, and that is when they go back to Mexico; in contrast, the men return home between October and December.

Even though Mexican women workers are employed in a variety of food production processes, and have longer work trajectories than previously, and long-term employment contracts and constitute a stable group of workers, there have been no significant changes in wages for temporary farmworkers in the SAW Program. By 2008, for example, in Ontario their wage in Canadian dollars was $8.75 for fruits, vegetables, flowers, Christmas tree and tobacco; and in 2013, it was $10.25 per hour (Pujalte, 2008; HRSDC, 2013a). Many workers do not complain about the low or unpaid wages because they fear being deported, registered on a blacklist or dismissed from the SAW Program. In 2010, in Simcoe, Ontario, over 100 migrant farmworkers from Mexico, Jamaica, Trinidad and Barbados, employed at Ghesquiere Plants Ltd., faced an imminent repatriation (deportation) after staging a wildcat strike demanding thousands of dollars in unpaid wages (Ramsaroop, 2010). Only two provinces, Alberta and Saskatchewan, routinely track complaints made by migrant workers; Ontario is among the provinces that do not track complaint claims by type of claimant. In 2013–14, it saw 242 workplace complaints from migrant workers, just a few less than its yearly average of 245, and wages and overtime issues topped the list (Hildebrandt, 2014). Research has revealed that temporary foreign agricultural workers have become essential to the Canadian agriculture sector as fewer and fewer Canadian citizens and permanent residents are willing to accept the low wages and onerous working conditions characterizing that industry. It is likely that real wages paid to SAW Program workers will continue to decline as they have done over the past decade.

Age

To qualify for the SAW Program, workers must be 22 to 40 years old. Most of the workers (64 percent) come from poor, rural areas in Mexico. In 2001, 55 percent of migrant women were young workers aged 18 to 34. But this changed by 2005 when the largest group (49 percent) was 35 to 44 years old; and in 2010, 43.5 percent were in that age range. A reason for the change is that some of the women who entered the Program two decades ago now participate as middle-age workers and have a significant work history in Canada. The *average* age for female workers in 2010 was 38 years old. As a result, there are now two generations of mothers who are employed in the SAW Program. One worker described this phenomenon as follows:

> I have [for] 17 years [been] working in Canada. My youngest daughter also comes to Canada, but to Alberta. She has already [been] coming [for] four years to work on crop flowers that are sold to greenhouses [i.e., nurseries]. She is 30 years old. It's sad because we have [gone] almost a year without seeing each other.

Education Level

Participants in the Program must have at least three years of education and a maximum of 12 years. In 2010, 54.6 percent (339) of female workers had finished primary school and 42.8 percent (266) had completed junior high. However, an analysis of schooling by five-year periods reveals an increase in female workers with junior high school education from 25 percent (70 of 280) in 2001 to 42.8 percent (266 of 621) in 2010 and a decrease in those with only primary school education from 72.9 percent to 54.6 percent in the same time span. The reason for this shift could be the high rate of unemployment and demographic changes in rural Mexico, which have resulted in increased migration of young mothers who have a junior high school education.

Marital Status

The women workers tend to have children whether they are married or without a partner. Of the female Mexican migrants who worked in Canada in 2010, 45.7 percent (284 of 621) were single mothers, 27.7 percent (172) were separated from their husbands, 8.4 percent (52) were single, 6.1 percent (38) were widows, 5 percent (31) were divorced, 5.3 percent (33) were married and 1.8 percent (11) lived in common-law unions. To sum up, workers who were mothers with young children but who did not have a partner represented 86 percent of the total number of women (henceforth, I refer to this group as "working mothers with no partners"). In contrast, 80.6 percent of the SAW Program men were married.

Children

In 2009, 92.4 percent (563) of the mothers who were migrant workers had one to six children. Over the past decade, the number of women workers in the Program with four children has increased from 73 percent (207 of 280) in 2001 to 86.2 percent (525 of 609) in 2009, while the percentage of single women workers has fallen from 17.9 percent (50 of 280) in 2001 to 7.4 percent (45 of 609) in 2009. This means that the probability of single women obtaining employment through the Program has progressively shrunk. Data indicate that the SAW Program favors young mothers with no partners. In contrast, 80.6 percent of male workers are married and 84.9 percent (12,497 of 14,731) of the male workers have one to eight children.

Other Dependents

The women migrant workers live in extended family households in Mexico that include adult family members who may be financially dependent on them. The number of these relatives is relevant because it determines their eligibility for entering the SAW Program, and it serves as a political mechanism for insuring that the women workers return to Mexico at the end of their contract. Furthermore, it has implications for the caregiving arrangements that mothers are able to make when they migrate. In 2009, 99 percent

(603 of 609) of the migrants had one to six economic dependents in their families. Between 2001 and 2009, about 6 percent of the migrant workers had five to eight dependents. The interviews revealed that those dependents are usually an elderly parent, a disabled relative or an unemployed husband or brother.

As mentioned earlier, for two decades the Canadian policies governing temporary migration for female Mexican farmworkers have been based on employing primarily mothers (with no partners) who are heads of family with multiple dependents. When the women migrate under the SAW Program, their families and homes fragment. Each of the resulting transnational families has more than one residential and family reference (Glick-Schiller, Basch and Blanc-Szanton, 1992; Bernhard, Landolt and Goldring, 2009).

TRANSNATIONAL MOTHERHOOD AND FAMILY TRANSITIONS

Transnational Families

There is consensus in the literature that there exists a wide mosaic of family configurations before and after migration experiences and that the family group is no longer a homogeneous unit (Hondagneu-Sotelo and Avila, 1997; Fox, 2001; Mummert, 2005; Ariza and D'Aubeterre, 2009). Comparative analysis reveals the breadth and depth of variation in the types of families that daily negotiate the multiple border-crossing relationships (Parreñas, 2005; Landolt and Da, 2005; Pedone, 2007; Parella, 2007; Huang, Yeoh and Lam, 2008; Nyberg, 2008; Herrera, 2008; Ojeda, 2009; Puyana, Motoa and Viviel, 2009; Bernhard, Landolt and Goldring, 2009; Yépez, Ledo and Marzadro, 2011). Transnational family models are dynamic structures and entities that transgress the traditional family paradigm of the nuclear or extended family, which lives in one physical space. Such families occupy two or more physical spaces and various frontiers, and their adult members develop strategies to ensure the survival of their families (Parella and Cavalcanti, 2010). One or more family members live in two or more countries, but they do not separate themselves from their societies of origin. Rather, they live certain aspects of their lives simultaneously in their country of origin and the destination nation. Although the family members live part or most of the time apart from each other, they are able to create links that allow them to feel as though they are part of a family unit and manage their well-being as a collective (Bryceson and Vuorela, 2002). Such ties can be maintained, strengthened or weakened, to the extent that members change their loyalties or initiate new affective relationships that can alter the transnational family's sense of belonging (Parella, 2012). In other words, their management of affection and care links are affected by the migration experience (Skrbis, 2008). So, while transnational families act as supports and sources of identity, at the same time their structure produces ongoing risks and fragmentations (Herrera, 2005). Moreover, the social networks of migrants and their transnational families are not necessarily spaces of equality with respect to gender (Hondagneu-Sotelo, 2001).

Transnational Mothering: Theoretical Framework

The practice of motherhood entails caring for, raising and preparing children for adult life. It is not predetermined to take one unique form; rather, it is a historical, social and cultural construction (Pedone, 2010). In the study that is the basis of this chapter, transnational motherhood was conceptualized as the relationships constructed by female migrant workers under conditions of long-term geographical separation from their children and other family members, the transfer of reproductive work in home communities and long-distance child-care arrangements resulting in the creation of new challenges for and meanings of motherhood (Parella and Cavalcanti, 2010; Pedone, 2010). For mothers who are migrant workers, transnational mothering becomes a transitory mothering strategy, and it becomes part of the life cycle of the domestic group. But however transitory these modalities may be, their impact is strongly felt by the mothers and the children.

Since Hondagneu-Sotelo and Avila's 1997 article, "I'm here, but I'm there," a vast body of literature has been published on transnational motherhood, stimulating debates about the situation of the children left behind, the weight of gender ideologies in shaping conceptions of women migrant workers and their families, the agency of women migrants in reconstructing their family ties and the reshaping of the practice of mothering in the context of migration (Herrera, 2008). Theories and models that aim to explain transnational motherhood are many and varied. One key theoretical approach uses social reproduction in the context of globalization to posit that the withdrawal of the welfare state in the North and the crisis in the systems of social protection in southern countries have resulted in an expansion of transnational networks of child care among women migrants and, thus, revealed the inability of nation-states to guarantee economic and social rights for their citizens, especially women and their children (Bakker and Gil, 2003; Ehrenreich and Hochschild, 2004). Using that theoretical framework, this chapter understands the challenges of transnational mothering faced by the female workers in the SAW Program as the product of a state failure to ensure the socioeconomic rights of women and children.

Goals and Challenges of Transnational Mothering for Women in the SAW Program

If one starts from the idea that gender shapes migration patterns, processes and experiences for both men and women as argued by Hondagneu-Sotelo (1994), then one must analyze the implications of male workers leaving their children with their wives, while female workers do not have an analogous option. The situation is especially difficult for mothers with no partners, because women's decision to migrate depends on the arrangements they are able to negotiate with a female family member—usually a grandmother, aunt or the eldest daughter—who agrees to perform child-care functions and take on other domestic responsibilities while they are working abroad, as in the case of Mexican women migrants in North Carolina in the United States (Vidal, Tuñón, Rojas and Ayús, 2002). In the past two decades, the migration of Mexican mothers as farmworkers has caused multiple profound changes in the structure of their families. One implication is the greater child-care demands on the female family member left in charge.

In Mexico, any mother (whether she is single, separated, widowed, divorced, in a common-law union or married) who wants to participate in the SAW Program has to get approval from the Sistema Nacional para el Desarrollo Integral de la Familia (SNDIF) (the National System for Integral Family Development). The aim of the SNDIF is to strengthen and foster the well-being of Mexican families. The SNDIF program is gender-biased; fathers who migrate do not have to get SNDIF approval because it is assumed that their wives will be the caregivers for the children. Migrant workers who are mothers have to identify in writing for the SNDIF the person who will be responsible for their children while they are working in Canada. That caregiver must satisfy certain conditions, such as be financially stable, have a "good moral character" and have an "honest" job. The SNDIF assumes that the father will be the first in line of possible caregivers, followed by the maternal grandparents, the paternal grandparents, aunts and uncles. As many of the women who participate in the SAW Program are mothers with no partners, they usually give the responsibility for caregiving and other household activities to their mothers, sisters or older daughters. One of the interviewees commented that her children's maternal grandmother was rejected by SNDIF because of her age (she was 60 years old) and because she was unemployed. So, she named one of her sisters as the person who would care for her sons while she migrated for work to Canada as part of the SAW Program.

For the purposes of this project, families were considered transnational families if they had participated in the SAW Program for more than two years. The transnational family arrangements are the product of the structure and restrictions of four decades of migration policy governing the temporary workers program. Several of the interviewed mothers had been living in transnational families and practicing transnational motherhood in Canada and Mexico for over a decade, as the case of a single mother who works on a strawberry farm illustrates:

> *I'm a single mother, and I've been going to Canada to work for ten years, five years for five months contracts and the others for seven months. The first time I went, my son was five . . . now he's about to turn 16. My son and my mother are my dependents.* (Female worker, 38 years old, Irapuato, October 2009)

Migrant workers' homes generally have at least two sources of incomes per family. In contrast, one-parent households are at a substantial financial disadvantage, and most female Mexican migrant workers in the SAW Program head such households. The majority of the women are motivated by the hope of obtaining a better life for themselves and their families. The interviews identified that as a common theme. Some women told us that "we're here because of men, 'cause they never took responsibility for their children."

The SAW Program contracts for female migrant workers average 6.5 months per year, so the mothers engage in transnational mothering during that period. The experience of transnational mothering is heterogeneous; it depends on the number of years (two to fourteen) that women have worked in Canada and if they are mothers with no partners or married mothers with partners, and it also depends on the number of children they have and the life course of the family. The annual migration to Canada lightens the burden of reproductive work for mothers who are heads of households because they can temporarily delegate some of the responsibility for caregiving and other household activities to another woman in the family. But besides sending money for their children and other dependent relatives, they have to attend to certain child-care obligations from a distance. For example, over the phone the mothers give advice about food, school, illness, discipline issues and the wise use of remittances to the person who has assumed their child-care responsibilities. They also help their children do their homework and provide love and guidance in phone conversations.

As part of transnational mothering, many women migrant workers use their situation to motivate their children to do well in school:

> *I've been coming to work in Canada for ten seasons. [Working here] means things will be better for my children, both economically and socially; for me that means school. There has to be communication and trust, even though you're here and they're over there. We communicate by telephone once a week. We have to explain to them why we're here, that we expect them to respond by doing well at school. That's why we come, to make things better for them and do everything we can for them.* (Female worker interviewed in Niagara, July 2004)

However, once the women make the decision to work in Canada, leaving behind their families in order to provide for them, they struggle to fulfill their role as mothers in their new transnational life as long-distance mothers. They have to renegotiate their power and authority within their families. The status of mothers is eroded when they are reproached or rejected by relatives, children or others in their community. One of the mothers interviewed in Niagara in 2009 who was separated from her son for eight months at a time over a period of five seasons in the SAW Program told us about the negotiation strategy she employed to restore her maternal status, authority and loving relationship with her child. It allowed her to resolve tensions between her 13-year-old son and herself and the conflict between him, his grandmother and his schoolteacher that was caused by his misbehavior and poor school performance:

> *They [the children] get used to it a bit when I let them know that I go there only for four months and then I return. But my boy told me, "Don't go anymore. I need you here, I feel lonely." Sometimes I think a lot about that. He was in sixth grade when his teacher asked my mom to come to school [to talk to her]. My mother said to me, "You should talk to your child because he does not obey me." She said, "When I went [to your son's school], the teacher told me, 'I will refer you to a psychologist'." [Then] the child began to have other behavior[ial problems]. We had [conversations like], "Now I'm not your mom, I'm your friend." At that time I could not scold him. But when I said, "Now I am your mother, "then we talked and I [could] say, "This is wrong". So that way we got confidence. Also, then he asked me, "Tell me how is your job? Do you talk with another person other than my dad?" [Then] he told me, "Now I'm not your son, I'm your friend." Later he said to me, "Today is the day when you are my friend, because I'll tell you something." I listened to my child, but I had to stay calm, I had to endure.*

Mothers also face the possibility of being displaced by the new primary caregiver. There may be conflict between the mother and the oldest daughter who has assumed caregiving responsibility for the younger children's care. In some cases, as the children get older, they challenge their mother's authority. Long-distance motherhood includes discussions over the phone in which mothers have to try to regain their power and authority. An interviewed mother told us, "When I call I say something like, 'Put your brother on the phone, what?! How is it he is not there?! I will call you tomorrow and I want to find everyone there! I want all of you on the phone!' And when I hear them all, I feel that they are fine." However, there are some mothers that cannot negotiate these challenges and so they feel frustrated. One of the women who participated in the study explained it as follows: "Sometimes there are problems there [in Mexico], and I call by phone and they tell me 'this is happening and this and this . . .,' it makes me feel helpless because I'm not there."

Upon return to Mexico, they once again assume the responsibilities they had delegated to a female family member. The family conflicts that they face when they come home tend to be frequent, and usually as mothers and as women they are called upon to resolve them. As mentioned earlier, these conflicts have to do with maternal authority and the tensions generated by cross-border care work. The use of the remittances by the children can be a source of conflict, and there are many other problems that the mothers confront when they return home. The children no longer obey them or they are performing poorly in school or they do not want to study or their affection has shifted to the caregiver or the caregiver provided them with the physical necessities but did not give them moral guidance and discipline or the grandparents enforced very strict traditional rules and practices, such as spanking the children. In many cases, the women have to handle these problems as they look for employment.

The tension between the productive role and the reproductive responsibilities intensifies for female migrant workers in proportion to the length of their absence (Parella and Cavalcanti, 2010). For mothers, the principal contradiction or dilemma is that in order to maintain the family, they find themselves forced to leave it. It is generally acknowledged that this cultural mandate is imposed on fathers who are migrants, but it is rarely recognized in the case of migrant workers who are mothers. That failure is attributable to the persistence of the gender ideology that only men are the breadwinners.

A second dilemma for the mothers is their own and their children's experience of the physical and emotional temporal separation. The cost of family separation for the children is enormous. It can be a highly disruptive and traumatic experience for children, which they express in feelings of abandonment, loneliness, depression, sadness, confusion, guilt, insecurity, rebellion against maternal authority and misbehavior. For the children, the bonds of love, affection and care are ambivalent and conflicted because, after such a long separation, the family group changes, such that the mother's return constitutes a new rupture and beginning, one that takes place under changed circumstances. The separations experienced by the families and the temporary care arrangements can become permanent and in the process there is an erosion of maternal status.

Given the economic circumstances that require leaving their children and given cultural expectations about mothering, the women experience feelings of guilt, anxiety, hopelessness, stress, confusion, loneliness, depression, frustration and loss of identity. Feelings of depression and hopelessness may persist during the period of reunion with their children. The testimony of a single mother (who had worked for five seasons in Canada) who sees motherhood as a "parabola" is illuminating:

> *I'm there with them for four months, I enjoy it but sadness is always with me [because] I'm constantly thinking that I have to go back. When I get to the airport on my way back [to Canada], it's just cry, cry, and cry. It's their mother who calls them "my love," who gives them everything. She is their mother over the telephone for eight months and it is only four months [of the year] that she attends to them completely. I'm like a parabola. [My children say], "I have a mom. She's just over there [in Canada], it's not like she's dead, because maybe she is already dead and I will not see her again. But she is there [in Canada -virtually], but nothing else." I'm not a mother for eight months, until I return and attend to them in every way. I always carry this sense of guilt inside*

> me because I can't take care of them all year round, so when I do get back to Mexico, I devote myself to them totally. When I arrive [in Mexico], I'm mom once again [but] when I leave them with her [my sister], they're her responsibility. (Female worker, Niagara, October 2009)

The mothers experience strong feelings of guilt:

> What happens to us is that when we return to Mexico, we tell our children right to their faces that it's because of them that we go away to work in Canada. When we come back [to Mexico], we're always really happy, we bring presents and everything, but the magic soon wears off because we start to see, or find out, that they misbehaved, so we get really mad and might even give them a good spanking, we yell at them that it's their fault we're going to work in Canada. But what we're doing [to them] is wrong. (Female worker, Niagara, July 2004)

Working mothers also have to resolve the internal contradictions between their self-sacrifice and their ability to experience themselves as human beings beyond their role as mothers.

Nevertheless, transnational mothering is not simply synonymous with children's grief, and it is not necessarily destructive or traumatizing. There are many cases where life has improved despite the pain. But the current mainstream discourse about motherhood stigmatizes these women; it does not take into consideration the diversity and complexity of their lives.

Most of the women described the struggles and achievements of transnational motherhood through their experience as mothers with no partners. The majority of these workers were mothers and only a few did not have any offspring, but when they had to defend themselves, then as a group their response was: "We're all single mothers here, we all have children in Mexico, and none of us is alone." Framing themselves as single mothers allowed them to confront the stereotype of "bad mother" and close ranks in the face of work-related problems.

One of the stigmas the women often confront is that they are fracturing their families. They are blamed, and they may feel guilty for intrafamily violence, sexual abuse, alcoholism, violent behavior, school failure and teenage pregnancies:

> I'm a single mom. When I came to Canada the children I left behind were still really little, just five and eight [years old]. But I had to leave . . . because I didn't have anybody to support me. My son is a teenager now and I'm afraid that while I'm here in Canada he'll start doing drugs, drinking, drifting away from me, [and] that's the last thing I want. Sometimes I think maybe I won't stay away so long, [that] I'll ask for a contract for five months instead of eight, because I'm here for a long time, far away from my kids. I always think about my children,

how I leave them alone, that I'm away from them for a long time, and lots of things could happen that I might regret, and I don't want that. (Female worker interviewed in Leamington, 2003)

When they return home to Mexico, their children usually encourage them to keep working in Canada. Thus they simultaneously experience harmony and disharmony, as they oscillate between love and guilt and moments of acute loneliness and overwhelming joy:

When I talk with my children I feel encouraged [because] I know they're okay. Then I tell them I get pretty tired at work [and they say], "No, mom, you went all the way to Canada, so give it all you got, don't give up, we're here waiting for you, don't be sad, don't worry about us." But you feel bad anyway, I mean you've abandoned your children and up here you feel alone. [But] when you go back home, the children are waiting for you with their arms wide open. Getting home and seeing them makes us happy too. (Female worker, Niagara, July 2004)

In some cases, the women also support elderly parents, disabled or unemployed husbands or siblings. A woman interviewed as part of the study explained that her daughter supported her and her father:

I'm 68 and my husband is pretty old too, we're both dependent on our daughter, that's why she goes to work in Canada; she's been going for five years now. (Worker's mother, Irapuato, October 2009)

Other mothers whose lives have been transformed and whose families have been reshaped by the SAW Program are the wives of Mexican male migrant workers. In 2012, there were more than 17,600 Mexican men in the Program. The wives of those men almost always remain in Mexico where they take charge of childrearing, care of the rest of the family and manage the household. Some, however, eventually get fed up with their husband's prolonged absences and tell them: "You said you were only going [to Canada] to work for three years, but it's been fifteen, so you're not going back anymore. The next time you come home, you won't find me here." Other women have left their husbands to remarry, or live with a new partner and try to reconstruct their lives and families. There are also cases of wives who never see their husbands again because they die in accidents at work while in Canada. These are the grim family dramas that are part of the Program's legacy.

The experiences of fathers who are migrant farmworkers in Canada parallel those of male Mexican migrant workers in the United States. The fathers interviewed as part of the study reported losing parental authority and the patriarchal privileges they enjoyed in their homes in Mexico. The majority of the fathers spoke about the emotional costs of their absence. For example, those who had been in the SAW Program for more than five seasons said they missed not only the births of their children, but also watching them grow up. Some added that upon their return they find that their children no longer see them as fathers nor do they see the youngsters as their children.

CANADA'S POLICIES FOR MIGRANT FARMWORKERS: GENDERED AND EXPLOITIVE

This chapter analyzes the SAW Program in light of local, regional and global economic policies because that allows for the identification of temporary work regimes organized on the basis of gender, race, class, ethnicity, nationality and citizenship status (Collins, 1995; Ong, 1987; Fudge and McPhail, 2009). Like other highly competitive industries, Canada's agro-alimentary sector aims to maximize profits by strategically mobilizing federal and local institutions and policies.

The SAW Program employers use Canada's temporary work visa program to create a workforce that is segmented along cultural, linguistic and gender lines. Employers readily admit that these hiring strategies are designed to create divisions within the workforce that will reduce socialization among the laborers. They also enable them to control their workers and keep wages low. For that reason they hire Mexicans women for one season and Caribbean women for another, increasing or decreasing the number of women hired, replacing women with men or employing Mexican and Caribbean women workers on the same farm.

The treatment of women workers from Irapuato, Guanajuato, by Canadian strawberry-growing companies exemplifies the strategies used by the SAW Program employers to engage in the gendered exploitation of the migrant workers. Canadian strawberry producers use the temporary worker visa program to specifically request women workers from Irapuato, Guanajuato, to take advantage of the skill the women have developed over several generations for cultivating and processing the fruit. For example, in Quebec in 2000, 20 women were given jobs in a strawberry-producing company; one year later, the number of women hired at that same farm was doubled to 43 workers. In 2001, on Prince Edward Island, 25 women were hired by one farm because of their experience in strawberry processing (STPS, n.d.). Despite their experience and dexterity, the women were not paid as skilled workers, although their expertise enabled their employers to save a substantial amount in training costs. In fact, it is common practice for employers to ask migrant women workers to convince other experienced female strawberry workers in their hometown to sign up for the Program. That frees them from the need to train workers and strictly supervise them. As one producer remarked, "Mexican workers never tire and need no supervision; they know what they have to do."

Discrimination, exclusion and racism are a daily reality for the migrant workers. Canadians consider Mexican migrants desirable as workforce but not as persons. A Canadian citizen interviewed as part of the research project described that attitude:

> In Latin America, social injustice is exposed, but in Canada social injustice is hidden, the [migrant workers'] lack of knowledge of [the local] language is used to take advantage [of them]. They [Mexican migrants] come here to work. [Here] they are nobody, they are nothing; they have no rights. In Canada there is more vigilance than in the U.S. [because there] the illegal workers can hide more easily; just in California, there are many more Latin American people [than here] and . . . the region is so large [that] no one can watch them. [Here] since they are not numerous . . . , they cannot hide so easily. Here [it] is much easier to monitor them.

The SAW Program employers are obligated to cover certain costs for their employees, including housing costs (except in British Columbia where the temporary foreign workers are responsible for part of the hiring cost) and part of the round-trip airfare (full cost in British Columbia). They also have to ensure that the workers are covered by a health insurance plan and registered with the provincial workers' insurance scheme. Not all employers abide by the terms of the employment contract. Some employers fail to provide workers with compensation payments (for work-related illnesses or accidents) or purchase nonoccupational medical insurance coverage for them. Workers are not provided with safety equipment or protection when they use dangerous agrochemical substances that may have severe repercussions on their health. They are not offered the services of translators. Workers are not always paid on time, even though most migrants work long hours and earn 15 percent less than Canadian workers. These working conditions have been widely documented in several studies (see Basok, 2002; Binford, 2002; Preibisch, 2004; Verduzco and Lozano, 2004; Becerril, 2004; 2007; Fairey et al., 2008; UFCW, 2011).

Canada has legislation against job discrimination, and the SAW Program offers political mechanisms (i.e., employment contracts) that are designed to protect temporary migrant workers, but they are not consistently implemented. Migrant workers find it is very difficult to exercise any rights because of their temporary legal status; so, unlike workers who are Canadians, they have unequal access to resources. That makes them even more vulnerable to exploitation (Sharma, 2001; Gómez, 2011). The female Mexican workers who are mothers and the main providers for their families keenly 'feel' the impact of the SAW Program's gendered policies and practices. Their ability to access resources is more limited than their male peers because the contracts for female workers are shorter than those of male workers. A previous study (Becerril, 2011) found that in 2006 most women workers (77 percent) were hired for an average of

6.5 months, while male workers received the vast majority (98 percent) of the 8-month contracts. Thus men have more opportunities to earn more than the women; a fact that may account for the gendered difference in their remittances to their families in Mexico and the impact of those earnings on those households.

Often the women are labeled "bad mothers," stigmatized as sexually subservient to their male counterparts and subject to sexual harassment. Many employers implement curfews and place restrictions on female migrant workers' visitors, making it very difficult for the women to socialize or access outside resources. Pregnancy often results in repatriation.

Migrant workers are generally not protected by Canadian labor regulation. They pay into the pension plan yet receive no benefits. They pay the premium for unemployment insurance but they are not eligible to receive the benefits. Recently things have taken a turn for the worse. While they were not explicitly included in the *Employment Insurance Parental Benefits* program until December 2012, the SAW Program workers were eligible for the benefits if they had a child during their employment contract period. They could receive benefits for up to 35 weeks; the length of the SAW Program contract determined that limit (Keung, 2012). In December 2012, Prime Minister Harper's conservative government made them ineligible for the unemployment insurance program's special parental, maternal and compassionate benefits, even though on an annual basis foreign migrant workers contribute an estimated $3.4 million every year to the Canadian Employment Insurance system (Keung, 2012). This policy change is not gender neutral. It has particular significance for mothers who had a SAW Program contract when their child was born. It is evident that Canada has failed to live up to its commitment to gender equality.

Discriminatory policies and practices are not consistent with the Canadian values established in the Canadian Constitution of Laws and Freedoms. They violate the labor and human rights of temporary foreign workers. The state is complicit in these violations as it continues to ignore the dangerous work and poor housing conditions that many of the workers endure. For instance, many employers house their workers in small rooms that serve as dormitories or in run-down trailers, but government inspection of those living quarters is sporadic at best. One study participant described her living conditions in Canada as follows:

> *We are as [if] in a jail the way that our beds are placed as bunk beds, [the] beds are in a row and in the middle of the room are closets, all continuous . . . here there are one, and further there is another one, and so on. Beds are too close. What divides our spaces are our curtains that we put around our bed.*

The failure of the state to respect the human and labor rights of the workers is not an unintentional oversight. There is a strong link between Canadian policies governing temporary labor migration and the state's goal of growing the economy (Gómez, 2011).

Today, many of the workers in the SAW Program live and work longer in Canada than in their nation of origin. They make important contributions to the economy and facilitate the maximization of profits in key sectors of the economy by performing jobs for low wages under precarious conditions. However, like their male counterparts in the SAW Program, the women workers are not eligible to apply for Canadian permanent residency and, thus, citizenship. Their temporary status and noneligibility for permanent residency renders them dependent on their employer such that they need to be "confirmed" as employees every season to continue working in Canada. That makes them particularly vulnerable to exploitation.

Mexico, too, in many cases has failed to protect or defend the rights of its citizens who are migrant workers, who are mothers. For instance, it has not insisted on better work conditions for Mexican female farmworkers in Canada. In part, this is attributable to the assumption that the Program is for male workers or that "because there is only a small number of female workers in the Program, it is not important to pay attention to their situation." Given the prospect of unemployment in Mexico, there is a strong competition among female migrants to remain in the SAW Program. The women do not report their poor working conditions because of the fear of losing their jobs and, thus, their family's primary income. These then are some of the direct pernicious ramifications of Canada's immigration and labor policies for migrant farmworkers from poorer countries.

CONCLUSION

Both Canada and Mexico need to make policy changes to improve the work and life conditions of Mexican female migrant farmworkers in the SAW Program. To address the problems faced by them and their families, the Canadian government should develop relationships between institutions at different levels (for example, federal and provincial governments, municipalities, the Foreign Agricultural Resource Management Services (FARMS), the Fondation des Entreprises en Recrutement de Main-d'œuvre agricole Étrangère (FERME),[3] churches and migrant-serving organizations). Canada should also create migration policies and programs that allow the mothers in the SAW Program to easily maintain frequent contact with their children. It should also provide training at different institutional levels about the situation of migrant women workers, specifically, the barriers they face in accessing public health care, the risks they endure at work and the violations of their rights. It should enforce the existing SAW Program employment standards, and it should consider ways for improving their living and working conditions on Canadian farms. It should review the farm labor contracting system and develop new protections for mothers with no partners and it should designate funding for service-providers so that they can assist migrant mothers whose young children are in Mexico. Moreover, Canada should ratify the United Nations' Convention on the Protection of the Rights of All Migrant Workers and Members of Their Families.

Mexico has also failed these women and their children. It needs to protect its female citizens who are part of the SAW Program; it should insist on work contracts and employment practices that are fair and responsive to the needs of that population. It should provide medical services, including psychological care to mothers who are migrant workers and their young children in Mexico. It should also fund public campaigns and awareness workshops in Mexico and Canada about the impact of family separation. These are crucial steps that both nations—Mexico and Canada—must take if the SAW Program workers who are mothers and their children are to be treated fairly.

NOTES

1. This chapter is based on a tri-national collective research project titled, "Transnational Work, Gendered Labor Policies and Family Organization: Temporary Mexican Female Transmigrants to the United States and Canada." The multidisciplinary group was composed of Dr. Kerry Preibisch (University of Guelph, Canada), Dr. David Griffith and Dr. Ricardo Contreras (East University, Carolina, United States), Dr. Elizabeth Juárez and Dr. Ofelia Becerril (El Colegio de Michoacán, México). The study was supported by PIERAN at El Colegio de México. Also, it presents the results of fieldwork conducted in Leamington and Niagara, Ontario, in summer 2009, financed by Canada-Latin America-Caribbean Awards from the International Council for Canadian Studies (ICCS).
2. The employment contract signed by Mexican migrants and their Canadian employers establishes a nominal workers system in which the employer agrees that from the eighth working day the employee shall be considered a "nominal worker." The contract also states that if the employee has been selected by name by the employer, in case of repatriation, the total cost will be paid by the employer. In case a nominal worker is unavailable to travel from Mexico, the employer agrees to accept a substitute worker (Trejo and Alvarez, 2007; HRSDC, 2013b). However, in reality, "nominal workers" are workers who have a history of working with a particular employer who requests their return because of their high level of productivity.
3. FARMS and FERME are the private sector entities authorized by Human Resources Skills Development Canada (HRSDC) to process the requests for Caribbean and Mexican workers for the SAW Program.

REFERENCES

Ariza, M. and D´Aubeterre, M.E., 2009. Contigo en la distancia . . . Dimesiones de laconyugalidad en migrantes mexicanos internos e internacionales. In: C. Rabell, coord., ed. 2009.*Tramas familiares en el México contemporáneo*. Estado

de México, México: Universidad Nacional Autónoma de México, El Colegio de México, pp.353–91.
Bakker, I. and Gill S., 2003. *Power, production and social reproduction*. London: Palgrave.
Basok, T., 2002. *Tortillas and tomatoes: Transmigrant Mexican harvesters in Canada*. Montreal and Kingston: McGill-Queens University Press.
Becerril, O., 2004. Políticas laborales de género, trabajo transnacional y experiencias vividas: Trabajadores y trabajadoras agrícolas migrantes en Canadá. *Antropología. Boletín Oficial delINAH*, 74 (abril/junio), pp.96–111.
Becerril, O., 2007. Transnational work and labour politics of gender: A study of male and female Mexican migrant farm workers in Canada. In: L. Goldring and S. Krishnamurti, eds., 2007. *Organizing the transnational: Labour, politics, and social change*. Canada: UBC Press, pp.228–48.
Becerril, O., 2011. *¡Soy un Tunante, cual loco caminante! Transmigrantes mexicanos a Canadácontendiendo el género, la sexualidad y la identidad*. Zamora, Michoacán: El Colegio deMichoacán.
Bernhard, J. K., Landolt, P. and Goldring, L., 2009. Transnationalizing families: Canadian immigration policy and the spatial fragmentation of care-giving among Latin American newcomers. *International Migration*, 47(2), pp.3–31.
Binford, L., 2002. Social and economic contradictions of rural migrant contract labor between Tlaxcala, Mexico and Canada. *Culture and Agriculture*, 24(2), pp.1–19.
Bryceson, D. and Vuorela, U., eds., 2002. *The transnational family: New European frontiers and global networks*. Oxford: Berg.
Citizenship and Immigration Canada (CIC), 2010. *Canada facts and figures. Immigrant overview permanent and temporary residents*. [pdf] Otawa: CIC. Available at: < http://www.cic.gc.ca/english/pdf/research-stats/facts2010.pdf> [Accessed 4 August 2011].
Collins, J. I., 1995. Transnational labor process and gender relations: Women in fruit and vegetable production in Chile, Brazil and México. *Journal of Latin American Anthropology*, 1(1), pp.178–99.
Ehrenreich, B. and Hochschild, A.R., 2004. *Global woman: Nannies, maids and sex workers in the new economy*. New York: Henry Holt and Company, LLC.
Fairey, D., et al., 2008. Cultivating farmworker rights: Ending the exploitation of immigrant and migrant farm workers in BC. *An economic security project report*. Vancouver: Canadian Centre for Policy Alternatives BC Office, Justicia for Migrant Workers, Progressive Intercultural Community Service, BC Federation of Labour. [pdf] 18 June. Available at: <http://www.policyalternatives.ca/sites/default/files/uploads/publications/BC_Office_Pubs/bc_008/bc_farmworkers_full.pdf. [Accessed 26 May 2011].
Fox, B. and Luxton, M., 2001. Conceptualizing family. In: B. Fox, ed. 2001. *Family patterns, gender relations*. Dont Mills, Ontario: Oxford University Press, pp.22–33.
Fudge, J. and McPhail, F., 2009. The temporary foreign worker program in Canada: Low-skilled workers as an extreme form of flexible labour. *Comparative Labor Law and Policy Journal*, 31, pp.101–39.
Georges, E., 1992. Gender, class, and migration in the Dominican Republic: Women's experiences in a transnational community. In: N. Glick-Schiller, L. Basch and C. Blanc-Szanton, eds. 1992. *Toward a transnational perspective on migration: Race, class, ethnicity and nationalism reconsidered*. New York: Annals of the New York Academy of Sciences, pp.81–99.
Glick-Schiller, N., Basch L. and Blanc-Szanton, C., 1992. Transnationalism: A new analytic framework for understanding migration, toward a transnational

perspective on migration. In: N. Glick-Schiller, L. Basch and C. Blanc-Szanton, eds. *Toward a transnational perspective on migration: Race, class, ethnicity and nationalism reconsidered.* New York: Annals of the New York Academy of Sciences, pp.1–24.

Goldring, L., 1992. La migración México-EUA y la transnacionalización del espacio político y social: perspectivas desde el México rural. *Estudios sociológicos*, X(29), pp.315–40.

Gómez, T., 2011. Low skill temporary work and non-access to permanent residence. *FOCAL*, Canadian International Development Agency. [pdf] June. Available at: <http://www.focal.ca/images/stories/Gomez_Labour_Mobility_Low-skill_workers_and_nonaccess_to_permanent_residency_e.pdf> [Accessed 8 November 2011].

Herrera, G., 2005. Mujeres ecuatorianas en las cadenas globales del cuidado. In: G. Herrera, C. Carrillo and A. Torres, eds. 2005. *La Migración ecuatoriana. Transnacionalismo redes eidentidades.* Quito: FLACSO Sede Ecuador-Plan Migración, Comunicación y Desarrollo, pp.281–303.

Herrera, G., 2008. Políticas migratorias y familias transnacionales. In: G.. Herrera and J. Ramírez, eds. 2008. *América Latina migrante: Estado, familias, identidades.* Quito: FLACSO, Sede Ecuador, Ministerio de Cultura del Ecuador, pp.71–86.

Hildebrandt, A., 2014. Few provinces track complaints by temporary foreign workers. Only three provinces record how often vulnerable employees file complaints. *CBC News Canada*, [online] 27 May. Available at: <http://www.cbc.ca/news/canada/few-provinces-track-complaints-bytemporary-foreign-workers-1.2648734> [Accessed 11 August 2014].

Hondagneu-Sotelo, P., 1994. *Gendered transitions: Mexican experiences of immigration.* Berkerley and Los Angeles: University of California Press.

Hondagneu-Sotelo, P. and Avila, E., 1997. 'I'm here, but I'm there': The meanings of Latina transnational motherhood. *Gender and Society*, 11(5), pp.548–71.

Hondagneu-Sotelo, P., 2001. *Doméstica: Immigrant workers cleaning and caring in the shadows of affluence.* Berkeley: University of California Press.

Huang, S., Yeoh, B. and Lam T., 2008. Asian transnational families in transition: The liminality of simultaneity. *International Migration*, 46(4), pp.3–13.

Human Resources and Skills Development Canada (HRSDC). Employment and Social Development Canada. Government of Canada. 2010. Temporary Foreign Worker Program. Seasonal Agricultural Worker Program. Available at: <http://www.esdc.gc.ca/eng/jobs/foreign_workers/lmo_statistics/annual-agriculture.shtml> [Accessed 14 January 2014].

Human Resources and Skills Development Canada (HRSDC). Employment and Social Development Canada. Government of Canada. Wages by commodity. Agricultural Stream and the Seasonal Agricultural Worker Program. 2013a. Available at: <http://www.esdc.gc.ca/eng/jobs/foreign_workers/agriculture/commodities.shtml#h2.2> [Accessed 14 November 2013].

Human Resources and Skills Development Canada (HRSDC). Employment and Social Development Canada. Government of Canada. 2013b. Agreement for the Employment in Canada of Seasonal Agricultural Workers from Mexico - 2013. Available at: <http://www.esdc.gc.ca/eng/jobs/foreign_workers/agriculture/seasonal/sawpmc2013.shtml> [Accessed 14 January 2014].

Kueng, N., 2012. Seasonal migrant workers stripped of parental benefits. *Thestar.com*, [online] 11 December. Available at: <http://www.thestar.com/news/canada/2012/12/11/seasonal_migrant_workers_stripped_of_paretal_benefits.html> [Accessed 19 June 2013]

Landolt, P. and Da, W.W., 2005. The spatially ruptured practices of transnational migrant families: Lessons from the case of El Salvador and the People's Republic of China. *Current Sociology*, 53(4), pp.625–53.

Mummert, G., 2005. Transnational parenting in Mexican migrant communities: Redefining fatherhood, motherhood and caregiving. *The Mexican International*

Family Strengths Conference, Cuernavaca. Morelos, Mexico 1–3 June 2005. [pdf] Available at: <http://www.ciesas.edu.mx/proyectos/mifs2005/papers/03/gail_mummert.pdf> [Accessed 9 March 2008].
Nyberg, N., 2008. La familia transnacional de latinoamericanos⁄as en Europa. In: Grupo Interdisciplinario de Investigador@s Migrantes, coord. *Familias, niños, niñas, y jóvenes migrantes*. 2010. Madrid: IEPALA, La Casa Encendida, pp.259–79.
Ojeda, N., 2009. Reflections on Mexico-US: Transborder and transnational families. *Frontera Norte*, 20(42), pp.7–30.
Ong, A., 1987. The gender and labor politics of postmodernity. *Annual Review of Anthropology*, 20, pp.279–309.
Parella, S., 2007. Los vínculos afectivos y de cuidado en las familias transnacionales. Migrantesecuatorianos y peruanos en España. *Migraciones Internacionales*, 4(2), pp.151–88.
Parella, S., 2012. Familia transnacional y redefinición de los roles de género. El caso de lamigración boliviana en España. *Papers*, 97(3), pp.661–84.
Parella, S. and Cavalcanti, L., 2010. Dinámicas familiares transnacionales y migración femenina: Una exploración del contexto migratorio boliviano en España. In: Grupo Interdisciplinario de Investigador@s Migrantes, coord. *Familias, niños, niñas, y jóvenes migrantes*. 2010. Madrid: IEPALA, La Casa Encendida, pp.93–106.
Parreñas, R. S., 2005. *Children of global migration: Transnational families and gendered woes*. Stanford: Stanford University Press.
Pedone, C., 2007. Familias transnacionales ecuatorianas: Estrategias productivas y reproductivas. In: V. Bretón, F. García, A. Jové, M.J. Vilalta, eds. 2007. *Ciudadanía y exclusión: Ecuador y España frente al espejo*. Madrid: Catarara, pp.251–78.
Pedone, C., 2010. Introducción. Más allá de los estereotipos: Desafíos en torno al estudio de las familias migrantes. In: Grupo Interdisciplinario de Investigador@s Migrantes, coord. *Familias, niños, niñas, y jóvenes migrantes*. 2010. Madrid: IEPALA, La Casa Encendida, pp.11–16.
Pessar, P., 1999. Engendering migration studies. *American Behavioral Scientist*, 42(3), pp.577–600.
Preibisch, K., 2004. Migrant agricultural workers and processes of social inclusion in rural Canada: Encuentros and desencuentros. *Canadian Journal of Latin American and Caribbean Studies* 29(57–58), pp.203–39.
Pujalte, C., 2008. Programa de Trabajadores Agrícolas Temporales México-Canadá. Consul de México en Toronto, Secretaría de Relaciones Exteriores. Monterrey, México: Centro de Diálogoy Análisis sobre América del Norte, Tecnológico de Monterrey. [online] Available at: <http://cedan.org.mx/sites/default/files/Pujalte_Programa_de_Trabajadores_Agricolas_Temporaes_0.pdf]> [Accessed 16 October 2011].
Puyana, Y., Motoa, A. and Viviel, A., 2009. *Entre aquí y allá: Las familias colombianas transnacionales*. Unión Europea, Universidad Nacional de Colombia, Fundación Esperanza. Colombia: Bogotá.
Ramsaroop, C., 2010. Migrant farm workers stage wildcat strike to demand thousands of dollars in unpaid wages: Employer responds with deportation. Justicia for Migrant Workers (J4MW). [online] Toronto: Ontario. Available at: <www.justicia4migrantworkers.org/index_archive.htm> [Accessed 7 March 2011].
Rivera, L., 2008. Los trayectos internos e internacionales en la dinámica de formación decircuitos migratorios transnacionales. In: G. Herrera and J. Ramírez, eds., 2008. *América Latina migrante: Estado, familias, identidades*. Quito: FLACSO—Sede Ecuador, Ministerio de Cultura del Ecuador, pp.89–116.
Rouse, R., 1988. *Mexican migration to the United States: Family relations in the development of a transnational migrant circuit*. Ph.D. Stanford University.

Secretaría del Trabajo y Previsión Social (STPS). (n.d.). Informe de evaluación de las temporadas 1998- 2004 y datos de 2000-2012. Programa de Trabajadores Agrícolas Temporales Mexicanos a Canadá. Distrito Federal, México: STPS. [online] Available at: <http://www.stps.gob.mx/bp/secciones/conoce/areas_atencion/areas_atencion/servicio_empleo/trabajadores_agricolas.html> [Accessed 12 May 2013].

Sharma, N., 2001. On being not Canadian: The social organization of 'migrant workers' in Canada. *Canadian Review of Sociology and Anthropology*, 38(4), pp.415–39.

Skrbis, Z., 2008. Transnational Families: Theorising migration, emotions and belonging. *Journal of Intercultural Studies*, 29(3), pp.231–46.

Trejo, E. and Alvarez, M., 2007. Programa de trabajadores agrícolas temporales México Canadá, Centro de Documentación, Información y Análisis, Dirección de Servicios de Investigación y Análisis, Subdirección de Política Exterior. Distrito Federal, México: Cámara de Diputados, LX Legislatura. [pdf] Available at: <http://www.diputados.gob.mx/sedia/sia/spe/SPE-ISS-CI-15-07.pdf> [Accessed 23 October 2010].

United Food and Commercial Workers, Canada (UFCW). 2011. 2010–2011 National reports on the status of migrant farm workers in Canada. [pdf] Toronto, Canada: UFCW, Agriculture Workers Alliance. Available at: <http://www.ufcw.ca/templates/ufcwcanada/images/awa/publications/UFCW Status_of_MF_Workers_2010-2011_EN.pdf> [Accessed 5 November 2012].

Verduzco, G. and Lozano, M.I., 2004. *Mexican workers' participation in CSAWP and development consequences in the workers' rural home communities*. Ottawa: North-South Institute.

Vidal, L., Tuñón, E., Rojas, M. and Ayús, R., 2002. De paraíso a Carolina del Norte. Redes de apoyo y percepciones de la migración a Estados Unidos de mujeres tabasqueñas despulpadorasde jaiba. *Revista Migraciones Internacionales*, 1(2), pp.29–62.

Yépez, I., Ledo, C. and Marzadro, M., 2011. Las cadenas que encadenan al cuidado. Migración femenina y reconfiguraciones familiares en Cochabamba. In: FLACSO (Facultad Latino americana de Ciencias Sociales sede Ecuador), *IV Congreso de la Red Internacional de Migración y Desarrollo*. Quito, Ecuador 18–20 May 2011. Quito: FLACSO.

Part IV
Care for Care Workers

8 "A Place to Call Home"
The Catholic Church and Female Foreign Domestic Workers in Singapore

Theresa Devasahayam

INTRODUCTION

In Southeast Asia, transnational migration for work has been spurred by globalization as countries become increasingly economically interlocked with each other. The experiences of migrant workers have been highly variegated, with low-skilled workers faring poorly. The lack of protective measures for low-skilled workers in the labor sending and receiving countries makes them particularly vulnerable to labor abuse. The vast majority of those migrant workers are caught in webs of asymmetrical relationships of power in various stages of the migration process so that their experiences are often shaped by marginality (Parrañes, 2008; Oishi, 2005; Yeoh et al., 2004). Moreover, from the standpoint of this group, the migration process often entails experiences of disruption, conflict, tension and pain because of the physical separation from their home and family (Parrañes, 2005; Sobritchea, 2007; Devasahayam and Yeoh, 2007; Chambers, 1994) and, in many instances, those experiences are made worse by the low-status work they perform in the destination country.

The theorizing in the migration literature about such cases conceptualizes 'location' as infused by the dichotomies of 'here' and 'there' and problematizes it as the root of the tensions and disruptions that migrants feel. The assumption is that migrants identify primarily with their homeland and that they suffer a disruption in their lives as a result of moving from one locale to another (Braidotti, 1994; Yeoh and Huang, 2000; Hondagneu-Sotelo and Avila, 1997). It is also assumed that this disruption is especially heightened among those who occupy temporary and marginal spaces in the destination nations that are not welcoming to them. Yet 'home' is never a distinct category from 'migration,' as compellingly argued by Ahmed, Castañeda, Fortier and Sheller (2004). They contend that home and migration should be understood as "specific processes, modes and materialities of uprooting and regroundings, in different contexts and on different scales" and as "the workings of institutional structures" (Ahmed, Castañeda, Fortier and Sheller, 2004, p.2).

Drawing inspiration from that thesis, this chapter discusses the efforts of the Roman Catholic Church in Singapore to create a 'home' for low-skilled women migrants who are employed in the domestic work sector and, thus, mediate their experience of 'uprooting' and 'regrounding.' To that end, the Church has established the Archdiocesan Commission for the Pastoral Care of Migrants & Itinerant People (ACMI), a nongovernment organization (NGO). The aims of this chapter are twofold. First, it interrogates the efforts of the ACMI to fill a moral gap in the political landscape by attempting to provide a 'home' to low-skilled migrant workers. Second, it discusses women migrant workers' perceptions of and experiences with the efforts of the Church to create a 'home' for them.

The Church sees itself as playing a moral role when it responds to the social needs of migrants, especially those who take on low-paid and low-status employment in Singapore. Its stance is based on a commitment to social justice and social inclusiveness, coupled with the ideological position of doing what is right for the greater good of society, including those persons who occupy marginal positions. Moreover, ACMI's goal of being "family to migrants" aims at fostering a sense of 'belonging' among the migrant women who are separated from their families (Archdiocesan Commission for the Pastoral Care of Migrants & Itinerant People, 2012a), because Singapore's labor laws prohibit low-skilled migrants from bringing their families with them (Devasahayam, 2010; Abdul Rahman, 2005). Thus, while the state considers low-skilled migrant workers to be a temporary feature of the labor structure of the country (Singapore has created a myriad of labor rules and policies that have stripped this group of their rights to basic entitlements; the aim is to reinforce their sense of detachment from the nation-state and undermine their attachment to it), the Church regards all social relationships within the context of 'family' and seeks to create a home for them, irrespective of their nationality, ethnicity and socio-economic class. One way in which the Church aims to be a 'home' to the migrant women workers is through the ACMI programs it hosts at its training Center. But the research project that is the basis of this chapter revealed that for the women having a sense of belonging at the Center seemed not to have as much importance as the practical gains from learning new skills through its classes.

The 2012 research project involved a survey of 251 migrant women who were participants in the ACMI programs. The findings were later confirmed in face-to-face interviews conducted by the author of this chapter. The survey, consisting primarily of closed-ended questions and a handful of open-ended questions, was designed by the author in conjunction with a research associate working at the Institute of Southeast Asian Studies. The survey was then distributed by the staff of ACMI on several Sundays when the women attended the programs at the Center. In 2013, the author decided to supplement the surveys with face-to-face interviews with ten migrant women attending ACMI's programs. Volunteers at the Center were also interviewed with the aim of gaining a larger picture of the Center's operations.

THE SOCIALLY CONSCIOUS CATHOLIC CHURCH

Religion and morality are often thought to be closely intertwined and almost inseparable (Reynolds and Tanner, 1995). Being a moral agent is tied to one's relationships with other people. In the case of the Catholic Church, being socially conscious is as important as practicing one's faith (Pontifical Council for Justice and Peace, 2004). The teachings of the Church direct its followers to look to a higher being, and Catholics are also called to reach out to others around them. Thus, beyond having faith, the members of the Church are asked to act on their faith. As doing what is right for the greater good of individuals in society is fundamental to the Church's teaching, it is committed to social justice. According to the Church's perspective, it is about giving to each person what is due to him or her as a person in all his or her fullness as a social being since she/he is made in the image of God. The social teachings of the Church are also concerned with the preservation of the dignity of persons and facilitating their growth and development (Pontifical Council for Justice and Peace, 2004).

The Church believes that it has a duty to respect the dignity of every person, including migrants. In striving "to fulfil the duties inherent in her [the Church's] mandate of salvation for all mankind, a mandate entrusted to her by Christ[,] . . . [the Church] has been especially careful to provide all possible spiritual care for pilgrims, aliens, exiles and migrants of every kind" (Apostolic Constitution of Pius XII, 1952, p.2). The position of the Church is encapsulated in the following phrase: "In the foreigner a Christian sees not simply a neighbour, but the face of Christ Himself, who was born in a manger and fled into Egypt, where he was a foreigner, summing up and repeating in His own life the basic experience of His people" (cf. Mt 2 v.13ff). It is this phrase which provides the theological grounds that compel the Church to reach out to migrants, a teaching spelled out in the Pontifical Council's Instruction called "Erga migrantes caritas Christi" (The love of Christ towards migrants) (Pontifical Council for the Pastoral Care of Migrants and Itinerant People, 2004, p.11).

In Singapore, historically and in recent years, the Catholic Church has acted on its faith in a myriad of ways. Notable among its efforts in reaching out to the poor, for example, is the Catholic Welfare Services. Since its inception in 1959, this "action arm" of the Church has been "initiating, assisting, coordinating and carrying out social services to alleviate poverty and distress among the people of Singapore, regardless of race or creed" (Catholic Welfare Services, 2010). The Church has also been actively meeting the needs of the poor through the Society of St. Vincent de Paul, which has branches in all the parishes[1] to attend to the needs of the poor in those communities by providing them with financial assistance and food rations (Caritas Singapore Community Council, n.d.).

Migrant workers in Singapore have also been the beneficiaries of the skills training programs of the Church. Its efforts on behalf of the migrants predate the establishment of the ACMI by several decades. In the late 1970s, at the local parish level, the Church had responded to the needs of Filipina women who had come to work in Singapore as domestic workers. The common problems that the women encountered were physical and psychological abuse by their employers, nonpayment of salary, poor living and working conditions and insufficient time for rest (Archdiocesan Commission for the Pastoral Care of Migrants & Itinerant People, 2012b). For this group, "adjusting to a new environment" proved to be a "traumatic experience" and "the Catholic Church felt an obligation to reach out to them" as it saw them as a " 'people of God on the move,' meriting justice and compassion" (Wijeysingha, 2006, p.179). The 1980s saw a greater influx of foreign workers from Thailand, Bangladesh, India and Indonesia as Singapore turned to them as labor source countries. It was then that the Catholic Young Christian Workers movement was formed with the intention of ensuring the well-being of migrant workers (Wijeysingha, 2006). In particular, the movement sought to help workers forge bonds among themselves, listen to each other and to recognize their dignity and worth as they were away from their families and in a nation that marginalized them. It was also at that time that the Catholic Welfare Center for Foreign Workers in Geylang was established. Its members were a group of Catholic Singaporeans who were inspired by Development Theology that was gaining momentum in Roman Catholic churches all over the world, following the Second Vatican Council. In a nutshell, Development Theology "was directed at championing the cause of people in all situations of life and the creation of a more just society" (Wijeysingha, 2006, p.196). Unlike the Catholic Young Christian Workers movement, social workers and lay workers attached to the Catholic Welfare Center aggressively lobbied for higher wages, social security benefits, job security and better working conditions for foreign workers in Singapore (Mauzy and Milne, 2002). However, in May 1987, things started to go downhill when the state of Singapore accused the Center of being "a cover for political agitation" (Haas, 1989, p.59; Daniel, 1987) and arrested 22 Center workers under the Internal Security Act. They were detained without a trial (Rodan, 2004, p.20), an event which subsequently prompted the closure of the Center.

Following that incident, the Church did not advocate for migrant workers' issues again until 1995 when Flor Contemplacion, a Filipina domestic worker charged with murdering a Singaporean child and a fellow domestic worker, was executed (Archdiocesan Commission for the Pastoral Care of Migrants & Itinerant People, 2012b). Although the Church had become cautious about intervening in migrant workers' issues, it did not completely retreat from trying to meet their needs. Along with hosting mass in languages such as Bahasa Indonesia and Tagalog, the Church gave help to domestic workers who had problems with their employers (and who were forced to 'runaway' in an attempt to seek a solution) by putting them in touch with their embassies (Archdiocesan Commission for the Pastoral Care of Migrants & Itinerant People, 2012b). It was also during this time that a priest, Father Andy Altamirano from the Congregation of the Immaculate Heart of Mary, established a support group for Filipina domestic workers and other Catholic migrant communities. Under his leadership, ACMI was established in June 1998. It had been decided by the Catholic Archdiocese that given the growing number of foreign workers, a specialized migrant ministry at the diocesan level would be more effective for the purposes of helping migrant workers than individual parishes working on their own (Archdiocesan Commission for the Pastoral Care of Migrants & Itinerant People, 2012b). From its inception, ACMI did not restrict its activities and services to Catholics; it reached out to all migrants regardless of religion and nationality. Increasing numbers of Indonesian women and men from Bangladesh were coming to Singapore to work as domestic workers and construction workers, respectively. Also by this time, the ruling party, the People's Action Party, began to set parameters on the work of what it called a 'civic society.' Civic organizations were expected to know their limits and not overstep their mandate but "work . . . together with a responsible Government" (Worthington, 2003, p.7). Given that the Church had been accused by the Singapore government of being a member of a Marxist plot, ACMI's work tended to be largely focused on activities aimed at meeting the needs of migrant workers, while partnering with the "government to address the question of individual treatment of foreign workers by employers, rather than dealing with broader questions of labor laws, immigration laws, or citizenship rights" (Archdiocesan Commission for the Pastoral Care of Migrants & Itinerant People, 2012b).

As the Singapore state had set strict limits on the activities of civic organizations, ACMI saw and still sees itself and functions as a religion-based organization with a charitable- and service-oriented focus. It thus fits squarely in the category of a local NGO. In Singapore, the state encourages civic society groups to step in and provide social and welfare services to the community, reinforcing the ideology of self-reliance and the values that were outlined in the government's Shared Values White Paper. According to that policy document, Singapore "aim[s] to create a citizenry that is self-reliant, productive and independent" (Kuah-Pearce, 2008, p.173). In this way, a strategic partnership exists between the state and certain civic groups in the delivery of social services to the people of Singapore. However, unlike many other charitable organizations, which are not-for-profit and whose services benefit the community, ACMI does not receive any funding from the Singapore government and, therefore, is independent of the state. Instead it is funded only by the Caritas Singapore Community Council, the official social and community arm of the Catholic Church in Singapore, which is also a member of Caritas Internationalis, a global federation of 165 humanitarian organizations (Caritas Singapore Community Council, 2013).

HOW ACMI REACHES OUT TO MIGRANTS

Headed by a Filipino priest as the Spiritual Director and managed mostly by Singaporeans, ACMI has a wide-ranging lineup of programs, assisting over 3,000 migrants and feeding more than 143,000 migrant workers (Archdiocesan Commission for the Pastoral Care of Migrants & Itinerant People, 2012c). Under the Commission established in 1998, the Befrienders and the Bread Basket programs were started. The Befrienders program reaches out to migrants in hospitals and migrants who may be facing problems and are unable to leave their homes, and the Bread Basket program distributes basic provisions and food in the dormitories housing migrant workers (although these workers may have their own food as well as cooking facilities). The aim is to express appreciation for the contributions of foreign workers to Singapore's development. The ACMI also renders assistance to migrant workers facing work-related or social problems by connecting them to members of the Catholic Lawyers Guild and other volunteer lawyers who are willing to provide legal aid on a pro bono basis. Additionally, counseling is provided to migrants, and the ACMI arranges for the use of a temporary shelter that is provided by the Good Shepherd Center (Archdiocesan Commission for the Pastoral Care of Migrants & Itinerant People, 2012d). Moreover, the Center has been partnering with catechists[2] from the Church of St. Ignatius and St. Vincent de Paul to help in the packing and delivery of 'goody' bags[3] for the Bread Basket program, with the aim of increasing awareness among Singaporean youth of the plight of low-skilled migrant workers (Archdiocesan Commission for the Pastoral Care of Migrants & Itinerant People, 2012e).

Networking has been instrumental in enabling ACMI to do its work. Since its inception, the organization has partnered with the various Family Service Centers,[4] hospitals and various embassies to help migrants more effectively. In addition, ACMI works with parishes that are scattered across the country. One of its most recent collaborative partners has been the Family Life Society (FLS), a nonprofit organization whose patron is the Catholic Archbishop of Singapore. The FLS offers counseling and care services (including pregnancy crisis services) as well as educational programs and resources to families and individuals (Archdiocesan Commission for the Pastoral Care of Migrants & Itinerant People, 2012f). The partnership has been beneficial for ACMI because FLS, with its team of trained para-counselors, has been providing counseling to the students enrolled in the Center's classes and foreign spouses of Singapore nationals who approach ACMI for assistance.

Additionally, the ACMI programs include a training Center that organizes classes primarily for women migrants. Since 2001, the Center has trained more than 4,000 women migrants from Indonesia, the Philippines, India, Myanmar and Sri Lanka. The survey revealed that more than half of the women enrolled had worked in Singapore for five years or more and that more than 27 percent of students took more than one course at the center.

Taught by volunteers, classes are conducted in English on a range of skills, including baking, caregiving, cooking, dressmaking, hairstyling and nail and beauty care. Migrant women are also given the opportunity to learn computer skills, improve their English proficiency and receive instructions about starting small-scale business enterprises. The women pay only an annual nominal fee of Singapore $90–100 to attend the classes, because the cost of running these activities is heavily subsidized by ACMI. The classes, held over a period of eight months and over two semesters a year, are on Sundays when the women have their day off from work. Usually classes meet every other Sunday; prior to January 2013 it was more common for the vast majority of migrant domestic workers to get every other Sunday off from work rather than every Sunday. In January 2013, the Singapore government legislated that all foreign domestic workers (in the year 2013 there were 210,000 such women) get a day off every Sunday (AWARE 2012).

The ACMI programs are "led from above" (Berger, 2005, p.18) in terms of their ideological rationale, but their goal is to meet the social, psychological and intellectual needs of the migrant women. The migrants experience alienation, anxiety and uncertainty as they have been compelled to leave their home nations for political and economic reasons. For example, by ensuring that the migrants receive 'gifts' of food through the Bread Basket program and, thus, do not starve, the Church believes that the migrant women workers will feel at home and not like strangers in a foreign land. The Church is cognizant that it is meeting their physical needs; the women may not have easy access to food because of their work and living conditions. In contrast, the justification for establishing the training Center is that the women migrant workers should have a place to go on their day off and, thus, develop a sense of belonging and security in a foreign country, while learning a skill that might be useful to them during their stay in Singapore or on their return to their home countries.

The Singapore state failed in its ethical duty to meet the needs of these migrant women until 2005 when it established the Foreign Domestic Worker Association for Skills Training (FAST) program (Foreign Domestic Worker Association for Skills Training, 2012). However, state support for programs that aim to better the lives of migrant women is mostly thin and lukewarm. For instance, FAST receives only partial funding from the Ministry of Manpower, a government ministry dealing with labor practices. The bulk of FAST's funding comes from multiple private-sector sources.

ACMI as well as other civil society organizations were established prior to FAST and most of them are faith-based entities. Some parishes have independently organized skills training programs for migrant workers, such as the Holy Family Filipino Group Skills Training Program based at Holy Family Church. There are also Church-wide programs that extend beyond the parish level, for example, the Novena Filipino Community Skills Development Program supported by Marymount Convent, the Filipino Ongoing Development Program managed by the Franciscan Missionaries of Mary and ACMI. Similar training programs are run by different Protestant denominations, such as the organization called Go Forth Services which holds its program at Lucky Plaza—the haunt of domestic workers, mainly Filipinas—as well as Trinity Christian Center, which hosts the Life Skills Course program. Such programs have been organized by some mosques and Buddhist temples too, although they may include religious courses. Embassies are also keen on training programs for their female citizens abroad. The skills training programs organized by the Filipino Overseas Workers in Singapore is jointly hosted by the Philippine Embassy and the Aidha, a microfinance business school known for its financial literacy and entrepreneurship courses.

CONTEXTUALIZING 'HOME': STATE AND CHURCH CONSTRUCTIONS

The Singapore state considers low-skilled migrant workers to be the 'other' within its borders. That these migrants are only sojourners in Singapore is signaled by the fact that they are employed on work permit passes, which allow them to stay in Singapore for a duration of two years only (Devasahayam, 2010). Their temporary status is reconfirmed by discriminatory state policies that subject them to particularly stringent labor laws. In contrast, high-skilled migrants are regulated by an entirely different compendium of rules and they are encouraged to consider making Singapore their permanent home (Leong, Rueppel and Hong, 2014; Kaur, 2007). The labor laws for low-skilled migrants, such as (female) domestic workers and (male) construction workers, prohibit them from bringing their families with them to Singapore for extended periods of time. They are also not permitted to marry Singapore nationals. Women migrant domestic workers if found to be pregnant are deported, as are those who are identified as HIV positive. Male low-skilled workers also face deportation if they are HIV positive. These laws and practices reinforce low-skilled migrants' experience of Singapore as a place that will never be a home to them even though the "diasporic processes of separation and lived experience 'elsewhere' casts doubt over the naturalness of home" (Ramji, 2011). According to state discourse, migrant loyalties, identities and desires and, thus, home are in the "places [they] left behind."

Singapore is a transit point for low-skilled workers' migration trajectory. As discussed earlier, for these workers, the state has created policies that ensure their detachment from Singapore. They are compelled to see Singapore as a "liminal space" (Walsh, 2007, p.509) in the migration process even though the law permits them to stay in the country beyond their two-year contracts as long as they are employed. In fact, scores of women migrant domestic workers have been working in Singapore for 10, 15 and even 20 years. For this reason, the term 'temporary' applies not only to the low-skilled migrant workers' jobs but also to how they are expected to relate to and experience Singapore.

In spite of the state's constructions of the migrants as a 'temporary' population that has no real claim on Singapore, the Church believes it has an obligation to be their 'family' and to provide a 'home' to them. It is to affect that end that ACMI has established various programs for migrant women domestic workers. The executive director of ACMI explains the Church's position:

> Here, we stress the community. . . there is a sense of safety. . . a place where they can come . . . it is like most religious organizations . . . the women know that they will not be exploited . . . when they go outside for courses . . . like there are commercial agencies that organize free courses . . . like how to start your own business . . . but they later find out that they have to take a loan from the organization to complete the course . . . there is nothing out there by way of law to protect them . . . for us, they also know we don't charge an exorbitant fee . . . and they know the church is a reputable organization . . . subsequently they can trust the people running the courses.

The Church sees itself as a critical agent in providing the migrants with a sense of stability and security, but the programs are not meant to remind them of their home life. Instead, the migrant women's experience of home as created by the Church in Singapore is meant to foster a sense of belonging and familiarity. So it is a 'temporary belonging' which forms the experience of the women given the time-delimited nature of their presence in Singapore.

RESPONSES AND REFLECTIONS

Sundays are busy days at the ACMI. Since the mandatory day off law came into effect, ACMI has seen a 30 percent jump in enrollment in its courses compared to previous years. In an interview, one student told me that initially she was turned away because the class she had wanted to enroll in was full. But later she was permitted to enroll when a woman who had registered earlier could not attend the class. Because a large number of women approach the Center for its courses, those who are turned away are usually advised to try other similar training centers in the country.

The students usually find out about the Center by word of mouth. Many of the students (32.7 percent) heard about ACMI through fellow domestic workers. A handful, however, learned about it by attending other similar training centers in Singapore. A few learned about the Center through their employers; the survey revealed that only 13.5 percent of the students had come to ACMI at the recommendation of their employer. Crisanta,[5] a 40-year-old Filipina, found out about the Center through her female employer who came across a flyer detailing its activities. Crisanta now attends the international culinary course at the encouragement of her employer who knows that she has a keen interest in cooking.

Many of the women are 'newbies' who have been attending classes for a year or two, but there are a significant number of students who are 'veterans.' They have become volunteers at the Center after starting as students. Graduating from being a student to a volunteer is not uncommon, particularly among those who have been employed in Singapore over several work contracts. Such has been the experience of Felicia, a 46-year-old woman from the Philippines, who has been a volunteer teacher at ACMI for nearly nine years. She started off by learning the basics of hairstyling at other training centers in Singapore before coming to ACMI. Proving herself to be the "best student" in the class, she was handpicked from a group of more than 13 students to receive additional training at the advanced level.

Both Singaporeans and migrant women volunteer at ACMI. Felicia was clear that her intention in volunteering was to "give something back" to ACMI; the motivation of the Singaporean volunteers was more in keeping with the broader objective of ACMI of making the migrants feel welcomed and at home in Singapore. A volunteer, who has been teaching the hairstyling course, reiterated the dual objectives of the Center. He explained that the courses offered by the Center are meant to provide the migrant women domestic workers with a place to go to on their day off from work. ACMI is also a place where they can receive support. They can use their day off in a purposeful way by learning new skills that could be useful either in their current jobs or in the future should they choose to set up a small business. He also claimed that the fact that the Center serves as a place where the women can learn a new skill has implications for how employers view granting them a day off:

> They [i.e., the employers] would definitely want their maids to spend their time . . . qualitatively (sic) . . . So if they come here, they would know that this is good quality spending of time . . . So I think we should reach out to more of the employers that we have this kind of help for their workers . . . They would be more open to them coming here to learn more skills (sic) . . . Because a lot of them . . . don't give off day and they pay them to stay at home . . . because they don't want them to mix up with the wrong people . . . So it is important that we get them to know us . . . So they are more open to sending their helper here for more courses . . . [and for] more knowledge.

Echoing a more obvious objective of the ACMI, the male volunteer stated that developing a new skill would be a way of bringing about change in the lives of the women. It would give them a certain degree of social mobility as they could take on other work besides domestic work.

Although being a home to the migrant women is a fundamental ACMI objective, the Center was important to the women because it provided them with the opportunity to learn new skills. The Center as a site for building friendships and forging relationships did not have much importance for them. In the survey conducted in May–June 2012, the majority of women (57.4 percent) indicated that they came to ACMI because they wanted to learn a new skill to improve themselves. Some explicitly connected improving their skill set to being more efficient in their work and, in turn, improving their employability. The possibility of starting up a business with their newly acquired skill was also on the minds of many of the students (47.4 percent). Some of the women felt that they wanted to do something useful on Sundays instead of loitering in the streets or meeting up with friends (20.3 percent). In the interviews, two women mentioned that attending the Center's activities was a productive way of spending their time on Sundays, and it kept them out of 'trouble,' which they associated with getting into relationships with the opposite sex. Rista, a 33-year-old woman from Indonesia, who had studied English and basic computer skills at the Center remarked:

> It is good to go out and meet with the good people [on their day off] . . . but if you meet with people who are not good, that is difficult (sic) . . . because I don't want to follow them by doing (sic) something wrong.

The women had positive feelings toward ACMI and spoke about how they felt "at home" at the training center because of the friendships they had established with the staff members or their classmates. In fact, approximately 28 percent said that they chose ACMI over the other training centers because it gave them "a sense of belonging." What this meant varied. For instance, Rista, a survey participant, said that she enjoyed her classes at ACMI because the people she met were nice and friendly and she was happy to take more classes. She felt at home at ACMI because the Center is run by Catholics, although she is Protestant. She also said that: "I can meet people from my country . . . and if we have something in our heart, we can talk to others . . . I am also happy to see them and to chat and to ask how they are . . . and how they are doing with their employers and to find out how they solve their problems with their employers."

On this same topic, Felicia, a migrant domestic worker, remarked:

> I do feel at home [at the Center] . . . if you have a problem, you can open up to your friends . . . the Center can also open up to you if you want . . . open to help you . . . to advise you . . . you can talk to them . . . the management . . . you can open your problems to them . . . they can advise you . . . they are friendly people . . . so far it is not my problem . . . concerning other students . . . if they come to me and tell their problem . . . then I will refer to them . . . then they will arrange talking to them [about the problem].

The interviews established that those who had recently joined the Center (for instance, in the past year) were less likely to report feeling a sense of home there, but they tended to acknowledge that they found the teachers to be friendly and kind and that they treated the students as their equals rather than as maids. As many of the women had been introduced to the Center by their friends, it appeared to serve as a venue where friends could gather rather than a site where they might develop new friendships and a sense of community, although the latter could occur.

It would seem that religious affiliation would be integral to enhancing the sense of 'feeling at home' for the female migrant domestic workers, but the interviews with the Catholic as well as Protestant Filipinas and Indonesian migrant women revealed otherwise. For example, Felicia did not think that religious affiliation was an important factor in her feeling a sense of home at ACMI: "It is not like I feel close to the people at ACMI because I am Catholic . . . it is because of the people around [that is who they are as individuals] . . . it is not about religion." Carolyn, a 35-year-old from the Philippines, echoed those sentiments: "I think not. . . . even if you [are] Indonesian or from Myanmar . . . same treatment right? . . . Anyone can join and feel at home [at the Center]."

Although the migrant women cited the atmosphere of camaraderie among teachers and students and between students as the reason for feeling a sense of home at the Center, their religious affiliation might have been a key factor in strengthening their sense of belonging, even though they might not have seen it that way. In fact the interviews revealed that the Indonesian women who were Muslim and the domestics from Myanmar (most of whom were Buddhist) did not report feeling at home at the Center to the extent that the Catholic and Protestant Christian women did. The Catholic women explained that they enjoyed meeting domestics from other countries and learning from each other about their different cultures and ways of life.

The survey found that Indonesians constituted the majority of students at 40.1 percent of a total of 251 students. As the majority of the students were Muslims, religious or, in this case, the Catholic origins of the Center did not appear to deter them from taking courses at the Center; but whether or not they felt a sense of home at ACMI differed greatly among individuals. Noorsarkina, a 42-year-old woman, said that she did not mind that the training center was run by Catholics although she is a Muslim. She did not sign up for classes at a mosque in Singapore, which ran similar courses, because ACMI's Center was located near her employer's home, and she did not wish to travel the longer distance to the mosque for the same purpose. She also said that she did not find it a 'problem' attending courses offered by a Catholic-run Center despite her religious affiliation. For her, what mattered most was mutual respect (*menghormati*) between those of different faiths and that she was not expected to convert to Christianity. At the same time, Noorsarkina mentioned that she felt treasured (*menghargai*) by the

ACMI community and was motivated to become a volunteer after two years of being a student.

Evi, a 27-year-old, remarked that being a Muslim did not deter her from attending classes at ACMI. She explained:

> This place is not only for Catholics or Christians, . . . Muslims can also come, so I am happy . . . Going to a mosque is *selesa* (calm) but here it is also *selesa* (calm) . . . Here there is all kinds of religion (*agama*) and races (*bangsa*).

As to whether she has made good friends at ACMI, Evi further explained that her closest friends were enrolled at similar courses at a mosque or at other training centers. But because ACMI was close to her employer's home and she found the teachers at the Center to be excellent, she decided to stay at ACMI, having already finished one semester of the basic computer course and an English language course. Nurida, a 25-year-old Muslim woman, had a similar position:

> Never mind . . . we are different religions . . . but communication is just nice . . . I enjoy sharing with them (sic) . . . I enjoy being at ACMI (sic) . . . It is okay. . . because all of us are like friends . . . the teacher and the classmates.

Moe, a 30-year-old from Myanmar, also made a similar point. It did not make a difference to her that the Center was run by Catholics; it was a place where she could learn a new skill, which was her priority:

> Everybody [at ACMI] is warm . . . it makes me happy to be here . . . If I have problems, I will talk to my friends here . . . But studying is more important . . . because when I go back to Myanmar, I want to open [a] hair salon.

Moe's position was the same as that of the majority of the women interviewed and those who participated in the survey. Learning a new skill was first and foremost on the minds of the women; cultivating friendships and feeling a sense of belonging to the community at the Center were viewed as secondary outcomes by them.

DISCUSSION

In Singapore, a myriad of organizations—both secular and faith-based—host training programs aimed at helping migrant women domestic workers from other nations. Undeterred by the possibility of duplicating the efforts of those organizations, the Church has pursued its mission of reaching out to the migrants. It sees them as strangers who deserve to be welcomed. Recognizing that migrants are in need of a 'family' because of their marginalized status, the Church has striven to be inclusive by creating a space that they can call 'home.' That has been and will be its position regardless of how the migrant women perceive their sojourn in Singapore, which is as a temporary feature of the migrant labor landscape and "a social 'other,' subordinate directly to their employers and more generally to the urban host society" (Momsen, 1999, p.1).

Ong reminds us that the concept of the 'other' is intrinsically bound up with notions of "neoslavery . . . emerg[ing] out of a postcolonial intersection of racialized nationalism, neoliberal strategies, and disjunctive moral economies . . ." (2006, p.198). Thus in countries such as Singapore, poor female non-citizen migrant workers who perform low-status jobs are subject to numerous exploitative practices. The dismal work conditions of the women in conjunction with Singapore's discriminatory labor policies, which define this migrant group as the 'other,' have created an environment where the women are virtually slaves (Devasahayam, 2010; Yeoh and Huang, 1999). Moreover, their 'otherness' is reinforced by the fact that they fill low-prestige, low-paying jobs, rendering them pariahs in Singaporean society. But the women make the most of their experiences in Singapore, tolerating injustices for the sake of their jobs, because work in Singapore is a financial passport to a better life for their families and themselves (Yeoh and Huang, 1999).

In its intent and purpose with respect to migrant workers, the Catholic Church is driven by an 'internal' factor and an 'external' one. It is motivated by an ethical impulse that is rooted in a theological ideology that requires it to be inclusive of and charitable towards the 'other.' Thus reaching out to the 'other' in its midst is an intrinsic, unchanging value of the Church. Although it has retreated from advocating for the rights of the women as workers, it is obligated by its values and goals to try to explicitly meet the social, psychological and intellectual needs of this migrant group. In a sense, reaching out to marginalized migrants who are the 'other' is integral to its character and, thus, it is part of the way it functions.

The Church's moral motivation sets it apart from the other organizations that aim to meet the needs of the migrant women domestic workers. For example, its attempt to create a place where the women can go on their days off are bolstered by the "moral" position of wanting to help them "stay out of trouble" and lure them away from "wasting their time and loitering in the streets." Steering the women away from 'trouble' is in keeping with the Church's moral teachings regarding sexual relationships outside of marriage and pregnancy out of wedlock. In fact, the Church sees it as its responsibility to do everything it can to provide a 'refuge' for the women. The Church's perceptions of the women mirrors and, in turn, reinscribes the stereotypes about them that are held by their employers, the Singapore state and the women's nation of origin. They also conceptualize the migrant women domestic workers as weak willed and unable to abide by moral codes and, therefore, vulnerable to a host of temptations around them. Controlling the movement of the women is not an explicitly stated goal of ACMI, but by [']helping['] them submit to their lot through religious disciplining and forbearance" (Ong, 2006, p.210) it covertly aids the Singapore state, employers and the nation of origin of the women in 'governing' them.

There is also an external factor that has provided the Church with a moral basis for its work with Singapore's female migrant domestic worker population. The fact that the Singapore government has largely failed to intervene positively on behalf of this migrant population, thereby leaving an ethical gap, has been critical in spurring the Church's efforts to reach out to the women. In fact, in reaching out to this migrant group, the Church has "introduced an ethical debate . . . (about) the plight of female migrants, articulating political claims for their moral dignity beyond a condition of neo-slavery" (Ong, 2006, p.198). But as mentioned earlier, it now treads carefully having learned from its experience in the late 1980s of the dangers of a direct confrontation with the state. Thus, in contrast to its predecessors, ACMI has a narrow focus that aims to avoid a severe political fallout. Rather than advocating for the rights of migrant workers, it has been primarily concerned with fostering the interests of migrant women domestic workers through its provision of social services.

CONCLUSION

In recent decades, the forces of globalization enveloping Southeast Asia have resulted in increasingly intertwined economies and transnational job opportunities. With limited options for a better life in their nation of origin, migrant women (from poorer countries in the Southeast Asian region) who work in Singapore in the domestic work sector have little choice but to "navigat[e] . . . transnational routes to and from 'home' and 'host'. . . . perpetuated by the [country's] disciplinary policies of use and discard" (Yeoh, 2006, p.150). The migration experience for temporary workers in Singapore is not a seamless process; they can never forget that they are a temporary feature in the receiving country's employment landscape and they must return to their nation of origin.

In a nation where until 2005 the state had limited interest in responding to low-skilled female migrant workers' social needs, the Catholic Church has attempted to reach out to them through its programs and services. Although it aims to "blur the distinction between here and there" for them (Ahmed, Castañeda, Fortier and Sheller, 2004, p.4), the women's experience of living in Singapore is the product of state policies that marginalize them as the 'other.' This does not indicate a failure on the part of the Church; rather, as this chapter has argued, the situation is more complex. The Church has been successful in meeting the practical needs of the migrant women who desire to improve themselves by acquiring new skills, but it has generally not been able to convince the women to see ACMI as a 'home.' In the future, they may come to view it as a 'home' if the state chooses to not discriminate against them but to treat them with the same respect that it extends to citizens of Singapore.

NOTES

1. A parish is the smallest unit of the larger Church organization which comes under the administration of a priest.
2. Laypersons who teach the principles of the Church to individuals interested in being admitted into the Church as members.
3. These are bags containing little gifts or candy usually distributed at a party or a celebratory event.
4. These are community-based focal points and social service providers that assist families in need.
5. All names cited in this chapter are pseudonyms in order to protect the identity and confidentiality of the women who were willing to participate in this study. In fact, informed consent was received from each woman and all participants were assured that their identities would be protected.

REFERENCES

Abdul Rahman, N., 2005. Shaping the migrant institution: The agency of Indonesian domestic workers in Singapore. In: L. Parker, ed. 2005. *The agency of women in Asia*. Singapore: Marshall Cavendish.

Ahmed, S., Castañeda, C., Fortier, A. and Sheller, M., 2004. Introduction: Uprootings/regroundings: questions of home and migration. In: S. Ahmed, C. Castañeda, A. Fortier and M. Sheller, eds. 2004. *Uprootings/regroundings: Questions of home and migration*. Oxford: Berg Publishers.

Apostolic Constitution of Pius XII, 1952. *Exsul Familia Nazarethan*. [pdf] Available at: <http://acmi.sg/Files/Documents/Exsul_Familia-en-sp.pdf> [Accessed 26 May 2013].

Archdiocesan Commission for the Pastoral Care of Migrants and Itinerant People, 2012a. *Archdiocesan commission for the pastoral care of migrants & itinerant people*. [online] Available at: <http://www.acmi.org.sg/> [Accessed 25 May 2013].

Archdiocesan Commission for the Pastoral Care of Migrants and Itinerant People, 2012b. *The care of migrants in Singapore*. [pdf] Available at: <http://acmi.sg/Files/Documents/The%20Care%20of%20Migrants%20in%20Singapore%20paper.pdf> [Accessed 6 June 2013].

Archdiocesan Commission for the Pastoral Care of Migrants and Itinerant People, 2012c. *About us*. [online] Available at: <http://www.acmi.org.sg/node/3> [Accessed 25 May 2013].

Archdiocesan Commission for the Pastoral Care of Migrants and Itinerant People, 2012d. *Services*. [online] Available at: <http://www.acmi.org.sg/node/9> [Accessed 25 May 2013].

Archdiocesan Commission for the Pastoral Care of Migrants and Itinerant People, 2012e. *Partnership with parish cathecists*. [online] Available at: < http://www.acmi.org.sg/node/37> [Accessed 25 May 2013].

Archdiocesan Commission for the Pastoral Care of Migrants and Itinerant People, 2012f. *Network partners.* [online] Available at: <http://www.acmi.org.sg/node/26> [Accessed 25 May 2013].
Association of Women for Action and Research (AWARE), 2012. Transient Workers Count Too. *TWC2 launched anti-discrimination T-shirts,* 15 February. [online] Available at: <http://www.aware.org.sg/2013/02/twc2-launches-anti-discrimination-t-shirts/> [Accessed 18 February 2014].
Berger, P., 2005. Religion and global civil society. In: M. Juergensmeyer, ed. 2005. *Religion in global civil society.* Oxford: Oxford University Press.
Braidotti, R., 1994. *Nomadic subjects: Embodiment and sexual difference in feminist theory.* New York: Columbia University Press.
Catholic Welfare Services, 2010. *A lifetime of caring. . . since 1959.* [online] Available at: <http://www.catholicwelfare.org.sg/aboutus/history.html> [Accessed 25 May 2013].
Caritas Singapore Community Council, n.d. *Our affiliates.* [online] Available at: <http://www.caritas-singapore.org/affiliates&associates/ouraffiliates_SVDP.html> [Accessed 25 May 2013].
Caritas Singapore Community Council (CSCC), 2013. *Living our social mission.* [online] Available at: <http://www.cscc-singapore.org/about-us/living-our-social-mission/#.Ufc8dKy6vcs> [Accessed 27 July 2013].
Chambers, I., 1994. *Migrancy, culture, identity.* London: Routledge.
Daniel, P., 1987. Safety found in the 'ready cover' of the Catholic Church. *The Straits Times,* 10 Jun, p.15.
Devasahayam, T.W., 2010. Placement and/or protection?: Singapore's labour policies and practices for temporary women migrant workers. *Journal of the Asia Pacific Economy,* 15 (1), pp.45–58.
Devasahayam, T.W. and Yeoh, B.S.A., eds., 2007. *Working and mothering in Asia: Images, ideologies and identities.* Singapore and Denmark: National University of Singapore Press and Nordic Institute of Asian Studies.
Foreign Domestic Worker Association for Skills Training, 2012. *Enhance capabilities and life-long employability through FAST.* [online] Available at: <http://www.fast.org.sg/> [Accessed 10 June 2013].
Haas, M., 1989. The politics of Singapore in the 1980s. *Journal of Contemporary Asia* 19, pp.48–77.
Hondagneu-Sotelo, P. and Avila, E., 1997. "I'm here, but I'm there": The meaning of Latina transnational motherhood. *Gender and Society,* 11(5), pp.548–71.
Kaur, A., 2007. International labour migration in Southeast Asia: Governance of migration and women domestic workers. *Intersections: Gender, History and Culture in the Asian Context,* [e-journal] 15. Available at: <http://intersections.anu.edu.au/issue15/kaur.htm> [Accessed 30 June 2011].
Kuah-Pearce, K.E., 2008. The poetics of religious philanthropy: Buddhist welfarism in Singapore. In: B. Turner, ed. 2008. *Religious diversity and civil society.* Oxford: The Bardwell Press.
Leong, C., Rueppel, P. and Hong, D., 2014. Managing immigration and integration in Singapore. In: *Migration and integration: Common challenges and response from Europe and Asia.* Singapore: Konrad Adenauer Stiftung.
Mauzy, D.K. and Milne, R.S., 2002. *Singapore politics under the People's Action Party.* London: Routledge.
Momsen, J.H., 1999. Maids on the move: Victim or victor? In: J.H. Momsen, ed. 1999. *Gender, migration and domestic service.* London: Routledge.
Oishi, N., 2005. *Women in motion: Globalization, state policies, and labor migration in Asia.* Stanford: Stanford University Press.
Ong, A., 2006. *Neoliberalism as exception: Mutations in citizenship and sovereignty.* Durham, NC: Duke University Press.

Parrañes, R.S., 2005. *Children of global migration: Transnational families and gendered woes.* Stanford: Stanford University Press.
Parrañes, R.S., 2008. *The force of domesticity: Filipina migrants and globalization.* New York: New York University Press.
Pontifical Council for Justice and Peace, 2004. *Compendium of the social doctrine of the church* (Philippine Edition). Manila and Makati, Metro Manila: Catholic Bishops' Conference of the Philippines and Word & Life Publications.
Pontifical Council for the Pastoral Care of Migrants and Itinerant People, 2004. Instruction-erga migrantes caritas Christi (The love of Christ towards migrants). [pdf] Available at: <http://acmi.sg/Files/Documents//ErgaMigrantesCaritasChristi.pdf> [Accessed 26 May 2013].
Ramji, H., 2011. "British Indians 'returning home': An exploration of transnational belongings. *Sociology*, 40 (4) pp.645–62.
Reynolds, V. and Tanner, R., 1995. *The social ecology of religion.* Oxford: Oxford University Press.
Rodan, G., 2004. *Transparency and authoritarian rule in Southeast Asia: Singapore and Malaysia.* London: Routledge.
Sobritchea, C.I., 2007. Constructions of mothering: Female Filipino overseas workers. In: T.W. Devasahayam and B.S.A. Yeoh, eds. 2007. *Working and mothering in Asia: Images, ideologies and identities.* Singapore and Denmark: National University of Singapore Press and Nordic Institute of Asian Studies.
Walsh, K., 2007. 'It got very debauched, very Dubai!' Heterosexual intimacy amongst single British expatriates. *Social & Cultural Geography*, 8 (4), pp.507–33.
Wijeysingha, E. in collaboration with Rev. Fr. R. Nicolas., 2006. *Going forth: The Catholic Church in Singapore 1819–2004.* Singapore: Titular Roman Catholic Archbishop of Singapore.
Worthington, R., 2003. *Governance in Singapore.* London: Routledge.
Yeoh, B.S.A., 2006. Mobility and the city. *Theory, Culture & Society*, 23 (2–3), pp.150–2.
Yeoh, B.S.A. and Huang, S., 2000. "Home" and "away": Foreign domestic workers and negotiations of diasporic identity in Singapore. *Women's Studies International Forum*, 23 (4), pp.413–29.
Yeoh, B.S.A. and Huang, S., 1999. Singapore women and foreign domestic workers: Negotiating domestic work and motherhood. In: J.H. Momsen, ed. 1999. *Gender, migration and domestic service.* London: Routledge.
Yeoh, B.S.A., Huang, S. and Devasahayam, T.W., 2004. Diasporic subjects in the nation: Foreign domestic workers, the reach of the law and civil society in Singapore. *Asian Studies Review*, 28, pp.7–23.

Part V
The Way Forward

9 Transnationalization and the Capitalization of Labor
Female Foreign Domestic Workers

Stuart Rosewarne

INTRODUCTION

International migration is a key feature of globalization, with women comprising almost half of the world's migrant worker population. Most of them are employed as domestic workers and care workers and their work generates a transnational flow of funds. This chapter argues that these women are exploited within the households where they work and across the transnational labor market plane. It contends that the commodification of reproductive labor is 'organized' by a multilayered, institutional architecture that 'supports' international migrant workers. Those institutions take advantage of female migrant domestic and care workers by appropriating an unduly high portion of their wages for themselves and, thus, they function as an exploitive global circuit of capital that runs parallel to the global care chain.

Research on the gendered dimension of globalization has largely been the province of feminist researchers, who have focused on three key features of women's labor migration. The one that has perhaps received the most attention has been the "global care chain" and the transnational transfer and redistribution of reproductive or emotional labor (Hochschild, 1997; Parreñas, 2006). A second area of study has explored the subordinate and precarious position of foreign domestic workers and care workers in the global labor market, a subject that now has particular resonance in light of the conclusion of the International Labour Organization (ILO) Domestic Workers Convention in 2011 (Piper, 2008; Phillips, 2009; Elias, 2010; Rosewarne, 2013). The third focus takes the form of the 'migration-remittances-development nexus' discourse. It assesses the opportunity labor migration affords women to attain the means to contribute to the material well-being of their families, if not their own empowerment (UNDP, 2009; UN-INSTRAW, 2006; Rosewarne, 2012). Each of these strands of research makes a contribution by illuminating globalization as consisting of economic, political and, above all, gendered processes.

Although these research foci recognize the interplay of the different facets of the transnationalization of domestic work, they have primarily concentrated on examining migrant women's experiences. A particular area of concern has been the exercise of women's emotional labors, especially as it occurs across a transnational plane. The emphasis has generally been on elucidating women's subjectivity and the challenges of meeting multiple familial demands. This has tended to result in the analysis of the economic dimensions of transnational domestic work being marginalized. Even in those instances where there is an initial and explicit appreciation of the value of migrant domestic workers' labor, the concern has been that framing such work in the same terms as those of labor engaged in the production of commodities understates the different character—the emotional and affective labor—that these workers bring to reproductive labor. Notwithstanding that this waged work generates financial resources that can enhance the material well-being of workers' families, the significance of the economic transaction is generally not regarded as worthy of further critical reflection (Hochschild, 1997; Yeates, 2004; Gutiérrez-Rodríguez, 2010). This neglect of the 'economics' of foreign domestic labor (insofar as this takes the form of waged labor and which sets in motion a transnational flow of funds) is a significant lacunae in the research on the dynamics of transnational domestic and care work. Drawing on fieldwork on labor migration and the employment of foreign domestic and care workers in Southeast and East Asia, I argue that additional insights into the dynamics and challenges of transnational domestic work can be gleaned by expanding the notion of a 'global care chain' so that it acknowledges that 'emotional labor' or 'reproductive labor' is based on waged work that engenders a chain of transnational money flows. The distinguishing feature of the 'global care chain' is that it is founded on the commodification of domestic work and care work and this necessarily entails an appreciation of the need for such labor, the institutional architecture established to organize this labor, the state regulation of international migrant labor and, crucially, the appropriation of a significant proportion of workers' wages by labor brokers, moneylenders, recruitment and placement agencies, money transfer companies and others across the spectrum of the transnational labor market.

I argue here that even as the key catalyst engendering migrant domestic work is women's entry into the international labor market (as a personal and familial survival strategy), there are multiple actors who are crucial to the institution of the 'global care chain' and who lay claim to the flow of funds that are generated from the commodification of reproductive labor. The workers' home states promote offshore employment as an export-revenue generating strategy, and the policies of most host states—and all host states in Southeast and East Asia and the Gulf states that are the principal destinations for Asian domestic and care workers—circumscribe migrant workers' employment rights and proscribe opportunities for settlement in ways that both impel and oblige workers to repatriate their income. The commodification of reproductive work is further facilitated by other actors in the labor migration architecture—the moneylenders, the labor recruiters, deployment and placement agencies, the state bureaucrats and the money transfer agencies—who foster labor migration with the object of capturing a share of the wages of the workers. Migrant domestic worker advocacy groups, in contrast, campaign to improve workers' rights and employment conditions, with a key aim of securing a greater net return for them for their labor. I contend that acknowledging that the 'global care chain' is built on the foundation of a transnational chain of money flows, or a global (exploitive) circuit of capital, provides for a richer understanding of the nature of globalized domestic and care work (including the transnational transfer of emotional labor) and the potential development impetus of such work for the labor-supply economies of the global South. This perspective also helps elucidate the forces shaping the subordinate and precarious status of such workers.

This chapter first considers the significance and shifting dynamics of Asia's transnational domestic workforce and the employment restrictions that institutionalize remittances as a defining feature of transnational labor. The subsequent section examines the institutional architecture of the labor recruitment and placement process and the mechanisms that facilitate the financial foundations of the labor trade. The extent of the claims made by those institutions on the workers' earnings is also discussed. In considering how the migrant worker experience in this 'global care chain' is constituted as a 'global circuit of capital,' this chapter argues that efforts to enhance the well-being of workers reinforce the instrumental approach to labor. In the concluding section, possible measures to challenge the instrumentalist approach for improving the standing of female migrant domestic workers are outlined.

THE SHIFTING DYNAMICS OF ASIA'S TRANSNATIONAL DOMESTIC AND CARE WORKFORCE

Labor migration has become a significant economic policy objective of several poorer nations in Southeast Asia and South Asia; it is promoted by the governments of those countries with the aim of generating export income in the form of workers' remittances. One catalyst for this policy objective was the decision of several countries in East and Southeast Asia—most notably Hong Kong, Singapore, Malaysia, Taiwan and Brunei Darussalam and Macau—and the Gulf states to open their borders to foreign domestic workers and care workers (Cheng, 2003; Lan, 2006; Quratul-ain, 2013; Ho, 2010). Indeed the Asian countries have become increasingly important destinations for migrant workers. There are several countries in Europe that have also been important destinations for Filipina domestic workers (and Italy to a lesser extent for Sri Lankan workers), and a distinguishing feature of these destinations is that they allow these workers to apply for permanent resident rights.

There are a substantial and growing number of foreign domestic workers employed across Asia. Precise numbers are not available because the number of undocumented workers is difficult to estimate (for instance, some of these workers entered the receiving nation on a tourist visa whereas others crossed borders without a visa). There are, for example, more than 300,000 migrant domestic workers employed in Hong Kong and over 200,000 are employed in Singapore. The number of foreign domestic workers employed in Malaysia was estimated to have grown to 300,000 prior to Indonesia refusing to allow Indonesian women who wanted to work in Malaysia permission to do so (however, the overall numbers of foreign domestic workers may have recovered to previous levels given that irregular migrants comprise a significant percentage of Indonesian workers in Malaysia) (AWARE, 2010; Yi, 2011). There are some 200,000 international migrant workers employed in Taiwan as domestic workers and care workers (Fuchs, 2011; Anon, 2011). There are over 100,000 registered migrant domestic workers in Thailand, although the actual number of migrants employed as domestic workers and care workers is much greater given the scale of undocumented migration from Myanmar. As Thailand is not a signatory of the 1951 UN Refugee Convention, it considers refugees from Myanmar to be undocumented persons rather than refugees. Although now they are able to register with Thailand's Office of Foreign Workers (as can workers from Laos and Cambodia), most of the million-plus Burmese migrants do not do so (Boontinand, 2010; Pearson and Kusakabe, 2012, p.39). Even though Japan and Korea have historically prohibited the employment of domestic workers from Southeast Asia, they have relaxed the restrictions somewhat to help meet the growing demand for care workers for their elderly citizens. In 2006, Japan negotiated an Economic Partnership Agreement with the Philippines to recruit nurses and care workers. The latter group of migrant workers would be recruited for limited-term, four-year contracts that could be extended for a further three years if they met the performance criteria of their job (Onuki, 2009). Post-arrival training was funded by official development assistance monies. Japan negotiated a similar agreement for the recruitment of nurses with Indonesia. This agreement was more restrictive; Indonesian nurses could work in Japan as nursing aides or trainees, not as registered nurses (Purba, 2013; Stott, 2008).[1]

The governments of the Philippines, Sri Lanka and Indonesia have been enthusiastic about taking advantage of these international employment opportunities for their citizens. They have built the institutional infrastructure to support the recruitment of their citizens to work overseas as domestic workers and care workers. In all three nations, a substantial proportion of those recruited found work as domestic workers, and women constituted the vast majority of those employed as domestic workers and care workers.

I became interested in the dynamics of labor migration in this part of the world because of evidence of the shifting composition (in terms of nationality) of the international migrant domestic worker labor force and the substantial interest of sending governments in promoting labor migration as an export-revenue generating policy. I was particularly interested in the increasingly robust organizing effort among migrant workers (especially in Hong Kong) that was engendering transnational forms of organizing. During 2003–7, I conducted semistructured interviews with 16 migrant workers in Hong Kong and Singapore, and I organized group discussions involving approximately 30 workers. I also met with representatives of 20 migrant worker organizations and migrant worker advocacy groups in the Philippines, Hong Kong and Singapore. The more prominent advocacy groups I met with in Hong Kong included Unifil, the Asian Pacific Mission for Migrants and the Asian Migrant Centre. I also met representatives of the Filipino Migrant Workers Union and the Indonesian Migrant Workers Union in Hong Kong. The Singaporean government prohibits independent organization of migrant workers, although they may join established trade unions. But that is not useful for them because domestic workers are not covered by labor regulations. I also met with a couple of civil society groups, mostly associated with the different branches of the Catholic Church, which lobby and provide refuge for migrant women. In the Philippines, the more prominent organizations whose representatives I met included DAWN and Migrante International.

The research project that is the basis of this chapter examined the shift in the source of international migrants employed as domestic workers and care workers. Hitherto, the Philippines had been the prime source country. Malaysia and Thailand were important source countries for the recruitment of domestic workers, but they had also become employers of substantial numbers of migrant workers, including migrant women domestic workers. Malaysia was a significant destination country for Indonesian workers and Thailand for Burmese refugees. During the first decade of the new century, Indonesia had emerged as the leading source of domestic workers for Hong Kong and Singapore and domestic workers and care workers for Taiwan (Lan, 2006; Anon, 2011). The dynamic character of labor migration was also evident in the way in which the recruitment net is now cast more widely than it was previously. Workers are being recruited from provinces in the Philippines and Indonesia that were formerly marginal sources for migrant labor. There are also some comparatively new source countries, such as Cambodia, Laos, Myanmar, Nepal, Bangladesh, Mongolia and Vietnam.

Several factors have contributed to this change in the labor source. On the supply side, governments see economic advantage in promoting labor migration as a strategy for addressing systemic trade imbalances. They also consider these employment opportunities as the answer to high unemployment within their borders and this interest has been fostered by the World Bank and the Asian Development Bank, which view labor migration as a key development initiative throughout the region. Households are drawn to it because it is one of the few ways in which they can generate an income.

The growing demand for migrant domestic workers and care workers has been prompted by changes in the receiving nations, such as changes in family structure, the increasing participation of women in paid employment, ageing populations coupled with a lack of institutional care facilities and the enhanced social status associated with employing a domestic worker. In their determination to meet the demand for these workers, the labor-importing countries are casting their net ever more widely across Asia.

The distinguishing feature that sets this industry of migrant domestic workers apart from many of the other forms of labor migration, and especially skilled migration, is that there are at least two universally shared conditions that define it. The first is the tendency of the governments of source countries to consider labor migration as an economic strategy for 'correcting' external trade imbalances (and that motivates them to establish the institutional architecture for promoting labor migration and the mechanisms that allow workers to repatriate their income). It has also resulted in the labor-exporting states quite consciously fostering an ideological milieu that is designed to reinforce and celebrate workers' sense of belonging to their country of origin (more on this strategy later).

Secondly, the governments of destination countries restrict the duration of residence and employment rights of migrant domestic workers, placing a limit of two to three years on employment contracts and in most instances requiring migrant domestic workers to return to their country of origin to renew their employment contracts. Labor-importing states also circumscribe the right of workers to be joined by their family members. The force of these restrictions has been highlighted recently with the unsuccessful attempts by Filipina workers in Hong Kong to apply for permanent residency.[2] In addition, with the exception of Hong Kong, and to some extent Taiwan, the terms and conditions of paid domestic work are generally not subject to any regulation, and waged domestic work is universally excluded from the protections of labor laws. A condition of employment for most domestic workers is that they live-in and, in effect, be on call to work on a 24/7 basis.[3] In conjunction, these restrictions make for highly precarious employment and, thus, increase the vulnerability of the undocumented or irregular migrant workers who make up the migrant domestic worker labor force.

The experiences of migrant domestic workers are not uniform in part because of the variation in the personal interactions between workers and their employers (Anggraeni, 2006). Their experiences are also framed by a range of systemic and structural factors, including differences in workers' education background and skill profile, language proficiency, level of self-confidence, workers' own familial contexts, the measure of support afforded by home governments or advocacy groups, and the workers' capacity to socialize with their peers or to join with others in lobbying for worker rights. Differences in employment opportunities also reflect the influence of employer preferences, which are shaped by stereotypical assumptions about workers' race, nationality, age, language capabilities and perceptions about workers' assertiveness or possible involvement in migrant worker campaigns. The different regulatory environments and the implementation of the regulations make for considerable diversity in workers' experiences.

One manifestation of that is the wide variation in rates of remuneration both across the various destination nations as well within countries. Wages and conditions of employment within a nation can be quite different, especially on the basis of workers' nationality. This is the case even in the instance of Hong Kong where all foreign domestic workers are supposed to be guaranteed a minimum wage (Asian Migration Centre, 2007; Ong, 2006; Briones, 2009); my research confirmed this practice.

Acknowledging the variations in the experiences of migrant workers demands a somewhat qualified approach to any generalizations about the foreign domestic workers' experiences. Nevertheless, migrant workers share at least two critical things in common. First, their primary ambition of enhancing their own and their families' material well-being is constrained by a labor market in which they have limited employment rights and are relatively impotent in their capacity to negotiate the terms and conditions of employment and the rate of remuneration. Second, in seeking and securing overseas employment, labor migration is characterized by multiple, onerous claims on workers' earnings by a number of the institutional architects who facilitate the transborder movement of workers.

THE RECRUITMENT, DEPLOYMENT AND RETURN OF MIGRANT DOMESTIC WORKERS: A CIRCUIT OF CAPITAL

The 'global care chain' is entwined with the labor migration project that has as its object the generation of remittances, which is contingent upon labor-importing states restricting the duration of migrant domestic workers' employment. The 'global care chain' 'forces' foreign migrant workers to remit a proportion of their income because workers who are part of it can only get short term employment contracts and the labor-importing states do not give their family members visas that would allow them to stay for an extended period of time with them. In other words, their employment status obliges and compels the workers to repatriate money.[4] Coordination of Action on Research on AIDS and Mobility (CARAM Asia) has very neatly summed up one dimension of the instrumentalism in the making of this workforce: "Migrant women workers . . . are not treated as human beings but [are] like commodities to be exploited . . . and then disposed . . . [of when they] are no longer of value" (2013).

Some researchers have argued that the provision of care that occurs in the context of a system of unequal exchange is a system of "extracting resources from the Third World . . . [that entails] a global transfer of services associated with a wife's traditional role . . . from poor countries to rich countries" (Hochschild, 1997, p.4, 26). However, instead of developing a critique that would draw out the material manifestations of the system of unequal exchange, as would tend to occur in the unequal exchange literature, the analysis focuses on the subjective dimension of the phenomenon:

"Today . . . love and care become the 'new gold'" (Hochschild, 1997, p.26). In distinguishing such labor from the work involved in producing commodities that are sold in the market place, these theorists question the preoccupation with defining the value-producing character of reproductive labor in terms of its remuneration. Indeed, the very gendered and racialized framing of such work underscores the devalorization of transnational domestic labor and care workers, and these theorists contend that putting a price on such labor does not do justice to, and cannot capture the value of, the sensations and feeling that are a crucial feature of reproductive labor. While the exploitative nature of the work is acknowledged, the research question focuses more systematically on the analysis of transnational domestic and care work in terms of the transfer of emotional labor (Parreñas, 2006). The analytical concern concentrates on how emotional labor is managed across the transnational plane, as well as the sometimes deleterious consequences for the families, especially, the children, left behind.

A recent and more critical intervention also alludes to the idea of unequal exchange (Gutiérrez-Rodríguez, 2010). Gutiérrez-Rodríguez argues that the structural inequalities that impel migration and the feminization and racialization of domestic work results in the devalorization of this form of labor. Notwithstanding an appreciation of the value of domestic work and the waged form it assumes with the globalization of domestic work, Gutiérrez-Rodríguez focuses on exploring the relational nature of domestic work, emphasizing domestic work as affective labor, and distinguishing it from work organized for the production of tangible commodities. So, the notion of value in a Marxist sense is discarded. Conceptualizing domestic work as affective labor recasts the employment relationship between the waged domestic worker and her employer as one in which the power relationship is diffused or muted. The social interactions within the household are represented as occurring in a space that is potentially convivial. The result, I want to suggest, tends to replicate the shortcomings of certain feminist analyses of the emotional labor that define domestic work and care work. Barker (2012) has critiqued those analyses as follows: When extended to the sphere of the global care chain, the preoccupation with affective labor downplays the asymmetry of the power relationships in this work space and neglects the exploitative character of domestic work undertaken by migrant workers. The focus on affective labor disregards the quite overt forms of disciplining and control that can be even more pronounced in the private space of the household. Indeed, the focus of some predeparture training programs that I observed is quite cognizant of this power dynamic because, while acquainting workers with their employment rights, the programs encourage workers to be compliant and deferential toward their employers in order to avoid projecting any impression that they will prove too adversarial in asserting their employment rights (Constable, 1997; Loveband, 2009; Gutiérrez-Rodríguez, 2010).

It is significant that this focus on the nature of relationships within the household marginalizes any critical reflection on the forces that impel women to migrate and the institutional contexts that frame the management and execution of their financial affairs. As a result, crucial aspects of the form of this labor, specifically, the acute asymmetry in the power relationships and the exploitative nature of this transnational labor market, are ignored. The preoccupation with affective labor overlooks the value-producing character of migrant domestic work and care work, the translation of care work into exchange value (albeit devalorized labor), the import of the commodified labor and the vested interests that seek to capture a share of the capitalized labor.

THE MULTIPLE CLAIMANTS ON CAPITALIZED LABOR

The commodification of domestic work has provided an opportunity for women of the global South to contribute to the material well-being of their families by selling their labor power. But the globalization of reproductive labor is more than the exercise of individual preferences. For the labor-supply states, migrant workers are a source of export revenue. They are 'foreign exchange heroes,' as Indonesia's president, Susilo Bambang Yudhoyono, declared in 2007 (Bustanuddin, 2007; Loveband, 2009). The Philippines president, Gloria Macapagal-Arroyo, celebrated them as a source of capital, calling them 'investor heroes' (Rodriguez, 2008; 2002). In effect, it is the capitalization of labor that is of paramount importance for the labor-exporting state.

The state is not alone in regarding migrant domestic workers in this way. The commodification of labor sets in motion a global circuit of capital, because the institutional architecture that facilitates the labor migration and the associated exchanges and transfers of monies is founded and maintained by an assemblage of stakeholders who seek to secure for themselves a share of the wages that are earned by the migrant workers. The organization of the global care chain rests on the imprimatur of the state (of both labor-exporting and labor-importing states), but the links that set the chain in motion are dominated by a host of private enterprises. These include the local agents who introduce the idea of working overseas to the women and liaise with recruitment and training agencies that organize their overseas placements; the moneylenders who provide some of the financial support that allows individuals to commence their journey; the businesses that provide predeparture training, including the NGOs that are contracted by governments to provide the service; the employment agencies in the labor-importing countries, as well as the money transfer agencies (that are used by workers to send money to their families); and, finally, the organizations that facilitate return migration and reintegration. In servicing the global care chain, each entity lays claim to a share of the future earnings of the domestic workers. The services rendered and the financial costs imposed on workers both structure and condition the lived experiences of migrant domestic workers. The globalization of reproductive labor and the migrant experience cannot be fully understood without considering the bases on which these workers have been incorporated into a transnational labor force that ignites and maintains a flow of funds that feed a global circuit of capital.

Viewed from this perspective, the globalization of care work and domestic work subjects female migrant workers to the control of a global market in which the disciplining process is affected through multiple institutional layers. The policies formulated by the labor-exporting states to promote and regulate the recruitment of labor establish the foundation of this chain. These policies may be partly motivated by the aim of affording some protection for the workers, but they impose a range of costs on them. These include the costs of passports and welfare insurance, as well as the costs associated with the time involved in navigating the bureaucratic maze. Moreover, there are the additional costs linked to bureaucratic corruption that has been a systemic feature of the state's engagement with labor migration programs, particularly in the Philippines and Indonesia. Indeed, the protracted business of obtaining the necessary documentation prompts many prospective migrants to seek work as irregular workers, and this has exacerbated the extent of bureaucratic corruption and multiplied the costs that migrant workers are required to meet (Hugo, 2009).

Migrating for work can be an expensive proposition, and many first-time migrant workers do not necessarily have the financial resources to meet the initial costs of pursuing employment. Some draw on the resources of family, and others turn to financial institutions, although it is more frequently the case that they have to rely on moneylenders who charge them exorbitant rates of interest. The differential burden of migrant worker indebtedness has recently been noted in a World Bank study. It identified Indonesian women, who overwhelmingly tend to seek work as domestics or care workers, as being more reliant on male moneylenders to fund their search and travel for work than their male counterparts; and as a consequence they incur greater levels of private debt than them, which invariably comes at a considerable cost to them (World Bank, 2009; IOM and ERCOF, 2010).

Governments were initially involved in organizing the recruitment and placement of workers, but private recruitment and placement agencies have come to dominate the industry, and this has been institutionalized with the regulation and licensing of recruitment agencies. The agencies are in the business of organizing prospective migrants so that they connect with the recruitment system, often facilitating access to lenders, arranging documents and organizing training. Because the recruitment agencies' motivation is to profit from this enterprise, their place in the global care chain comes at a considerable cost to workers. My research (and much of the other published research) on the subject indicates that the financial burden it imposes on workers varies considerably, but the debt incurred by first time migrant workers is generally equivalent to six-to-eight months of their wages (Ananta, 2009; Varia, 2007; Constable, 1997). Reflective of the lack of any substantive competition in the transnational labor market, the relative cost of securing employment through a recruitment and placement agency appears to be comparable irrespective of the employment destination: A worker who seeks employment in Hong Kong or Taiwan, where foreign domestic workers' wages are the highest in the region, will pay recruitment and placement fees that amount to about the same proportion of her earning as those paid by a worker seeking employment in Singapore or Malaysia.

In some contexts, there are explicit regulations that proscribe or set legal limits on the charges that can be imposed on workers; however, it is not uncommon for these to be ignored or for agents and recruiters to charge for other services (Tan, 2013; Pan, 2013; Gooch, 2012; Constable, 1997). Such additional costs add to the financial burden of migrant domestic workers, and it is the recruitment and placement agencies that generally have the first claim on workers' earnings until the debt is settled, and, thus, this obligation will usually be included in the employment contract. Thus the employment assumes the form of debt bondage or servitude and that is used by many agents and employers as justification for confiscating workers' passports and other documents, even though the practice is illegal.

Irregular migrants are equally, if not more, subject to the disciplining effects of the succession of stakeholders they have to navigate in their quest to secure employment. Acquiring the 'paper work' for irregular migration may not be as time consuming as the drawn out bureaucratic procedures for getting authorization for overseas employment, but recourse to unofficial agents and lenders and covert payments to border officials means an especially high financial burden on undocumented migrant workers (Boontinand, 2010).

CAPITALIZED LABOR AS DEVALORIZED LABOR

The circuit of capital is, of course, predicated on the opportunities for migrant workers to be recruited into the global care chain. As contributors to the debate on migrant domestic workers and care workers have argued, the appeal of migrant workers lies in their labor being undervalued. As noted, rates of remuneration vary considerably, differing from one destination country to another and varying according to the skill and education profile of workers, language proficiency, their country of origin (and even the province within a country), religion and age. Historically, Hong Kong is the only labor-importing country that has set a minimum wage for migrant domestic workers; rates of remuneration are set within a broad band linked to the local market rate, but are subject to negotiation between the recruitment agency, the worker and the placement agency. Depending on workers' proficiency in negotiating and understanding contracts, there is considerable scope for workers misunderstanding what a recruitment agency promised or actually negotiated and the recruitment agencies misrepresenting what is expected of workers (IOM, 2008). For instance, workers can discover on arrival at their destination that their contracts have been substituted by others that provide for lower remuneration or more onerous conditions of employment. They can also find themselves subject to additional charges imposed on them by the placement agency.

Thus one of the paradoxes of the globalization of domestic work as a state-led economic strategy is that the value of this export industry and the workers themselves are vulnerable to exploitation by recruitment and placement agencies because of the general lack of meaningful employment regulations in the labor-importing countries. As a result of considerable pressure from migrant worker advocacy groups, as well as a vested interest in maximizing the flow of funds, the governments of the Philippines and Indonesia have attempted to contain the costs imposed on migrant workers and to adopt and enforce employment contracts that mandated a minimum wage and other entitlements.[5] The Philippines government, for instance, has threatened to restrict the placement of Filipina workers by employment agencies in Singapore that do not require of employers that they meet the workers' placement and return travel costs. Specifically, it has said that it would veto the licenses of Philippine recruitment agencies that partnered with those Singaporean agencies (Tan, 2013). The Philippine's government has only now taken a stand (to protect its female citizens), even though the requirements having been in place for almost a decade.

Efforts by labor-exporting states to institute and enforce minimum wages for their citizens employed as domestic workers in other nations can have the undesirable effect of eroding the demand for those workers. This was the reason that Hong Kong's and Singapore's demand for Filipina migrant domestic workers declined and their demand for Indonesian domestic workers increased (Basu, 2011). The shift was also linked to Indonesian labor recruiters' determination to increase the appeal of Indonesian workers for Chinese families by incorporating Mandarin or Cantonese language lessons in Indonesian migrant workers' training programs. These changes point to a pervasive shift in the countries from which migrant domestic workers and care workers are sourced; the changes directly impacted the employment prospects of Filipina workers, and Indonesia's moves to mandate minimum wages and conditions for its migrant women workers has prompted governments in destination countries to explore other sources for labor. Singapore's Ministry of Manpower Planning is considering recruiting domestic workers from Cambodia, Myanmar, Bangladesh and Sri Lanka in the wake of the Indonesian government's demand that the minimum wages for domestic workers who are Indonesian citizens be increased (Tan, 2012b). Hong Kong has recently signed a memorandum of understanding with Bangladesh for the recruitment of up to 100,000 Bangladeshi women as domestic workers (Rahman, 2013). Malaysia is recruiting more women workers from Sri Lanka and Bangladesh and has begun to recruit Cambodian women to work as domestics (Human Rights Watch, 2011). The Macau administration is proposing to recruit domestic workers from China (Ho and Chan, 2012). Vietnam has become an important labor source country for Taiwan, which is also interested in Mongolia as a labor source for domestic workers.[6]

This ever-widening net for recruiting is partly driven by the objective of meeting the growing demand for domestic workers and care workers in light of the efforts of labor-exporting states (particularly the Philippines and Indonesia) to enforce greater protections and improved rates of remuneration for their citizens who are migrant workers. It is also influenced by the determination of labor-importing states to contain the cost of employing migrant foreign domestic workers. Hong Kong and Taiwan, for instance, have refused to provide foreign domestic workers with the periodic increases in minimum wages received by their citizens who are domestic workers (Loveband, 2009; Inquirer.net, 2011).[7] The administration in Macau sought to limit workers' capacity to negotiate wage increases by banning foreign domestic workers from 'job hopping' (US Consulate Hong Kong, 2009). A still more striking illustration of this determination was Singapore's Competition Commission's 2011 decision to fine 16 employment agencies for discussing the merits of instituting a pay raise for Indonesian domestic workers in order to make Singapore a more attractive employment destination (Tan, 2011; Toh, 2012). The Commission ruled that the agencies were colluding to set salaries that "should be determined by market forces."

The increasing intensity of competition in this labor market is acting as a fetter on efforts to improve migrant domestic workers' wages. Yet there appears to be little change in the claims that are made on their earnings by the institutions responsible for the global labor chain, and this is amply demonstrated in the costs that workers incur in remitting income to their families. The World Bank in particular regards the exorbitant transmission fees as a principal impediment to the development potential of remittances. Despite the Bank urging that labor-exporting states encourage commercial banks to become more actively involved in the money transfer business, money transfer agencies still dominate the business, and the fees they charge for their services continue to be a drain on the income remitted (World Bank, 2006).

Returning migrants do not escape this chain of claims on their earnings either. Labor-exporting states have adopted a range of measures to assist workers' return. For instance, in an initiative designed to assist the return of migrant workers, the Indonesian government opened a designated point of entry, 'Terminal 3,' at the Soekarno-Hatta International Airport through which returning migrant workers could be expeditiously processed. The special facility was established to "provide formal, state-regulated, safe and reasonably priced transportation to take [returning migrant] workers back to their home villages" (Silvey, 2007, pp.265–6). However, rather than prevent the corrupt overcharging and exploitation of migrant workers that it was designed to circumvent, personal links between the airport management and the relevant Government Minister has served to institutionalize the corrupt practices.

The labor-exporting states have also established reintegration programs with a view to pressuring workers to channel their earnings into business enterprises or community development ventures. This reflects the instrumental approach to labor migration that international financial institutions, and especially the World Bank, have impressed upon labor-exporting states (ADB, 2006; World Bank, 2006). The World Bank and other financial institutions have encouraged labor-exporting states to get workers to repatriate their funds through official banking channels, because this not only provides a clear measure of the labor-exporting strategy, it also provides an indication of the magnitude of future remittance flows, serving as a potential flow of export revenue against which governments, as well as businesses, can borrow. The capacity to leverage against future remittance flows for funding additional investment in the nation is believed to underscore the developmental significance of the labor-exporting strategy, but it also locks governments into maintaining labor migration as a crucial part of their economic program (Bevacqua, 2008).[8] This instrumentalist approach contributes to institutionalizing the migrant worker experience as one framed by the generation of capital. It highlights the integral link between the global care chain and the global circuit of capital, which is an association that entails the capitalization of labor.

Empowering Migrant Domestic Workers and the Value of Domestic Labor

With the different stakeholders seeking to maximize their returns from involvement in the global care chain, the different points of the chain of labor migration and money exchanges (that have their roots in the commodification of labor) thus become sites of contestation. This multilayered conflict, I contend, frames the migrant labor experience. The different institutional stages of the migration-remittance chain (that underpin the multiple layers of the claims made on workers' earnings) have become a defining feature of the efforts to empower migrant workers. The importance of investing in empowerment has been a particular focus of the discourse on women workers. This is fundamentally about employment protections; a major concern has been pursuing measures that enhance the rewards of temporary labor migration. Given the argument here, it should come as no surprise that empowerment is conceptualized in financial terms. The economic imperative is, of course, a principal motivating factor for migrants, and this is an understandable preoccupation of financial institutions and, most notably, the World Bank and the Asian Development Bank, as it is for the labor-exporting states (World Bank, 2006; ADB, 2006). However, the association of empowerment with efforts to increase the magnitude of remittances and to secure the remittances for workers' families, has also come to define those institutions whose mission is advancing migrant worker rights (ILO, 2012; Rahman, 2009; Ong, 2006).

The ILO considers changing the power relationships in the labor market and the related capital one to be crucial for migrant workers' empowerment. Some of the initiatives that could be taken toward realizing this end have been outlined by the ILO (2006); it advocates that commercial banks should provide loans to migrant workers to fund their search for employment and cover their travel costs.[9] The ILO considers systematic regulation of recruitment agencies to be essential, and it also supports regulation of the large number of agencies that are currently clandestine and many of which are set up by registered agencies. The inefficiencies in state processing of visa applications, expediting the procedures, reducing the imposition of unnecessary charges and limiting the fees associated with predeparture training should also be addressed.[10] More informative predeparture briefings to better acquaint workers with their employment rights should be introduced. Additionally, the ILO advocates more concerted efforts to regulate recruitment and placement of workers to reduce the incidence of irregular labor migration. It considers enhancing consular support for workers in destination countries as essential to this task. Moreover, the ILO emphasizes the importance of assisting returning migrant workers and their families in their reintegration by increasing employment opportunities for them. For instance, loans would enable those workers to establish business ventures that could counteract the economic pressures that drive people to migrate.

Economic empowerment is the overriding preoccupation, although other aspects of empowerment, such as 'sociocultural empowerment and social protection' and 'political empowerment,' including, "*participation in discourses of important national policy*, [and] particularly issues that directly relate to their status as migrant workers' (*sic*) are regarded as important" (Ofreneo and Samonte, 2005, pp.19–20). But, as was clearly articulated in the ILO empowerment program for Filipina workers, the paramount objective was fair wages:

> The payment of [decent] wages . . . will enable them not only to maintain a decent standard of living while working overseas, but also allow them the capacity to save and productively use their earnings in anticipation of their resettlement in the Philippines. (*loc.cit.*)

The ILO is not the only organization that focuses primarily on improving the material fortunes of migrant workers; enhancing the economic rights of workers has been a key concern of other migrant worker advocacy groups (as Briones (2009) has noted), and it is generally one that they have pursued to the neglect of other rights for those workers, such as the right to citizenship. This has served to reinforce the emphasis on the economic benefits of labor migration by focusing on 'savings and investment mobilization,' and developing policies that are designed to promote investment and *entrepinoy* (entrepreneurial) endeavor and which buttress the economically instrumentalist approach to labor migration.

Expressed in these terms, the value of migrant labor is reduced to a somewhat narrowly defined economic reckoning, and enhancing the value of labor necessarily means contesting the efforts of the different stakeholders to extract a share of the proceeds of workers' earnings. This aligns with the more noteworthy concrete initiatives pursued by the governments of the Philippines and Indonesia to mandate minimum wages and work conditions for migrant domestic workers and to have these enforced in labor-importing countries. The Philippines government has made a concerted effort to secure minimum wage agreements to bolster the earning potential of migrant domestic workers. The government set a target minimum wage of $US400 a month, an increase from the average market rate of some $US350 a month and has mandated this be incorporated into employment contracts as a requirement before it will issue an exit visa. The government has successfully concluded a bilateral agreement with the Singaporean government endorsing this provision and is now pursuing this target with the Gulf states (ABS-CBNnews.com, 2012). The Indonesian government has recently followed suit, concluding a similar agreement with Singapore that sets a minimum wage of $US360 a month, and is seeking to negotiate this minimum wage agreement with other states, including Malaysia and some of the Gulf states (Tan, 2012a; CAW, 2009; CARAM Asia, 2013; Cochrane, 2013). The difficulty that these governments face in ensuring that the terms of such minimum standards are honored is in countering the practice that some recruitment agencies have adopted of getting workers to sign two contracts. One is worded to meet the minimum remuneration standards and employment conditions; the other has inferior terms and conditions, reflecting the 'market rate' of terms and conditions that are afforded to workers recruited from other source countries where governments have not set minimum standards.[11]

As the primary rationale driving individuals to seek offshore employment is to enhance their families' and their own material well-being, how they can maximize the return on their work efforts is an important consideration. Their capacity, however, to limit the claims made on their earnings is somewhat constrained. As the World Bank study of migrant domestic workers established, women who work as domestic workers tend to have access to fewer financial resources than their skilled-worker counterparts or male migrant workers (World Bank, 2009). Their ability to negotiate employment conditions and rates of remuneration with recruitment agencies is constrained by the institutional arrangements that privilege the agencies' interests over that of the women's on the grounds that those agencies are the conduits that make it possible for the women to enter the international labor market. By indicating their preferred employment destination, women who are employed as domestic workers could exercise some control over their employment options and earning possibilities. However, as I was informed by a number of workers, the exercise of preferences is subject to their capacity to meet the additional costs associated with seeking employment in the higher-paying destinations. Many of the women who were employed in Singapore indicated their preferred employment destination was Hong Kong, but they had been persuaded to accept work in Singapore; the recruitment agency had advised them that an established employment history would stand them in good stead when they sought employment in the higher-paying destination.

Migrant domestic workers have some recourse to redress contract abuses. Migrant worker advocacy groups in the Philippines and Indonesia have pressured labor-exporting states to provide labor attachés at their embassies, and this has enhanced the ability of women migrant domestic workers to try to ensure that their rights as workers are respected. But as residence rights are contingent on employment, the extended length of time it takes to pursue redress can result in workers being expelled before their case is heard by the courts, utterly frustrating the exercise of their rights. With labor-importing countries sourcing workers from an ever-growing number of countries, the competition to secure work has become more intense for migrant workers. The fear that they could be replaced by workers paid lower wages and employed on more onerous terms has discouraged workers from asserting their rights. Some migrant worker organizations have reported that labor attachés at their home nations' embassies were reluctant to exert much pressure on the host nation because of the fear that that could jeopardize the demand for workers from their nation and, thus, the stream of export revenue.

The link in the global care chain where workers are most able to avoid claims on their earnings is in the remittance of their wages. A number of workers I interviewed indicated that they prefer having their friends (who were returning to their home nation) act as money couriers and, thus, avoid the fees charged by money transfer agencies. It also allowed some of them to circumvent the scrutiny of their financial affairs by the government. This, however, was not an entirely risk-free strategy, because there is the danger that the monies could be stolen or lost. The experience of many Indonesians who were taken advantage of when returning through 'Terminal 3' at the Soekarno-Hatta International Airport is evidence of this problem.

MOVING FORWARD?

Migrant worker organizations and advocacy groups have made important advances in their efforts to improve remuneration standards and to reduce the magnitude of claims made on workers' earnings by state and non-state actors, thereby enhancing the financial benefits of migration for workers. They have been able to pressure the governments of labor-exporting countries and (some) labor-importing countries to better regulate the institutional arrangements that facilitate labor migration. They have also contested government regulations that enhance the market power of the politically powerful recruitment agencies (IOM, 2008; Morgan and Nolan, 2011). For instance, they have campaigned against the restrictions that lock workers into agreements with particular recruitment agencies (England, 2008).

The migrant worker campaigns have served as a catalyst that has forced labor-exporting states to adopt more proactive initiatives to promote workers' interests and rights. These efforts have contributed to ameliorating the disciplining effects of the labor markets that define the global care chain in East and Southeast Asia. However, they do not engage with the significant financial burden the institutional architects of the global care chain place on women migrant domestic workers. The salience of the ILO's Domestic Worker Convention (C189) cannot be overstated. The momentum in promoting employment protections for migrant domestic workers will likely be sustained. The Convention provides additional leverage to migrant worker advocacy groups and other civil society organizations for pressuring labor-exporting states that have ratified the Convention to institute more meaningful measures to afford greater protections for workers. Such pressure should also strengthen the resolve of labor-exporting states to invest more effort in negotiating bilateral and multilateral agreements with labor-importing states to improve workers' employment rights and ensure conditions for their meaningful exercise.

It is however important to acknowledge the limitations of the Convention as an instrument for enhancing the employment rights of migrant domestic workers. The Convention sanctions the global care chain but is silent on the question of the capitalization of labor and the claims on the earnings of migrant domestic workers by various entities. There is nothing in the Convention that speaks directly to the need to address the exploitative nature of the global circuit of capital in which these female workers are caught. It fails to recognize that regulating the excessive charges of moneylenders, recruitment and placement agencies and money transfer agents is crucial if some degree of balance is to be introduced in the labor markets. The Convention also sanctions temporariness as the foundation of the global care chain, without acknowledging that it undermines migrant domestic workers' rights. Temporary resident status means that migrant domestic workers do not have the freedom to negotiate with an employer of their choice, or to find work in a preferred location or pursue any employment claims. Most migrant workers do not seek to migrate and resettle permanently, but some do (Ong, 2006). Crucially, however, recognizing some form of resident rights, on terms that are comparable to those enjoyed by skilled and professional migrant workers, would seem a reasonable basis for countering the subordinate status of migrant domestic workers and the devalorization of their labor as well as for enhancing the civil and political rights that are so vital to the exercise of these workers' employment rights.

CONCLUSION

The research on the global care chain has highlighted the organization of emotional or reproductive labor across the transnational plane, capturing a very important dimension of the experience of migrant domestic workers. Similarly, research about remittances has identified the role that temporary labor migration can play in improving the material well-being of migrant workers' families and, more generally, the development potential of the global South. These research emphases must be supplemented with an appreciation of the material significance of transnational labor and how the experience of migrant domestic work is framed by the commodification of labor as a means for enhancing the financial well-being of workers and their families. The commodification of domestic labor and care work requires an appreciation of the effort of the workers to simultaneously manage the multiple demands of their workplace and their families. The experience of labor migration, however, should not simply be reduced to elucidating the nature of their work in terms of the transfer of emotional and affective labor across the transnational plane. The paramount rationale for labor migration is to exchange labor for a payment, a wage; thus to overlook the costs incurred by domestic workers and care workers in securing transnational work and the claims made on their earnings when they attempt to repatriate their savings or return to their country of origin is to ignore the considerable financial costs borne by those domestic workers and care workers. As I have argued, the opportunity to engage in transnational work sets in motion a flow of capital that is usually considered by institutions like the World Bank and sending and receiving nations as igniting development in the global South. But this flow of capital also results in multiple claims on the workers' wages by the institutional forces that contribute to the organization of the transnational labor market: the moneylenders, the labor agents, recruitment and placement agencies, the money transfer agencies, as well as the state.

A rich appraisal of the migrant worker experience will acknowledge that the exercise of emotional labor (that constitutes the global care chain) is predicated on waged labor, which in turn engenders a global circuit of capital. This circuit generates a multiplicity of disciplining forces and this is evident in a labor market that, through a number of institutional arrangements, circumscribes workers' human rights and employment rights. The general disciplining aspects of this labor market is compounded by the micro characteristics of domestic work, especially the requirement that workers meet the particular demands of the employer within the intimacy and privacy of the home of the latter. Of course, these effects can be ameliorated by the extent to which migrant domestic workers are able to successfully negotiate the terms and conditions of their employment; the role of various advocates for workers in challenging the subordinate position of workers (by promoting their employment rights in the global labor market) has been crucial in enhancing this capacity. Clearly, the conclusion of the ILO's Domestic

Workers Convention is one of the achievements of this advocacy. But a more complete grasp of the disciplining effects of the global capital circuit on workers requires taking into account the efforts of the workers to navigate their way through the maze of financial transactions associated with transnational labor (engaging in migrant domestic work comes with substantial monetary costs). These costs erode not only the real material benefits of the transnational employment venture, they also engender obligations and claims on workers that can discourage them from exercising their limited employment rights. The manner in which migrant domestic work generates an international flow of funds, engaging with the global circuit of capital, can underscore the disadvantage that defines work in the global care chain.

NOTES

1. Taiwan has also relaxed restrictions on the recruitment of Indonesian care workers (Hsiao, 2013).
2. Hong Kong's Court of Final Appeal ruled that Evangeline Banao Vallejos and Daniel Domingo would not be allowed to settle permanently in Hong Kong although they had been residing in the city for over seven years, which is the period that normally qualifies foreigners the right to become permanent residents under the constitution. (Ms. Vallejos has worked in Hong Kong for 27 years and Mr. Domingo for 28 years.) Following the Hong Kong's First Court of Instance ruling in September 2011, that legislation restricting foreign domestic workers from qualifying for permanent residence contravened the Hong Kong Basic Law and, thus, held up the right of Ms. Vallejos to apply for permanent residence, almost one thousand migrant workers applied for permanent residence.
3. The Hong Kong administration mandates workers' right to one day free of work each week. Taiwan has a similar provision, although this can be negotiated away, and Singapore has recently adopted a similar provision following the Taiwan model, which will apply to new recruits.
4. The residency restrictions in all destination countries in South East and East Asia that govern the issue of migrant domestic worker visas proscribe family reunion possibilities as well as any scope for resettlement, and the consequence is that workers necessarily retain a continuing association with their country of origin, an association that is generally underscored by continuing family responsibilities.
5. These initiatives have prompted governments of other Asian labor-export states, such as Nepal, to try to negotiate minimum wage agreements with governments in the Gulf states (Joshi, 2012)
6. The shift in Taiwan's labor sourcing is partly motivated by international political considerations. In the wake of the Philippines' Coast Guard firing on a Taiwanese fishing vessel in the contested territorial waters of the South China Sea and killing two fishermen, Taiwan flagged its intention to restrict the recruitment of Filipino workers (Einhorn, 2013).
7. Despite the Hong Kong administration agreeing to increase the minimum wage for foreign domestic workers in 2011, the wage is still below the 1998 level when it was subsequently reduced to accommodate the difficult circumstances (United for Foreign Domestic Workers' Rights, 2011) faced by employers in

the wake of the Asian financial crisis (United for Foreign Domestic Workers' Rights, 2011).
8. This report published by the Economist Intelligence Unit report was funded by the money transfer company Western Union.
9. Enlisting microfinance to provide funds to assist migrant workers is another strategy being advocated (Barnes et al., 2007).
10. See also International Domestic Workers Network (2012). Paradoxically, the World Bank acknowledges that the exercise and abuse of market power by recruitment agencies results in workers incurring substantial costs. However, the Bank argues against labor-exporting states strengthening the regulation of recruitment and labor placement industries for fear such interventions could place labor-exporting countries at a competitive disadvantage. This contrasts with the efforts of the Committee on Payment and Settlement Systems and IMF to establish a voluntary code of principles for remittance service providers (World Bank, 2006).
11. This practice of migrant domestic workers being provided with two different contracts of employment, one of which is designed to meet the minimum employment standards set by the government of the labor-exporting state, mirrors the practice (mentioned above) of workers discovering upon their arrival in the employment destination that their contract has been substituted for one that has inferior terms and conditions than those promised to them by the labor recruitment agency.

REFERENCES AND FURTHER READINGS

ABS-CBNnews.com, 2012. Singapore employers' upgrade of maids' pay hailed. [online] Available at: <http://www.abs-cbnnews.com/global-filipino/12/18/12/singapore-employersupgrade-maids-pay-hailed> [Accessed 1 March 2013].

Ananta, A., 2009. Estimating the value of the business of sending low skilled workers abroad: The Indonesian case. [online] Available at: <http://iussp2009.princeton.edu/papers/91804>.

Anggraeni, D., 2006. *Dreamseekers: Indonesian women as domestic workers in Asia*. Jakarta: Equinox Publishing/ILO.

Anon, 2011. Taiwan—Indonesian agreement on domestic workers. *The Jakarta Post*,[online] 5 May. Available at: <http://udfwrs.blogspot.com.au/2011/05/taiwan-indonesiaagreement-on-domestic.html> [Accessed 8 May 2013].

Asian Development Bank (ADB), 2006. *Workers' remittance flows in Southeast Asia*. Manila: ADB.

Asian Migrant Centre, Indonesian Migrant Workers Union and the Hong Kong Coalition of Indonesian Migrant Workers Organization, 2007. *Underpayment 2: The continuing systematic extortion of Indonesian migrant workers in Hong Kong: An in-depth study*. Hong Kong: AMC.

Association of Women for Action and Research (AWARE), 2010. Transient Workers Count Too, 2012. Fact sheet: Foreign domestic workers in Singapore (Basic Statistics), 16 November. [online] Available at: <http://twc2.org.sg/2011/11/16/fact-sheet-foreigndomestic-workers-in-singapore-basic-statistics/> [Accessed 1 May 2013].

Barker, D., 2012. Querying the paradox of caring labor. *Rethinking Marxism: A Journal of Economics, Culture and Society* 24 (4), pp.574–91.

Barnes, F., Shuaib, F., Shaw, J. and Eversole, R., 2007. *Leveraging remittances with microfinance: Indonesia country report*. Brisbane: The Foundation for Development Support.

Basu, R., 2011. Where have Singapore's Indonesian maids gone? *Straits Times*, [online] 27 March. Available at: <http://www.thejakartaglobe.com/archive/where-have-spores indonesian-maids-gone/> [Accessed 15 May 2013].

Bevacqua, R., 2008. *Building a future back home: Leveraging migrant worker remittances for development in Asia*. London: Economist Intelligence Unit.

Boontinand, V., 2010. *Domestic workers in Thailand: Situation, challenges and the way forward*. Bangkok: International Labour Organization.

Briones, L., 2009. *Empowering migrant women: Why agency and capability are not enough*. Farnham, Surrey: Ashgate.

Bustanuddin, 2007. RI's migrant workers are foreign exchange "heroes." *The Eco-Soc Rights News Monitor*, [online] 1 June. Available at: <http://ecosocmonitor.blogspot.com.au/2007/06/ris-migrant-workers-are-foreign.html> [Accessed 12 February 2013].

Cheng, S. A., 2003. Rethinking the globalization of domestic service: Foreign domestics, state control, and the politics of identity in Taiwan. In: M. K. Zimmerman, J. S. Litt and C.E. Bose. eds. 2006. *Global dimensions of gender and carework*, Stanford: Stanford University Press, pp.128–44.

Cochrane, J., 2013. Indonesia asks Saudis to extend deadline for undocumented workers. *The New York Times*, [online] 10 June. Available at: <http://www.nytimes.com/2013/06/11/world/asia/indonesia-asks-saudi-arabia-to-extenddeadline-for-undocumented-workers> [Accessed 11 June 2013].

Committee for Asian Women (CAW), 2009. *Indonesia pushes for better migrant-worker protection*. [online] Available at: <http://www.cawinfo.org/2009/10/indonesia-pushes-forbetter-migrant-worker-protection/> [Accessed 26 March 2010].

Constable, N., 1997. *Maid to order in Hong Kong: Stories of Filipina workers*. Ithaca: Cornell University Press.

Coordination of Action on Research on AIDS and Mobility (CARAM Asia), 2013. *Governments in Asia and the Middle East ensure a comprehensive right protection program for migrant workers through a committed regional cooperation*. Press statement, 11 June 2013. [online] Available at: <http://www.caramasia.org/?p=1607> [Accessed 14 June 2013].

Einhorn, B., 2013. As the Philippines and Taiwan fight, migrant workers suffer. *Bloomberg Businessweek*, [online] 16 May. Available at: <http://www.businessweek.com/articles/201305-16/philippines-and-taiwan-fight-and-migrant-workers-suffer> [Accessed 25 May 2013].

Elias, J., 2010. Making migrant domestic workers visible: The rights based approach to migration and 'the challenges of social reproduction'. *Review of International Political Economy* 17 (5), pp.840–59.

England, V., 2008. Indonesian migrant workers fight for fairness. *South China Morning Post*, [online] 17 February. Available at: <http://webcache.googleusercontent.com/search?q=cache:nWW3PGM6YLoJ:www.scmp.com/article/626470/indonesian-migrant-workers-fight-fairness+&cd=1&hl=en&ct=clnk&gl=us > [Accessed 07 July 2015].

Fuchs, R., 2011. Migrant domestic workers in Taiwan. *International Training Workshop on the Implementation of CEDAW*. [online] 1 December. Hope Workers Center. Available at: <http://tw.migrantworkers.org/index.php?option=com_content&view=article&id=100:interntional-training-workshop-on-the-implementation-of-cedaw&catid=1:latestnews&Itemid=58&lang=in> [Accessed 6 February 2013].

Gooch, L., 2012. Malaysia urged to protect domestic workers. *The New York Times*, 3 December. [online] Available at: <http://www.nytimes.com/2012/12/04/world/asia/malaysia-urged-to-protect-domesticworkers.html?_r=0> [Accessed 4 December 2012].

Gutiérrez-Rodríguez, E., 2010. *Migration, domestic work and affect: A decolonial approach on value and the feminization of labor.* New York: Routledge.
Ho, Cecilia, 2010. Macau overlooks migrant workers' hardships and contributions. *Macau Daily Times,* [online] 12 April. Available at: <http://deltabridges.com/macau-news/ceciliaho-macau-overlooks-migrant-workers-hardships-and-contributions> [Accessed 15 May2013].
Ho, J. and Chan, T., 2012 Move to welcome mainland helpers welcomed in Macau. *The South China Morning Post,* [online] 24 November. Available at: <http://www.scmp.com/news/hong-kong/article/1089442/move-allow-mainland-helperswelcomed-macau> [Accessed 15 April 2013].
Hochschild, A.R., 1997. Global care chains and emotional surplus value. In: W. Hutton and A. Giddens, eds. 1997. *On the edge: Living with global capitalism.* London: Jonathan Cape, pp.13–146.
Hsiao, A., 2013. Group slams care services draft act. *Taipei Times,* [online] 9 March. Available at: <http://www.taipeitimes.com/News/taiwan/archives/2013/03/09/2003556658> [Accessed 8 May 2013].
Hugo, G.J., 2009. Best practice in temporary labour migration for development: A perspective from Asia and the Pacific, *International Migration,* 47 (5), pp.23–74.
Human Rights Watch, 2011. *'They deceived us at every step': Abuse of Cambodian domestic workers migrating to Malaysia.* New York. [pdf] Available at: <http://www.hrw.org/sites/default/files/reports/cambodia1111webwcover.pdf> [Accessed 4December 2012].
Inquirer.net, 2011. *Foreign maids in Hong Kong to get HK $160 Pay Rise.* Pinoy.com, [online] 2 June. Available at: <http://www.pinoy-ofw.com/news/11836-domestic-helperwage-increase-160.html> [Accessed 1 May 2013].
International Domestic Workers Network, 2012. UN CEDAW committee recommendations should sound alarm bells in Indonesia and Hong Kong. [online] Available at: <http://www.idwn.info/news/un-cedaw-committee-recommendations-should-sound-alarmbells-indonesia-and-hong-kong> [Accessed 1 May 2013].
International Labour Organization (ILO), 2006. *Using Indonesian law to protect and empower migrant workers: Some lessons from the Philippines.* Jakarta. [pdf] Available at: < http://www.ilo.org/jakarta/whatwedo/publications/WCMS_122285/lang—en/index.htm> [Accessed 4 February 2013].
International Labour Organization (ILO), 2012. Providing better economic protection to Indonesian migrant workers. Press release, 19 March 2012. [online] Available at: <http://www.ilo.org/jakarta/info/public/pr/WCMS_176878/lang—en/index.htm> [Accessed1 May 2013].
International Organization for Migration (IOM), 2008. Summary of Proceedings regional conference-workshop. In: *Organizing the association of employment agencies in Asia: Moving forward to action on ethical recruitment.* Manila, Philippines 3–4 April, Manila, Philippines: IOM.
International Organization for Migration and Economic Resource Center for Overseas Filipinos (IOM and ERCOF), 2010. *International migration and migrant workers' remittances in Indonesia: Findings of baseline surveys of migrant remitters and remittance beneficiary households.* Makati City, Philippines: IOM.
Joshi, Y.R., 2012. Minimum wage for domestic workers to the Gulf. *The Himalayan Times,* 28 June [online] Available at: <http://udfwrs.blogspot.com.au/2012/06/minimum-wage-forsouthasian-domestic.html> [Accessed 8 May 2013].
Lan, P., 2006. *Global cinderellas: Migrant domestics and newly rich employers in Taiwan.* Durham, NC: Duke University Press.

Loveband, A., 2009. *Nationality matters: Indonesian foreign domestic workers in contemporary Taiwan*. Ph.D. University of Wollongong.

Morgan, G. and Nolan, C., 2011. *Step up: Improving recruitment of migrant workers in Indonesia*. Jakarta: BSR. [pdf] Available at: <http://www.bsr.org/reports/Improving_Migrant_Worker_Recruitment_in_Indonesia.pdf> [Accessed 5 May 2013].

Ofreneo, R. E. and Samonte, I. A., 2005. Empowering Filipino migrant workers: Policy issues and challenges. *International Migration Papers*, 64. Geneva: International Labour Office.

Ong, A., 2006. *Neoliberalism as exception: Mutations in citizenship and sovereignty*. Durham: Duke University Press.

Onuki, H., 2009. Care, social (re)production and global migration: Japan's 'special gift' toward 'innately gifted' Filipino workers. *New Political Economy*, 14(4), pp.489–516.

Pan, X., 2013. Greedy practices put some domestic workers into a state of indentured servitude. *Domestic Worker Project*, [online] 17 March. Available at: <http://www.domesticworkerproject.com/2013/03/17/debt-and-despair/> [Accessed 1 May 2013].

Parreñas, R. S., 2006. *Servants of globalization: Women, migration and domestic work*. Stanford: Stanford University Press.

Pearson, R. and Kusakabe, K., 2012. *Thailand's hidden workforce: Burmese migrant women factory workers*. London: Zed Books.

Phillips, N., 2009. Migration as development strategy? The new political economy of dispossession and inequality in the Americas. *Review of International Political Economy* 16 (2), pp.231–59.

Piper, N., 2008. Political participation and empowerment of foreign workers—gendered advocacy and migrant labor organizing in Southeast and East Asia. In: N. Piper, ed. 2008. *New perspectives on gender and migration: Livelihood, rights and entitlements*. London: Routledge, pp.249–73.

Purba, K., 2013. Commentary: EPA with Japan only a means to get cheap Indonesian nurses. [online] 18 January. Available at: <http://www.thejakartapost.com/news/2013/01/18/commentary-epa-with-japan-only-ameans-get-cheap-indonesian-nurses.html> [Accessed 15 May 2013].

Quratul-ain, B. B. S. B., 2013. NGOs study plight of domestic helpers. *The Brunei Times*, [online] 8 April. Available at: <http://www.bt.com.bn/news-national/2013/04/08/ngos-study-plight-domestic-helpers> [Accessed 1 May 2013].

Rahman, Md M., 2009. *Gender dimensions of remittances: A study of Indonesian domestic workers in East and Southeast Asia*. Bangkok: Unifem.

Rahman, Z., 2013. Hong Kong to recruit 100,000 Bangladeshi female workers. *The Independent*, [online] 4 January. Available at: <http://www.cawinfo.org/?p=4253> [Accessed 10 May 2013].

Rodriguez, R. M., 2002. Migrant heroes: Nationalism, citizenship and the politics of Filipino migrant labor. *Citizenship Studies* 6 (3), pp.341–56.

Rodriguez, R. M., 2008. The labor brokerage state and the globalization of Filipina careworkers. *Signs: Journal of Women in Culture and Society* 33 (4), pp.794–800.

Rosewarne, S., 2012. Temporary international labor migration and development in South and Southeast Asia. *Feminist Economics* 18 (2), pp.63–90.

Rosewarne, S., 2013. The ILO's Domestic Worker Convention (C189): Challenging the gendered disadvantage of Asia's foreign domestic workers? *Global Labour Journal* 4 (1), pp.1–25.

Silvey, R., 2007. Unequal borders: Indonesian transnational migrants at immigration control. *Geopolitics*, 12 (2), pp.265–79.

Stott, D. A., 2008. The Japan-Indonesian economic partnership: Agreement between equals?' *The Asia-Pacific Journal: Japan Focus*, [online] 13 July. Available at:

<http://www.japanfocus.org/-David_Adam-Stott/2818/article.html> [Accessed 07 July 2015].
Tan, A., 2011. 16 employment agencies fined for fixing maids' salaries. *The Straits Times Indonesia*, [online] 1 October. Available at: <http://www.thejakartaglobe.com/archive/16maid-agencies-fined-for-price-fixing/> [Accessed 10 May 2013].
Tan, A., 2012a. Singapore to increase Indonesian maid salaries after November. *The Straits Times*, [online] 13 August. Available at: <http://www.thejakartaglobe.com/archive/singapore-to-increase-indonesian-maid-salariesafter-november/> [Accessed 10 May 2013].
Tan, A., 2012b. Talks under way to source maids from Cambodia. *The Straits Times*, [online] 22 September. Available at: <http:www.straitstimes.com/breakingnews/Singapore/story/talks-under-way-source-maids-from-cambodia> [Accessed 10 May 2013].
Tan, A., 2013. 10 maid agencies face temporary ban. *The Straits Times*, [online] 11 April. Available at: <http://www.straitstimes.com/the-big-story/case-you-missed-it/story/10-maidagencies-face-temporary-ban> [Accessed 10 May 2013].
Toh, H.L., 2012. Challenges on cartel enforcement. In: *7th East Asia conference on competition law and policy*. Kuala Lumpur, Malaysia 2 May. Competition Commission of Singapore, [pdf] Available at: <http://www.adbi.org/files/2012.05.02.cpp.sess2.4.li.challenges.cartels.enforcement.pdf> [Accessed 15 May 2013].
United for Foreign Domestic Workers' Rights, 2011. Asian migrants say 'OK to 4K.'[online] 23 May. Available at: <http://udfwrs.blogspot.com.au/2011/05/asian-migrants-sayok-to-4k.html> [Accessed 8 May 2013].
United Nations Development Programme (UNDP), 2009. *Human development report 2009—overcoming barriers: Human mobility and development*. New York: Palgrave Macmillan.
United Nations International Research and Training Institute for the Advancement of Women (UN-INSTRAW), 2006. *Gender, migration, remittances and development*. New York : UN-INSTRAW.
US Consulate Hong Kong, 2009. New Macau labor law to prevent 'job hopping' by foreign workers. Ref Id09HONGKONG2156, aka Wikileaks id #23616, [online] 24 November. Available at: <http:www//.cablegatesearch.net/cable.php?id=09HONGKONG2156>[Accessed 15 May 2013].
Varia, N., 2007. Indonesia, Malaysia: Overhaul labor agreement on domestic workers Human Rights Watch, [online] 22 February. Available at: <http://www.hrw.org/news/2007/02/20/indonesiamalaysia-overhaul-labor-agreement-domestic-workers>.
World Bank, 2006. *Global economic prospects: Economic implications of remittances and migration*. Washington, DC: International Bank for Reconstruction and Development/World Bank.
World Bank, 2009. *Workshop on enhancing access to formal financial services enhancing access to finance for migrant workers in Indonesia* (report). World Bank and IFC projects and studies on gender in economic sectors: Empowering female migrant workers and their families through improving access to finance. Washington, DC: International Bank for Reconstruction and Development/World Bank.
Yeates, N., 2004. Global care chains: Critical reflections and lines of enquiry. *International Feminist Journal of Politics* 6 (3), pp.369–91.
Yi, B.L., 2011. Malaysia suffers shortage in foreign domestic help. *Inquirer Global Nation*, [online] 25 January. Available at: <http://globalnation.inquirer.net/news/breakingnews/view/20110125-316477/Malaysiasuffers-shortage-in-foreign-domestic-help> [Accessed 15 April 2013].

10 Hopes and Expectations Dashed
Migrant Women, the Informal Welfare State and Women's Labor Force Participation in Greece[1]

Antigone Lyberaki

INTRODUCTION

Since the 1990s, women from Eastern Europe have been employed by middle class Southern European families as care workers and domestic workers. Using Greece as a case study, this chapter examines the features of Greek society and economy that created this employment niche. It also assesses the effect of the economic crisis on Albanian women migrant workers in Greece and considers their future prospects in that country.[2] It argues for a state supervised market in care services and domestic work that does not discriminate against migrant workers.

Greek economic history can be categorized into two distinct periods. The first is the period leading up to the crisis—the times of plenty. In 2010, the economic model supporting that period collapsed in the most spectacular way with Greece's near bankruptcy. The subsequent crisis period has been characterized by the realization that the *status quo ante* was not feasible and hence had to change. The process of seeking a postcrisis state of affairs that does not reproduce old dilemmas, but can still somehow accommodate the aspirations of the Greek population, is underway; although, at the time this chapter was written in 2014 it was far from complete.

Prior to and during the present crisis period, migrant workers played a key role in Greek economy and society. Since the early 1990s, women migrant workers facilitated middle class Greek women's entry into the labor force and liberation from parochial and patriarchal roles. The spread of prosperity meant fast growth throughout the period; the development of a part-time care work market passed the benefits lower down the social scale. This newly formed market in domestic work and care services served as a partial solution to key structural problems within the Greek economy and society, and it alleviated some of the pressures on the welfare state and an economy suffering from a labor shortage.

Women immigrants in Greece found a niche in a two-speed society that was divided between 'insiders' and 'outsiders.' Greek society was characterized by the coexistence, on the one side, of privileged small groups, chiefly in the public or large corporate sector and, on the other side, larger groups of less fortunate individuals in the small-scale private sector (primarily in the wholesale and retail trade sectors) and in the service industries (such as financial intermediation, hotels and restaurants and health and personal service). The privileges of the 'insider' groups were evident in their higher salaries, greater labor market protection and more generous social protection. When the recession set in, this system (and immigrants as the most exposed 'outsiders' in the system) came under acute pressure. Shrinking incomes, high unemployment and falling demand threatened their achievements; their environment also became increasingly hostile and intolerant, characterized by instances of xenophobia, hate and violence.

So, even though migrant women performed crucial functions that allowed Greek society and economy to thrive, what their role will be in the *new* postcrisis equilibrium—when and if that is attained—remains an open question. Depending on the shape of things to come, their dreams of prosperity might be salvaged. A lot will depend on the success of structural reforms currently under way and the termination of Greek's two-speed society. If Greece becomes a society where there is a level playing field between the native born (i.e., Greek citizens) and the migrants, migrant women workers may be able to compete on fair terms and benefit from their hard work. The alternative scenario might be a Greece with an economy that is very much like the one that existed prior to the crisis, however, it will be one in which migrant workers will earn much less than they did previously and will be more marginalized than before.

This chapter provides a framework to illuminate this conundrum. I begin by surveying the available theoretical and empirical literature, using primarily the lens of feminist economics. I place female migration in the larger context of the women's labor market involvement and more specifically in the realm of care work. This allows me to conduct a detailed examination of the issues of migration, including the recent feminization of migration. In the second section, I consider the roles played by migrant workers in Greek society—before, during and after the economic crisis. In section three, I examine the economic crisis and the yet unanswered questions regarding its likely impact on migration. Using as my case study the provision of long-term care for the elderly, I illustrate the importance of public policy in creating and configuring the employment niche for Albanian migrant women workers in Greece—historically the largest group of migrants. Depending on Greece's policy choices, the place of migrant workers in the economy could vary considerably. I argue that this wait-and-see attitude is apparently shared by the Albanian migrant women workers who I surveyed in early 2013. In the conclusion, I return to the big picture and ask about the prospects of female migrants and the extent to which they can be improved by Greece's policy decisions.

WOMEN ON THE MOVE IN SOUTHERN EUROPE

The 'Greek crisis' is emblematic of the 'Great Recession' and its impact on Europe. Before, however, analyzing Greece from a feminist economics perspective, I examine what is known about female migration and how the crisis affects it. This helps to set the context for addressing the Greek case later in the chapter.

Feminist economics considers four sets of issues to be of critical importance. First, women's participation in the labor market and the choices made by women given the existence of gender roles. Second, care provision and the nexus of state-family-market in care services. Third, the broader trends favoring the feminization of migration as a distinct facet of globalization, and the implications this has for the welfare and life prospects of women migrants and, more broadly, women in the labor-exporting and labor-importing countries. Fourth, the effects of the economic downturn and the financial crisis on the women's participation in the labor market, social and care services and female migrants' prospects.

Factors Affecting the Labor Supply of Women

Care needs and gender roles affect the real choices for women. The broad trend favoring women's increased involvement in paid work is apparent throughout the world, but the process is not uniform and neither are its rates of change. Understanding the stop-go phases of women's employment as well as the underlying facilitating and inhibiting factors are important both for analysis and policy. In Southern Europe (i.e., Italy, Spain, Portugal, Cyprus and Greece), women participate in the labor market to a considerably lower degree compared to the Nordic countries, the Anglo-Saxon economies and even Continental Europe. Although women in the Mediterranean South have been steadily increasing their labor market involvement, a significant employment gap persists. These are the economies where the family is 'strong' in function (i.e., it has a decisive role in allocating tasks and roles to its members) and 'long' in duration (it retains its role well after the official coming of age of children and performs solidarity functions among generations throughout the life cycle) (Bengston and Roberts, 1991; Reher, 1998; Kohli, Kunemund and Ludicke, 2005; Attias-Donfut, Ogg and Wolff, 2005). The persistence of the 'strong' and 'long' family not only interferes with women's economic independence options and influences whether women get paid jobs, but also the type of jobs that are deemed appropriate for them within the gendered division of roles and obligations.

The Family and Care Provision

Feminist economics is interested in the way the economy provides—or fails to provide—resources for the care of children and the elderly. Hence, many of the questions feminist economists ask are related to care work. Concern over the need to provide care for children and long-term care for the elderly in the context of ageing societies has motivated researchers to analyze the balance between the demand and the supply of care.[3] In theory, care needs can be provided by the state (social infrastructure), the market ('outsourcing' of care to private providers),[4] or the family. It could also be provided by some combination of the three approaches. The partial outsourcing (i.e., delegating) of the caring activities hitherto performed within the family has important implications for women's labor force participation. It is both a precondition and a result of greater paid work involvement of women. It has been estimated that between the 1960s and the 1990s, the average couple in the US was responsible for adding the equivalent of another part-time job in the economy in order to compensate for the reduction of time and effort spent on children and leisure (Schor, 1991), while equivalent (although lower) estimates have been made for the case of Europe (Esping-Andersen, 2002).

It is difficult to overstress the significance of the family in care provision in Southern Europe (Bettio and Villa, 1998; Ferrera, 1996; Gershuny and Sullivan, 2003). Although the architecture of the system was in the process of recalibration during the 1990s and early 2000s (Ferrera, 2010), the Mediterranean welfare state has remained strongly familial (i.e., the family is responsible for the bulk of care work for the young and the elderly), and gender roles remained unchanged to a far greater extent than elsewhere on the continent.

Nevertheless, there have been some changes. Over the past four decades, in Southern European nations, women's time spent on domestic work has been declining, while women's paid work has been on the rise (Kan, Sullivan and Gershuny, 2011). The decline in women's domestic work time was due largely to the fewer hours they spent on routine housework and only to a lesser degree attributable to men's greater domestic work involvement (Kan, Sullivan and Gershuny, 2011). Greater gender inequality is found in routine housework and care for children and other adults, while the less gender-stereotyped chores (such as gardening, shopping and DIYs) exhibited faster role convergence. This is particularly the case in the Mediterranean countries (Spain and Italy), where normative ideologies of gender roles remain deeply entrenched. Indeed, there is evidence that the continuing effects of gendered domestic work ideologies may operate dynamically through the life course (Kan, Sullivan and Gershuny, 2011 and also Kan and Gershuny, 2009).[5]

In Mediterranean countries over the past few decades, there has been a shift away from the 'family model' of care provision to the 'migrant-in-the-family' model. This refers to the transformation of the traditional family model of care into a new complex division of labor, whereby family carers (mainly women) provide the coordination for care and domestic work, while care work is entrusted to a female immigrant (Bettio, Simonazzi and Villa, 2006; Bettio and Solinas, 2009).[6] It appears that the familial Mediterranean welfare system with its traditional gender ideology (Risman, 2004) managed to accommodate change thanks to the invisible support of migrant women workers.

The Feminization of Migration

Migration is becoming increasingly 'feminized.' Of particular relevance are efforts to analyze the interconnections between the feminization of migration and changes in care regimes. The tasks of looking after children and the elderly were reassigned between the family (using its own resources), the private care market and state social services; the resulting division of labor entailed new roles for informal arrangements that made up for the gaps in the formal provision of care. The supply of care work is intricately linked with migrant women's labor. This is true for internal as well as for trans-border migration. Domestic tasks, which in the past had been performed by internal migrants, by the late twentieth century, became the object of female international migrants' work.[7]

This is a global phenomenon and in 2005, the number of female migrants globally was estimated at 94.5 million (49.6 percent of total). The share of women among migrants in Southern European countries was about 38.9 million (51 percent) compared with 45.2 million (51 percent) in the high-income countries, which belong to the Organization for Economic Cooperation and Development (OECD)[8] (Kofman and Raghuram, 2012). According to Kofman and Raghuram (2012), female migrants provide care in a range of contexts and sites. They find employment as domestic workers and as care professionals and facilitate the care of children, adults, the disabled and the elderly within households, in residential homes and hospitals.[9] The mobility of these women also leaves care gaps to be filled in the areas they leave behind. Hence, care demands are both being created and met through women's employment, underlining the complex causal relations that tie together migration, gendered labor and care regimes (Hochschild, 2000).

Migrants who perform care services and domestic work are less protected and more vulnerable to unfair treatment and exploitative practices than skilled health professionals. Women are concentrated in these employment sectors, recasting gender inequalities and women's subordinate labor market position within the global economy. The allocation of low-wage care work to migrant women reinforces the lower valuation of unpaid care within families and of women's labor (Herrera, 2012). After the pioneering work of Hochschild (2000), for instance, more recent work analyzing the case of Spain notes that migrant women working in the care and domestic sector face a double segregation, as they are more segregated than both native (Spanish) women and migrant men[10] (Del Río and Alonso-Villar, 2012).

The economic crisis in Southern Europe has worsened the situation of migrant women workers. To understand the impact of the crisis, I use Greece—where the crisis has been deepest and longest—as a case study.

GREECE IN GOOD TIMES

The case of Greece helps to illuminate some of the broader issues affecting women migrant workers in Southern European countries. Greece shares a number of features with its Mediterranean counterparts. It has 'strong' families and a weak (state run) social services system. Greece also experienced a reversal of historical migration pattern, from emigration to immigration. Moreover, a large part of the economy is informal and unregulated.

The Macro Background of the Greek Story: From Emigration to Immigration

Migration *to* Greece is a relatively recent phenomenon. For the greater part of the twentieth century, Greece was a country that people predominantly emigrated *from* in order to work elsewhere. Up to the 1960s, they went to the United States, Australia and Canada, while during the 1960s there was circular migration to Germany. During the period of emigration (up till 1975), Greece had dynamic macroeconomic growth, similar to that of developing countries that transferred labor from an underemployed rural sector to a booming urban sector (dual economy models). Part of the mechanism of Greek growth was emigration. In the prewar period, emigration was transcontinental and permanent. From the 1950s onward, it changed direction to the industrial economies of Western Europe (Germany, Belgium, the Netherlands and Sweden). The distinction is important because in the case of permanent (transcontinental) migration there remained fewer economic and social links with Greece. In the case of emigration to Europe, the families mostly remained in Greece, a fact that generated a steady stream of remittances, which were a major prop to the balance of payments. This allowed Greece to import investment goods (i.e., machinery, etc.), which fed into development of industry and (later) tourist services.

The shift of women from the rural to the urban sector had a paradoxical effect. In the rural environment (characterized by small family farms) women were fully involved in the family farm, but in the urban market opportunities for employment outside their homes were more limited. Women, nevertheless, still played an important role as unpaid labor in the very small family-run enterprises, which survived (and indeed multiplied) in the urban context during the postwar economic growth period, lasting to the 1980s.

The dual-economy fueled growth sputtered to a stop after the 1967–74 dictatorship. The 1974 fall of the dictatorship in Greece was accompanied by activism on the legal front and a general effort to build European-type institutions. This activism was nowhere more in evidence than in the case of gender. The 1975 constitution contained an explicit gender equality clause, which stated "all legal differentiation by gender is unconstitutional."[11] The advent of a socialist government in 1981 led to an avalanche of legislation aimed at gender equality, which placed Greece, in legal terms, at the forefront of Europe. However, this legal and institutional activism in favor of labor equality was mainly about statutory changes and was not informed by a feminist analysis of women's real position in the Greek economy and society. By ignoring the dual nature of the labor market and the dynamics of the economics of the family, well-intended legal interventions failed to change the situation on the ground and led to a type of reformist complacency termed 'legalistic formalism,' i.e., the proclamation of a problem as 'solved' after passing the relevant legislation, regardless of implementation (Lyberaki, 2010).

This approach was only marginally effective. It did not lead to any more than a paltry increase in women's labor force participation. That was the beginning of what has been termed 'the Mediterranean Paradox,' which refers to a dramatic fall in fertility in the early 1980s that was not accompanied or explained by greater paid employment involvement of women. The rapid increase in social expenditure after the 1980s was directed mainly at old-age pensions and expenditure on other types of social transfers, such as family benefits and child-care benefits, remained at low levels; it also crowded out possible new initiatives such as long-term care and other benefits in kind. Indeed, given that the formal welfare state gave out cash benefits, the 'real work' of care services and the creation and maintenance of a safety net was left to 'informal social protection.' In other words, the burdens remained on the family (Lyberaki and Tinios, 2012b; 2014). The gender equality legislation only made jobs in the public sector accessible to women. In large numbers, women found employment as government workers. In the private sector, their involvement was much more limited. Their chances of being hired in that sector were reduced because the state mandated that the extra cost of employing women be borne by employers.

Immigration and the Growth Revival of the 1990s

At the beginning of the 1990s, the Greek engine of growth appeared to have stalled. The economy was characterized by low labor productivity, low innovation, low competitiveness, rigid labor market regulations concerning work hours and wages and minimal mobility across sectors, regions and occupations. At the same time, there was a large untapped reserve of female labor supply, i.e., women who stayed at home. There were also a small number of women who had (profitably for themselves) joined the rank of insiders in the public service.

Other European economies, such as Sweden and Finland, were facing the same dilemmas. Like Greece, a previously successful economic model appeared to have reached its limits for them. Both of these countries responded with extensive reforms of the economy, the financial system and the social security system, almost reinventing themselves, which changed the way the economies worked and increased competitiveness (Hilson, 2008). Greece, in contrast, appeared to suddenly leave its low-growth, high-inflation stagnation without significant institutional change—almost as if by magic.

Explaining Greece's positive growth development is difficult. There was very little structural change as Greece had remained a two-speed society relying on the insider/outsider distinction. The public sector, if anything, had become more dominant (as reflected by its steadily increasing share in the Gross Domestic Production (GDP) to over 58 percent). One major difference in the economy during the late 1990s and early 2000s was the advent of large-scale immigration. With the opening of borders in the Balkans, large numbers of workers crossed into Greece from Albania, Bulgaria and Romania. The instability in the former Soviet Union and the Caucasus also led to the emigration of ethnic Pontic Greeks.[12] For the Greek economy, these workers were like 'manna from heaven.'

Migrant Workers' Niche in the Greek Economy

Contrary to widespread fears among the Greek population, the arrival of immigrants acted as a catalyst of positive developments in the labor market, in the macroeconomy and at a more micoeconomic/structural level (Lyberaki, 2008). The labor market effects were positive overall because, first, the immigrants alleviated severe geographical rigidity in labor supply because they settled in high-labor demand areas. Second, the initial integration of migrants into the informal/underground economy served as a filter that allowed them to eventually transition to more highly remunerated and stable jobs. This interconnection is evident in an examination of the regional correlation of unemployment and immigration; regionally, the higher the share of immigrants the *lower* the unemployment rate (Lianos, 2003).

The economic performance effects were undeniably strong and beneficial given that the arrival of large numbers of migrants helped to accelerate demand without inflationary pressures. Also, the supply of (mainly female) migrant labor had a positive direct impact on Greek women's labor participation rates (via the provision of care for the elderly and children). Thus native women could enter the labor market and 'delegate' their care duties to migrant female care workers without major alteration in the care work performed by men.[13] At the same time, this increase in the reservoir of labor served to arrest (to a certain extent) the delocalization of manufacturing activities to lower labor costs in neighboring economies (Lyberaki, 2011b).

The fiscal consequences of immigration in the short- and medium-term were positive for two main reasons. Most of the immigrants were younger and were thus net contributors to social security. Moreover, social security providers received a major short-term boost to finance state pensions. Although this did not provide a definitive solution to the structural problems with Greek society and economy, it provided a window of opportunity as it bought time for a much-needed major reform, which, unfortunately, is still stubbornly resisted by the Greek populace.

The Greek economy was able to absorb migrant workers smoothly because of three factors. First, the extensive European Union (EU) funded public works infrastructure construction projects connected to the 2004 Olympic Games created a demand for labor. Second, the rising living standards (corresponding to what could be called 'the new needs') generated a demand for workers. And third, the availability of flexible workers compensated for the rigidities of the formal labor market, such as the low occupational and geographical mobility as well as the high formal employment protection, which acted to discourage hiring (Burtless, 2001; OECD, Economic Surveys: Greece, 2005 and Nicoletti, Scarpetta and Boyland, 2000). This (third) effect was particularly marked at the lower end of the labor market. Most jobs were filled primarily by the domestic labor supply, but there were severe gaps at the lower end that could not be filled by the Greek population because of the lack of reserves of labor. Historically, labor reservoirs consisted of internal migration (rural exodus and urbanization), women and youths. By the 1980s, all three sources were depleted. Internal migration and urbanization had exhausted their potential, marking a sharp reversal from the historical trends. In any case, young labor force entrants (whose numbers were low to begin with because of the decline in Greek fertility) prolonged their stay in education,[14] thus further reducing the labor supply. Women were making a delayed and relatively slow entry into the labor market; their employment participation rates were still below 45 percent.

Thus immigration in precrisis Greece had the direct effect of increasing growth. Against a background of rising living standards, net job creation, real wage increases, substantial decline in inflation rates, revitalization of the rural areas (in both the demographic and economic sense) and of the property market (at the lower end of the real estate spectrum), immigrants saw clear improvement in all areas of their lives (their jobs, their wages, their living conditions and their general prospects—including regularization). The immigrants' contribution to the growth in production during the 1995–2004 upswing was between 0.3–0.4 percentage points annually.[15] If one also considers the second-round effects (i.e., induced investment, changes in relative factor prices and factor elasticities, complementarities in labor markets, raised domestic demand and higher demand for housing), then the actual effects were probably much greater.

Immigrants filled a general labor supply deficit; women immigrants went a step further and allowed the creation of a private unregulated care service industry, enabling Greek women to finally leave the home. This has been described as the mechanism of the *Deae ex Machina* (Lyberaki, 2011a). The core argument of the *Deae ex Machina* thesis rests on the observation that women's labor force participation increased in Greece from 41.1 percent in 1983 to 59.2 percent in 2008. After 1992, this increase was even greater for mothers of children under 12 years of age. By the end of the first decade of the twenty-first century, Greek women's labor force involvement stood somewhere between Spain's 66.7 percent and Italy's 55.1 percent. A large part of this change has to do with cohort effects. Women born after 1950 are more educated and have forged stronger career links than earlier generations of women. Historically, in Greek society, the need to provide care constrained the ability of women to leave the home to seek paid work. This was necessitated by a rigid allocation of responsibilities by gender; care of children and the elderly was seen as 'a woman's duty.' Greek men were unwilling to share care responsibilities, so Greek women could not work outside the home to the extent that women in other European countries (and even Spain) were able to do so. The arrival of a willing and cheap supply of migrant women workers who could perform care work allowed the care deficit to be made up without major changes in gender roles, hence the label of the phenomenon as the 'Deae ex Machina' effect[16] (Lyberaki, 2011a)—the care gap was (at least partly) solved 'as if by magic.'

Women Migrant Workers' Niches in Greek Economy before the Crisis

Beginning in the early 1990s, the composition of the population in Greece saw sea changes. The great majority of migrants came from neighboring Balkan countries, although waves of economic migrants and asylum seekers have also been arriving from Eastern Europe, the former USSR, the Middle East and several Asian and African countries. Initially, Greece was merely a stepping-stone in their preferred migration route westward; now, increasingly migrants are interested in long-term residence or even permanent settlement in Greece.[17]

According to the 2001 Census, the reported stock of foreigners living in Greece was 762,200 amounting to approximately 7 percent of the total population (OECD, 2004).[18] Officially they account for 9.5 percent of employment in Greece, but their actual share is probably higher (closer to 12 percent) as they tend to be underrepresented in the Labour Force Survey because of sampling and irregularity factors (Cavounidis, 2006). This large infusion of migrant labor does not seem to have affected labor force participation rates of indigenous men (as discussed earlier), but was strongly associated with the increase in native women's employment rates. In regional labor markets between 1998 and 2001, an increase of 1 percent in migrants was accompanied by a substantial 2.5 percent increase in Greek women's labor force participation (Lianos, 2003, p.117).

By the beginning of the twenty-first century, women made up 45.5 percent of all immigrants in Greece according to the official data. However, their involvement in the informal sector is probably larger, especially in lines of work that are notoriously underrecorded (such as household services[19]). So the official records may suffer from a gender bias. Although women make up almost half of the immigrant population, the gender composition of the various ethnic groups is uneven, ranging from less than 5 percent for migrants from Pakistan and Bangladesh to 50 percent of migrants from Albania and to over 75 percent for migrants from the Philippines and Ukraine.

Female immigrants tended to participate in the labor market at slightly higher rates compared to Greek women (58.8 percent versus 54.8 percent), although much less than the male immigrants (89.6 percent). A gender gap analogous to that existing between indigenous men and women persists among immigrants. The same is true with respect to the wage gender gap; it remains persistent and wide. Wages for migrants remained relatively low and near the statutory minimum wage for the economy. Immigrant men were paid comparable amounts to indigenous women, while immigrant women received lower wages.

Immigrant women working in the opaque sphere of the informal (unregulated) economy were faced with a nexus of dangers as well as opportunities. On the one hand, their access to the officially defined social protection schemes remained problematic because of insufficient social insurance contributions (access to social security, health care and child-care facilities, for what they are worth).[20] On the other hand, informality was a blessing because it offered them a degree of freedom of choice. It alleviated the burdens of time-consuming bureaucratic procedures and, more importantly, offered tax-free and contributions-free earnings. Hence the paradox: Women, especially middle-aged women whose previous experience in Eastern Europe was one of rigid regulation, discovered the attractions of a 'culture of informality' when they found employment in the informal care sector. These 'advantages' often make them reluctant to change their status to 'regulated' when the chance arises (Psimmenos and Skamnakis, 2008, pp.398–402).

How many Greek households would have had access to this new labor market? Rough calculations suggest that as many as 15–20 percent of all urban households may have employed migrant workers (Lyberaki, 2011a). For instance, as 20 percent of immigrants worked in domestic services, their number would have exceeded 200,000. Assuming a third of those worked full time, 130,000 would have had multiple employers, and if 50 percent worked for two or more households, then (as mentioned earlier) we arrive at an estimate of 15–20 percent. Alternatively, extrapolating from survey data from SHARE (Survey in Health Ageing and Retirement in Europe), Lyberaki (2011a) estimates that approximately 20 percent of households (with at least one member who was 50 years or older) used the market to meet their care needs. So it is fair to say that the availability of care workers made a substantial difference for middle class (primarily urban) families. The existence of a care market also favored the development of a part-time market, which benefited families with lesser means.

All in all, before the crisis, the care sector provided a point of entry into the labor market for many immigrant women. Although instances of poor remuneration and discrimination abounded and the job duties varied significantly, it would be a mistake to consider female immigrants in the hidden domestic economy to be passive victims. Partial control over the pace and their duties gave them some bargaining power, and the development of a personal relationship with the family often enhanced their satisfaction and the self-esteem they derived from their work (Papataxiarchis, Topali and

Athanassopoulou, 2008). Furthermore, it offered a 'way in' in a clientelistic society, where who you know is often of decisive importance. Evidence from fieldwork conducted from 2000 to just before the onset of the crisis clearly suggests that the domestic care sector involved the opportunity for upward mobility for some migrants (in the same or different line of activity), while it made possible for other women to make the opposite choice. They could move 'backward' to 'inactivity' as soon as the economic situation of their family allowed them to become 'housewives again.' Both these trajectories were particularly relevant in the case of female Albanian migrants in Greece (Kambouri, 2007, p.189; Lambrianidis and Lyberaki, 2001;Lyberaki and Maroukis, 2005).

GREECE IN BAD TIMES: THE CRISIS AND MIGRATION

The Onset of the 2007 Crisis and the Period of Stabilization

In retrospect, the symbolic apogee of the 'Greek success story' was the 2004 Olympic Games project. The entry into the euro (2001) led to a dramatic fall in interest rates, and Greece took advantage of it by vastly expanding its external borrowing capacity to prop up consumption. So, while in the 1990s growth was based on an expansion of productive effort, in the 2000s, living standards continued rising largely as a result of public borrowing to finance fiscal expansion.

The period of easy borrowing met its nemesis when, after 2009, Greece discovered the hard way that it could no longer find willing lenders to finance its national debt.[21] Given that the crucial decision was made to not leave the euro, the only way to reduce the deficit was internal devaluation (i.e., an absolute reduction in social benefits and wages in order to contain fiscal deficits and to aid competitiveness). This strategy, in conjunction with inflexibility and reform delays, led the country to a dramatic and protracted deflation, unprecedented in any advanced country since the war. Greece's GDP has fallen for six consecutive years resulting in a cumulative reduction of GDP per head by a quarter (23 percent) and an unemployment rate of 26.9 percent (second quarter 2013). The bailout organized by the troika of the International Monetary Fund (IMF), European Central Bank and EU Commission provided liquidity, which allowed the state to remain functioning, but it came at the cost of possibly one of the most severe fiscal rebalancing programs ever implemented.

In terms of immigration, this has meant that Greece is no longer a desirable destination. Immigrants view it as a conduit for further migration into the EU and particularly to the parts of the EU that have not been severely affected by the crisis (e.g., Germany, Austria and the Netherlands). Triandafyllidou et al. (2013) estimated the immigrant stock in Greece (December 2012) to be 831,000 persons, just under 8 percent of the resident population.²² Ongoing research in Albania (by far the largest source of Greek immigrants) suggests that there is a strong return migration flow (mainly from Italy and Greece) as a result of the recession and economic instability.²³ The economic performance and future outlook of the sending economies seem to be the reason for migrant workers returning home in increasing numbers; Albania, for instance, has been one of the fastest growing economies in Europe. From 2007 to 2012, the economy grew by 22 percent—almost the same percentage by which Greek GDP *shrank*—and despite the ongoing economic crisis, the country has been able to maintain its financial stability and positive growth rates. Although Albania witnessed a declining trend in remittances, this was partly offset by returning immigrants bringing back their savings. The unemployment rate remains at 13.3 percent, while the labor market conditions are improving somewhat. Bulgaria and Romania also grew during the crisis and are expected to grow in the future. Unemployment is lower in both countries compared to the situation in Southern Europe (at 12 percent and 7 percent, respectively).

My argument so far has been that immigrants in Greece played an important role precrisis in unwittingly enabling the delay of the 'time of reckoning.' The effect on the immigrants during the various phases of the crisis must be investigated. Equally important is the following question: What can their role be in possible postcrisis scenarios?

The Case of Long-Term Care Provision: A State-Family Demarcation of Responsibility

In Greece, the existence of a two-speed labor market and the delay of reforms created the migrant workers' employment niche. This niche was particularly vulnerable to the mechanism of the crisis. The crisis involved a very large reduction of private disposable incomes, which was felt disproportionately by the 'outsiders.' 'Insiders' were able to protect themselves by delaying structural reforms. Given that the overall fiscal stance could not be changed, tax rates and utility rates were increased by the state. In a two-speed labor market, protection of privileged sectors meant more of the overall adjustment was borne by the unprotected part; thus there was a quantum rise in unemployment in the private sector as well as a precipitous fall in wage rates in professions that were not protected by the law or by preexisting collective agreements (in other words, the wages fell mostly in public sector enterprises). Migrants, as the 'outsiders' *par excellence*, were disproportionately among the losers. Male immigrants were also disproportionately hurt as many of them were employed in the construction sector that was hit especially hard. Women immigrants were affected less than men; their sectors of employment were a little further from the crisis' firing line.²⁴

The issues raised by the mechanisms of the crisis and the interplay between public policy and migrants' choices are most obvious in the case of long-term care for the elderly. In that field, policy choices were responsible for the locus and forms of migrant employment niches. The continued existence or transformation of these niches will thus depend on the nature and direction of reforms.

Long-term care for the elderly, i.e., personal care services for the old and infirm, serves as an interesting case study of the evolution of social policy in Greece, the course of reforms and the role played by immigrants. Up to the late 1990s, 'formal' long-term care was limited to institutional care in old-age homes, most of which were set up as trusts and foundations by private donations. They frequently bore the founder's name and were (and are) often run by Church bodies. These charities provided very basic services to persons of very low levels of income; by the 2000s, partly because of stigma and partially because of rising incomes, they accounted for a small and shrinking part of care providers. The rapidly growing demand for care work for the elderly (that was attributable to an ageing population) was and is met by the family; and when the care recipient's care needs increase, they are frequently medicalized and provided for by inpatient services at hospitals at a greatly inflated cost and to the detriment of the quality of life of the beneficiaries.[25]

Responsibility for decisions and financing was borne by the family. This meant that women in the family were expected to care for elderly or disabled parents or relatives, frequently in parallel with their responsibility for their young children. The arrival of female immigrants who were prepared to supply these services (at a cost which could be met by an average urban family) kick-started a new unregulated market for personal services. In contrast to the rigidly regulated and bureaucratic nature of state care, private care obeyed no rules, lacked quality control and operated on the basis of classified advertisements and word of mouth.

At the close of the 1990s, the state had a chance to intervene to manage demand and ensure the quality of long-term care facilities for the elderly by providing consumers with information and reassurance that would allow the private market to develop and cover the population's need in a more thorough manner. The EU Community Support Framework provided generous financing for interventions in long-term care for the elderly. The National Action Plan for Inclusion 2001 singled out long-term care as an area of strategic importance for society. Furthermore, it recognized that direct state funding could meet only a small percentage of need and could not dent the larger problem. Should the aim have been to cater to the underlying demand, the way would have been open for the state to implement a two-pronged strategy. First, it could have created a policy of accreditation, provision of information and quality control that would allow a private market in long-term care to develop that would meet the needs of the elderly. Second, the state could have established and enforced minimum quality standards in a consistent and transparent manner that the private sector would have to meet. It could have used the funds provided by the EU as a lever to support quality development of services that could cover the entire Greek population.

Despite official statements about the urgency of meeting the challenge (e.g., in the First National Action Plan for Inclusion ('NAPincl') in 2001 —NAPincl 2001) what actually happened was very different from the strategic vision. A new program—Help at Home—was started and devolved to municipalities, which chose to implement it with their own employees. In those places where the program was endorsed by the municipality, it proved extremely popular with the people it could reach. However, they were only a small proportion of the total. The way the program was administered (and its relative size) had minimal impact on the unregulated sector, which continued to operate as it had previously. The program, despite being new, developed in a manner mirroring the way the public sector had been operating. It soon became focused on the needs and privileges of *suppliers* (the municipalities, the new employees hired to implement it), for instance, by limiting the times services were available to match the timetables of the providers as opposed to the needs of the recipients. The new service was frequently planned to maximize 'absorptive capacity' of the EU funds utilized; planned policies often prioritized spending, rather than delivery of the planned outcomes or the welfare of their beneficiaries. New social programs were seen by many municipalities as an onerous new chore to be undertaken because of the availability of funds, and not as crucial obligations of the state to its citizens. Once the funds dried up (the EU funds are supposed to finance one-off, investment-like expenditures and not to bankroll social policy on a permanent basis), programs in many municipalities were placed at risk or were discontinued, as local authorities were not willing to transfer monies from other programs to fund them.

The case of the Help at Home program illustrates the role of immigrant women in meeting Greek citizen's care needs—both what actually happened and could have happened (and might still happen in the future). The *old* equilibrium was characterized by the implicit acceptance on the part of the state of a deep formal-informal divide. The understanding was that, given its limited resources, the state would do what it could; specifically, it would directly provide services with its funds. It was also assumed that someone else would be responsible for catering to the unmet bulk of demand for social services if the state was either unwilling or unable to provide for them.

The old equilibrium is now threatened by a lack of funds because of retrenchment and an increase in demand for safety-net services that is attributable to the crisis. There may still be an informal market for care workers' services, but these workers will suffer the consequences of their employers' lower incomes. Their wages will be lower than what they earned prior to the crisis, which could further compromise their quality of life.

The (possible) new equilibrium in Greece might entail a retreat from the ambition to provide services from state resources, replaced by the state's assumption of responsibility for monitoring needs and regulating the supply by enforcing accreditation and minimum quality standards for long-term eldercare facilities. This will allow a new market to develop, free from the constraints of the informal market and the gray economy. Given the level of demand and its potential for growth, the new equilibrium may well prove to be a more stable environment in which immigrant labor may be utilized and, more importantly, it may hold better prospects for those workers' fuller integration into Greek economy and society.

Albanian Migrant Women Workers' Perception of the Greek Crisis and Their Future Prospects

A large number of life-altering decisions that the migrants and their families will have to make depend on how they understand the change in their circumstances and whether they believe their migration project to be in ruins. No a priori theorizing can be a substitute for their perspective, in their own words. To answer those questions, in early 2013, I conducted a small-scale survey of migrant women in Athens. The sample was composed of 146 women from Albania (predominantly from the south of the country), living and working in the greater Athens area. Face-to-face interviews took place during the months of February and March 2013. Most of the respondents (37 percent) were between 45 and 54 years of age, another 26 percent were 35–44 years old and 20 percent were between 25 and 34 years of age. The low representation of younger women was partly addressed by 25 additional in-depth interviews in Athens in April and May. Two thirds of the survey respondents had completed upper secondary education, while 14.1 percent had a tertiary education degree. Most were employed in cleaning (one out of two) and care work (including nursing). Twenty-eight percent were homemakers. Almost all had some work history and experience (90 percent), mostly for over 10 years (70 percent). Most of the women were married (93 percent) with children (87 percent). Around 60 percent of those children were less than 18 years of age. Half of the respondents also had older parents living with them; the migration was a multigenerational family project for them. Finally, 72 percent arrived between 1993 and 2000 (only 10 percent came after 2000).

Competition for jobs with other immigrant women was perceived as a threat by 80 percent of the respondents. This group of Albanian women considered their direct competitors to be women migrants from Bulgaria, Romania, Russia and the Ukraine. They also believed that they were undercutting their wages. A key part of the questionnaire attempted to determine the effect of the crisis on their everyday lives.

Wages
Wage rates had increased steadily in the period before the crisis, but wages and hours declined considerably after the onset of the recession. As these women were working in the unregulated part of the market, wage rates fell more than hours. In the realm of care work in particular, 33.8 percent reported fewer hours, 14.9 percent reported that their job was discontinued,

while 51.4 percent reported wage declines. Women who were employed as cleaners reported higher incidences of job loss; their employers could not afford to replace them (more jobs were lost in the cleaning sector than in the care sector). This suggests that although the Greek households employing 'migrant-in-the-family' for caring functions needed to contain costs, they found it hard to reduce hours. In a sense, the demand for some care services was inelastic.

Unemployment

Currently only 14 percent of the respondents are unemployed. That rate is considerably lower than the rate of unemployment among women in general and also lower than the unemployment rate of third country nationals who are women. But many had experienced spells of unemployment during the past years. They fell into two groups: those who experienced short-term unemployment (under a year) and those who experienced very long-term unemployment (over two years). In 40 percent of the cases, the respondent's husband had lost his job, a third of them for longer than two years. Construction workers (comprising two out of three of the unemployed spouses) faced higher unemployment risks. Job mobility was very low, while residence mobility was higher. Some 50 percent managed to successfully renegotiate their rent downward as a result of the crisis.

The survey participants had been visiting their home country less frequently during the crisis. Two out of three admitted that they had thought about going back (or moving to another country), but in reality this was a very unpopular option. Very few respondents knew of someone who had made such a decision. The reason they did not go back to Albania was because of concerns about their children's education and life prospects, the hope that things would eventually improve, and, to a lesser extent, the pressing need to send remittances to Albania to help the family left behind. Thus, while the differentials have changed because of the crisis, the lower level of income in Albania is still the decisive factor. However, according to 96.2 percent of respondents, their situation in Greece deteriorated during the crisis, with increasing unemployment and financial difficulties being the most serious threats. The children's future is the main reason for the women's decision to remain in Greece. When asked about their aspirations and expectations concerning their offspring, half of the respondents mentioned going to university, while 16.4 percent hoped to see their children become entrepreneurs.

Future in Greece

Among the respondents, two out of three agreed with the statement, "*The crisis will pass and I am going to remain here in Greece,*" while strongly disagreeing with the statement, "*The crisis is pushing us back to our country.*" The key reasons for their decision to remain in Greece were: first, the way of life; second, work opportunities; and third, friends. Thus, while prospects are grimmer for immigrants, the existence of a superior social and educational infrastructure, a legacy effect of the good times, still convinces many female migrant workers to remain in Greece.

The sample size is small, but it was obvious that among the women, on the one hand, there was a distinct pattern of success and optimism, and, on the other hand, a feeling of having reached an impasse or dead end. There were some notable success stories regarding the overall immigration experience: Upon arrival, almost all had no familiarity with the Greek language, but they acquired it gradually. They first found work as cleaners. From then on, the 'successful group' followed different trajectories, such as: i) passed exams in Greek in order to acquire additional skills for a career as an aesthetician or a cosmetologist; ii) moved to personal care of the elderly in their homes; iii) became a caregiver for children; or iv) found a nursing job as a private night nurse in a hospital.

Regardless of the specific career pattern, the success scenario frequently involved the purchase of an apartment or land in Athens, Albania or both venues. Successful immigrants tended to be rather optimistic and did not consider moving back to Albania. They had plans for their children.

In contrast to the successful migrant workers, there were some women who felt they had reached a dead end. A number had started out in the cleaning sector and choose not to shift to any other kind of work. For a while, working as a cleaner was an attractive proposition (good wages, amenable hours, personal autonomy) such that they were not motivated to find another line of work. These women are now facing the greatest difficulties because of job loss, wage declines and fewer work hours. Operating informally in the gray economy with no registration and no social security contributions made good financial sense during the time of economic growth, but it turned out to be an additional problem during the crisis. They have no access to social benefits, including unemployment benefits or health insurance. However, it must be stressed that although the women feel highly pessimistic, they do not consider leaving Greece an option. Thus the respondents appear to remain committed to their original choice of remaining in Greece. They have not given up hope of maintaining their well-being or their situation improving with time. Their 'wait and see' attitude amounts to a vote of confidence about their prospects in Greece.

CONCLUSION: ALTERNATIVE SCENARIOS FOR MIGRANTS' WELL-BEING

As this chapter was being written in 2014, the Greek crisis was still unfolding. While some of the major dangers, such as exiting the Eurozone (known as Grexit) or a catastrophic bankruptcy, have been avoided so far,[26] what will ultimately transpire is not at all clear. Even if the bailout program is followed to the letter, it is only a plan to navigate the crisis, and it says nothing about how the country will be organized after the crisis. The lay of the land will be very different, but in what way will depend on events yet to occur and decisions yet to be made.

So, with respect to immigrants in general and migrant women workers in particular, the jury is still out and will remain out for some time. There are two possible scenarios for their future, depending on the success or failure of the structural reforms underway; those reforms will have the effect of altering immigrants' niche in Greek society, and, thus, they will determine their future.

My analysis has pinpointed two key areas of reform. First and necessary for fiscal balance is the reduction of the dominant role of the state in the Greek economy and society. Second, a level playing field will have to be established such that the sharp distinction between insiders and outsiders is smoothed and a common set of rules enforced, whether it be for employment protection, tax laws or social protection entitlements.

In the case of the success of the reform project, the erstwhile role played by immigration (to fill the gaps left by state provision and to provide for missing labor force flexibility) will cease to exist. Immigrants will no longer be relegated to a *functionally* inferior position in the division of labor. They will therefore lose their niche, but they will be in a better position to take advantage of new and wider opportunities. Indeed, should the Greek economy, in opening up, be more closely integrated into world production networks, migrants (from the 1990s) might even be able to use their familiarity with their country of origin as a kind of comparative advantage (Labrianidis and Lyberaki, 2004). Women immigrants are also likely to benefit from the development of a private care industry that has a sounder foundation, which includes a social insurance mechanism that guarantees access to social services to all.

However, another scenario is also possible. Greek society might very well react to the crisis by retreating from some of the gains of the past two decades. Increase in male unemployment has given rise to concern in Greek society about 'jobless households,' i.e., households where the male breadwinners are unemployed. This may result in the clawing back of some of the gains in gender balance. A similar phenomenon occurred in the US in the Depression of the 1930s, when much of the gender balance progress that had occurred since the start of the Great War was clawed back. Such a development in Greece—a country where gender equality was legally enshrined but only enforced fully in the public sector—is not inconceivable. Indeed, there is evidence of priority being given to male employment during the crisis (see Lyberaki and Tinios, 2012a). This situation would be exacerbated if the growth trajectory out of the recession involves, as previously, 'jobless growth.'

In such a situation where the dearth of jobs makes indigenous women retreat to the home, the situation of immigrant women will be more difficult than it was precrisis. As immigrant women supplying care are complementary to indigenous women's employment, loss of a job by a native (Greek) woman would lead to a double job loss—as it would cost the immigrant care worker her job as well. In such situations, it is likely immigrant women will try to reproduce the precrisis employment model. However, given their employers' loss of income and jobs, they will receive lower wages than before and will have fewer prospects. Similarly, if the state remains committed to the notion that its only role is in the direct provision of care services, then immigrant women will have to remain in the informal market. During the precrisis period the market's informality used to be a financial advantage (tax evasion aided in keeping costs down), but it will no longer be a benefit. In Greece, fiscal reform has resulted in fewer opportunities for tax avoidance and evasion.

The thread running through this chapter is that immigration to Greece of the 1990s was successful because migrants performed functions that answered real needs of the Greek economy and society. Their continued presence will depend on the kind of role they can find for themselves in the changed circumstances of the country. But their ability to do so depends on how well they are integrated in the fabric of Greek society. If they are perceived and treated as a foreign body or as a threat, the chances are magnified that their presence will be seen more as a problem than a solution. To avoid that possibility, Greece and the EU have identified their inclusion in Greek society as a strategic priority, with the goal of enhancing their potential contribution. That may seem to be a positive sign, but both Greece and the EU are also erecting a 'Fortress Europe' to keep new migrants out of their borders. Thus the future prospects of women migrant workers in Greece remains unclear and requires further study.

NOTES

1. Valuable assistance was received from Ermela Giana and Stavros Vouyoukas.
2. The terms 'migrant' and 'immigrant' are used here interchangeably to refer to foreign-born workers, although strictly an immigrant is someone who moves into a country, while a migrant is someone who moves in any direction (emigrant is the term to describe the people that move out of their country). Interestingly, this distinction does not exist in the Greek language. Internal (rural-urban) migrants are not included in the migrant population, because the data do not record mobility within borders. Similarly, in Greece as in other EU countries, a key legal distinction is between European Nationals (EU) nationals (who do not need work permits) and third-country (non-EU) nationals who do. In this way, Bulgarians and Romanians counted as third-party migrants until those countries accession to the EU in 2008. Although it is estimated that around half of migrants in Greece have a more-or-less regular status (the other half are either undocumented or their permits expired), there are insurmountable obstacles in acquiring refugee status, while the acquisition of citizenship is virtually blocked to non-Greeks. The process of naturalization

in Greece is such that only a tiny minority of immigrants (who are not ethnic Greeks) can acquire Greek citizenship; as a result, individuals who have been in the country since 1992 may not be distinguishable from recent arrivals (Triandafyllidou et al., 2013).
3. Although it is more or less accepted that the delegation of the hidden, unpaid household realm care work to migrant women workers has liberated women who used to perform these tasks, crucial issues related to the quality of care purchased from the market remain a point of contention (see debate on commodification and, in particular, McCloskey (1996), Himmelweit (2005), Nelson (1999) and England and Folbre (1999)).
4. Market provision of care services can be either formal/regulated or informal/unregulated. In practice there are various combinations of the two (Daly and Lewis, 1998; 2000; Lewis, 2002).
5. These findings used data from the Multinational Time Use Study (MTUS), which, unfortunately, does not include Greece in the sample.
6. A variant of this literature is the 'migrant-carer model' (Simonazzi, 2009).
7. In the mid-twentieth century it was expected that domestic service would wither away with the development of modern capitalism and the extension of the welfare state provisions. This proved not to be the case. In fact, domestic services show signs of revival in contemporary societies. Indeed, the provision of care today is situated at the crossroads of important themes such as migration, gender inequalities and informal work (Sarti, 2005, p.1).
8. Large-scale migration for care purposes characterizes South to North movement, OECD and non-OECD countries such as Hong Kong Special Administrative Region (SAR), Saudi Arabia, Singapore and the United Arab Emirates (UAE).
9. Women also move for other reasons, such as family migrants, agricultural or manufacturing workers, sex workers, etc.
10. Migrant women in Spain are 26 percent more occupationally segregated than migrant men (Del Río and Alonso-Villar, 2012).
11. Article 116, paragraph 1.
12. Many ethnic Greeks from the southern shores of the Black Sea (The Pontus) had been displaced to the USSR after 1922 and were subsequently relocated to the Caucasus or to Central Asia. A significant number of them were offered Greek citizenship after 1992, partly in order to avoid conflicts in the Caucasus. This group of immigrants thus came to Greece with full citizenship and legal rights. A parallel may be seen with Russian Jewish emigration to Israel in the same period.
13. Time-use data do not exist in Greece, but casual empiricism reveals that men assume far smaller burdens of care than in other countries. See also Karamessini, 2005.
14. They also tended to stay longer at their parents' home, a phenomenon that has been aptly called "Hotel Mama" (Coomans, 2001).
15. IMF, 2006: 14
16. Deae ex Machina, or goddesses from the machine, is the female form of 'Deus ex Machina' meaning a person who appears or is introduced into a situation suddenly and unexpectedly and provides an artificial or contrived solution to an apparently insoluble difficulty. The term was first used in Ancient Greek and Roman drama where it meant the timely appearance of a god to unravel and resolve the plot. Since ancient times, the phrase has also been applied to an unexpected savior that brings order out of chaos.
17. This reversal caught both society and policy makers by surprise (on the issue of attitudes see Triandafyllidou, 2000, and on the gradual formation of "migration policy" see Triandafyllidou, 2005). Policy has been designed in order

to cover the needs of the original majority of migrants, i.e., men, so it is not only male-orientated but also family-orientated, adopting a rather patriarchal approach toward migrants. This stands in sharp contrast to the new reality and the fact that there is a growing trend toward the feminization of migration (Liapi and Vouyioukas, 2006, p.8).
18. Given their irregular status, the total number of immigrants is probably greater than in official statistics. Fakiolas (2000) estimated that migrants not enumerated in 2000 were 400,000 persons (i.e., 20 percent of the total).
19. Research on migrants working in the supply of services to Greek households has taken off only recently (Kambouri, 2007; Psimmenos and Skamnakis, 2008; Lyberaki, 2011a; Papataxiarchis, Topali and Athanassopoulou, 2008).
20. Social protection is skewed heavily toward pensions, which makes it largely irrelevant to immigrants' needs. On the other hand, system fragmentation allows immigrants to "purchase" health insurance coverage at minimal cost (Tinios, 2003).
21. The abrupt cessation of access to funds has much to do with the uncovering of the 'Greek statistics' budget overruns of 2009—when a budget deficit originally projected to be 2.9 percent of GDP was proved in October to have been in excess of 15 percent. This gave rise to indignant reminders in German public opinion of the 'no bailout' clause in the Euro treaty—which markets appeared to have forgotten in framing loan terms up to then. After October the difference between Greek and German government borrowing took off to levels reminiscent of credit card debt.
22. About half of them are estimated to be undocumented (either because they never had a valid permit or because they did not manage to renew it). Composition-wise, Albanians remain the dominant group at 60 percent of the total, followed by Bulgarians, Georgians, Romanians and Pakistanis, Bangladeshis and persons from the Philippines (Maroukis, 2012).
23. Study on the Economic Impact of the Greek Crisis in Albania, conducted by the Albanian Centre for Competitiveness and International Trade (ACIT, 2012).
24. The unemployment rate *by nationality and gender* developed as follows between 2008 and 2012: for men third country nationals (TCN) it started from 5 percent to 11 percent, 12 percent, 27 percent and reached 40 percent in 2012. For women TCN it started from 11 percent to 13 and 18 percent and escalated to 29 percent and to 35 percent in 2012.
25. National Action Plan for Social Inclusion (NAPIncl.Gr) 2001 makes extensive references on this matter. For the Plan itself and further analysis on the issues, see Lyberaki and Tinios, 2002.
26. Abandoning the euro in favor of reinstituting a national currency would, almost certainly, result in a sharp devaluation and would carry the danger of inflation and further unemployment. Refusal on the part of the state to repay debts would bar Greece from international borrowing and would make financing essential imports very difficult. Both scenarios would have severe immediate effects, as well as long-term social impacts.

REFERENCES AND FURTHER READING

Albanian Centre for Competitiveness and International Trade (ACIT), 2012. *Study on the economic impact of the Greek crisis in Albania*. [pdf] Available at: <http://www.usaid.gov/sites/default/files/documents/1863/USAID%20Study%20on%20Greek%20Crisis.pdf> [Accessed 7 July 2014].

Attias-Donfut, C., Ogg, J. and Wolff, F.C., 2005. Family support. In: A. Börsch-Supan et al., eds. 2000. *Health, ageing and retirement in Europe. First results from the survey of health, ageing and retirement in Europe*. Mannheim: Mannheim Research Institute für the Economics of Ageing, pp.171–8.

Bengtson, V. L. and Roberts, R. E., 1991. Intergenerational solidarity in aging families: An example of formal theory construction. *Journal of Marriage and the Family*, 53 (4), pp.856–70.

Bettio, F. and Villa, P., 1998. A Mediterranean perspective on the breakdown of the relationship between participation and fertility. *Cambridge Journal of Economics*, 22 (2), pp.137–71.

Bettio, F., Simonazzi, A. and Villa, P., 2006. Change in care regimes and female migration: The 'care drain' in the Mediterranean. *Journal of European Social Policy*, 16 (3), pp.271–85.

Bettio, F. and Solinas, G., 2009. Which European model for elderly care? Equity and cost-effectiveness in home based care in three European countries. *Economia & Lavoro*, 43 (1), pp.53–71.

Burtless, G., 2001. The Greek labor market. In: R.C. Bryant, N.C. Garganas and G.S. Tavlas, eds. 2001. *Greece's economic performance and prospects*. Athens and Washington: Bank of Greece and the Brookings Institution, pp.453–93.

Cavounidis, J., 2006. Labor market impact of migration: Employment structures and the case of Greece. *International Migration Review*, 40 (3), pp.635–60.

Coomans, G., 2001.The role of women in the labor market in ageing societies. In: E. Kikilias, C. Bagavos, P. Tinios, and M. Chletsos, eds. 2001. *Demographic Ageing, Labour Market and Social Protection: Trends, Challenges and Policies*. Athens: National Labour Institute Editions (in Greek). pp.187–98.

Daly, M. and Lewis J., 1998. Introduction: Conceptualising social care in the context of welfare state restructuring. In: Lewis, ed., 1998. *Gender, social care and welfare state restructuring in Europe*. Cheltenham: Ashgate. pp.1–24.

Daly, M. and Lewis, J., 2000. The concept of social care and the analysis of contemporary welfare states, *British Journal of Sociology*, 51 (2), pp.281–98.

Del Río, C. and Alonso-Villar, O., 2012. Occupational segregation of immigrant women in Spain. *Feminist Economics*, 18 (2), pp.91–123.

England, P. and Folbre N., 1999. The cost of caring. *Annals of the American Academy of Political and Social Science*, 561 (1), pp.39–51.

Esping-Andersen, G., 2002. A child-centred social investment strategy. In: G. Esping Andersen, D. Gallie, A. Hemerijk and J. Myles, eds. 2002. *Why we need a new welfare state*. Oxford: Oxford University Press, pp.26–67.

Fakiolas, R., 2000. Migration and unregistered labor in the Greek economy. In: R. King, G. Lazaridis and C.G. Tsardanidis, eds. 2000. *Eldorado or fortress*. London: Macmillan, pp.57–78.

Ferrera, M., 1996. The southern model of welfare state in social Europe. *Journal of European Social Policy*, 6 (1), pp.17–37.

Ferrera, M., 2010. The South European countries. In: Castles, et al., eds. 2010. *The Oxford handbook of the welfare state*. Oxford: Oxford University Press, pp.616–29.

Gershuny, J. and Sullivan O., 2003. Time-use, gender and public policy regimes. *Social Politics*, 10 (2), pp.205–28.

Herrera, G., 2012. Starting over again? Crisis, gender, and social reproduction among Ecuadorian migrants in Spain. *Feminist Economics* 18 (2), pp.125–48.

Hilson, M., 2008. *The Nordic model: Scandinavia since 1945*. London: Reaktion Books—Contemporary Worlds.

Himmelweit, S., 2005. *Can we afford (not) to care? Prospects and policy*. GeNet Working Papers 2005-11. Cambridge: Gender Equality Network of the Economic and Social research Council.

Hochschild, A.R. 2000. Global care chains and emotional surplus value. In: W. Hutton and A. Giddens, eds. 2000. *On the edge: Living with global capitalism*. London: Jonathan Cape, pp.130–46.
International Monetary Fund (IMF), 2006. *Country Report: Greece*, no 6 (5), January. Washington, DC: IMF.
Kambouri, H., 2007. *Gender and migration: Everyday life of female migrants from Albania and Ukraine*, Athens: Gutenberg (in Greek).
Kan, M.Y. and Gershuny, J., 2009. Gender and time-use over the life-course. In: Btynin and Ermish, eds. 2009. *Changing relationships*. New York and Oxford: Routledge. Ch. 9.
Kan, M.Y., Sullivan, O. and Gershuny, J., 2011. Gender convergence in domestic work: Discerning the effects of interactional and institutional barriers from large-scale data. *Sociology*, 45 (2), pp.234–51.
Karamessini, M., 2005. *Reconciliation of work and private life in Greece—The Greek national report*. European Commission's Expert Group on Gender, Social Inclusion and Employment. Luxembourg: Office for Official Publications of the European Communities.
Kofman, E. and Raghuram, P., 2012. Women, migration, and care: Explorations of diversity and dynamism in the global South. *Social Politics* (Fall 2012), 19 (3), pp.408–32.
Kohli, M., Künemund, H. and Lüdicke, J., 2005. Family structure, proximity and contact. In: A. Börsch-Supan et al., eds. 2000. *Health, ageing and retirement in Europe. First results from the survey of health, ageing and retirement in Europe*. Mannheim: Mannheim Research Institute für die Economics of Ageing, pp.164–70.
Labrianidis, L. and Lyberaki, A., 2001. *Albanian immigrants in Thessaloniki*. Thessaloniki: Paratiritis (in Greek).
Labrianidis, L. and Lyberaki, A., 2004. Back and forth and in-between: Returning Albanian migrants from Greece and Italy. *Journal of International Migration and Integration*, 5 (1), pp.77–106.
Lewis, J., 2002. Gender and welfare state change. *European Societies*, 4 (4), pp.331–57.
Lianos, T., 2003.*Contemporary migration to Greece: An economic analysis*. Athens: Centre for Economic Planning and Research (KEPE) (in Greek).
Liapi, M. and Vouyoukas, A., 2006. Policy formation and policy implementation affecting the integration of new female immigrants in Greece: National report on key informants' interviews. *Working Paper no. 10*, WP2, Centre for Research on Women's Issues (KETHI).
Lyberaki, A. and Maroukis, T., 2005. Albanian immigrants in Athens: New survey evidence on employment and integration. *Southeast European and Black Sea Studies*, 5 (1), pp.21–48.
Lyberaki, A., 2008. The Greek Immigration Experience Revisited. *Journal of Immigrant & Refugee Studies*, 6 (1), pp.5–33.
Lyberaki, A., 2010. The record of gender policies in Greece 1980–2010: Legal form and economic substance. *GreeSE Paper No 36*. Hellenic Observatory Papers on Greece and Southern Europe. London School of Economics.
Lyberaki, A., 2011a. Migrant women, care work and women's employment in Greece. *Feminist Economics*, 17 (3), pp.103–31.
Lyberaki, A., 2011b. Delocalization, triangular manufacturing and windows of opportunity: Some lessons from Greek clothing producers in a fast-changing global context. *Regional Studies*, 45 (2), pp.205–18.
Lyberaki, A. and Tinios, P., 2002. *Work and cohesion: The Greek national plans for employment and social inclusion*. Athens: Papazisi (in Greek).
Lyberaki, A. and Tinios, P., 2012a. Labour and pensions in the Greek crisis: The micro-foundations of disaster. *Sudost-Europa*, 60 (3): pp.363–86.

Lyberaki, A. and Tinios, P., 2012b. The crisis as handmaiden of social change: Adjusting to the 21st century or settling old scores? In: O. Anastasakis and D. Singh, eds. 2012. *Reforming Greece: Sisyphean task or Herculean challenge?* [e-book] Oxford: South East European Studies at Oxford, pp.65–70. Available at <http://www.sant.ox.ac.uk/seesox/publications/ReformingGreece3.pdf> [Accessed 7 July 2014].

Lyberaki, A. and Tinios, P., 2014. The informal welfare state and the family: Invisible actors in the Greek drama. *Political Studies Review*, 12 (2), pp.193–208.

Maroukis, T., 2012. *Update report Greece: The number of irregular migrants in Greece at the end of 2010 and 2011* [pdf] Available through Database on Irregular Migration <http://irregular-migration.net/fileadmin/irregular-migration/dateien/4.Background_Information/4.5.Update_Reports/Maroukis_2012_Update_report_Greece_2.pdf> [Accessed 7 July 2014].

McCloskey, D., 1996. Love and money: A comment on the markets debate. *Feminist Economics*, 2 (2), pp.137–40.

National Action Plan for Social Inclusion (NAPincl) 2001–2003. Greece, 2001. In: A. Lyberaki and P. Tinios, eds. 2002. *Work and cohesion: The national action plans for employment and social inclusion*. Athens: Papazisi [in Greek].

Nelson, J., 1999. Of markets and martyrs: Is it ok to pay well for care? *Feminist Economics*, 5 (3), pp.43–59.

Nicoletti, G., Scarpetta, S. and Boylaud, O., 2000. *Summary indicators of product market regulation with an extension to employment protection legislation*. Economics Department Working Papers (No. 226), Paris: OECD Publishing.

Organisation for Economic Cooperation and Development (OECD), 2004. Trends in International Migration. Paris: SOPEMI.

Organisation for Economic Cooperation and Development (OECD), 2005. *Economic Surveys: Greece*. Paris: OECD.

Papataxiarchis, E., Topali, P. and Athanasopoulou, A., 2008. *Worlds of domestic work: Gender, migration and cultural transformations in Athens in the early 21st century*. Athens: Alexandria (in Greek).

Psimmenos I. and Skamnakis C., 2008. *Domestic work by female immigrants and social protection: The case of women from Albania and the Ukraine*. Athens: Papazisi (in Greek).

Reher, D.S., 1998. Family ties in Western Europe: Persistent contrasts. *Population and Development Review*, 24 (2), pp.203–34.

Risman, B.J., 2004. Gender as a social structure theory wrestling with activism. *Gender & Society*, 18 (4), pp.429–50.

Sarti, R., 2005. Conclusion: domestic service and European identity. In: Pasleau, Sarti and Schopp, eds. 2005. *Final report: The socio-economic role of domestic service as a factor of European identity*. The Servant Project HPSE-CT 2001-50012. Available at: <http://www.uniurb.it/scipol/drs_servant_project_conclusion.pdf> [Accessed 7 July 2015].

Schor, J.B., 1991. Global equity and environmental crisis: An argument for reducing working hours in the north. *World Development*, 19 (1), pp.73–84.

Simonazzi, A., 2009. Care regimes and national employment models. *Cambridge Journal of Economics*, 33 (2), pp.211–32.

Tinios, P., 2003. *Development with solidarity: A framework for pensions in the 21st century*. Athens: Papazisi (in Greek).

Triandafyllidou, A., 2000. Racists? Us? Are you joking? The discourse of social exclusion of immigrants in Greece and Italy. In: R. King, G. Lazaridis and C.G. Tsardanidis, eds. 2000. *Eldorado or fortress*. London: Macmillan, pp.186–207.

Triandafyllidou, A., 2005. *The Greek migration policy: Problems and prospects.* [pdf in Greek]. Available at: <http://www.eliamep.gr/wp-content/uploads/2008/07/triand.pdf> [Accessed 7 July 2014].

Triandafyllidou, A. et al., 2013. *Migration in Greece: People, policies and practices.* [pdf] IRMA Project Report, no. 7, June 2013. Available at: <http://irma.eliamep.gr/wp-content/uploads/2013/02/IRMA-Background-Report-Greece.pdf> [Accessed 7 July 2014].

Contributors

Maria Jose Alcalá is the Director of the High-Level Task Force for the International Conference on Population and Development Secretariat. She was the Chief of Section and Senior Advisor of the Ending Violence against Women Section at UN Women (2007–12). She also headed the United Nations Trust Fund to End Violence against Women. She was the lead author and senior researcher of *A Passage to Hope, Women and International Migration, UNFPA State of the World Population Report 2006*.

Delali Badasu is a Senior Research Fellow at the University of Ghana. She coauthored *Socio-Cultural Dimensions of Migration in Ghana* (2011) and coedited *Child Care in a Globalizing World: Perspectives from Ghana* (2012). She is currently a coinvestigator on a research project titled, "Migration Dynamics and Domestic Work in Ghana," and she is working on a paper titled, "Informal Sources of Social Protection among International Sub-Saharan African Migrants."

Ofelia Becerril (formerly Ofelia Becerril Quintana) is a tenured Researcher and Professor at El Colegio de Michoacán. Her previous publications include¡*Soy un tunante! Cual loco caminante. Transmigrantes mexicanos en Canadá, contendiendo el género, la sexualidad y la identidad*. She has also published the book chapters, "Trabajo transnacional y organización familiar de las mujeres migrantes mexicanas de las visas H-2 en Estados Unidos" (*Ellas se van: Mujeres migrantes en Estados Unidos y España*, 2013) and "Transnational Work and the Gendered Politics of Labour" (*Organizing the Transnational: Labour, Politics, and Social Change*, 2007). She is currently working on a project titled, "Mujeres transmigrantes temporales de México a Estados Unidos y Canadá".

Theresa Devasahayam is Visiting Senior Research Fellow in the Asia Research Institute at the National University of Singapore. She recently published *Gender and Ageing: Southeast Asian Perspectives* (2014). She coauthored *Gender, Emotions and Labour Markets: Asian and Western*

Perspectives (2011). She is the editor of *The Singapore Women's Charter: Roles, Responsibilities and Rights in Marriage* (2011); *Gender Trends in Southeast Asia: Women Now, Women in the Future* (ISEAS, 2009); and she coedited *Working and Mothering in Asia: Images, Ideologies and Identities* (2007). She has published in numerous international and regional journals and local and regional newspapers. Her views on migrant women, Singaporean women and fertility choices and ageing have been cited by CNN, Bloomberg, Channel News Asia and The Straits Times. She served as an Associate Population Affairs Officer in the Emerging and Social Issues Division of the United Nations Economic and Social Commission for Asia and the Pacific (2004–5) and she provided technical expertise to the United Nations Population Fund and United Nations Women (formerly UNIFEM) on sustainable development-related projects in Cambodia, Myanmar, the Philippines, Thailand, Timor-Leste and Vietnam.

Graham Finlay is a Lecturer in the School of Politics and International Relations, University College Dublin. His previous publications include "Comprehensive Liberalism and Civic Education in the Republic of Ireland" (*Irish Political Studies*, 2007, 22.4). He coauthored "'Citizenship Matters': Lessons from the Irish Citizenship Referendum" (*American Quarterly*, 2008, 60.3). He is currently Principal Investigator at University College Dublin for two large research projects in these areas funded by the European Commission: FP7 FRAME, which works for coherence in the European Union's human rights policies, and FP7 bEUcitizen, which examines barriers to European citizenship for both migrants and EU citizens.

Antigone Lyberaki is Professor of Economics at Panteion University in Athens. She has a Ph.D. in economics and an M.Phil in development studies from Sussex University. She has taught at the University of Crete, the City University of New York (Queen's College) and the École des Hautes Études en Sciences Sociales, Paris. Her current research interests are small- and medium-sized firms, migration, ageing societies and gender/feminist economics. She has also participated in official reports for European institutions on the gender impact of the crisis.

JoAnne M. Mancini is Senior Lecturer in the Department of History, Maynooth University. A primary focus of her current research is the migration of people and things. Her forthcoming and recent publications include, *Art and War in the Pacific World* (forthcoming) and J.M. Mancini and Keith Bresnahan, eds., *Architecture and Armed Conflict* (2015).

Zahra Meghani is an Associate Professor in the Philosophy Department at the University of Rhode Island. Her areas of research interest include, global justice (including migrant health care workers), neoliberalism, health-care ethics and environmental ethics. She has published in journals such as *Developing World Bioethics*, *International Journal of Health Services* and *Journal of Agriculture and Environmental Ethics*.

Sonya Michel is a Professor of History at the University of Maryland, College Park. She is a founding coeditor of the journal *Social Politics: International Studies in Gender, State and Society*; author of *Children's Interests/Mothers' Rights: The Shaping of America's Child Care Policy* (2000); and coeditor of *Mothers of a New World: Maternalist Politics and the Origins of Welfare States* (1993), among others. Her current research is on women, migration and the work of care.

Amaia Pérez Orozco holds a Ph.D. in international economics and development. Her previous publications include *Subversión feminista de la economía: Aportes para un debate sobre el conflicto capital-vida* (2014), *Global Care Chains: Towards a Rights-Based Global Care Regime* (2010) and *Perspectivas feministas en torno a la economía: El caso de los cuidados* (2006). She is currently working for the UN Women Training Center, and she is responsible for the course, "Why We Care about Care." She is also a member of the International Association for Feminist Economics.

Stuart Rosewarne is an Associate Professor in the Department of Political Economy at the University of Sydney. His teaching and research draws on Marxist and feminist theory to focus on the dynamics of the global political economy with an emphasis on international labor migration and transnational organizing. His recent research on migrant domestic workers has been published in the *Austrian Journal of Development Studies*, the *Global Labour Journal*, *Feminist Economics* and *Work Organisation Labour and Globalisation*, and on migrant construction workers in the *Journal of Industrial Relations*.

Sarah van Walsum (1955–2014) was a Professor of Migration Law and Family Ties at VU University. Her work focused on migration law, family law and relations of care. She was the author of *The Family and the Nation: Dutch Family Migration Policies in the Context of Changing Family Norms* (2008). Her other important works include her inaugural lecture "Intimate Strangers" (VU University Amsterdam, 2012); "Sex and the Regulation of Belonging: Dutch Family Migration Policies in the Context of Changing Family Norms" (*Gender, Generations and the Family in International Migration*, 2011); "The (Non)Regulation of Domestic Work in the Netherlands," (*Canadian Journal of Women and the Law*, 2011, 23 (1)); and "Transnational Mothering, National Immigration Policy, and European Law" (*Migrations and Mobilities: Gender, Citizenship, Borders*, 2009).

Index

ABD (Asian Development Bank), 203, 212
Abdul Rahman, N., 180
ACA (Patient Protection and Affordable Care Act), 64, 65
accession states, 25, 26–7, 30, 32
ACMI (Archdiocesan Commission for the Pastoral Care of Migrants and Itinerant People), 180, 183, 184–5, 187–91, 193. *See also* Catholic Church; nongovernmental organizations
advocacy efforts, 63–7, 201, 203, 210, 213–14, 215–16. *See also* NGOs
Africa, 78, 86, 89. *See also* Ghana
Agarwal, B., 125n17
Agenjo Calderón, A., 123
agricultural workers. *see* Seasonal Agricultural Workers (SAW) Program
Agyepong, I., 150n6
Ahmed, S., 179, 193
Albania, migrants from, 236, 239–43
Alonso-Villar, O., 228, 244n10
Alston, P., 35
Altamirano, A., 183
Alvarez, M., 172n2
Ameringer, C.F., 55, 56, 61, 65
Amissah, M., 89
Ananta, A., 209
Anarfi, J., 86
Anderson, B., 133
Anderson, J., 117, 121, 124n2, 124n7
Anggraeni, D., 204
Anonuevo, A. T., 142
Appiah, E. N., 89
Archdiocesan Commission for the Pastoral Care of Migrants and Itinerant People (ACMI), 180, 183, 184–5, 187–91, 193. *See also* nongovernmental organizations
Ardayfio-Schandorf, E., 89
Ariza, M., 160
Armas, A., 125n12
Arthur, J. A., 87
Artico, C., 84
Asia, 201–2, 203. *See also individual countries*
Asian Development Bank (ADB), 203, 212
Asian Migration Center, 205
Asiedu, A., 87
assistance programs, 7. *See also* public services; social security/protections; welfare
asylum seekers, 24, 25, 27–8, 32, 35, 38, 40, 41, 44, 45, 46n6, 47–8n16, 233
Athanassopoulou, A., 235, 245n19
Attias-Donfut, C., 226
autonomy, 2, 12, 63, 108, 113, 137, 140–2, 143, 149, 241
Avila, E., 82, 84, 160, 161, 179
Awumbila, M. O., 88
Ayús, R., 162

Baataar, C., 85, 90
Badasu, D. M., 76, 78, 85
Baker, D., 7
Baker, N., 26
Bakker, I., 161
Balbo, L., 81–2
Ban, C., 6
banking, exclusion of irregular migrants from, 61, 142, 143, 146, 149
Banks, J., 29

Barker, D., 206
Barnes, F., 219n9
Barrett, A., 30, 46n9
Barry, U., 29
Basch, L., 155, 160
Bashi, F., 145
Basok, T., 169
Basu, R., 210
Becerril, O., 169, 172n1
benefits, 61, 170. *See also* public services; social security/protections
Benería, L., 124n3
Bengston, V. L., 226
Benhabib, S., 13, 18n7
Berger, P., 185
Bernhard, J. K., 160
Bettio, F., 76, 77, 227
Bevacqua, R., 212
Billingsley, A., 94n10
Billstein, H., 89
Binford, L., 169
birth rates, 77, 78–9, 93n3, 93n4
birth tourists, 27
Blanc-Szanton, C., 155, 160
Böcker, A., 145
Bolivia, 101, 102, 107, 108, 109, 110, 112, 113, 116, 121, 122. *See also* global care chains
Boontinand, V., 202, 209
borders, open, 2–3
Boris, E., 53, 54, 56, 57, 58
Bose, C. E., 13, 124n6
Bosman, I., 139
Bosniak, L., 3
Boyd, M., 92
Boylaud, O., 232
Braidotti, R., 179
Briones, L., 205, 213
Bryceson, D., 160
Burtless, G., 232
Butler, J., 104

CAG (Caring Across Generations), 63, 65–7
calamity funds, 138
Campillo Poza, I., 113
Canada, 17n3, 154–72. *See also* Seasonal Agricultural Workers (SAW) Program
capability theory, 24, 36–8, 39, 40–1, 45, 47n15
capital, global circuit of, 199, 201, 207, 208, 212, 216, 217, 218

capital accumulation, 79, 102, 105, 106–7, 122, 123
CARAM Asia (Coordination of Action on Research on AIDS and Mobility), 205
"Care and Nutrition of the Young Child" (UNICEF), 80
care/care work: analysis of, 205–7; arrangement of, 114–16, 161–2; for children of female migrants, 1–18, 75–94, 179–94, 224–46; commodification of, 105, 111–12, 146; culture of care, 104; and demand for female foreign workers, 7; denial of, 124n4; effects of migration on, 1–18, 75–94, 110–11, 116–17, 179–94; globalization of, 103–4, 208; and illusion of self-sufficiency, 104–5; intersection with other issues, 140–2; invisibility of, 105, 106; lack of labor laws for, 12, 23–48, 53–69, 101–25, 179–94, 199–219; live-in arrangements, 108; and malnutrition, 80–1; need to consider in development policies, 1–18, 101–25; under neoliberalism, 6–7 (*see also* neoliberalism); notion of, 102–3; in objectives of development, 106; other-mothers, 83–4; privatization of, 23–48, 75–94, 106, 110–12, 131–50; provision of in Southern Europe, 227; public responsibility for, 1–18, 110–14, 120; reactionary ethos of, 106, 115, 116, 122, 124n5; redistribution of, 1–18, 23–48, 75–94, 134–5, 154–72, 224–46, 228; skill needed for, 17n2, 199–219; social conceptions of, 104; systemic link with inequality, 116–19; transfer of, 1–18, 23–48, 75–94, 101–25, 154–72, 224–46; unpaid care, 77, 228; and women's labor market involvement, 1–18, 23–48, 75–94, 154–72, 179–94, 224–46. *See also* domestic work; global care chains; home health workers
care crisis, 124n6, 124n8
Carens, J. H., 3, 18n9, 18n10, 47n14

Index   257

care rights, 104, 117
Carer's Allowance, 29, 30
care systems, unjust, 101, 102, 104, 106, 107, 110–19, 122. *See also* global care chains
care workers: demand for, 7, 30, 203–4; organization of, 147–8 (*see also* nongovernmental organizations)
Caring Across Generations (CAG), 63, 65–7
Carrasco, C., 103, 104, 108, 124n4
Castaneda, C., 179, 193
Castles, S., 84, 88
Catholic Church, 28, 115, 124n5, 180, 181–3, 184–5, 187–93
Cavalcanti, L., 160, 161, 165
Cavounidis, J., 233
CEDAW (Committee on the Elimination of All Forms of Discrimination against Women), 34–6, 37–8, 41, 43, 47n14
Central Intelligence Agency, 9
Chamberlain, M., 85, 89
Chambers, I., 179
Chammartin, G. N., 5
Chan, T., 211
Cheng, S. A., 201
Child Benefit, 26, 27, 30, 31–2
child care, 5, 6, 7, 29, 30, 31, 39, 41, 77, 79, 81, 85, 89, 112, 161, 162, 163, 234. *See also* care/care work; global care chains
citizens, mushroom, 105, 124n4
citizenship: in Canada, 154–72; and care rights, 104; in Greece, 243–4n2, 244n12; in Ireland, 24–5, 26, 32; in Netherlands, 131–50; in Singapore, 179–94; in US, 65–6
Clare, S., 55
Clark, D., 46n9
Clark, P., 46n9
class, 56, 155, 168. *See also* poverty; low skilled
class inequalities, denial of, 67
Clemens, M., 94n11
clinics, free, 55–6, 65, 68n4
Cochrane, J., 214
Cohen, R., 44
Cohn, D., 60, 62
Coke, E., 57–8
Collins, J. I., 168

Committee on the Elimination of All Forms of Discrimination against Women (CEDAW), 34–6, 37–8, 41, 43, 47n14
community health centers, 68n4
Conaghan, J., 147
conditional cash transfers, 93–4n6, 116
Constable, N., 206, 209
contracts: and benefits, 136; limits on, 204, 205; in SAW program, 156, 157, 163, 169, 170, 172; substitution of, 210, 214, 219n11; temporary, 132
Contreras, J., 125n12
Contreras, R., 172n1
Convention on the Rights of the Child (CRC), 34, 47n13
Coomans, G., 244n14
Coordination of Action on Research on AIDS and Mobility (CARAM Asia), 205
corruption, bureaucratic, 208
Cortés, R., 91
Corvers, F., 150n2
Cranford, C. J., 147
CRC (Convention on the Rights of the Child), 34, 47n13

Da, W. W., 160
Daly, M., 92, 244n4
Darnell, J. S., 55
D'Aubeterre, M. E., 160
DCWs (direct care workers), 54, 55, 63–7. *See also* care workers; home health workers
Deae ex Machina, 232, 233, 244n16
debt, of migrants, 208, 209
Deere, C. D., 124n3
De Grip, A., 150n2
De Lange, T., 136, 150n5
Del Rio, C., 228, 244n10
democracies, liberal, 1–3, 4, 11, 12, 13, 17, 62–3
democratic governance, commitment to, 2–3
dependency, 77, 104, 113, 137, 140–2, 143–6, 149, 156
Dependency Law, 113, 116, 123
deportation, 3, 18n10, 27–8, 32, 33, 55, 144, 158, 186
Devasahayam, T. W., 179, 180, 186, 192
development, 1–18; care in objectives of, 106; contribution of

remittances to, 87–8; indicators of progress, 80; and maternal migration, 86, 93; migration as tool for, 88, 203; migration-development nexus, 77, 88, 93, 200; migration's potential to undermine, 91–2; Millennium Development Goals, 75, 79, 91; nation-building as, 133; and neoliberalism, 133 (*see also* neoliberalism); OECD, 78; priorities of, 122; social issues in, 79–80; UNDP, 79. *See also* Asian Development Bank; international financial institutions; International Monetary Fund; World Bank

direct care workers (DCWs), 54, 55, 63–7. *See also* care workers; home health workers

domestic work: analyses of, 205–7; devalorization of, 206; and human rights violations, 117, 179–94, 199–219; as indicator of public responsibility for care, 120; international market in, 135; lack of protections for, 12, 136–7; need for men to take responsibility for, 1–18, 17, 23–48, 101–25, 154–72, 224–46; neglect of economics in, 200; organization of, 147–8; redistribution of, 1–18, 23–48, 101–25, 134–5, 154–72, 224–46; regulation of, 1–18, 23–48, 101–25, 109–10, 179–94, 199–219, 224–46; research on, 200; revival of, 244n7; women channeled into, 1–18, 17n2, 23–48, 101–25, 154–72, 179–94, 199–219, 224–46

domestic workers, 1–18, 23–48, 101–25, 131–50, 179–94, 199–219, 224–46; ability to control employment options, 214–15; appropriation of wages of, 200–1, 208, 209, 211–12, 214, 216, 218; competition in market for, 211; demand for, 203–4; demographics of, 103; difficulty in addressing abuses of, 23–48, 53–69, 101–25, 179–94, 199–219; efforts to set minimum wages for, 214; excluded from social security/protections, 56–7, 101–25, 137, 179–94, 224–46; home health workers construed as, 56; and home-work life reconciliation, 118; lack of protections for, 47n10, 57, 109, 117, 204, 215; live-in arrangements, 111, 140, 142, 144, 204; and power relationships, 101–25, 131–50, 179–94, 206–7; promotion of employment rights of, 199–219; recruitment of, 210–11 (*see also* recruitment agencies); and residency restrictions, 1–18, 23–48, 53–69, 101–25, 131–50, 179–94, 199–219, 218n4; social security/protections for, 1–18, 23–48, 53–69, 101–25, 131–50, 140; wages of, 205, 209–10; working conditions of, 101–25, 131–50, 179–94, 199–219, 204

Domestic Workers Convention (ILO), 199, 216, 217–18

Domínguez, M., 108

double day, 82

double presence, 82, 154–72

Doward, J., 47n16

Duncan, P., 46n7

Eckenwiler, L., 68n1

economic rights, focus on, 213–14

economics, feminist, 103, 105, 106, 124n4, 125n17, 225, 226, 229

economy, informal, 125n11, 229, 231, 233, 234, 238, 239, 241, 243

Ecuador, 107, 108, 121, 122, 125n12. *See also* global care chains

education, 17n2, 27, 62, 75, 76, 77, 78, 79, 83, 87, 89, 90, 111, 116, 133, 158–9, 239, 240, 241

Ehrenreich, B., 13, 161

Einhorn, B., 218n6

elder care, 5–7, 13, 16, 23, 30, 31, 46n7, 53, 58, 77, 146, 237–8. *See also* care/care work; direct care workers; global care chains; home health workers

elderly, population of, 78, 79

Elias, J., 199

Emergency Medical Treatment and Labor Act, 55

Index 259

empowerment, 212–13. *See also* advocacy efforts
Engbersen, G., 143
England, P., 124n4, 244n3
England, V., 216
equality, 36–8, 62–3. *See also* inequalities
equality, gender, 83, 91. *See also* gender inequalities
Equality Act, 40
Escobar, A., 104, 122
Esping-Andersen, G., 227
Europe, demographics of, 78
Europe, Eastern, 224. *See also* Albania
Europe, Southern, 226, 227. *See also* Greece; Spain
European Commission, 9
European Convention on the Legal Status of Migrant Workers, 40
European Union (EU), 25, 26–7, 43–4, 47–8n15, 136, 231, 243n2
Eurozone, exiting, 241, 245n26
Euwals, R., 150n2
exploitation, 1, 46n1, 53, 144, 149, 169, 179, 187, 199, 205, 228
Ezquerra, S., 123

Fairey, D., 169
Fair Labor Standards Act (FLSA), 57, 58, 63, 64, 67
Fajujonu v. Minister for Justice, Equality and Law Reform, 28
Fakiolas, R., 245n18
families, transnational, 88, 90–1, 112, 120, 132–3, 145, 154, 160–2. *See also* migration, maternal; mothering, transnational
familism, 111, 119
family, 28–9, 146, 226, 227, 229
Family Life Society (FLS), 184
family reunification, 1–18, 23–48, 92, 101–25, 154–72, 179–94, 199–219; criteria for in Spain, 117; and immigration policies, 7–8, 12; in Ireland, 25, 26, 31; option of sponsoring families, 18n18; and residency restrictions, 1–18, 23–48, 101–25, 131–50, 154–72, 179–94, 199–219, 218n4; and Singapore labor laws, 180
family wage, 29
Fanning, B., 42, 46n4, 46n5

farm workers. *see* Seasonal Agricultural Workers (SAW) Program
FAST (Foreign Domestic Worker Association for Skills Training), 185
fathers, migrant, 167–8
Ferguson, J., 135, 145
Ferrera, M., 227
Fiawoo, D. K., 89
Finch, J., 145
Finlay, G., 26
FLS (Family Life Society), 184
FLSA (Fair Labor Standards Act), 57, 58, 63, 64, 67
Folbre, N., 86, 244n3
Foreign Domestic Worker Association for Skills Training (FAST), 185
Fortier, A., 179, 193
fostering, of children, 85–6, 89–91
Fox, B., 160
Fraser, N., 56
Fuchs, R., 202
Fudge, J., 135, 147, 168

Garcia, R. J., 60, 69n11
García, V., 125n9
García Domínguez, M., 124n2
Garza, C., 80
Gasper, D., 47n15
Gavanas, A., 125n11
Gebeloff, R., 68n7
gender: and arrangement of care, 1–18, 74–94, 101–25, 131–50; in dilemmas for maternal migrants, 1–18, 74–94, 101–25, 131–50, 165; and division of labor, 32, 119, 244n10; and exclusion from protections, 136–7; and exploitation of workers in SAW program, 168; and labor market involvement in Greece, 226; and labor policy, 155; and Mexico's failure to respect rights of migrant workers, 171; and migration, 155, 161; and migration policy in Greece, 244–5n17; and migration policy in Ireland, 31–3; norms of and children's expectations, 84; norms of in Greece, 226; norms of in Ireland, 24, 28–31, 32, 34–5, 38, 41, 43; in policies of SAW, 169–70; in unjust systems of care, 114–16. *See also* care/

care work; care workers; domestic workers
gender equality, 13, 83, 90, 91, 170, 229, 230, 242
gender inequalities, 67, 227, 229–30, 242
gender justice, 12, 36, 47n15
gender mainstreaming, 91
gender roles, 28, 108, 120–1, 226, 227, 233. *See also* gender
Georges, E., 155
Germano, R., 10
Gershman, J., 7
Gershuny, J., 227
Geschiere, P., 133
Ghana, 17n4, 77, 85–90, 138–9, 141, 149
Giana, E., 243n1
Giddens, A., 79
Gil, S. L., 104, 105, 118, 124n2, 125n15, 161
Giullari, S., 76, 82
Glick-Schiller, N., 155, 160
global care chains, 120–1, 200, 201; analyses of, 217; and compulsion to repatriate money, 205; concept of, 102–3; and conflict between capital and care, 107; and financial burden on women migrant workers, 216; formation of, 103–4; and inequalities, 120; link with global circuit of capital, 212, 217; private enterprises in, 207–8 (*see also* placement agencies; recruitment agencies). *See also* care systems, unjust
globalization, 5, 199–200. *See also* neoliberalism
Goldring, L., 155, 160
Gómez, T., 169, 171
Gooch, L., 209
Goodin, R., 46n1
Goody, E. N., 85, 89
Gordon, L., 56
Goss, S., 10
Greece: care in, 237–8, 243; citizenship, 243–4n2, 244n12; division of society in, 224–5; economic crisis in, 225, 235–6, 245n21, 245n26; economic history of, 224, 229, 230–1; effects of migrants on labor market in, 231–2; family in, 229; future of, 241–2; gender and migration policy in, 244–5n17; gender in, 226, 229–30, 233, 242; health insurance in, 245n20; informal economy in, 234, 241, 243; marginalization of migrants in, 225; migrants' choice to remain in, 233, 240–1; migrants in, 224–5, 233–5, 239–43; migration patterns in, 229, 231; possible new equilibrium in, 238–9; possible scenarios for migrants in, 242; social security/protections in, 229, 231, 234, 245n20; unemployment in, 240; women in labor force in, 229, 230, 231, 232–3
Griffith, D., 172n1
Griffith, K., 58, 59, 68n5
Grossman, A., 84
Guevarra, A. R., 135
Gutiérrez-Rodríguez, E., 200, 206

Haraway, D., 122
Harvey, D., 6, 7, 67
Hayek, F. v., 6
health care, 6, 7, 10, 18n10, 37, 55–6, 64, 65, 68n4, 69n9, 138, 234
Health Care and Education Act, 64
health insurance, 55, 64–5, 138–9, 149, 245n20
health workers, 86, 94n11. *See also* home health workers; nurses
Help at Home, 238
Henrici, J., 53, 54, 66, 68n3
Henry, S., 85
Herrera, G., 101, 110, 113, 115, 120, 124n2, 160, 161, 228
Hess, C., 53, 54, 55, 66, 68n3
Hewitson, G. J., 124n4
Hilbers, P., 150n2
Hildebrandt, N., 76, 158
Hill, M., 28, 29
Himmelweit, S., 244n3
Hinsliff, G., 47n16
Ho, J., 211
Hobbes, T., 124n4
Hochschild, A., 13, 82, 102, 135, 161, 199, 200, 205, 206, 228
Hoffman Plastic Compounds Inc. v. NLRB, 60, 64
Hogan, G., 32, 33, 47n12

Holding, R., 18n5
Holland, K., 47n11
home health workers, 30, 53–8, 63–7. *See also* direct care workers
home-work life reconciliation, 78, 103, 118
Hondagneu-Sotelo, P., 54, 82, 84, 155, 160, 161, 179
Hong, D., 186
Hong Kong, 202, 204, 218n2, 218n3
Houwing, H., 150n2
Hsiao, A., 218n1
Huang, S., 160, 179
Hugo, G. J., 208
Human Development Report 2009 (UNDP), 5
human rights, 4; applicability to migrants, 43, 45; capability theory, 24, 36–8, 39, 40–1, 45, 47n15; CEDAW, 34–6, 37–8, 41, 43, 47n14; and domestic workers, 23–48, 101–25, 179–94, 199–219; instruments governing migration, 11, 33–6, 40, 172; and intersectionality, 36; violations experienced by women migrant workers, 11–13, 23–48, 101–25, 179–94, 199–219. *See also* Canada; Ireland; Spain
Humphries, J., 125n17

ICCPR (International Covenant on Civil and Political Rights), 34, 35
identity, shared sense of, 2–3, 18n8
IFIs (international financial institutions), 6, 7, 8. *See also* Asian Development Bank; International Monetary Fund; Structural Adjustment Programs; World Bank
ILO (International Labor Organization), 34, 41, 103, 199, 213, 216, 217–18
IMF (International Monetary Fund), 6, 8, 9, 18n15, 43, 93n1, 133, 235
Immigration and Nationality Act (INA), 59
immigration policies, 1, 12. *See also individual countries*
Immigration Reform and Control Act (IRCA), 59, 60, 64, 68n5

INA (Immigration and Nationality Act), 59
Indonesia, 202, 203, 207, 208, 210, 211–12, 214, 215
inequalities, 67, 116–20. *See also* gender inequalities
informal work/economy, 4, 12, 30, 39, 125n11, 228–9, 231, 233–4, 238–9, 243, 244n4, 244n7. *See also* unregulated work
insurance, 138–9. *See also* health insurance
International Convention on the Protection of the Rights of All Migrant Workers, 11, 33, 172
International Covenant on Civil and Political Rights (ICCPR), 34, 35
international financial institutions (IFIs), 6, 7, 8. *See also* Asian Development Bank; International Monetary Fund; Structural Adjustment Programs; World Bank
International Labor Organization (ILO), 34, 41, 103, 199, 213, 216, 217–18
International Monetary Fund (IMF), 6, 8, 9, 18n15, 43, 93n1, 133, 235
International Organization for Migration (IOM), 4, 6, 9, 210
International Research and Training Institute of the United Nations for the Advancement of Women (UN-INSTRAW), 123–4n2, 199
intersectionality, 36
IOM (International Organization for Migration), 5, 6, 9, 210
IRCA (Immigration Reform and Control Act), 59, 60, 64, 68n5
Ireland: asylum seekers in, 27–8, 32, 40, 41, 44, 46n6, 47–8n16; attempts to implement CRC in, 47n13; barriers to permanent settlement in, 25–6, 32; barriers to social protections in, 26–7; care work in, 44, 46n7; citizenship in, 24–5, 26, 32; Constitution, 28–9, 33, 34, 43; construction of gender in, 24, 38; dependence on EU, 43–4; diversity of, 24; economy of, 45; gender norms in, 28–31, 32, 34–5, 41, 43; immigration

policies in, 24–8; injustices to migrant workers in, 23; just response to situation of female migrants in, 33–6; labor flow in, 23; labor inspection in, 41, 44, 48n17; lack of protection for workers in, 33; migrants from accession states in, 26–7; migration policy and gender in, 31–3; nurses in, 44, 46n7; objections to recommendations for, 42–5; outflow of workers from, 45; Proclamation of the Irish Republic, 33; recent migration to, 24–5; recommendations for state response to situation of migrant workers, 40–2; right to enter, 44–5; view of care work in, 29; women in workforce in, 29; work permits in, 25–7, 30, 40, 41

Irwin, A., 7
Isiugo-Abanihe, U. C., 89

Japan, care workers in, 202
Jenson, J., 79, 81, 91, 93, 93n6
Jiménez, E., 101, 114, 122, 124n2
Jiménez Tostón, G., 125n16
Joshi, Y. R., 218n5
Juárez, Elizabeth, 172n1
justice, 37, 45, 47n15

Kabeer, N., 124n3
Kabki, M., 138
Kambouri, H., 235, 245n19
Kan, M. Y., 227
Karaagach, D., 143, 145
Karamessini, M., 244n13
Kaur, A., 186
Keenan, B., 30, 32
Kelly, J. M., 32, 33, 47n12
Keung, N., 170
Kirk, G., 7
Klein, J., 53, 54, 56, 57, 58
Knegt, R., 147
Kofman, E., 228
Kohli, M., 226
Kollmann, G., 57
Korea, care workers in, 202
Kösters, L., 150n2
Kristof, N., 43
Kuah-Pearce, K. E., 183

Künemund. H., 226
Kunz, R., 93n1, 93n2
Kusakabe, K., 202
Kymlicka, W., 2

Labonte, R., 18n15
labor, affective. *see* care/care work; domestic work
labor, emotional, 206. *See also* care/care work; domestic work
labor, productive, 131
labor, reproductive, 207. *See also* care/care work; domestic work
labor flow, 4, 5–6, 7, 13, 23, 31. *See also* migration
labor inspection, in Ireland, 41, 44, 48n17
labor law. *see* labor regulations/law; *individual countries*
labor market test, 25–6, 40
labor policy, 136, 155. *See also* labor regulations/law
labor regulations/law: and home health workers, 56; lack of for domestic/care work, 12, 136–7; lack of protections for domestic/care workers, 57, 109, 204; protection of undocumented workers, 58, 60. *See also under individual countries*
labor relationships, flexibility of, 25, 108, 134, 136, 147, 150n2, 232
Labrianidis, L., 235, 242
Lally, C., 27
Lam, T., 160
Lan, P., 201, 203
Landolt, P., 160
Latham, M., 80–1
Ledo, C., 160
Lee, E. Y., 65, 69n9
legalistic formalism, 230
Lentin, R., 32
Leong, C., 186
Levitt, P., 84
Lewis, J., 76, 82, 244n4
Lianos, T., 233
Liapi, M., 245n17
Liebert, S., 55, 56, 61, 65
life: commodification of, 105; sustaining, 102, 106–7 (*see also* care/care work; welfare; welfare state); vulnerability of, 104
Lima, F. H., 92

Litt, J. S., 13, 124n6
live-in arrangements, 54–5, 108, 111, 140, 142, 144, 204
Lobe and Osayande case, 28
Long Island Care at Home v. Evelyn Coke, 57–8
Los Angeles, unionization of domestic workers in, 147
Loveband, A., 206, 211
low skilled, 1, 3, 7–8, 12–3, 15. See also professional hierarchy
Lozano, M. I., 169
Lüdicke, J., 226
Lutz, H., 76, 85, 92, 135, 142
Lyberaki, A., 230, 231, 232, 233, 234, 235, 242, 245n19, 245n25

Macapagal-Arroyo, G., 207
Mac Éinrí, P., 46n3
Maher, V., 135
Mahon, R., 76, 79
Malaysia, 202, 203
Mancini, J. M., 26
Manuh, T., 77, 87, 90
Mapp, S., 76, 83, 87
Marchetti, S., 143, 144
Maroukis, T., 235, 245n22
Martin, S., 54, 68n3
Martínez Franzoni, J., 112
Marzadro, M., 160
maternity: expansion of, 115; neomaternalism, 81. See also migration, maternal; mothering, transnational; mothers
maternity leave, 29, 41, 81, 117
Mauzy, D. K., 182
May, V. H., 57
Mazzali, A., 141
Mazzuccato, V., 85, 88, 91
McCloskey, D., 244n3
McKenzie, D. J., 76
McKeown, Adam, 149
McPhail, F., 168
MDG (Millennium Development Goals), 75, 79, 91
Medicaid, 55, 64, 65, 68n7, 69n9
Medina, J., 148
Meghani, Z., 9, 68n1
Mellon, G., 48n16
Mexico, 53–69, 154–72. See also Seasonal Agricultural Workers (SAW) Program
Michel, S., 76, 77, 94n7, 94n9

migrants: attitudes toward, 44; complaints about, 9–10; concerns about future care for selves, 142 (*see also* social security/protections); contributions of, 9–10; discrimination against, 2; labor conditions for, 117–18; number of, 5; protections for, 11; sources of, 16–17, 203 (*see also* South, global; *individual countries*); support of family in home countries, 4; as temporary population, 186–7; undocumented, 3–4, 10, 13, 58, 59–62, 66, 209
migrants, maternal. *see* migration, maternal; mothering, transnational
migrants, returning, 142, 211–12
migrant workers, women: blamed for social harms, 101; employment prospects of, 11–12; injustices experienced by, 1–2; in low-skill professions, 13; motivations of, 108; number of, 5. See also migration, maternal; mothering, transnational
Migrant Worker's Convention (ILO), 33, 35, 39, 40
migration: cost of, 18n17, 208–9; as development initiative, 203; as economic policy, 201; ethics of, 47n14; feminization of, 107–8, 228; and globalization, 5; motivations for, 38–9, 112, 133; right to, 44–5; temporary/circular, 92, 136 (*see also* Seasonal Agricultural Workers (SAW) Program); understanding of, 179; as vulnerability factor, 117; by women, lack of data on, 4. *See also* labor flow
migration, culture of, 117
migration, maternal, 1–18, 74–94, 101–25, 154–72. See also mothering, transnational; Seasonal Agricultural Workers (SAW) Program
migration-development nexus, 77, 88, 93
migration-remittance chain, 212

migration-remittances-development nexus, 75–93, 200
Millar, S., 48n17
Millennium Development Goals (MDG), 75, 79, 91
Miller, D., 2
Miller, M. J., 84
Milne, R. S., 182
mobility, upward, 118, 235
Moerbeek, S., 143, 145
Molano Mijangos, A., 124n2
Molyneux, M., 79, 81, 93, 93n6, 116
Momsen, J., 13, 192
moneylenders, 18n17, 200, 207, 208, 216, 217
Moodysson, L., 84
Moore, H. L., 86
Morgan, G., 216
mother blaming, 85, 166
mothering, transnational, 74–94, 161, 163–6. *See also* migration, maternal
mothers, 75–6, 80, 86, 115, 116, 162. *See also* migration, maternal; mothering, transnational
Motoa, A., 160
movement, freedom of, 44
Mullin, M., 29
Multilateral Framework for a Rights-Based Approach to Labour Migration (ILO), 34, 41
Mummert, G., 160
Mundlak, G., 147
Murphy, C., 91
Murphy, K., 46n6
Murray, T., 47n11
Myanmar, migrants from, 202

Nabigne, E., 85
NAPincl (National Action Plan for Inclusion), 237, 238
National Labor Relations Act (NLRA), 57, 58, 59, 60
nation-building, 133
needs, social construction of, 118
Nelson, J., 244n3
neoliberalism, 1–18, 53–69, 74–94, 101–25, 131–50, 179–94, 199–219, 224–46; development of, 6; effects of, 7, 9, 76, 87, 115–16, 133, 134; elements of, 68n6; hierarchy of workers in, 62; and MDGs, 79; Ong's conception of, 62; view of development in, 133; Washington Consensus, 87; and workers' rights, 67
neomaternalism, 81
neoservility, 119
neoslavery, 192
Netherlands, 140, 142–3, 144, 148, 150n2, 150n10
New Deal, 56
New Poverty Agenda, 79
New Social Policy, 116
NGOs (nongovernmental organizations), 63–7, 75, 76, 142, 143, 182, 203, 207. *See also* ACMI; advocacy efforts
Nicoletti, G., 232
Nielsen, K., 2
NíLaoire, C., 25
NLRA (National Labor Relations Act), 57, 58, 59, 60
Nolan, C., 216
nongovernmental organizations (NGOs), 63–7, 75, 76, 142, 143, 182, 203, 207. *See also* ACMI; advocacy efforts
non-state actors, 35, 42. *See also* NGOs
Northants Co. Council v. A.B.F., 33
Nukunya, G. K., 85, 89, 90
nurses, 44, 46n7, 86, 87, 202
Nussbaum, M., 47n15
Nyberg, W., 160
Nyonator, F., 86

obligation, in capability theory, 37, 38
O'Brien, Á., 84
OECD (Organisation for Economic Co-operation and Development), 78, 79, 224n8, 228
Ofreneo, R. E., 213
Ogg, J., 226
Oishi, N., 179
Ojeda, N., 160
Okazawa-Rey, M., 7
Ong, A., 62, 68n6, 155, 168, 192, 193, 205, 213, 216
Onuki, H., 202
Oppong, C., 76, 85, 90
Organisation for Economic Co-operation and Development (OECD), 78, 79, 228, 244n8
organization, of migrants, 203. *See also* unions

Orozco, A., 103, 113
Orozco, M., 94n11
other-mothers, 76, 83–4. *See also* mothering, transnational
Owens, R., 135, 147

Pan, X., 209
Pandey, G., 133
Papataxiarchis, E., 234, 245n19
Paraprofessional Health Institute (PHI), 63–5, 66–7
Parella, S., 160, 161, 165
parental leave, in Ireland, 29
Parreñas, R. S., 76, 82, 83, 84, 92, 114, 160, 179, 199, 206
Passel, J. S., 60, 62
passports, confiscation of, 209
Pateman, C., 124n4
paternity, immobility of, 115
Patient Protection and Affordable Care Act (ACA), 64, 65
Pearson, R., 202
Pedone, C., 160, 161
Peet, R., 6, 7, 8, 9
Peng, I., 76, 77
Pérez Orozco, A., 108, 118, 123, 124n2, 125n15
Perry, M. F., 57
Peru, 107, 108, 121. *See also* global care chains
Pessar, P., 155
Petrozziello, A., 123n1
PHI (Paraprofessional Health Institute), 63–5, 66–7
Philippines, 30, 46n9, 135, 141, 142, 202, 203, 207, 208, 210, 214
Philips, S., 42
Phillips, N., 199
Picchio, A., 103
Pieterse, J., 47n15
Pillinger, J., 24, 34, 40, 41, 47n10, 87
Piper, N., 81, 92, 199
placement agencies, 208, 209, 210, 213
Pogge, T., 47n14
Ponder, C.S., 67
Pool, C., 144
poverty, 8, 18n15, 53, 55, 68n7, 75, 77, 79, 88, 89, 107, 134, 181. *See also* Millennium Development Goals
power relationships, 59–60, 206–7, 213. *See also under* domestic workers

Pratt, G., 77, 82, 83, 84
Preibisch, K., 169, 172n1
professional hierarchy, 1, 4, 12, 13. *See also* class; poverty
professionalism, 119
profits, and commodification of care, 105
progress, indicators of, 80. *See also* Millennium Development Goals
Promotion of Personal Autonomy and Attention to Persons in a Situation of Dependency (Dependency Law), 113, 116, 123
Psimmenos, I., 234, 245n19
public services, 7, 10, 87, 133. *See also* social security/protections
Purba, K., 202
Puyana, Y., 160

Quartey, P., 87
Quratul-ain, B. B. S. B., 201

race, 1, 2, 4, 11, 36, 56, 61, 67, 102–3, 118–9, 147, 168
racial inequalities, denial of, 67
Raghuram, P., 228
Rahman, Md M, 213
Rahman, Z., 211
Ramakrishnan, U., 80, 81
Ramji, H., 186
Ramsaroop, C., 158
Ratzinger, J., 115, 124n5
Razavi, S., 103, 124n3
recruitment agencies, 1–18, 208, 209, 210, 213, 219n10
Regan, C., 55, 68n8
Régimen Especial de Empleados de Hogar (REEH), 109
Reher, D. S., 226
religion, 28, 115, 180, 181–3, 184–5, 187–93
remittances, 9, 94n8, 199–219; amount of, 18n11; appropriation of, 12, 17; contributions to human development, 87–8; costs of, 18n16, 211; effects of, 116; and empowerment, 213; as export income, 4, 7, 9, 201; and global care chain, 205; and immigration policies, 7; as informal social protection, 89, 111; and regular banking,

142–3; remitted by women, 12; via mobile phone, 146; workers' control over, 215
remittances, reverse, 85, 91
residency, 218n2; in Asia, 204, 218n2, 218n4; contingent upon employment, 113, 215; desire for in Greece, 233; in EU, 136; in Hong Kong, 218n2; in Ireland, 25–6, 31, 32, 38, 39, 40, 42; lack of focus on, 216; of non-EU parents, 46n7; possibility of acquiring, 1, 7, 17n3; restrictions on, 204, 218n4; SAW Program workers' ineligibility for, 171
Resnick, J., 13, 132, 134
Reynolds, V., 181
rights, human. *see* human rights
rights, negative, 37
rights, positive, 37
Risman, B. J., 227
Rivera, L., 155
Rivera-Batiz, F.L., 59
Robert, E., 124n2
Roberts, R. E., 226
Robeyns, I., 125n17
Rodan, G., 182
Rodriguez Enríquez, C., 125n13
Rojas, M., 162
Rosewarne, S., 199
Rosnick, D., 7
Rossi, A., 76, 94n13
Rouse, R., 155
Rueppel, P., 186
Ruhs, M., 30
Russell, H., 29
Rust, A., 30, 46n9

Sackey, B., 85
Salazar, C., 101, 114, 122, 124n2
Samonte, I. A., 213
SAPs (Structural Adjustment Programs), 7, 9, 18n15, 87, 107, 133, 135. *See also* globalization; neoliberalism
Sarti, R., 244n7
Sassen, S., 107, 125n11, 133–4
Satterthwaite, M., 36
Saulny, S., 93n4
SAW (Seasonal Agricultural Workers) Program. *see* Seasonal Agricultural Workers (SAW) Program
Scarpetta, S., 232
Scheman, N., 148
Schmalzbauer, L., 76, 82, 83, 84, 94n10
Schor, J. B., 227
Schrecker, T., 18n15
Seasonal Agricultural Workers (SAW) Program, 154; complaints by workers in, 158; employers' failure to comply with regulations, 169; experience of fathers in, 167–8; gender in policies of, 169–70; treatment of workers in, 168–71; wages for workers in, 158; wives of male migrants in, 167; women in, 156–60, 162. *See also* Canada
Segura, D. A., 76
self-definition, right to, 2
self-sufficiency, 79, 104–5
Sen, A., 24, 36–8, 45, 47n15
services, public. *see* education; health care; public services; social security/protections
servility, 119, 144
Shakow, A., 7
Shamir, H., 147
Sharma, N., 169
Shaw, W., 2
Sheller, M., 179, 193
Shue, H., 46n1
Silvey, R., 212
Simonazzi, A., 227, 244n6
Simpson, M., 84
Singapore: ACMI in, 180, 183, 184–5, 187–91, 193; experience of domestic workers in, 182; failure to meet needs of migrant women, 185; faith-based programs for migrants in, 185–6; labor regulations/law in, 180, 186; limitations on civic organizations in, 183; mandatory day off in, 185, 187, 218n3; migrants in, 183, 186–7, 193, 202; prohibition of organization of migrants in, 203; training programs in, 185, 191; work conditions in, 192
Sistema Nacional para el Desarrollo Integral de la Familia (SNDIF), 162

Skamnakis, C., 234, 245n19
Skrbis, Z., 160
Smith, B., 27
Smith, L., 87, 138, 139, 140, 141, 150n7
Smyth, J., 27
SNDIF (Sistema Nacional para el Desarrollo Integral de la Familia), 162
Sobritchea, C. I., 179
social contract, 104–5
social investment paradigm, 77, 78, 79, 87–8
social justice, commitment to, 2–3
social networks, 144–6, 149
social policy, 136. *See also* public services; social security/protections
social protections. *see* social security/protections
social relationships, transnational, 143
social remittances, 12, 138–9
social reproduction, 110–14, 124n6, 124n7
Social Security Act, 56–7
Social Security Administration, 10
social security/protections, 17; absence of, 112; alternative forms of, 133, 149; decline of, 87, 107, 132, 133, 146; denial of based on status, 145; exclusion of domestic workers from, 56–7, 137; exclusion of migrants from, effects of, 139–42; guaranteed by EU, 44; inclusion of migrants in, 139, 142; lack of in global South, 1–18, 74–94, 101–25, 131–50, 154–72; new approaches to, 131; paradigms in, 131, 133, 134; received by migrants, 10; remittances as, 89; transnational arrangements, 137–43. *See also* welfare; welfare state
social services. *see* public services; social security/protections
solidarity, transnational, 148
Solinas, G., 227
Spain: care crisis in, 107, 108; care in, 111–12, 113, 114; criteria for family reunification in, 117; Dependency Law, 113, 116, 123; domestic workers in, 108–10, 111–12; familist discourse in, 111, 119; gender roles in, 108, 114; migration policies, 113; migration to, 108; occupational segregation in, 244n10; professionalist discourse in, 119; regulation of domestic work in, 109–10; rhetoric of equality in, 121; shift to neoliberalism, 6–7; situation of domestic workers in, 109–10; social reproduction crisis in, 123
Sri Lanka, promotion of migration in, 202
Staab, S., 103, 124n3
Stacey, J., 135
Stack, C., 84
Staring, R., 145, 150n10
Steiner, H. J., 35
Stewart, A., 131, 134, 135, 136, 148
Stewart, J., 46n9
St. Martin, D., 79
Stott, D. A., 202
Structural Adjustment Programs (SAPs), 7, 9, 18n15, 87, 107, 133, 135. *See also* globalization; neoliberalism
Sullivan, O., 227
Sure-Tan, Inc. v. NLRB, 60
Suzuki, E., 8

Taiwan, 202, 218n3, 218n6
Tan, A., 209, 210, 211, 214
Tanner, R., 181
Tavernise, S., 68n7
taxes, paid by migrants, 10
Tetteh, E. K., 85, 88, 89
Thailand, 202, 203
Tinios, P., 230, 242, 245n20, 245n25
Tinnemans, W., 143, 145
Toh, H. L., 211
Topali, P., 234, 245n19
Tormey, A., 27
Trejo, E., 172n2
Triandafyllidou, A., 244n2, 244n17
Tuñón, E., 162
Twum-Baah, K., 87

UNDP (United Nations Development Programme), 5, 79, 199
unemployment, after Greek crisis, 240, 245n24
UNICEF, 80

UN-INSTRAW (International Research and Training Institute of the United Nations for the Advancement of Women), 123–4n2, 199
unions, 11, 41, 42, 44, 120, 143, 144, 147–8, 149, 203
United Nations, 4, 11, 123–4n2, 133, 199. *See also* Millennium Development Goals
United Nations Development Programme (UNDP), 5, 79, 199
United Nations Population Fund (UNPFA), 4, 5, 6, 9
United States, 8, 53–69, 93n4, 147; FLSA, 57, 58, 63, 64, 67; home health workers in, 53–8, 63–7; immigration law in, 59–60, 64, 68n5; NLRA, 57, 58, 60
Universal Declaration of Human Rights, 4
UNPFA (United Nations Population Fund), 4, 5, 6, 9
unregulated work/ economy, 4, 12, 229, 232, 234, 237–9, 244n4. *See also* informal work/economy

Vachani, N., 84, 89
Van den Berg-Eldering, M., 144
Van der Leun, J., 143, 145
Van Walsum, S., 92, 136, 141, 142, 143, 145, 150n5
Varia, N., 147, 209
Vásconez, A., 125n12
Vega Solís, C., 104, 108, 115
Verduzco, G., 169
Vidal, L., 162
Villa, P., 227
visas, 7, 92, 145, 205, 218n4. *See also* work permits
Viviel, A., 160
Von Benda-Beckmann, K., 145
Vonk, G., 136, 145, 150n5
vote, right to, 18n5
Vouyioukas, A., 245n17
Vouyoukas, S., 243n1
vulnerability, 46n1. *See also* exploitation; dependency
Vuorela, U., 160

wages: after Greek crisis, 239–40; appropriation of, 200–1, 208, 209, 211–12, 214, 216, 218; for DCWs, 63–4; of domestic workers, 205, 209–10; effects of migrants on, 10; and empowerment, 213; family wage, 29; of home health workers, 58; of low-skilled noncitizens, 4; minimum wage, 58, 63–4, 210, 214; overtime pay, 58, 63–4; of undocumented migrants, 59. *See also* remittances
Walsh, K., 186
Wanderley, F., 101, 114, 122, 124n2
Warner, D.C., 55
Washington Consensus, 87
Watson, D., 29
WB (World Bank), 6, 8, 9, 18n15, 79, 86, 93n1, 133, 203, 211, 212, 214, 217, 219n10
Weber, D. P., 59
Weisbrot, D., 7
welfare, 112–13, 133. *See also* public services; social security/ protections
welfare recipients, assumptions about, 56
welfare states, 76–7, 93, 106, 131–7, 149
Wellman, C., 2, 47n14
White, A., 46n3
Whittaker, W. G., 58
WHO, 94n11
Whyte, G., 32, 33, 47n12
Wijeysingha, E., 182
Williams, F., 131
Wilper, A. P., 55
Wolff, F. C., 226
Wong, M., 88, 89
worker, ideal, 8
workers, mushroom, 105, 113, 120, 124n4
work-life reconciliation, 78, 103, 118
work permits, 25–7, 30, 40, 41, 243n2. *See also* visas
World Bank (WB), 6, 8, 9, 18n15, 79, 86, 93n1, 133, 203, 211, 212, 214, 217, 219n10
World Trade Organization (WTO), 135
Worthington, R., 183
Wyly, E., 67

Yeates, N., 124n3, 200
Yeboah, I., 85, 88
Yeoh, B., 84, 160, 179, 192
Yépez, I., 160
Yi, B. L., 202
Young, I. M., 148
Yudhoyono, S. B., 207

Zaguirre, A., 109, 113
Zambrano v. Office national d l'emploi, 46n7
Zimmerman, M. K., 13, 124n6, 147
Zinsser, J.P., 79
Zlotnick, H., 81